Master Sportsman
the story of Norman Borrett

RICHARD SAYER

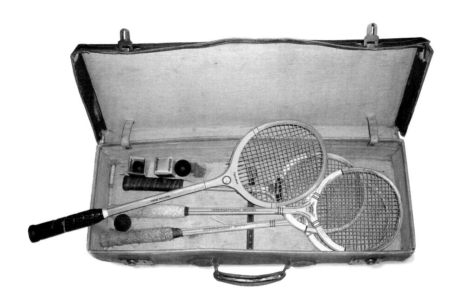

TO MULLIE

Master Sportsman
the story of Norman Borrett
by Richard Sayer

First Published in 2011 by Albert Publications
in association with
The Society of Old Framlinghamians
www.oldframlinghamian.com

Reprinted February 2012

ISBN 978-0-9562872-1-2

DESIGNED BY CHRIS KEEBLE, KEEBLE+HALL
PRINTED IN SUFFOLK ON ELEMENTAL
CHLORINE-FREE PAPER,
SOURCED FROM SUSTAINABLE FORESTS.

CONTENTS

FOREWORD
by Denys Carnill

I was delighted to be asked to write this Foreword to Richard Sayer's well-researched and hugely entertaining book which I am sure will be much enjoyed by those who knew Norman and the many more who knew of him. His record speaks for itself. What an all-round talented sportsman he was! And one wonders how much more he could have achieved if the Second World War had not intervened.

Of his hockey I write later in the book, and of his other sports I am not qualified to speak, though I do recall one occasion in late 1949 when, after we had both been playing for Jack Meyer's 'West of England Wanderers' against Oxford University, Norman arranged to play against the University squash champion as a warm-up for the Amateur Championship later in the week. He did not just beat his opponent, he annihilated him. Norman was ruthless, as he was later when, playing in the quarter-final of that Championship against Alan Seymour-Hayden, the Royal Navy's top player, The Times reported that Norman kept striking the gallant commander when the latter was looking out to sea. The competitive spirit, the will to win, was always there.

'Carnill at right-back was in such mood of magnificence that he not only answered for the sins of others, but would have played the Welshmen quite adequately on his own. The timing of his interceptions, the way he gathered and controlled the ball on forehand and backhand alike, won admiration and received applause. It was a performance that might not have displeased some of the famous cricketers from 'W.G.' to Wally Hammond, whose stroke-play is still a memory treasured on this Bristol cricket ground'.

REPORT ON THE ENGLAND v WALES GAME AT BRISTOL IN HOCKEY NEWS.
APRIL 1952.

Denys Carnill captained Oxford University, Cheltenham, England and Great Britain. Won 45 England and 27 GB caps, 1950-1960.

Denys pictured above – in Hockey News September 1952.

As well as his cricket, where the statistics speak for themselves, he was at one time asked to play at Wimbledon but had to decline because it cut across other sporting commitments.

He was a great sportsman, a true Master Sportsman whom you will enjoy reading about. Thank you Norman for the pleasure you gave us, and thank you Richard for all your efforts.

Denys Carnill

INTRODUCTION

All schools have their distinguished alumni, and Framlingham College, "The Albert Middle Class College in Suffolk", is no different. Politicians, artists, military men, including no fewer than three winners of the Victoria Cross, High Court judges, businessmen, farmers, horse racing trainers of three Derby winners and international sportsmen, all feature in the distinguished former pupils section of the Old Framlinghamian archive.

This is a book about one of those former pupils who became a master at the College, spending more than 50 years connected in one form or another to his alma mater. He wrote two books and they are in the College Library. But there is nothing in that library, or available elsewhere, which records his story. Those who knew him, particularly those who saw him in his sporting prime, grow old, and if the story is not told now, it will be lost.

What can be gleaned from the sporting record offers no insights into the man. What does appear suggests that there was, to put it neutrally, something unusual about his talent. Here, in the clipped tones of a reference book, is how the Oxford Companion to Sports and Games, edited by John Arlott, summarises Norman's career:

'Although he represented Cambridge for 3 years before 1939, it was not until after the war that he burst upon the squash scene and, virtually unknown, won the amateur championship in December 1946. He won the title for the next 4 years and then retired from the game. He returned however to captain the British team in South Africa in 1955. As an international hockey player he captained the British Olympic team, as a forward, in 1948 and was capped 37 times at hockey by England or Great Britain. He also played cricket for Essex and Devon.'

As a pupil at the College from 1956 to 1961 I knew Norman from the sport I played there, rather than from the classroom, where we did not coincide, my having been permitted, sadly, at the age of 13, to give up

the study of Geography. Like many others I kept in touch with him in later life. I saw more of him in his last years than before, having secured, not without difficulty, his agreement, and then his active support, for this biography.

He was a difficult subject, which will not surprise those who knew him well, because notwithstanding a self-confidence which appeared to many as arrogance, he was naturally disinclined to talk about himself and his achievements, only being prepared to reveal glimpses of his beliefs and thoughts. That a story has been produced at all is entirely due to the support I received from Mullie and the family, who were interested in learning more about this private husband and father, as well as the contributions received from so many of his former pupils and fellow masters, and a host of his friends and colleagues from the world of sport.

If the text is dominated by sporting record that is because sport informed Norman's entire existence. It is hoped that the words of the contributors, both favourable and critical, will provide some leavening to this sporting diet. The biography has a sub-text: the story of the sports people whom Norman encountered who, like him, were all-rounders, gifted in different sports. The final chapter seeks to bring those threads together in a short review of these sporting polymaths of Norman's era. For those who have an interest in the close detail of his career on pitch, court and field, appendices are provided. I am responsible for all errors therein and in the text.

Richard Sarge

RJS
Hampshire February 2011

1

OLYMPIC HOCKEY SILVER

The eleven weary men climbed the stairs to the right of the box, turned left at the top and followed the slim figure at their head along the front of the box. They stopped and watched as their leader halted, grasped the hand of Princess Elizabeth and with a nod of the head accepted the silver medal attached to its ribbon. As he turned to look at the cheering Wembley crowd, enthusiastically applauding their Great Britain hockey team, Norman Borrett felt the conflicting emotions of achievement and disappointment.

He had captained his side to a second place, an achievement which would not be equalled for forty long years until the 1988 Olympic hockey gold was won. But that satisfaction was tempered by the fact that they had lost. It did not matter to him that their Indian victors, Olympic champions in 1928, 1932 and 1936, were unanimously regarded as the best team in the world. Borrett did not like, and was not accustomed to, losing, particularly by four goals to nil. That August 1948 result was not often to be repeated in his later career.

The Olympic Games had been held in London for the first time in 1908, and London had been promised them again for the 1944 Games, but that event had evaporated in the smoke of war. In 1946 London accepted the IOC's invitation to host the first post-war Olympiad, and agreed, in order to maintain the four yearly cycle, to put them on with a scant two year preparation in 1948. The Austerity Games, as they were later dubbed, saw the 6,000 competitors from 59 countries housed in military buildings, with the GB team's training camp situated at Butlins, Clacton.

The most crucial occasion in the history of sport...

The IOC president, speaking after the Games, described, with perhaps forgivable hyperbole, the staging of the Olympic Games in London as "the most crucial occasion in the history of sport". He went on to say that "in the threadbare and impoverished world of 1948, it was a challenge to the British genius for improvisation for Britain to hold the Games in a city afflicted by an unparalleled housing shortage". There was no purpose-built stadium, just a temporary running track at the Wembley home of football. Dutch athlete Fanny Blankers-Koen, a mother of two who won four gold medals and was later voted the female athlete of the century, reached the stadium for her events by taking the underground train and walking the rest of the way. Food was still rationed and so was

LEFTT: The Olympic Final at Wembley Stadium, August 1948. Norman second left and Micky Walford second right. Note the difference between the English and the Indian head sticks, and also the uneven grass surface.

clothing. The Australian Hockey Association offered to send food parcels to selected British hockey players to enhance their performance, an offer which was declined with sincere thanks.

Crowds in excess of 80,000 flocked to Wembley, as a public hungry for sporting entertainment on the grand scale attended the first Olympiad for 12 years. Mullie, Norman's widow, recalls the thrill of attending the opening ceremony at Wembley on Thursday July 29th. British ceremonial tradition produced a pageant which, although simple, created a wonderful cosmopolitan and friendly welcome to the Games.

Mullie attended the first match of the hockey tournament two days later. A total of thirteen countries had entered the event, and were placed in three round-robin groups, two of four and one of five. The winners of the four-team groups, plus the winner and runner-up of the five-team group, would progress to the semi-finals.

Post-war it was possible to divide the hockey world into two parts, referenced by the type of hockey stick used in each country. The traditional, so called English head stick, with its long curving striking area, remained the weapon of choice in most of the world. Only a few countries had adopted the Indian head, a shorter, stubbier-headed stick, more easily manoeuvrable when playing on the difficult reverse, left, side of the body (hockey being a game which, unusually, requires everyone to play right-handed). Of the leading teams competing in the Olympics of 1948, the Asian sides, India, Afghanistan and Pakistan used the new-fangled version, whilst the Western participants, Great Britain, Holland, France, Belgium, Spain, Switzerland, Argentina and the United States stayed traditional. Acceptance in Britain of the Indian stick was to take a long time; Denys Carnill, writing as the 1952 British Olympic captain, wrote an article encouraging such acceptance as late as January 1953.

The first four-team group was won easily by India, the only surprise being that the Spanish side, concentrating on packing their defence, held them to two goals. In their other two preliminary games India scored eight and nine goals. The five-team group was won by Pakistan who were unbeaten. They were held to scores of 2-1 and 3-1 by Belgium and France respectively, but defeated Holland 6-1. The Dutch team nevertheless qualified for the semi-finals as runners-up by winning their other three games.

Great Britain was considered likely to have little trouble in winning its four-team group. But the first match, on Saturday 31st July against Switzerland, at the Guinness Sports Ground at Park Royal in North West London, produced a surprise. The Great Britain team, comprising five Scots, one Welshman and five English, and playing the traditional, and rigidly applied, five-three-two formation, lined up with Brodie in goal; Sime and William Lindsay at full back; Micky Walford, Reynolds, and Robin Lindsay at half-back; and in the

forward line Peake, White, Adlard, Norman Borrett, and Griffiths.

The Swiss, like the Spaniards, concentrated on a massed defence, and although Great Britain attacked almost continuously, they did not show quite enough imagination in pressing home their advantage. The press considered that Sime and Lindsay at the back, and Borrett and Griffiths up front, did well, but the 0-0 draw was a big disappointment to Norman's team.

The next match, six days later at Chiswick Polytechnic, against USA, bronze medallists at the 1932 Olympics, saw a much improved performance from an unchanged GB team. The London Evening Standard reported that: *'Great Britain played brilliant hockey at Chiswick last night against the United States and after leading by 4 goals at half-time eventually ran out winners by 11 goals to none. Goals were scored by Borrett six, Adlard two, White, Peake and Reynolds.'* This scoreline remains today Great Britain's only double-figure victory.

The side had only two days rest before their last group match, on Saturday 7th August against a skilful Afghanistan side. On the perfect grass of the Lyons' Sports Club, Sudbury, Great Britain started slowly, going two up by half-time. Norman's interval talk again had a dramatic effect, the team putting six more past keeper A. J. Nuristani (one of five Nuristanis in the team). Norman's personal tally was four, with two from White and one each from Griffiths and Adlard. Jim Blythe, an Old Framlinghamian, remembers Norman telling him in all seriousness some years later that the Afghan goalkeeper applied for asylum after the game, fearing that he would be unwelcome in his

home country after this performance.

Switzerland having been held to a draw by the Argentine, Britain headed the group, and went through to the semi-final, a further two days later on the Monday. Holland showed much better form against India in their semi-final than they had against Pakistan, and they were thought by many spectators to be unlucky not to draw instead of losing 2-1, after being two goals down at half-time.

The Evening Standard previewed GB's next match, at 7.15pm on August 10th with the headline '*Ten goal Borrett in semi: we play Pakistan*'.

The Pakistanis, playing in their first Olympiad after partition and containing several players from the great Indian pre-war team, faced an unchanged GB side. It was a desperately hard game, and GB had to be at their best on the lush turf of Wembley Stadium to hold their opponents goalless at half-time. The second half saw the home team stronger in the heavy conditions and two goals from centre forward Adlard saw them through 2-0, a result described in the newspapers as GB's great day of the tournament.

The team's stamina was tested by the short recovery period permitted before the final, which was played at 6pm on Thursday August 12th. The opponents, India, were strongly fancied, the best team in the world, winners of the previous three Olympics, and now with a brilliant new crop of players - the average age of the side being not much more than twenty.

Buoyed by a dozen or more telegrams wishing him luck, from friends, hockey clubs, the squash world, Framlingham staff, old Cambridge

OLYMPIC HOCKEY MEN ON TRIAL

The British Olympic hockey trial match sides to play at Weston-super-Mare on June 26 are:

REDS: D L S Brodie (Glasgow), G B Sime (Glasgow), P Whitbread (London), M M Walford (Sherborne), F O Reynolds (Army), F R Lindsay (London and Army), J M Peake (Navy), W N White (Cambridge), R E Adlard (Cheltenham), N F Borrett (Dorset), W S Griffiths (Newport).

WHITES: E G Highman (Cardiff), F A Stephens (Bath), W L Lindsay (Dublin), P O Stanley (Bristol), D B Thomas (Cardiff), H T Lake (Devizes), A H Young (Glasgow), R Davies (Cardiff), W A Pitt (Bristol), A Morris (Swansea), W O Green (Army).

Olympic hockey Test

The Great Britain team to meet Oxford and Cambridge touring side in an Olympic hockey trial at Park Royal, London, next Saturday will be: D L S Brodie (Scotland), G B Simes (Scotland), P Whitbread (England), M M Walford (England), F O Reynolds (England), R F Lindsay (Scotland), J M Peake (England), W N White (Scotland), R E Adlard (England), N F Borrett (England), W S Griffiths (Wales).

OLYMPIC HOCKEY TRIAL

FROM OUR HOCKEY CORRESPONDENT

In a trial game at Park Royal on Saturday the British Olympic side, although without N. F. Borrett, gave a brilliant display of hockey against a combined Oxford and Cambridge side who will visit South Africa at the end of the month, and won very easily by eight goals to one.

The training and tactics developed during the past months under the combined management of Captain G. S. Grimston and C. E. Newham showed the Olympic side to be a machine-like combination, and well as the Universities played, they stood no chance with a really fit side, who went at full stretch from start to finish. The forwards combined very well indeed and the defence had a perfect understanding with one another. The game was one of the best seen for years.

The English centre, R. E. Adlard, was at his best, scoring five brilliant goals, R. Davies, J. Peake, and W. N. White scoring the remainder. J. S. McCormick scored for the Universities.

BRITISH OLYMPIC XI.—D. L. S. Brodie (Scotland); G. B. Sime (Scotland), P. Whitbread (England); M. M. Walford (England), F. O. Reynolds (England), F. R. Lindsay (Scotland); J. M. Peake (England), R. Davies (Wales), R. E. Adlard (England), W. N. White (Scotland), W. S. Griffiths (Wales).

OXFORD AND CAMBRIDGE.—J. B. Lewis (Cambridge); R. M. Argyle (Cambridge), J. B. Dosseter (Oxford); W. Vans Agnew (Cambridge), A. J. Robinson (Midlands), R. J. L. Altham (Oxford); J. S. Maples (Cambridge), R. A. Fletcher (Oxford), C. J. Studdert Kennedy (Oxford), J. P. McCormick (Cambridge), A. N. Other.

GAMES HOCKEY DRAW

AMSTERDAM, Sunday.—Great Britain, the Netherlands, India and Pakistan, the four strongest hockey countries, have been placed at the head of the four pools into which the 17 entries for the Olympic tournament have been divided. Eire's entry was not accepted. The pools are:

POOL A.—India, Austria, Argentina, Palestine, Poland.

POOL B.—Great Britain, Czechoslovakia, Hungary, Spain.

POOL C.—The Netherlands, Afghanistan, Switzerland, the U.S.

POOL D.—Pakistan, France, Belgium, Denmark.

Britain will play three matches within six days—against Hungary on July 31, Spain on Aug. 3, and Czechoslovakia on Aug. 5.—Reuter.

DRAW AT HOCKEY

There was no score in the preliminary round of the Olympic hockey match between Great Britain and Switzerland at Park Royal.

Britain, with all the play in the first half, might have had a commanding lead had it not been for the brilliant saving tactics of the Swiss goalkeeper, F. Stuehlinger.

In the second half Britain continued to dominate the game, but were foiled by the strong Swiss defence.

British forwards N. F. Borrett and W. S. Griffiths played well, and defenders W. Lindsay and Sime were prominent. Results:

Great Britain 0, Switzerland 0; Holland 4, Belgium 1 (at Park Royal). India 8, Austria 0, Denmark 2, France 2 (at Sudbury).

Borrett's four

BEATING Afghanistan 8—0 in the last of the preliminary Olympic HOCKEY rounds, Great Britain have entered the semi-final. After his six goals against U.S.A. on Thursday, N. F. Borrett (inside-left) scored four.

Britain soon forced a number of short corners. After 25 minutes White put Britain ahead. Borrett then beat both backs and dribbled the ball into the net.

Britain increased their interval lead when Borrett (2) and W. Griffiths scored from short corners, but the best goal of the match came from White, who snatched the ball with reversed stick from the goal-line. Borrett cracked home another and R. Adlard scored Britain's eighth.

HOCKEY

Great Britain played brilliant hockey at Chiswick last night against the United States, and after leading by four goals at half-time eventually ran out winners by 11 goals to none. The United States goalkeeper made many good saves, but the side was outclassed by the speed and stick-work of the British team. Goals were scored by Borrett (6), Adlard (2), White, Peake, and Reynolds.

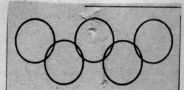

Hockey

10-goal Borrett in 'semi'

WE PLAY PAKISTAN

Standard Hockey Reporter

BRITAIN'S team for to-night's Olympic hockey semi-final against Pakistan, at Wembley Stadium (7.15), will be that which, in their last two matches, against U.S.A. and Afghanistan, scored 19 goals and conceded none.

Pakistan are considered by good judges to be a better side than India. If that estimate is correct they should be good enough to win the Olympic title.

But the British team have not yet been seriously extended. They are improving rapidly and, when really extended, as they will be to-night, may well surpass previous performances.

Top scorer

Norman Borrett, the British captain, sets a fine example. Not only does he make innumerable openings in midfield, but he is our most dangerous forward. He has scored ten of Britain's present total of 19 goals. Borrett, a schoolmaster at All Hallows, is also our amateur squash rackets champion.

Both teams are confident; but the heavy rain of the last few days must work in our favour, since we are accustomed to soft pitches, whereas the Pakistanis play a game better suited to the hard, fast surfaces natural in their own country.

There is a good chance of a British win.

Hockey Highlight

Imagine a forward line of S. H. Shoveliers and you will get some idea of the brilliant hockey played in the Olympic Games by the team of Indians who won the trophy. One shudders to think how many goals they would have scored against Great Britain in the final at Wembley if the ground had been as hard as some of those they play upon in their own country.

Appearance of a British team in the Olympic Tournament after a very long absence was a heartening feature; by reaching the final our team have given English hockey the biggest fillip it has ever had. Naturally all attendance records for hockey in this country were broken at Wembley.

Our All-Rounders

In one thing I think we had the pull over the Indians—many members of our team were all-rounders, with outstanding records at other games. N. F. Borrett, inside-left, is the squash champion; M. M. Walford, right-half, plays cricket for Somerset and, like W. N. White, our other inside-forward, is a Varsity rugger Blue.

Charges to pay

_____ s. _____ d.

RECEIVED

POST OFFICE

TELEGRAM

Prefix. Time handed in. Office of Origin and Service Instructions. Words.

At ___6·15___ m **52**

From 2·51 PM EAST LONDON T 26

By

No.

OFFICE STAMP

9 48

At _____ m

To _____

By

BORRETT CAPTAIN BRITAIN HOCKEY TEAM EMPIRE

STADIUM WEMBLEY =

GOOD GAMES GOOD SHOOTING AND ALL THE BEST OF

LUCK FOR TODAY AND THURSDAY = ALL ENGLAND

WOMENS HOCKEY ASSOCIATION +

For free repetition of doubtful words telephone TELEGRAMS ENQUIRY or call, with this form at office of delivery. Other enquiries should be accompanied by this form, and, if possible, the envelope.

B or C

G.N.P.Co. Ltd. 51-7820

ABOVE: Captain and team received numerous good luck messages from friends and supporters.

colleagues, and the Irish hockey goalkeeper, Norman ran out on to the Wembley turf before a British record crowd for a hockey international of 25,000. GB's attack struggled from the start against a sound Indian defence, with Norman and his fellow midfielders forced to tackle back on the very fast and skilful opposing forwards. Neither side found play easy on the heavy, bumpy, pitch, which had not been improved by the ground having been the venue for the soccer semi-final only 24 hours beforehand. The Indians were expected to have the greater difficulty with conditions which were totally foreign to the fast, bare pitches of their home territory, but they had a genius for adaptation. If the ball didn't travel well along the ground they employed the aerial route.

Norman's 1950 instructional book 'Improving Your Hockey' describes this tactic: '_The scoop stroke, although legal, is a bad one as it is likely to lead to dangerous play. It is an ugly and unnecessary stroke. Perhaps the only excuse (if there is one) for using it is in very wet weather when the ball will not travel far on the ground. It was used repeatedly by the Indians against Great Britain in the final of the Olympic Games Hockey Tournament. Their forwards scooped the ball over the heads of our backs and chased it, for the ground was heavy and it was difficult for the defence to turn quickly and recover._'

The Indian wingers were put away to great effect by clever Indian passing and two goals before half-time gave the champions a comfortable lead. Norman had a chance to reduce the deficit but was unable to convert a penalty bully awarded against Pinto the Indian goalkeeper. Norman's half-time talk produced a spirited GB performance in the second half, but two more goals enabled the Indians to run out clear winners, 4-0. Norman in later life felt that "we had shot our bolt with the effort we had made to overcome Pakistan and the shortness of recovery time between matches made things difficult for us. The Indian inside-right was an outstanding player, full of wizardry." Bill Colwill, later the hockey correspondent of the Independent, was at the match: 'India were awesome, very young with magic skills which made the British players look pedestrian by comparison.'

The British hockey team, along with all other competitors, was invited by the Olympic Organizing Committee to a farewell party at London's Hurlingham Club, the night of the final day of the Games, and the following Wednesday to the High Commissioner of India's Farewell Reception to the Indian Olympic Team at India House. And that was it; no radio or television appearances, no clothing or stick sponsorship contracts, no mentions in the New Year's Honours list. For these were the days of amateur, unpaid, uncoached, unsponsored sport played by enthusiasts out of a love of the game, and this is the story of an amateur sportsman, who, if he had been born into a later age when winning sportsmen were glamourised and idolized, would no doubt from time to time have occupied some space on the back pages of our daily newspapers, even though his two main games, hockey and squash, continue to be regarded as minor sports.

2

CHILDHOOD, SCHOOL AND UNIVERSITY 1917–1939

MARSH GREEN FARM, NEVILL HOUSE AND STOKE PARK

ABOVE: Alice Borrett with Charles (left) and Norman.

There have been Borretts in East Anglia for many generations, since the first Huguenot Borrett arrived from France. Walter George Borrett, son of Charles Catchpole Borrett, a maker of candles from Fressingfield, Suffolk, was born in Poplar, London, in December 1870. He married Alice Frances Mecrow and became a farmer in the Dagenham countryside. There were two children of the union, late in Walter's life, the first, Charles Walter, in November 1916, and the second, Norman Francis, eleven months later, on 1st October 1917, born at Whipps Cross Hospital in Wanstead, Essex.

Charles and Norman's early education was at a kindergarten in Barking. When Charles was seven and Norman six they went to board at Nevill House, an Eastbourne prep school run by a Mr. Laming. From there at the age of eight the boys moved to another boarding school - Stoke Park Preparatory School at Guildford – where they stayed until reaching secondary school age.

In the 1920s prep schooling followed traditional lines, based on religion, exercise, sport and study, in something like that order. Norman and Charles adapted, as they had to, to life away from parental care, with only three exeat visits each term. That Norman enjoyed his prep school days, away from home from an early age, was down to two factors, the protective presence of his brother Charles and his love of and success in sport. Both boys were naturally good at games and enjoyed any pastime involving exercise, whether with or without a ball. There was no squash or hockey, these being specialized sports which they would not see until they were thirteen. As is often the case, the aptitude which both boys displayed on the games field came from no obvious source; neither parent was blessed with particular sporting skill, nor the grandparents. And is also frequently so, the younger brother, born to travel in the wake created by, and to be in competition with, his older sibling, was destined to be the more talented, and the more self-confident, of the two.

Norman's parents retained some of his childhood letters home to Marsh Green Farm in Dagenham, written in an immaculate hand, far more legible than the handwriting he was to employ later as a school

teacher. In May 1929 Norman recorded that he had been second in class with 69%, and that he had lost to Hoe Place playing for the A Cricket team. In the formal language of the time he concluded "I hope you are quite well; I am fit and happy." Norman's letter to his parents in Landermere, Frinton, in October 1930 advised that he had been third in class that week with 61%, that he had won his football game by five goals to three, but had lost his hockey match against the Royal Grammar School, Guildford, by seven goals to three. The conclusion to the letter was the same but with the added warmth of "fondest love, your affectionate son, Norman."

I hope that you are quite well. I am fit and happy…With fondest love, your affectionate son, Norman…

Between the dates of those two letters Marsh Green Farm had been sold by his parents. Walter Borrett had been approached by the Ford Motor Company who were planning to establish a Thames-side motor plant, and were keen to acquire the acreage which the farm offered for this purpose. Walter and Alice were reluctant to move. The price offered by Ford was however generous and Walter, realising he could secure the family's finances, accepted. The proceeds were invested in the new family home, Landermere on Fourth Avenue, near the sea-front on the Essex coast at Frinton, and in property in London which was rented out.

The two boys were fortunate that their natural skill and keenness at games was supported by the Stoke House staff. Sport was an integral part of the curriculum in those days, and the staff were enthusiastic and encouraging. School trips to sporting events were organized by willing masters. On such a trip Norman saw his first Test match, being taken to Lord's towards the end of the summer term on Saturday 28th June 1930 to see England play Australia in the second Test. On the first day England had scored 387 for nine, thanks to a century in his first Test innings by Duleepsinghi. Norman was lucky that the school chose the second day for the visit. In Norman's schoolboy pencilled hand his scorecard records a glorious day's play. After an opening stand of 162, the 21 year old Bradman came in to score a brilliant undefeated 155 by the close of play, when Australia were, at 404 for 2, well on their way to a seven wicket win. (And they say that fast scoring in Tests is a 21st century phenomenon). This remarkable day included not only a presentation on the ground of the two teams to King George V, but also the appearance over the ground of the ill-fated airship the R101.

FRAMLINGHAM COLLEGE

The first four years

The scout actor; an introduction to squash and hockey, under Charles' wing, the debating society, sport in the school holidays.

In September 1931, just before his 14th birthday, Norman followed Charles and became a boarder at Framlingham College in Suffolk, 'a school for the sons of gentlefolk' created in 1864 by a charter granted by Queen Victoria in memory of Prince Albert. The school was to become a significant part of the rest of his life. The story of Norman's schooldays at Framlingham was recounted in Bob Gillett's elegantly drawn history of the College from 1925, 'The Second Sixty Years', and the following account draws significantly on that source. Quotations are from the College magazines of the period.

Young Norman's sporting prowess was soon to show itself at the College, but the first impact he made was in a completely different area of activity. In his first term he joined the College scout troop and appeared before the adjudicator, Mr (later to become Sir) Cedric Hardwicke, the well-known stage and film actor, in the Patrol Play competition. He was '*made up perfectly as a modern flapper, with ginger hair, and a hat at a marvellous angle*'. He did not find, even at this tender age, anything particularly daunting about performing before an audience.

Magazine reports of his first year of sport contain a few pointers to the future. The Easter term of 1932 saw him playing hockey for the first time, in the Colts XI, where his skill earned early plaudits: '*A player of undoubted class…we watch his progress with interest*' and his first cricket term in the Colts team suggested he had '*some promise for the future*'. It was his second winter term, beginning in September 1932, that saw the first glimpse of his particular talent for squash racquets.

At barely 15 years of age he won all his matches for his house, Stradbroke, in the inter-house squash competition, open to boys of all ages.  This was the inaugural such contest, the College courts having only been constructed, and squash introduced for the first time into the college sports curriculum, only two years earlier.

ABOVE: The old open-backed courts built 1930. M. Garnett in foreground 1954.
BELOW: Framlingham Castle, across the Mere, from the front drive of the College, 1933.

ABOVE: College 1st XV 1934. Rev. Kneese back left, next to 17 year old Norman. Brother Charles is the Captain. Note the original open-backed squash courts in the background.

The two courts were each a foot or two short of later regulation size, with low overhead girders, and a gallery above the back of the court open to the cold Suffolk air. Most boys who learned their craft on those courts, playing no lobs and killing the slow ball with some ease in the cold atmosphere, would on leaving school find it difficult to adapt to the bigger, higher and hotter courts found almost everywhere else, especially at the main London venues which hosted the public school competitions, the Evans and the Drysdale Cups. Whilst we will see later that Norman Borrett's squash may also have suffered from the effects of the low roof structure, the cold air of those open-backed Framlingham courts nurtured an ability he never thereafter lost to kill the ball from anywhere in the court.

In only his second hockey term, Easter 1933, 15 year old Norman was picked for the 1st XI, along with his brother Charles. The magazine noted an improvement in footwork amongst the hockey players from the advent of squash, and Norman was himself later to attribute much of his success at the one game to his skill at the other. His second cricket term also saw him selected for the school 1st XI, and he did well with over 300 runs from his bat

helping the side to several wins.

In the winter term of his third year the young Borrett again won all his squash matches in the inter-house competition. Charles captained the College XV that term but was unfortunate to break a leg in October. This injury was not to heal quickly. He did not play sport for the rest of the year and even in the following year's rugby term he was forced to be non-playing captain, in which role he attracted 'a large measure of credit' for the spirit shown by his team.

After Christmas before the start of the Easter term, the enterprising Richmond Hockey Club organized a series of matches for leading schoolboy players. Norman, 16 years old, was chosen for the first of the three games, playing at centre-half in the same side as fellow Framlinghamian J.S. Woodbridge. The national press noted that Norman was one of the best half-backs on display.

On his return to school his hockey talent became obvious. In the view of one prescient critic 'there should be a future for him at this game'. On the College cricket ground, the Back, during the summer he demonstrated that a batsman with hand-eye coordination, balance and good footwork could hit the opposition bowling with ease. When winter came he played rugby, the main pre-Christmas game. Squash racquets was still a fledgling sport and there was no coaching and little competition, although an enthusiastic headmaster W.H.A. Whitworth arranged a number of representative matches for five strings in that winter term of 1934. Norman was a member of the team and played in matches against, amongst others, the Escorts from London, the Old Framlinghamians, HMS Ganges and RAF Martlesham, sides which were still on the college fixture list thirty years later. The inter-house contest again pitted the best in school against each other, and Norman won all his matches for the third year running.

Hockey had been introduced into the College curriculum in 1914 by headmaster F. W. Stocks, whose two brothers, Sir Denys Stocks, later President of the HA, and the Rev. F. C. Stocks, were both England internationals. F. W. himself played for Oxford and in the 1920s produced some excellent players at the College, among them one international, N. R. Salew, and several divisional and county players including L. G. Hayward (Southgate and South), B. W. Firkling (Hampstead and South) and W. A. Goodale (Wimbledon and Middlesex). After the death of Stocks in 1929, C. E. Thomas took over the hockey, and was to run it for the next twenty years. In 1930 three members of the 1st XI played for the English Schoolboys which toured Germany, one of whom F. G. Jerrey was later to play county and divisional hockey, both with and against Norman.

In the 1930s the game thrived and was played, alongside athletics, as the major game during the Lent term. Divisional, county, and Army and Navy players still appeared in good numbers. Fixtures with other schools, which had not been easy to arrange as there were few hockey schools within a reasonable distance of the College, grew in number. In March 1935 brother Charles, by now Head Prefect, moved the proposition at the College debating society that "Athletics should be abandoned in favour of a longer hockey season". In an acrimonious discussion, in which the motion was narrowly lost, Charles relied on both the local unpopularity and the excessively strenuous nature of athletics to make his point. It was a point evidently lost on his sibling who, apart from representing the school in the Norwich / Ipswich / Framlingham triangular schools meeting, participated in the College athletic sports day and won or was placed in no less than five events, an activity clearly not strenuous enough to prevent him playing for the school in sixteen hockey matches in term time. The full sporting diary to which Norman committed himself did not mean he ignored other duties and interests. He became secretary of the College debating society and, showing confidence on his feet, took part in a number of debates.

The pace of life did not slacken in the holidays. Norman played several hockey matches over the Easter break, including the Lowestoft hockey festival and a game for Cranleigh at Thames Ditton where he attracted a favourable mention from the watching Times correspondent.

Norman was made captain of cricket in his fourth summer term,

1935, but found that for all his efforts, 357 runs and a remarkable 60 wickets with his left arm spin bowling, his team struggled to match him, '*even in the virtues of courage and commitment*'. Tennis was not a recognised game, either at school or at house level, there being no hard courts until headmaster Whitworth's plea to the governors for £350 funding produced two such courts in Easter 1935, and Norman played only a little.

ABOVE: Participation in the CCF was compulsory. Norman is nearest the camera in the front row, his boots apparently about to attract comment from the inspecting officer.

The end of that College year saw the departure of Charles after five years of hard work and achievement. In the words of Bob Gillett: '*When Charles left the school he did so with a special blessing. He was Head Prefect, a senior NCO, captain of the XV and Cross Bearer. His intention was to seek ordination to the priesthood. After graduation at Cambridge he was indeed ordained priest in 1943, beginning a remarkable career in the Church as Curate of All Saints, Newmarket.*'

As Canon Borrett he was to be an occasional preacher at the College in later years, and it was as the Venerable Archdeacon Borrett that in 1988 he dedicated in the College chapel the Old Framlinghamian Lodge's fortieth anniversary gift of a carved crucifix.

The Borrett family Frinton summer holiday at Landermere in 1935 was a busy one as Charles got ready for Cambridge. He and Norman played cricket for Frinton, visited friends and talked of 'Fram' and how life there would differ for Norman without the presence of his older brother. Norman had been selected by Essex to play for their Young Amateurs side, and he played against the Young Amateurs of Suffolk, Hertfordshire, and Surrey. The Evening News reported that the Surrey bowling had proved too much for Essex '*though N. F. Borrett made 50 when things were going very badly.*'

The final year

*Head prefect, captain of squash, fives, hockey,
cricket, athletics and swimming; rugby and squash
at Christmas; hockey and squash at Easter;
Essex YAs, 63 runs at Lords, and Frinton cricket
in the summer.*

Succeeding his older brother as head prefect in his final year at school,
starting in September 1935, Norman's dominant position in school
affairs was remarkable. In the rugby 1st XV his play at stand-off half
made him a match-winner. Although '*he had much to learn… his innate
games sense proved of considerable value in directing the attacking policy of the
side*', and his 'genius' (not a word much bandied about in the sober
language of the College magazine reports of the day) was the influence
behind the general success of the team and in particular the win over
close rivals Ipswich School.

That same term he captained both the squash team and the
fives team, and participated in debates on, amongst other topics, the
Abyssinia-Italy dispute. During the next two terms he was captain
of hockey, cricket, athletics and swimming. If all this suggests that
life was hectic (apart from the need to keep up with the demands of
academic work) it ignores the lack of a break in the school holiday
as hockey, rugby and squash occupied most of his three weeks rest
from school. In the Christmas holiday of 1935 Norman played at
fly-half for the Eastern Counties Public Schools rugby XV in
several matches, and also had to find time to compete, amongst 47
other boys, in the Evans Cup, the Public Schools squash
tournament at Queen's Club. This tournament was played on
handicap from 1922 until 1949, and thereafter level. Little was
known of this pupil from East Anglia and the handicapper was
generous in his award of 'receive 2'. Norman sailed easily through
the second and third rounds, and reached the quarter-final. The
handicapper must have begun to doubt his judgement as Norman
went through to the semi-final with another three-games win,
showing a nice range of strokes, good positioning, and (interestingly,
according to The Times) '*reasonable speed*' about the court. The
semi-final gave him greater difficulty as he won 3-2 over an
opponent receiving 3.

In the final he played the favourite, the handicap back-marker,
R. S. Woodward from Lancing. Woodward had an impossible task on
his hands, owing 3 and giving 2 to Norman, a player who was clearly
as good as himself. This meant that he had to score 5 points before he
got level with Norman, and he fell into the trap of going all out for
winners, thus making many errors. Norman played safely and at times

brilliantly, with a nice touch on his drop-shots, as he won 9-1, 9-2, 9-4,
playing a number of shots which clung to the side-wall and several
winning drop-volleys as he clinched the match. The Daily Telegraph
took the view that '*Borrett's hitting to a length, drop-shots and general
court-craft suggest he is a very good player in the making.*' The strength of
Framlingham squash at this time is shown by the fine performance in
the Under 16 Junior event of J. D. Molyneux, who reached the final.

In the first week of the New Year Norman was on the train to
London again, to the Kensington Country Club, to play in the Club's
annual schoolboys tournament. He won the event with a straight-
games win over Yeats-Brown of Tonbridge, a player whom he was to
meet again post-war, in the Amateur.

The Easter term of 1936 saw the hockey colt who had four years
earlier been identified as '*a player of undoubted class*' become '*a polished
exponent of the game in every phase…he possesses a powerful shot…his
mastery of the
flick pass is
complete…he
always plays
with his head
and his
judgement is
rarely wrong.*'

…he always plays with his head and his judgement is rarely wrong

His influence, not just on his team, but on hockey's role in school life
was recognised:

'*As a captain he is both encouraging and inspiring and his stylish
exhibition has done much to improve the hockey in the School*'. He was a
class above all schoolboy opponents, and most club opponents as
well, scoring sixteen goals against Norwich and Ipswich schools in
just three matches, and leading the side to victories against several
club sides.

Ken Mayhew, eight months older than Norman, and a member of
the same College cricket and hockey teams as they progressed through
the school ranks, recently recalls, with the sharp memory of a fit and
alert 93 year-old, the words of advice given to Norman, at the end of
this, their last hockey term, by the hockey master C. E. Thomas, under
whose wise guidance Norman's play had developed: "When you go up
to Cambridge you should switch from your school position of centre
half to inside left. It is not difficult to play at centre half, but inside left
is far more demanding and the chances of your making a name for
yourself will be greater". Thomas lived to see the enormous impact
this advice was to have on English international hockey.

Athletics sports day in bitterly cold conditions in the first week of
April was dominated by the captain of athletics. In very heavy going
Norman demonstrated his stamina by winning the steeplechase for the

second consecutive year and his strength by winning the putting of the 16lb weight. He placed second in the mile, half-mile, long jump, relay and throwing the cricket ball, and third in the hurdles. Headmaster Whitworth duly handed the inter-house trophy to Norman as captain of his house, Stradbroke. The view that the College games committee took of all this is evident from its decision later in the year to prevent boys entering more than three races, excluding the steeplechase.

In the Easter holiday Norman captained the College hockey side at the Lowestoft Easter hockey festival, the side acquitting themselves well against adult competition, demonstrating *'quick footwork and clever combination'* in running the Dominoes off their feet, 8-2, Norman and Frank Jerrey each scoring three. The next week Norman went to London to compete, for the only time, in what was the annual unofficial 'Junior Amateur' squash competition, the Drysdale Cup, held at the RAC. 46 boys entered from a number of schools, Framlingham with five sending in the largest entry, followed by Lancing with four plus one old boy, the tournament being open to boys under 19. Norman won his first and second round matches but lost in the third, quarter-final, round, well beaten by D. M. Beadle, an undergraduate, who in turn lost, in five games, in the semi-final to the winner, C. M. Butler, formerly of Lancing. The Squash Rackets, Fives & Tennis and Rackets journal, in its November 1936 edition, noted that Framlingham's headmaster, Whitworth, had formerly taught at Lancing, *'but as he does not play squash this can have little connection with the victory of N. F. Borrett at Queen's Club (in the Evans Cup) and Framlingham's distinction in providing two players in the last eight of the Drysdale Cup'.*

C. F. M. Chapman was the other Framlinghamian mentioned, and he remained at the College for another year as captain of squash. The journal's article on Framlingham's squash prospects concluded:

'Chapman's chief difficulty is to obtain fixtures. The only school match is arranged against Lancing, to be played in London, and it is probable the Jesters may visit them. J. D. Molyneux and D. E. Wright are both old colours. If Framlingham can get the number of fixtures necessary to provide them with match experience, they should again be well represented at Queen's and the RAC'.

Norman's last term at Framlingham was, to put it mildly, a busy one. He had applied, in April 1935, for Cambridge and he now had to sit the entrance exam. He also had duties both as Stradbroke house captain and head prefect, as well as commitments on the dramatic front. In July the College staged, in the magnificent setting of Framlingham Castle, the bi-annual college play. His Casca in Julius Caesar was described as *'an efficient conspirator whose tremendous initial stab might have finished off a lesser man than Caesar'.* John Clymer, the pupil who played Caesar, might have wished for the stab to have come from any wrist other than that of the future amateur squash champion of England.

Clymer's survival enabled him to take a significant part in Old Framlinghamian affairs in future years, and it was he who in 1969, representing the Society of Old Framlinghamians, presented new squash courts to the College to replace those on which, until the year before, Norman Borrett had taught the game to generations of young Framlinghamians. The new courts, full in height and length and no longer open to the elements, would give future boys the facilities which Norman never had to work with.

As cricket captain in that last summer term Norman worked hard to develop his team but it still lost more matches than it won or drew. He did not have the benefit of the coaching support of a College

ABOVE: July 1935. Amidst the ruins of Framlingham Castle Norman plays Casca, second from the right, in Julius Caesar.

cricket professional; the first such appointment, that of the old Hampshire and England stalwart Philip Mead, the greatest run-scorer in the history of the English County Championship, not being made until the next year 1937. Nor, to divert for a moment, did Norman's team have the help of the famous Framlingham bowling-machine.

This remarkable contraption was built in 1908 by Reginald Brooks-King in Somerset, and donated anonymously to the College by a member of staff in July 1937. It is today the earliest extant such machine. It relied for propulsion on a very powerful spring releasing a bowling 'arm' on the lines of the Roman catapult system. It had a pin, fastened to a strap, which could be inserted into the ball to check its flight and hence exert a spin on the ball when it was fired. That was the theory. In practice the machine had a tendency to leap from its moorings at each delivery. In his September 1987 Cricketer magazine article on this singular piece of equipment, Scyld Berry, later to be editor of Wisden, recounts that Philip Mead, *'a bowling machine of no mean durability himself'*, made the machine redundant shortly after it had been installed, on his arrival at the College in 1937. It was sold to a scrap man but was spotted on the scrap cart by cricket-loving master Bob Gillett, who bought it, stored it in an out-house and then forgot about it until 1984 when he restored it and arranged for the Science Museum to display it alongside its more modern counterparts.

Norman Borrett's personal statistics for the 1936 season of 504 runs in 14 innings and 56 wickets spoke of an outstanding schoolboy talent. Contemporary accounts describe him as a batsman with all the strokes, including the one that has traditionally eluded even the finest exponents, the orthodox on-drive. He occasionally substituted for this shot *'a tremendous hit which, given connection, leaves the ground over mid-wicket's head'*. As a bowler he was rated as an indefatigable left-arm spinner and as captain *'he kept a fair grip on the game and spared neither himself nor his men'*.

A schoolboy blessed with such unusual sporting talent, in the days when prowess in that sphere would inevitably cause a culture of hero-worship from fellow pupils, might well struggle to prevent such achievements going to his head. Whilst Norman never lacked confidence, he did manage, in the opinion of two at least of his peers, Ken Mayhew and Patrick Howard-Dobson, to handle this schoolboy fame in a natural and unaffected way. They both felt that "he kept his feet on the ground and was popular with all of us".

Norman left Framlingham having matriculated successfully, scoring better in the arts than in the sciences. On his return to the College as a master in the 1950s he often related to the Common Room his struggle with pipette and burette, in C. E. 'Squiffy' Thomas's chemistry classes.

The summer vacation, longer than usual as the Cambridge term started later, meant cricket. Norman played for Essex Young Amateurs in several inter-county matches. This kept the name he had made for himself at school in the MCC's eye, with the result that at the end of July he received a letter from R. S. Rait-Kerr, MCC Secretary, inviting him to play for the Young Amateurs against the Young Professionals at Lord's on Friday and Saturday August 7th and 8th. This was a fixture designed to give a chance to appear at the headquarters of cricket to those boys who had missed out on selection for the main schoolboys' match - Lord's Schools versus The Rest - thus permitting the Public Schools selectors to see as many candidates as possible. Norman's side contained Alan Shirreff, a later captain of Kent, whilst the opposition included Leslie Compton, Brown, Routledge and Thompson, all of whom were to play regular cricket for Middlesex after the war. The Amateurs scored slowly *'but N. F. Borrett's innings was an exception'*, a freely-hit 63 coming at a critical time and stopping what looked like becoming a rot. When he came in, at number seven, he immediately enlivened the game with a fine drive to mid-off for an all-run five, and he continued to drive with great power until he was out to a mis-hit off fast bowler A. Nevell. Norman scored eight runs in the second innings, and bowled seven overs for eight runs and one wicket. Sixty five years later, sitting in front of the pavilion at Lords in the seat with his name on it, in the area reserved for those with over fifty years MCC membership ('Death Row' in common parlance), his companion, his pre-war Cambridge squash colleague, Michael Baring, recalled watching Norman hit a six over the old grandstand in that innings – a mighty blow for a youngster.

The following week the Frinton club hosted their traditional cricket week. For Norman this was if anything a step up in class of cricket, even after his Lord's experience, for the Frinton team included a number of current and future Essex county players, Arnold Quick, Frank Unwin, Frank Vigar and the Essex captain Tom Pearce. 18 year-old Norman's week went well as he scored 59, 67 and 56 in his first three innings, including two century partnerships with Pearce and Quick, which did no harm to any county aspirations he might have harboured. His seven innings that summer holiday for Frinton produced 397 runs, with a best of 152 against Felixstowe, and his bowling brought 12 wickets at 18 apiece, including 5-45 against Witham.

Clacton's Essex County week started later in August and Norman was there to watch the county play Nottinghamshire, Jack O'Connor scoring 111 off Larwood and Voce. The next time Norman was to see O'Connor was the next year, when the two of them played together for Essex against Cambridge University, when O'Connor was again to score 111. As a further coincidence, Norman's only post-war game for Essex was to be in at Clacton, against Nottinghamshire, exactly ten years later.

This card does not necessarily include the fall of the last wicket

2d. Lord's MCC Ground

Young Amateurs v. Young Professionals

FRIDAY & SATURDAY, AUGUST 7, 8, 1936.   (Two-day Match.)

	YOUNG AMATEURS.	First Innings.		Second Innings.	
1	R. H. Yeatman ....St. Paul's	c Goldsmith, b Routledge	18	c and b Lambert	24
2	J. Darbyshire ....Epsom	b Nevell	4	b Nevell	13
3	T. D. Heathcote ....Bradfield	c Brown, b Nevell	3	b Nevell	0
†4	D. E. Young...K.C.S., Wimbledon	l b w, (n) b Thursting......	6	st Compton, b Nevell.....	0
5	A. C. Shirreff ....Dulwich	l b w, b Thursting	20	l b w, b Nevell..............	1
6	A. K. Sharp ....Brighton	b Lambert	0	c Thompson, b Lambert..	58
7	N. F Borrett ....Framlingham	c Routledge, b Nevell ...	63	c Brown, b Nevell	8
*8	A. H. Holladay ....Bedford	b Nevell	0	l b w, b Lambert	3
9	D. R. Dalglish ....Ampleforth	b Nevell	13	l b w, b Nevell...............	7
10	D. C. Wilson ....Winchester	not out	20	not out	13
11	R. Campbell-Walker.....Sherborne	c Compton, b Nevell	2	b Nevell	0
		B 9, l-b 9, w , n-b 1,	19	B 1, l-b 6, w 1, n-b ,	8
		Total 168		Total 135	

FALL OF THE WICKETS.

1-9	2-28	3-36	4-48	5-49	6-80	7-81	8-107	9-153	10-168
1-24	2-30	3-42	4-42	5-46	6-52	7-55	8-123	9-135	10-135

ANALYSIS OF BOWLING.

Name.	1st Innings. O.	M.	R.	W	Wd.	N-b.	2nd Innings. O.	M.	R.	W	Wd.	N-b.
Nevell	22.1	6	44	6	...	...	18.4	5	47	7	...	...
Goldsmith.....................	5	2	9	0	...	1	...	...	...	...	...	...
Routledge.....................	7	3	9	1	...	...	4	1	10	0	1	...
Thursting.....................	16	2	59	2	...	...	4	0	13	0	...	...
Lambert	4	1	10	1	...	...	14	2	33	3	...	...
Thompson	4	1	18	0	...	...	...	...	...	...	...	...
Robertson.....................	...	...	...	...	...	...	4	0	24	0	...	...

	YOUNG PROFESSIONALS.	First Innings.		Second Innings.	
1	D'Arcy	c Dalglish, b C.-Walker..	19	c Young, b Borrett	31
2	Harrington	c Heathcote, b Yeatman..	5	c Darbyshire, b Dalglish..	4
†3	Goldsmith..............................	l b w, (n) b Dalglish	0	c Heathcote, b Wilson ...	7
4	Thursting................................	b Campbell-Walker	17	run out	12
5	Brown	b Campbell-Walker	2	c Yeatman, b Young......	28
6	Nevell	b Dalglish	17	not out	34
*7	Compton, L.	l b w, b Young..............	1	b Young........................	13
8	Thompson	run out	38	b Young........................	6
9	Routledge...............................	b Young	6	l b w, b Young...............	4
10	Robertson, J. S.	run out	1	run out	2
11	Lambert	not out	9	not out	0
		B 17, l-b 6, w 3, n-b 3,	29	B 17, l-b 1, w 1, n-b 1,	20
		Total 144		Total 161	

FALL OF THE WICKETS.

1-9	2-16	3-54	4-57	5-58	6-60	7-88	8-99	9-112	10-144
1-12	2-31	3-61	4-65	5-74	6-112	7-125	8-143	9-156	10-

ANALYSIS OF BOWLING.

Name.	1st Innings. O.	M.	R.	W	Wd.	N-b.	2nd Innings. O.	M.	R.	W	Wd.	N-b.
Dalglish.........................	19	11	20	2	3	...	8	5	16	1	1	1
Yeatman	4	2	5	1	...	...	1	0	1	0	...	...
Shirreff	9	4	8	0	...	...	12.2	1	27	0	...	...
Campbell-Walker	16	1	41	3	...	2	7	1	21	0	...	...
Young	15	2	36	2	...	1	18	5	42	4	...	...
Sharp	1	0	4	0	...	...	...	...	...	...	...	...
Borrett	3.1	2	1	0	...	...	4	1	6	1	...	...
Wilson	...	...	...	...	...	...	10	2	28	1	...	...

Umpires—Powell and Sweetland.   Scorer—Mavins.

The figures on the scoring board indicate the batsmen who are in.

Play begins 1st day at 11.30, 2nd day at 11.

Luncheon at 1.30.   †Captain.   *Wicket-keeper.

Stumps drawn at 6.30, half-an-hour extra on last day if necessary.

TEA INTERVAL—There will probably be a Tea Interval at **4.30-4.45** but it will depend on the state of the game.

(n) Signifies L.B.W. under the new experimental rule.

YOUNG AMATEURS WON THE TOSS.

CAMBRIDGE 1936–1939

Freshman Year

Squash for the University, but not hockey or cricket; the Amateur Squash Championship; and a County Cricket game for Essex.

A week after his 19th birthday, in October 1936, Norman went up to Pembroke College, Cambridge. His application for admission to Pembroke, made as long ago as February 1935, gave brief details of his Framlingham history: sub-prefect, Hockey XI, Colours '33, '34, '35, '36; Cricket XI, Colours '33, '34, '35, '36 Rugby Football XV, colours '34, '35, '36. He had passed his School Certificate in July 1934, with credits in

English, History, Geography, Mathematics, French, and thereby gained exemption from the whole of the Previous Examination except Latin. The Previous

…His application stated that he intended to read for the Geographical Tripos, with a view to a career as a schoolmaster.

Examination was the Entrance examination to Cambridge, which all had to take unless they obtained an exemption from all or part of it, usually on the strength of (Higher) School Certificate. His application stated that he intended to read for the Geographical Tripos, with a view to a career as a schoolmaster. He knew what he wanted to do.

Norman brought with him to Cambridge a squash reputation, based on his wins in the Evans Cup handicap and in the Kensington Club tournament the previous Christmas. He was invited to play in the first fixture of the Cambridge University season, against the Bachelor's Club on October 15th, and did well enough to be retained in the team for all the 13 matches up to the Varsity match on December 15th.

He thus got first class match experience against top London club and county players. The fixture list was impressive – Jesters, Queens Club, International Sportsmen, Princes Club and the Junior Carlton. His best result was to run Dr. J. F. Stokes, the top Surrey county player, close in a five game match against the Jesters.

By late November the composition of the Cambridge side had become clear, and Norman had established himself at second string, a fine achievement for a freshman. Just before the big day against

Oxford a major test of the side's prospects awaited. All five members of the prospective half-blue team entered the Amateur Squash Championship ("the Amateur") on December 4th. There were 64 competitors for Amr Bey's title, and Norman was mentioned in the press as an interesting entry amongst those younger men yet to win their championship spurs.

Norman was drawn in the first round against the experienced Desmond Backhouse, like his brother a previous runner-up in the Amateur, later to be capped by England in April 1938, and the winner in May 1936 of the Eton Fives national championship. The 19 year-old Borrett went on to the Bath Club 'B' court at 4 p.m. on Friday December 4th for the first of his many matches in the Amateur over the next 15 years. He lost, but was praised in the press for putting up a most promising show, running Backhouse close in the first game, winning the second on his merits, and nearly overhauling his opponent in both the third and fourth, before losing three games to one.

The Varsity match took place on December 15th, with Norman winning his half blue as second string. At first string was Cambridge's captain, Norman Yardley, a highly talented sportsman. His story is worth telling.

Whilst still a schoolboy at St. Peter's York in 1932, he won the North of England squash championships, a title he retained for the following five years. In 1933 he won the Drysdale Cup which he retained in 1934. His schoolboy squash feats were legendary, including a victory over the 1928 Amateur champion, and he was described as the most brilliant of all schoolboy players seen up to that date, '*close in class to Amr Bey*'. This was high praise indeed, as Amr Bey was himself said to be '*quite certainly the best squash player there has ever been*'.

Going up to Cambridge in 1935 Yardley carried all before him, winning a cricket blue as a freshman in 1935, and in 1936 heading the batting averages and playing a fine innings of 90 against Oxford. In August he played ten times for Yorkshire. In 1937 he scored two centuries for Cambridge and one for Yorkshire. As captain of the university cricket side in 1938 he presided over a team which did not win a match, but was chosen for the Rest in the Test trial and travelled to South Africa with Hammond's MCC side.

Yardley was a multi-skilled sportsman, excelling at cricket, squash and hockey, at each of which he gained a blue. In 1946 he played a full season for Yorkshire, toured Australia with Hammond in 1946-47, and was an obvious choice as captain of England in 1947. His squash suffered, as cricket claimed him, and he did not have the opportunities, particularly immediately after the war, to continue to develop his great talent for squash. A unique achievement of captaining England at both cricket and squash was thus lost.

Yardley was not well prepared for the 1936 Varsity squash match.

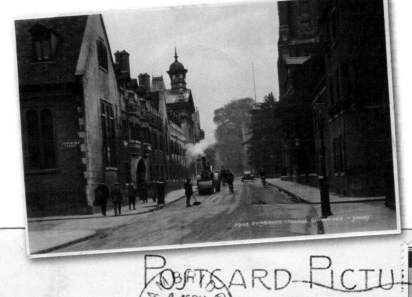

LEFT: The front and back of Norman's Pembroke College postcard to his father, in June 1935, on taking his entrance exam.

He had damaged an ankle at hockey, and had not done well in the recent Amateur squash championship, whereas his Oxford University opponent, Roger Pulbrook, had reached the semi-final, only losing to the great Amr Bey. Pulbrook was a distinguished rackets player and a promising squash player, who two years later was to win the South of England squash championship. The Daily Telegraph report of their contest, written by the well-known cricket writer R. C. Robertson-Glasgow, saw it as *'the match which stood out far above the others…Yardley, at his best, is among our first half-dozen amateurs, and Pulbrook has been playing first string for the Bath Club. Few finer things have been seen in squash rackets this season than Pulbrook's 'Rorke's Drift' defence and rally in the last game, when he drew up from 0-5 to 7-5 in one hand, almost on will-power alone.'* This effort was magnificent but in vain, as Yardley won 9-6, 9-5, 9-7.

Norman Borrett won 9-0, 6-9, 9-3, 9-3, at second string over R. C. Riseley. This was another remarkable match. Riseley played for Oxford at no less than four sports, squash, real tennis, lawn tennis, and rackets, this last a game at which he excelled. He was a hitter of merciless violence. He took the rackets technique, and the violence which is part of it, into his match against Norman, winning the second game according to the Evening Standard, *'by tempting Borrett to play rackets himself in self-defence, but did not succeed again.'* The Times' correspondent thought Riseley's thunderous style made the match *'rather amusing until Borrett's superior stroke-play prevailed'*. Robertson-Glasgow summed it up more prosaically: *'Borrett is a neat and excellent player, Riseley a strong man who plays terrific rackets strokes. Borrett was often outhit, but Riseley was too inaccurate to stave off defeat.'*

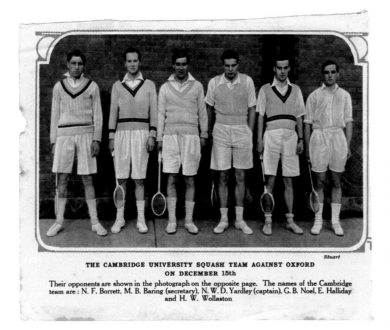

Stuart

THE CAMBRIDGE UNIVERSITY SQUASH TEAM AGAINST OXFORD
ON DECEMBER 15th

Their opponents are shown in the photograph on the opposite page. The names of the Cambridge
team are : N. F. Borrett, M. B. Baring (secretary), N. W. D. Yardley (captain), G. B. Noel, E. Halliday
and H. W. Wollaston

Cambridge completed a five-nil whitewash and defeated Oxford for the seventh year running. Norman's squash star was on the rise.

He played in the Pembroke hockey side, but struggled to get into the varsity team. He realized he needed to play regular top class club hockey if he was to persuade the Cambridge captain to pick him. Goodale, a fellow Old Framlinghamian, played for Wimbledon Hockey Club, and encouraged Norman to join the club. This he did, travelling each Saturday morning to play centre-half for the first team against the top London sides. In late October he impressed the Daily Telegraph reporter: '*A feature of the game (against the RAF, won 3-2 by Wimbledon) was the fine form of Borrett, the Wimbledon centre-half. He is at Cambridge and worthy of a trial with the light blues. He is however inclined to play too much on the attack, and give the opposing centre-forward plenty of scope.*'

Norman was of course keen to play well in Wimbledon's game against the University, a match which took place in late November. Cambridge won 8-1. '*Borrett at centre-half without neglecting defence tried hard to get his forwards going. It was not his fault that Wimbledon did not score more often; they had more than one chance*'. For Cambridge, Frank Hopkinson at inside-right and Norman Yardley at inside-left were outstanding, Yardley scoring three goals. This game gave the Cambridge captain, full-back P. L. Trevorrow, a close-up appreciation of Norman Borrett's abilities, with the result that he was then picked for several games in the varsity side. Although the Daily Telegraph described him as '*a prospective Blue and smart inside-left*', he did not gain selection for the varsity match, an omission which although with the benefit of hindsight may look odd, was not surprising given that the Cambridge insides, Yardley and Hopkinson, were both old blues, as was the centre-half, R. F. Marsh. Hopkinson was to play for England within one year and Norman within two. Norman was on the touchline in February at Beckenham to watch Cambridge lose the varsity match 3-0 to Oxford.

At the end of term he accepted an invitation to join the Cambridge University Muddlers – motto 'Post pugnam, prosit' - on its

Easter hockey tour to the Rheinland. Matches were played against Dusseldorf, Duisburg, and Mulheim, and the undergraduates, billeted at the homes of their hosts, had a rare opportunity to learn something of the changing situation in Germany.

The summer term began at the end of April. A pleasant surprise awaited his arrival at his lodging at 7 Brookside: a letter from the Hawks Club secretary inviting him to join this distinguished club for Blues and half-blues. The terminal subscription of £2, and the entrance fee of £1.10s, were not insignificant additional expenses to a young man with limited resources. He was finding that he was becoming a regular visitor to Messrs Ryder & Amies, 'Tailors, Hosiers, Robe Makers and Club Colour Specialists' of King's Parade, Cambridge, to purchase the blazers, ties, sweaters, and other paraphernalia demanded by sporting success. Membership of the Hawks Club gave status but more importantly the opportunity to get to know the leading sportsmen of the university in comfortable surroundings, based on those of a London gentlemen's club.

The cricket term was to be an interesting time for Norman. Already well known as a squash and hockey player he was inevitably going to be closely scrutinised for his cricketing prowess. He had a fine record at school, had performed well the previous summer at Lord's in the schools trial and at the Oval for Essex Young Amateurs, and he was well regarded by Essex, who had written to him in April enquiring as to his availability for the County during the 1937 season. Norman's reply brought this letter from Brian Castor, the Essex secretary, well-known for his directness, the original of which Norman kept in his scrapbook:

Dear Norman

Thank you for your letter of the 20th. I don't want to disappoint you, but my original letter was simply an enquiry the Committee threw out so that we should know how many amateur players might be available during the season. This doesn't mean that you are not going to get any cricket but I thought it only fair to warn you.

I saw Norman Yardley at Lord's and he spoke about you. If you are not playing for the Varsity against Essex we want you to play for us against the Varsity and will keep a place for you. If you would only keep your arm up and spin and flight the ball, you ought to get wickets. I am serious about this, but at risk of being thought a meddler, you can only make yourself into a bowler by persevering.

Yours sincerely

Brian Castor.

Norman was not impressed by Castor's technical advice at the end of the letter, as is shown by the two pencilled exclamation marks he inserted alongside it in the margin.

The immediate goal for Norman was to get into the varsity side, no mean task even with Yardley as a supporter. In the Pembroke College team Norman coincided not only with S. C. 'Billy' Griffith, later to become an England wicket-keeper, but also with George Mann, captain of England in 1949, both of whom played for the University. The University captain, Tindall, had six of the 1936 side still in residence, including John Cameron, a future West Indies Test player, and Paul Gibb, another future England wicket-keeper and opening batsman. The competition for places in 1937 was fierce, there being in effect only four places open, two of which were bound to be filled by opening bowlers. All four gaps were filled by seniors, even Griffith, who had gained his Blue in 1935, but had not played in 1936, failing to force his way into the team. Wisden's end of season commentary noted that: '*One of the most remarkable features of the season was that of fourteen public school captains in residence as freshmen (Norman*

being one) not one got into the eleven against Oxford, and without wishing to be considered over-critical one is inclined to the opinion that Tindall was not altogether wise in not giving more trials to some of them'. Despite this apparent strength the results were poor, and only Yardley, the secretary, was invited to play in the traditional Gentlemen versus Players match at Lords.

Norman was given his chance in the three day Freshmen's Trial, Tindall's side against Yardley's side, played at Fenners on May 8th, 10th and 11th. Batting second wicket down he scored 14 before being caught by Mann, and did not get to the crease in the rain-curtailed second innings. Bowling first change his spin was economical rather than penetrating as he returned figures of 0-12 from six overs as Yardley's side were bowled out for 88. He was given a second chance when invited by Tindall to play for the Etceteras in a three day match

BELOW: Norman pictured back left for the Etceteras v Perambulators. The latter were composed of those who came from Eton, Winchester, Harrow, and Rugby, whilst the Etceteras were selected from those who came "from other schools".

Photos.: Crisp

THE ETCETERAS (CAMBRIDGE) XI.

against the Perambulators, again on the Fenners' square, one week later. Norman missed out on this opportunity to state a case for inclusion in the University team, scoring only 16 batting at number seven, stumped off Bruce-Lockhart's leg-spin, and bowling a wicketless eight overs for fifteen.

Norman went to the Pembroke May Week Ball, but retired at a reasonable hour, as was his wont. He drank very little, a habit he maintained throughout his sporting career and one which he never found prevented his enjoyment of an occasion. Late in life he expressed his reasoning: "I couldn't see the point of behaving like a b.f. and then waking up with a headache."

> *He drank very little, a habit he maintained throughout his sporting career... "I couldn't see the point of behaving like a b.f. and then waking up with a headache".*

Brian Castor kept his promise and on June 16th, 17th and 18th 1937 the 19 year old Norman Borrett played his initial first-class game for his county against his university, at Brentwood. Norman received a number of messages wishing him good luck, including a telegram from Walter Winstanley, cricket master at Framlingham. The debutant's contribution was to bat at number eight, sadly to be run out for seven ("Jack O'Connor wouldn't run when I called him for a sharp single"), and to bowl two overs for one run in the University's follow-on. Essex were easy winners by an innings and 33 runs, with Maurice Nichols scoring 64 and O'Connor 111.

J. W. A. Stephenson, who would later become secretary of the MCC, took 8-46 in the first innings, whilst cousins Peter and Ray Smith took seven wickets between them in the second innings. Some thirty years later Norman Borrett and Ray Smith would be in opposition, Norman as cricket master at Framlingham and Ray as cricket professional at Felsted.

Norman headed for Frinton at the end of his first year at Cambridge, having gained a blue for squash, missed out on blues for hockey and cricket, and having played for Pembroke at hockey, squash and cricket. During the long vacation he played for Frinton and other local Essex sides. In one of these, playing for Clacton Casuals, he and Essex county cricketer Arnold Quick bowled out the opposition between them, Norman taking 5-28 and Quick 3-17.

Second Year

Squash and hockey for Cambridge; a second round defeat in the Amateur; Digby Flowerdew; a squash tour to the US; hockey for the East; no Cambridge cricket but another Essex County game.

The Michaelmas Term of 1937 saw a new captain in the University squash side, Maurice Baring. Norman Yardley, described in the Cricketer Spring Annual of 1937 as 'the most versatile games player in Cambridge at present', was a travelling reserve for Lord Tennyson's cricket team on their tour of India, and thus was out of the University from November to February. Early in the season Baring promoted Norman Borrett, the Hon. Secretary of the squash team, to first string, where he gained experience against a number of the country's best players. In the game against the International Sportsmen's Club he played, and lost in three straight games, to five time Amateur champion, F. D. Amr Bey. Cambridge beat ten of the leading London clubs on their way to the Bath Club clash with Oxford on December 14th.

The squash press commented that Norman had filled the position of first string for Cambridge *'with distinction and it will be interesting to see how he stands up to a major competition – his name being among those accepted for the Amateur.'* As in 1936, the Amateur, at the Bath Club, was held in the first week of December, providing a stern pre-varsity match test for several members of the two university teams. Whilst the timing of the Amateur was useful for them, it was highly inconvenient for others: *'The Amateur should be in January – December is an impossible month for schoolmasters'.* As we will see, this exhortation from the press was finally accepted eleven years later, to the benefit of Norman, by then himself a schoolmaster.

On Tuesday December 1st Norman donned rugby kit for the first time in two years as he returned to Framlingham as a member of the Old Framlinghamians rugby XV, which was beaten 9-8 by the College team in the annual OF fixture. It is inconceivable today that a competitor in the Amateur (let alone the principal member of the Cambridge squash team) would permit himself to risk injury in a rugby match three days before the event. But the times were different. On the evening of Friday December 4th Norman beat Essex's Alan Leiper 9-6, 9-6, 8-10, 9-0, in the first round of the Amateur. He then ran up against R. F. Lumb and despite establishing long leads in each of the first two games, frittered away his advantage and lost 8-9, 6-9, and 4-9. In a comment not aimed specifically at Norman, but which was in later years from time to time to be directed at him, the SRA's January 1938 annual

RIGHT: The Cambridge quintet for the December 1937 varsity match.

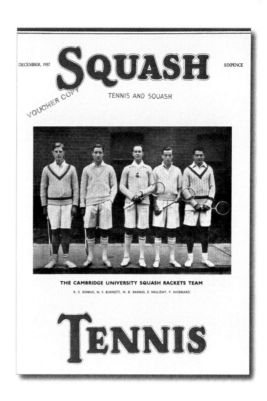

report on the Amateur '*regretted the tendency among some of our younger players to shadow too closely their opponent when he is about to play the ball*'.

Another Old Framlinghamian enjoyed a more successful Amateur. Dr. Digby Flowerdew had had a fine season the previous year, 1936-37, at first string for St. Thomas' Hospital, unbeaten in all his Cumberland Cup matches, playing with great consistency and not a little brilliance. Flowerdew came from a distinguished family. He was the only son of Dick Flowerdew who was the 13th of 15 siblings. The 12th sibling was Gordon Flowerdew, who, along with seven of his brothers, had attended Framlingham College in the early years of the century. He was awarded a posthumous Victoria Cross for valour at Moreuil Wood in France in 1918.

Digby Flowerdew, Gordon's nephew, in the Amateur of 1937 beat D. I. Burnett in the quarter-final 3-1 to reach an all-medical semi-final against Dr. J. F. Stokes, to whom he lost, narrowly, 10-8 in the fourth game. Stokes could then make little of the incomparable Amr Bey in the final.

Although Norman had played top string in the run-up to the Varsity match, captain Maurice Baring decided to take that burden on himself when, on December 14th, the match took place. The ploy almost back-fired as Baring lost a match which Cambridge should have won. At second string Norman's clear-cut win over Whitehouse was vital in securing a narrow three-two defeat of the traditional rivals. '*Borrett was much too good for Whitehouse after he found his touch in the middle of the second game. He is really good, although with a stroke-player's failure of looking, and probably feeling, rather dismal when matters are not going all his own way.*' Throughout his career Norman's squash court demeanour was serious, even severe, but this was better attributed to fierce concentration on the job in hand rather than to dismal response to the state of the game.

Norman's presence in the Cambridge hockey side in his second year was secure, his game having improved considerably. However the position in which he should play was a matter of some debate: '*Borrett is either a centre-half or an inside-left, and has gained quite a reputation in the centre-half position*' wrote the London Evening News. For the first match of the new season on October 18th against Beckenham Norman was selected at inside left.

In each press report of Cambridge's matches against London clubs in the build-up to the varsity hockey match, against Beckenham, Southgate, Richmond and Wimbledon, Norman was named variously as the outstanding forward, the cleverest player, or the brilliant provider and goal scorer. The University won most of its games, including a thrashing of a strong Essex side 5-3, all five being scored by centre forward Gower, for whose goals the main credit went to the insides, and Norman in particular for his unselfish support. Press comment described Norman as '*fairly certain to make his name in higher hockey circles before the end of the*

season, a class exponent and a consistent scorer.'

The East selectors picked the young undergraduate for the East divisional trial on December 18th at Luton, his first representative match. At inside left for Whites he scored a goal and impressed the selectors sufficiently to be chosen for the East's first game, against West, on January 8th 1938 at Bristol. Just before Christmas came another invitation, this time to play for the first time in the prestigious annual hockey match at Beckenham between the Cambridge University Wanderers and the Oxford University Occasionals. The fixture was essentially designed to maintain relationships between players on both sides who had appeared in varsity matches, but with seven international players on the Cambridge team and four for Oxford, the game had a high profile. '*Borrett's stickwork and passing were exceptionally good*' and he scored the decisive goal in a 3-2 win for his team.

The Gloucestershire County Cricket Ground at Bristol was the venue for Norman's debut in divisional hockey, which counted as an international trial. The England national selectors were present to watch Norman play out of position at centre forward for East against a strong West team including J. B. Evans the England goalkeeper and the gifted David Milford, England's inside left for the past seven years. The East team included two other Cambridge men, Self, who had won his blue in the 1937 match, and Skrimshire, like Norman not yet a blue. Norman did well enough but, as all university players were excluded from the next divisional match on January 29th between East and North at Warrington, due to the proximity of the varsity match, he did not make either of the teams selected after that game for the England Final trial.

With three weeks to go came the news Norman had been hoping for, an invitation from G. E. Hewan the University captain to play against Oxford at Beckenham on February 12th. He immediately

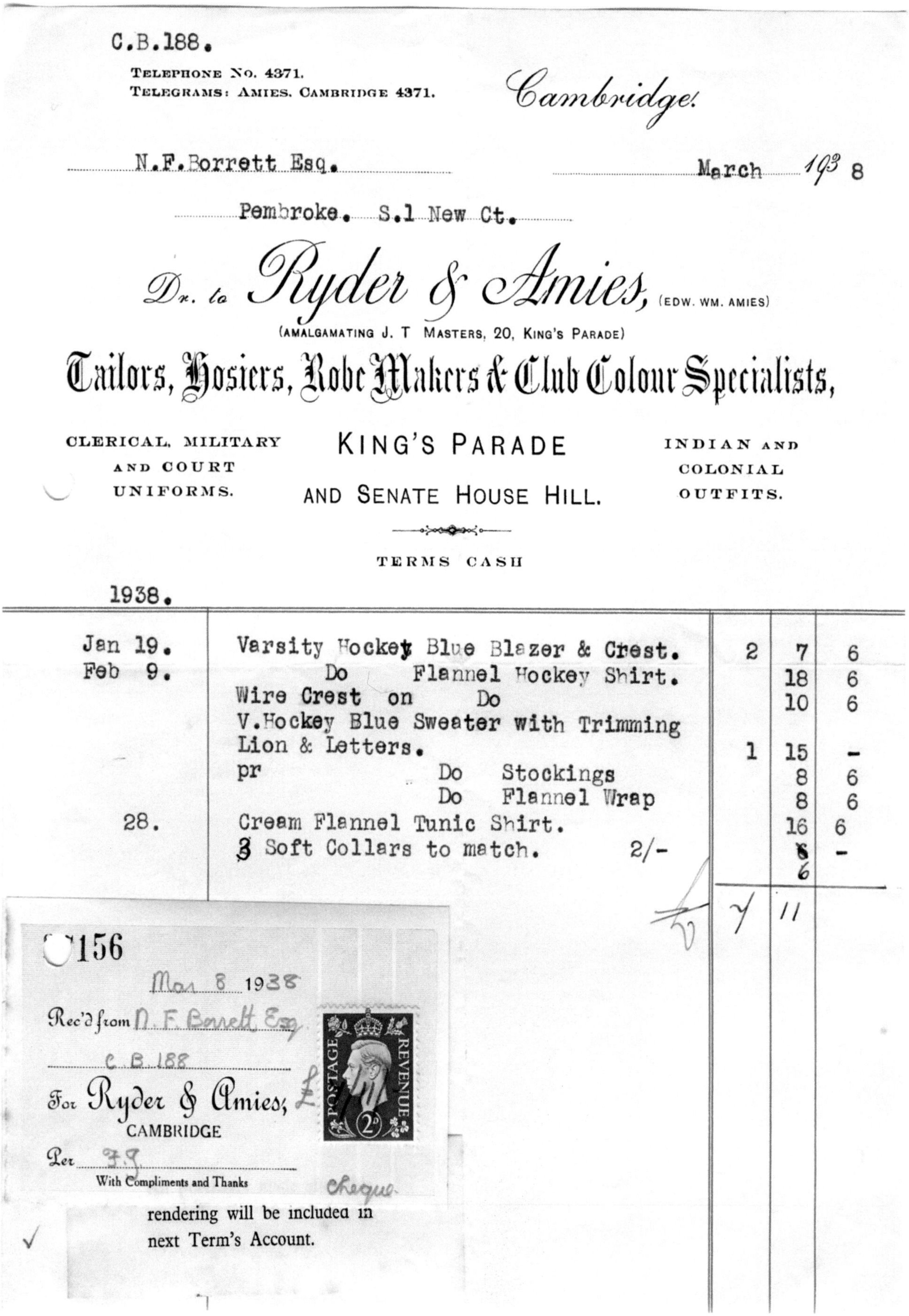

C.B.188.

TELEPHONE No. 4371.
TELEGRAMS: AMIES. CAMBRIDGE 4371.

Cambridge.

N.F.Borrett Esq.   March   19⁹ 8

Pembroke. S.1 New Ct.

Dr. to **Ryder & Amies,** (EDW. WM. AMIES)

(AMALGAMATING J. T MASTERS, 20, KING'S PARADE)

Tailors, Hosiers, Robe Makers & Club Colour Specialists,

CLERICAL, MILITARY AND COURT UNIFORMS.	KING'S PARADE AND SENATE HOUSE HILL.	INDIAN AND COLONIAL OUTFITS.

TERMS CASH

1938.

			£	s	d
Jan 19.	Varsity Hockey Blue Blazer & Crest.		2	7	6
Feb 9.	Do Flannel Hockey Shirt.			18	6
	Wire Crest on Do			10	6
	V.Hockey Blue Sweater with Trimming				
	Lion & Letters.		1	15	—
	pr Do Stockings			8	6
	Do Flannel Wrap			8	6
28.	Cream Flannel Tunic Shirt.			16	6
	3 Soft Collars to match. 2/-			8	—
				6	
			7	11	

156

Mar 8 1938

Rec'd from N. F. Borrett Esq

C B 188

For *Ryder & Amies,*   £

CAMBRIDGE

Per JS

With Compliments and Thanks   Cheque.

rendering will be included in
next Term's Account.

visited Ryder and Amies in King's Parade, and ordered his Cambridge hockey blue blazer, sweater, flannel shirt, stockings and a "cream flannel tunic shirt with 3 soft collars to match", a total investment of £7. 11s.

His selection was greeted with letters of congratulation from a number of friends and family. The press, previewing the match, described Norman as '*the brains of the Cambridge attack*', and forecast a close game between evenly matched sides. The prediction was correct, the match ending in a tight 1-1 draw. R. L. Hollands, writing in The Times, expressed disappointment with the Cambridge inside forward trio of Gotch, Wakeling and Borrett, '*whose passing was too square and who were not as quick or accurate in the circle as had been expected*'. Playing at inside left for Oxford, although by instinct a half back, was Micky Walford; his and Norman's paths would often cross in the future.

The Cambridge squash team made history when they toured the United States in March, travelling there and back on the liner Queen Mary – an experience in itself. The team's arrival date meant they were unable to play in the U.S. championships but a number of matches were arranged against Yale, Harvard, Princeton and several of the leading New York clubs. Norman played second string to the captain Michael Baring and despite winning his opening match against Yale, found the same difficulty as his colleagues in adapting to the longer American court, harder ball and heavier racket, as he lost to Harvard and to Hartford Golf Club. The social side was inevitably a major element of the tour, and Cambridge acquitted themselves well through the round of receptions and dinners: "They made such a hit" in the words of the captain of the next Cambridge side to visit USA, in March 1952. Norman sent a succession of detailed post cards to his parents and Charles, providing them with an interested visitor's view of Boston, Cambridge, the Ivy League Colleges, New York, baseball, hot dogs, the theatre, and gentlemen's clubs. There were only passing references to his squash games. "The University Club beat us 5-0; then they gave us a very good dinner, after which they took us to the Onyx Club. Three of us went on to another one after that, and I eventually got to bed at 3.30am. The next night we went to the Roseland dance place, but found it too wild and dangerous so we left and went to the Stork. This was a grand place and we had some good dancing. The first place was a good example of hot dancing which really is silly. You could easily get a kick, so we went for something more English."

Yardley, secretary the year before, was captain of University cricket in 1938. He selected Norman for the University Seniors' Trial, but Norman made only seven in the first innings, and, batting at number five in the second was 18 not out, in company with George Mann, when the declaration came. One over in the first and three overs for four runs in the second innings gave his bowling little opportunity to impress.

Three weeks after the Seniors' trial, on May 25th, Norman played his second first class match, again for Essex against the University, this time at Fenners. Batting at five he was bowled by the very man he wanted to impress, Yardley, for 9. Second time around he was promoted to three but did not have much chance to create an impact, being 15 not out when the match was won. In the Essex side were captain Denys Wilcox, later headmaster of Alleyns School, Maurice Nichols, England's leading all-rounder that year, and the Smith cousins, Ray and Peter. Wisden's review of the worst Cambridge University season in history, in which no game was won out of 13 played, focused on the poor bowling attack, no bowler being deserving of selection by any county (an interesting comment given that Yardley would be a regular England change bowler within 10 years). Paul Gibb was the leading batsman and was chosen for England during the season, whilst J. R. Thompson, the freshman, was the next best, '*indicating the makings of a brilliant batsman.*' Neither Yardley nor F. G. Mann, both future England captains, had a good season. If Norman had performed at his best in his trial and his Essex match, Yardley might have been tempted to give him a few matches as a spinner who could also bat, but it was not to be.

* * * * * * * * *

Graduation Year

Cambridge Squash captain; a lesson learned at the Amateur; hockey for Cambridge, the East; and… England, but no Cambridge Cricket.

Norman's last Cambridge year began in mid October 1938. On the first of the month he had celebrated his 21st birthday with a party at Landermere in Frinton. A scrapbook still preserves the handwritten greetings telegram from his mother and father wishing that his "future may be crowned with success, happiness and love."

For a sportsman undergraduate, competing in two sports at University level and seeking to make it three, time for study was at a premium. Norman had participated in every aspect of university life, working and playing hard. Now the thought of examinations at the end of the academic year meant he had to apply some focus, where there had to date been very little, on Geography lectures and tutorials. "Having done very little work previously I began turning up for morning tutorials."

Squash was the perfect game for the busy man. High in energy, short in duration, it provided valuable daily exercise and could easily be fitted around the call of the lecture hall. In the new year he would join and play occasionally for the famous wandering club, the Jesters, with its fixture list of over 200 fixtures a year, but for now he played squash with fellow members of the university team, occasionally with friends in Pembroke, and competitively for the varsity in the dozen or so Michaelmas term matches around East Anglia and London. He had two immediate goals – to captain the university to victory in the varsity match on December 9th, and to compete well in the Amateur Championship between December 2nd and 12th.

Competition for his time came from hockey. Although the varsity match did not take place until February 11th, preparation for that date started at the same time as squash, from the beginning of term, and continued with matches every Saturday and most Wednesdays against a number of the major hockey clubs on the London circuit. The first match was on October 15th at Cambridge against Beckenham, and the first two squash matches were on the 13th and 16th.

Norman scored three times in a 4-3 victory over Southgate and once in the win over Wimbledon and again in the defeat to Richmond, when he demonstrated '*some of the best stickwork of the match*.' The University then played Essex in the first East trial, winning 3-1, before travelling to Northampton, where Norman scored a hat trick in a 7-0 victory over the Bacchanalians. The next match was a twelve goal thriller against Lampard-Vachtell's XI. Of the latter side's seven goals, three came from David Milford and one from Freddie Brown, later to captain England at cricket; Norman scored twice in Cambridge's five goal reply.

Norman learnt much from the University's squash fixtures, most of which were against Bath Club Cup players. This was the gold standard. Roy McKelvie, outspoken sports journalist and Scottish squash international, wrote in November that year that '*The Bath Club Cup, the Amateur, and the Londonderry Cup are all that most of these players play in. One day a Bath Club Cup pundit will lose to a Cumberland Cup second section player*.' Norman lost at first string against the Royal Engineers, when the experienced D. I. Burnett beat him 10-8 in the fifth, but won against United Hospitals and the International Sportsmen's Club. Against T.C.S. Haywood's team, Norman again lost, this time in straight games to the brilliant K. C. Gandar-Dower, the favourite for the Amateur. In the match against the RAC Norman played, and beat 10-8 in the fifth, Brian Phillips, with whom he was to have many battles

over the next 17 years. In late November, Norman made the captain's traditional announcement to the press of the award of half blues to two members of his team to play Oxford on December 9th, holding back the choice of the fourth and fifth strings until later.

Amr Bey had retired, having won six Amateurs in the last seven years. In the new era, for the first time in the history of the event, seedings were introduced. There were eight players seeded, and Flowerdew was among them. The common belief was that the winner would come from this chosen elite, but there were those who, on seeing him in court, fancied the Cambridge captain to beat Snell and Hooper to reach the semi-final. Norman took the unusual step, for him, of missing a University hockey match (against Spencer on Wandsworth Common) on December 1st as he prepared for his first match in the Amateur the next day. His first round opponent was R. G. Shaw, runner-up in the RAF championship.

The Times reporter was impressed by '*the admirable form shown by the Cambridge captain N. F. Borrett, whose opponent was completely outplayed by the undergraduate. Borrett, who takes a very early ball, set a tremendous pace from the start, and Shaw, who relies on delicate drops and angle shots for his aces, never had time to make them*.'

In the second round Norman was not quite so impressive as in the first round, and dropped a game to A. R. Fyler, '*but with recovered concentration took the last game easily*.' The third round pitted him against Edward Snell, an England international, twice a runner up to Amr Bey, and now a seed. This match was a seminal moment in Norman's career, when he learned that speed and power do not succeed against canny play unless accompanied by accuracy and length. The game was of great interest to the pundits – the young tiger against the seasoned hunter. Norman set out to play as fast as possible, intent on storming his man. Snell countered by slowing down the play by every means in his power. At first Norman's strategy succeeded, and playing in hurricane fashion, with brilliant shots of every description, he won the first game. Snell, however, remained unperturbed, and seemed to be quietly studying his opponent's weak points. He returned everything, and played his shots to a better length. By some very judicious lobbing and clever placing, he gradually broke down his opponent's impetuous attack and caused him to play the game he dictated. Norman took the view at this point that he should play Snell at his own game, but like many before him, failed, and in the last three games he made only four winners.

The significance of the match to Norman is apparent from the clarity with which, in his eighties, he could recall the event: "I lost because I changed my game from my natural attacking one to a defensive one – like a b.f." For some players the severity of the reverse might have stalled their progress in the game. In Norman's case the opposite was the case: he concluded that it was important to play to one's strengths, and in his case to dictate play so as to prevent a skilful player from dominating the rallies. To do this would demand a level of physical fitness he did not currently have. By the time he re-entered the squash scene eight years later he had developed the hurricane attack into a consistent, focused weapon, which would kill off the strongest of opponents.

Digby Flowerdew again reached the semi-final, with a remarkable quarter-final performance which saw him reverse his 3-1 loss to Stokes the previous year. In the match of the championship he demonstrated why many had regarded him as on the brink of being a top class player. Sadly the effort had taken a deal out of him and he lost his semi-final to Burnett, who in turn was dismissed by Gandar-Dower, a victor over Snell in the semi, in a one-sided final.

One week after his loss to Snell, Norman was leading his Cambridge squash team into battle with Oxford, who were seeking their first win since 1930. Norman was the only player who had previous experience of the annual fixture. Having played second string the previous two years he now headed the list, playing R. S. Woodward, whom he had beaten in the final of the Evans Cup as a schoolboy two years before. Woodward had himself gone on to win the 1937 Evans Cup and he was described in the Daily Telegraph as '*a pretty player whose volleying was something out of the ordinary. He looked against N. F. Borrett a potentially better player, which is saying much, but it is little use being a stroke player if you do not win.*' Norman was the harder hitter and dismissed his opponent, not without difficulty, in straight games, 9-5, 10-8, 9-5.

J. R. Thompson, the gifted all-rounder who had won his cricketing blue as a freshman, and who was a world class rackets player, played second string and won 10-9 in the fifth game. He and Norman were to play each other in the final of the Amateur squash championship in 1948. The other ties all went Cambridge's way as they whitewashed the dark blues for the second time in Norman's three years in the side, winning the match for the ninth time in succession.

Term ended in mid-December. Norman's Michaelmas term bill, totalling £65.18s included 5s 4d for gate fines, 10s for hire of space in the bicycle shed and £1.4s 9d for coals in his room.

The Old Framlinghamians entered the Londonderry Cup, the Public School old boys squash competition, for the first time. The date for their first round match against Old Haileyburians however clashed with the East hockey trial on December 19th and Norman had to withdraw. As Digby Flowerdew was forced at the last minute to give a

walk over to Stokes, the OF team were soundly beaten 4-1.

The East hockey trial was held at Cambridge on December 19th. In a 2-2 draw Norman scored one of the goals, was described as the outstanding player, and earned selection for the divisional side. Thus on January 7th 1939, almost one year to the day after his debut for them, Norman played for the East against Combined Services at Brentwood. East won 3-1 and Norman was rewarded by being picked for East's next divisional match, against Midlands, at Eaton Park, Norwich, on January 28th. This match was also won, this time by 2-1.

The Varsity hockey match was scheduled for February 18th, and time was short to get the team in top gear for the big fixture. Matches were played against the Royal Navy, the Army, Beckenham and Mid Surrey, before a splendid final rehearsal on February 11th, against Acrostics, who were destroyed by the remarkable score of 12-1, Norman scoring 6 of the goals. Whilst the forward line was a settled unit, P. R. Oliver, the Cambridge captain, had a selection issue at centre half, where Jackson's performance had been inconsistent. This had driven Oliver to play Norman in three pre-Varsity matches, at centre-half, apparently out of position. Norman, who performed quite brilliantly there, had of course played nowhere other than at centre half throughout his Framlingham schooldays and had only switched to inside left on arrival at Cambridge at C. E. Thomas' suggestion to advance his hockey career. The Daily Telegraph described Norman as having '*shaped very well*' at centre half, following the switch at half time against Beckenham. But, the paper continued, '*previously Borrett had been brilliant at inside left*' and had scored one of the goals.

Unfortunately the player brought in to replace Norman at inside left, Coggan, scarcely rose to the occasion. Against Mid Surrey The Times noted that the lack of drive in the attack '*was accentuated by the fact that Oliver repeated the experiment, first tried at Beckenham last Saturday, of playing Borrett at centre half instead of inside-left. So far as Borrett was concerned the experiment succeeded. His defence was sound and he served his forwards uncommonly well, especially in the first half…Unfortunately there does not appear to be anyone approaching Borrett's standard to fill the gap at inside left, so that the loss entailed by the move is greater than the gain.*'

With one week to go, Oliver abandoned his plan, returned Norman to the attack and put his faith in Jackson at centre half. The resulting triumph over Acrostics restored the confidence of the whole side, and the Varsity match was won, narrowly, 3-2. One of the most exciting Varsity matches for a long time started dramatically when Norman, with a flick from the edge of the circle, scored in the third minute. From two goals down Oxford equalized with goals from a short corner and a break-away from Desmond Eagar (later to captain Hampshire at cricket) who was the fastest forward on the field. Harry

B or C

POST OFFICE TELEGRAPHS.

| Charges to pay | | No. | 64 |

Charges to pay
s.   d.

TIME OF
RECEIPT

AM10 24

From
T S B

If there is doubt about the
telegram ring "Telegrams
delivery for

accuracy of any part of this
Enquiry" or call at the Office of
free repetition.

This form, and if possible the envelope, should accompany any enquiry other than by telephone.

82

Prefix. Time handed in. Office of Origin and Service Instructions. Words.

82 10.7 FRINTONONSEA T 10

Office Stamp
1 3 MCH 39

THE INFORMATION OVERLEAF WILL INTEREST YOU.

BORRETT PEMBROKE COLLEGE CAMBRIDGE =

= CONGRATULATIONS GOOD LUCK FOR SATURDAY =

= MOTHER + +

ABOVE: One of many good luck telegrams for Norman's first England hockey cap, against Wales at the Oval, March 1939.

Haslam, the Daily Telegraph reporter, considered Norman to be the best forward on the pitch, whereas The Times felt that whilst '*he was brilliant in the first half, when he was always the chief danger to the Oxford defence, later in the game he was inclined to hang back too far and at times was almost a fourth half-back, but this was when Cambridge were holding on grimly to their one goal lead.*' Nevertheless the triumph belonged to the much maligned Jackson, who played well above expectations and scored the winning goal.

In late February Norman was again picked as centre half, this time for Essex who played Suffolk at Chelmsford. Harry Haslam in the Telegraph wrote that he '*played a grand game, and his brilliant stickwork and accurate ground passes to his forwards played a big part in his side's 5-1 victory.*'

Norman had been playing well, for University, County and Division, but, as a 21 year old inexperienced player, he had hardly contemplated being considered for full England honours. It was therefore a pleasant surprise for him to receive the HA's Match Secretary's letter of February 12th advising of his selection for the Possibles against the Probables in the final England trial, at Beckenham, on March 4th. Rail times from Holborn and Victoria were provided and '*tickets will be issued by Thomas Cook & Sons by post immediately I have received your acceptance*'. Following an unsatisfactory first England trial at Nottingham the week before, the old maestro David Milford had been dropped, Frank Hopkinson (Norman's old Cambridge

colleague and now a Canford schoolmaster) had been moved from inside right to centre forward and Norman took the place of Rothwell, who had been inside left in the previous year's internationals. '*Borrett is a really fine shot in the circle or from corners, and his trial is fully justified.*'

He did well for the Possibles as they held the Probables to a 2-2 draw, but The Times was cautious: '*Borrett scarcely made as much use of Pope at outside left as Pope deserved… Borrett frequently transferred play to the centre, when a quick return pass down the wing to Pope would have been more profitable.*' He had not taken his chance and he was not picked for the first international, against Scotland, on March 11th.

But fate then played a hand. It was found that the England centre forward, Adlard (who was to play in that position for Great Britain in the Olympics in1948) had fractured his wrist in the final trial. It was reasonable to assume the selectors would replace him with the player who had done well understudying him in the trial, Frank Hopkinson. Instead they picked a new cap who had not featured in the trial, Dickinson, and put Hopkinson at inside left against Scotland even though, as an inside right, '*he knew nothing whatever of this specialized job.*'

Although England won 1-0, the team did not fire, and Hopkinson struggled in his unaccustomed role on the left. Accordingly changes were made for the next game against Wales at the Oval. Hopkinson was dropped and replaced by Norman. The Observer liked the change: '*Borrett has most of the qualities demanded – good stickwork, the ability to dribble and pass either way equally well, speed, stamina, and some scoring*

RIGHT: C. E. Thomas, Norman's old chemistry master and hockey coach, wrote congratulating him on his first international cap.

FRAMLINGHAM COLLEGE,
SUFFOLK

Mar 14th: 39

My dear Borrett,

I write to congratulate you on your selection for England in Saturdays match. We have watched your rapid rise to fame with much eagerness & pleasure & hope that is only the prelude to a great number of "caps". I need hardly mention that the event is being duly celebrated with a half holiday so you will be very popular with the School.

I don't know whether you happen to have seen in the papers that we played the Germans boys from Düsseldorf. We drew 3-3. Uppingham beat the 1-0 but Seys lost 4-0 so I think our performance was very creditable. I am taking the team for a 10 days tour in Germany. I only wish you could come & play for us. They tell me it is pretty rough over there.

Best of luck on Saturday.

Yours Sincerely,
CE Thomas

power, though he has something to learn in the use of the flick shot, of which D. S. Milford was, and still is, the acknowledged master. If Borrett behaves in his best Cambridge manner and if the surface of the Oval be firm and true there may easily be a big improvement in the English forward play.' Norman was not to relinquish that place for fourteen years.

The pigeon-hole for his mail at the Hawks Club, and the table in his lodgings, were inundated with letters of congratulations from family and friends. One special one was a telegram wishing him good luck, signed by Frank Hopkinson. A remarkable one was from a friend on Travellers Hockey Club notepaper congratulating Norman on his selection and asking if he wanted to play for the Travellers against a Beckenham XI on Sunday, "the day after the international." Several messages arrived from Framlingham College, one a cable from the redoubtable Reverend Kneese, chaplain at Framlingham, and another a charming letter from "Squiffy" Thomas, Norman's chemistry and hockey master, advising that "the event is being duly celebrated with a half holiday, so you will be popular with the School." One from someone who was clearly a close friend, writing on Hurlingham Club paper, took a different tack: "Nice work – suppose it will make you even more conceited than ever and will afford but a further opportunity for more 'dog'…(I learnt of your selection when) your name caught my eye in the middle of a lot of rubbish obviously written by some reporter for whom you had been standing drinks."

The outfield at the Oval on March 18th was indeed firm and true; conditions ideal for Norman to employ his stickwork. Wales caused a surprise by scoring first but within a matter of minutes Tattersall broke down the English right wing and centred perfectly for Norman to hit a first-time shot past Pickford in the Welsh goal. England then took the lead when a penalty corner was hit out to Norman, who stopped it for Leeming to drive the ball home. In the second half England emphasized their superiority with further goals from Dickinson and Baylis. It was the Observer's view that 'the inclusion of Borrett improved the stickwork of England's inside forwards and, in his first appearance in an international, was successful.' R. L. Hollands in The Times thought 'Borrett had a great deal to do with the victory. He was at pains to get himself unmarked, took the ball cleanly, and his passes seldom failed to find the man they were intended for. He made the left wing a much more powerful striking force than it has been previously.'

The following Saturday, March 25th, Norman retained his place for what the Sunday Times described as the most important game of the international hockey season, England versus Ireland at Edgbaston cricket ground. Frank Hopkinson regained the place he had surrendered to Norman, replacing the injured Penn in his proper position of inside right. Norman worked hard at engendering the same attacking spirit which had demolished Wales but the Irish half back line dominated the game and forced Norman into much defensive work. The Irish 1-0 victory confirmed the superiority they had exercised over England in recent years.

England's performance the next week on April 1st against Holland was better, although the Telegraph considered that 'the dearth of forward talent which had been evident in all matches this season' remained an issue. The game, the first meeting between the two sides since 1935 in Amsterdam, was played on one of the best surfaces in the country, at Wardown Park, Luton. Hopkinson at inside right scored early on for England, and centre forward Dickinson the second. Smart

LEFT: Graduation day June 20 1939.
Norman with Alice and Walter, and
right, with Mullie.

inter-passing
between
Borrett and
Baylis on the
left wing
ended in
Borrett scoring
the third and
winning goal
with a neat push shot. The traditional post match dinner at the Hotel
Russell in London, with the two captains proposing toasts, and
Norman collecting Dutch team signatures on his menu card, was a
happy end to his first international season. It was to be the last
international for either side for eight long years. Only Wyatt, Rowan,
Tattersall, Baylis and Norman were to play for England again.

These hockey commitments inevitably brought clashes with
Norman's squash. He had in mid-February and early March played
first string for Essex in the 4-1 defeats of Cambridgeshire and Norfolk,
winning both his matches 3-1, which made Essex champions of the
East in the area county championship. He was then unavailable for the
national quarter-final loss to Yorkshire, the same day as his debut
hockey international.

The Frinton connection was helpful to Norman's cricket, when
in March Tray Grinter, captain of the Frinton side, and a City
businessman, wrote to Norman passing on requests from friends for
Norman to play in various cricket matches, and asking him to play for
Grinter's side to play Sir Julian Cahn's XI in Nottingham in August.
Cahn was a remarkable man, a millionaire whose love of cricket led
him to form his own team of first class and club players to play against
strong opposition, including international touring teams. Grinter's
letter ended with a wonderful example of the network in operation:
"As regards playing for Essex, if you are keen you might let me know
when you will be available and I will let the Chairman (who is a
personal friend of mine) know." Norman happily accepted the
invitation to play in Nottingham and spent the rest of his summer
vacation playing for Frinton and several occasional teams.

Norman's Cambridge cricket ambitions got no further than in his
first two summers. He was again selected for the Seniors Trial but
failed to impress, making only 4 when batting second wicket down.
Given only one over of bowling in the first innings, he proved to be a
difficult proposition for the batsmen in the second, taking 4-23 in five
overs on a rain-affected pitch. In Wisden's words *Borrett started the last
stage sensationally by doing the hat-trick,* one of those three victims being
Sam Silkin, later a Labour Attorney-General.

A little surprisingly to those who have observed his cricketing

career both before and after Cambridge, Norman did not do enough
to be given a game for the University. Wisden's summary of the 1939
University season, in which again the side failed to win a match,
referred to the captain's inability to find a clever slow spin bowler.
Norman's hat trick had presumably been disregarded as an isolated
occurrence. Another left-arm spin bowler was also overlooked by
Cambridge that season: 18 year old N. B. F. Mann played in the
Freshmen's Match, where he failed to take a wicket in either innings,
but never got a game for the varsity. He was to tour England with the
1947 South African side, going on to win 19 Test caps. Mann was
immortalised by John Arlott when, in the 1947 match between South
Africa and Middlesex, he caught and bowled F. G. Mann, an act which
drew from John Arlott the comment: "Ah, one more example of man's
inhumanity to man".

It is J. R. Thompson's view that in the immediate pre-war era
Cambridge cricket was significantly in the hands of the 'Lord's Schools'
– those senior Public Schools which played regular matches at the
Lord's ground. Thompson felt that his school, Tonbridge, was on the
edge of this area of influence, but that Framlingham would not have
been, and that Norman was probably not inclined to get to know the
men who wielded that influence. Stuart MacGregor, Old Allhallows
pupil, remembers being told by a Blue of Norman's time that Norman
"was not averse to speaking his mind and did himself no favours". The
fact remains that Norman had his chances to impress with weight of
runs and wickets in trials and other matches such as the Essex games,
but failed to take them.

Norman managed a few lectures in his final year: "I always tried to
get to the morning lectures", and achieved a 3rd in Part II of the
Geographical Tripos (having also taken a third in Part I in 1938) and
officially graduated BA on June 20th 1939, obtaining his MA by proxy
on January 22nd 1943. In his last two years he had gained his colours
for Pembroke at all three major sports, and won blues at hockey and
squash rackets, captaining the University in the latter sport. As Norman
reflected on his University career as he returned home at the end of
his final term, he knew that the career ambition, expressed in his
Cambridge application form in April 1935, was still what he wanted to
do. He had an aptitude for sport and a belief that he could make
something of a sportsman. To give that belief its opportunity he would
become a schoolmaster.

But these thoughts were overshadowed by the prospect of war.
Within a mere three months of graduating those fears became reality.
He was not to know it, but a career as one of the outstanding
sportsmen of his time was to be put on hold for nearly seven years.
The years between 22 and 28, when raw sporting talent broadens and
fills as physique and mental strength develop, were to be lost.

3

LOVE AND WAR

Muriel Knight-Rowe was born on January 20th 1920 in Niteroi, a town on a bay opposite Rio de Janiero. Her paternal grandfather, James Rowe, a vet in Weymouth, produced a son William. William left the UK at the age of 21 to make a new life in Brazil in the early days of the century. He soon met the English girl whom he would marry, and became managing director of a flour mill making spaghetti and other products.

William Rowe and his wife Madge produced 5 children, 3 boys and 2 girls, Mullie being the second oldest and the second daughter. All the children were sent to boarding school in England, and Mullie followed her older sister, at the age of 11, to board at Sandecoates School in Dorset. Their mother would travel to England once a year to see the children during their school holidays, except in the summer when they sailed back to Rio. During those annual UK

visits the family would stay at the Hawthorns Hotel, Bournemouth. It is still there today, under the name of the Wessex – *pictured right*. In the Christmas holidays of 1936, the Borrett family also holidayed there. Norman, 19, and Mullie, 16, met and quickly became good friends.

It was not permitted for the genteel ladies of Mullie's school to correspond with boys. Mullie, showing early signs of resourcefulness and persuasiveness, got various of her friends who were going out on exeat to post her occasional letters to Norman at Cambridge.

The Hawthorns Christmas for the two families was repeated in 1937, and the relationship between Mullie and Norman prospered.

…Norman dropped toilet rolls out of the window so they hung like streamers down the front of the building

Norman proved to be a hit with Mullie's siblings. Noel, Mullie's youngest brother, attending Mullie's 90th birthday party, recalled Norman with a smile: "He was very good company, and kept us all amused. He was always playing practical jokes. I remember going with him to the Metropole, a tall hotel near to the Hawthorns, getting into a room on the top floor, from where Norman dropped toilet rolls out of the window so they hung like streamers down the front of the building."

In the University summer vacation of 1938 the romance had developed to the point where Norman asked if he could spend his holidays with Mullie in Brazil; she had just left school and was now living in Rio with her parents. He travelled out on a passenger liner and the two of them spent two months together.

The following summer Mullie visited England with her parents. When Norman came down from Cambridge in July 1939, with plans to become a schoolmaster, he saw Mullie whenever he could. But by August, with war now looking inevitable, Mullie's father decided that he and her mother had to get back home to Rio and that Mullie must go with them.

"Norman's response to this was to say that we won't be able to see each other again for a long time, so let's get married. I immediately accepted and Norman asked my father for his permission to marry me. Father, facing the prospect of marrying off his second daughter only one year after his first, said he would consent if we delayed marriage for three years. To this we of course agreed, and our engagement was announced just before the day that war broke out. My mother stayed on for a short while with me in England, whilst father had to get back to his business in Rio. She followed not long after and was fortunate to catch the last ship to leave the UK for Brazil, praying that she would escape the threat posed by the Graf Spee off South America. My brothers Frank and Noel left Rio and went to Canada where they attended Ridley College."

The announcement of their engagement appeared in the papers early in September and, accompanied by a picture of the photogenic Mullie, in The Bystander's social columns on 6 September 1939.

"I was sixteen when I first met Norman in 1936: He'd just been up at Cambridge University for his first term. He was full of fun and that's what attracted me to him. I was never under any illusions as to

what was going to take priority in our marriage. When we got engaged he said: 'You realise my sport comes first.' and I said: 'Oh yes, I do know that.' It didn't worry me; in the three years we had known each other I'd always been used to him playing something or other and it didn't matter a thing to me. When Norman said that to me, I'd have been surprised if he had said anything else!"

Norman volunteered for the Army whilst living at Frinton and it was there he received his call-up papers. As Norman joined up, Mullie volunteered for the WRVS at Weymouth, where she attended to casualties as they came in.

Some months into a war which showed every prospect of lasting a long time, the prospect of staying unmarried for the promised three years was a bleak one. So the couple wrote to Mullie's parents to seek their blessing to a wedding in August 1940. They were happy to give that blessing, but were unable to attend the wedding, and indeed Mullie was not to see her parents again until 1947.

"We married on 31 August 1940 at the Colchester Garrison where Norman was based. There were very few guests at the ceremony as trains from London were being bombed, and we too had our scares, being diverted en route to the wedding into a bomb shelter.

Our reception was at the George Hotel in Colchester, and our first married home was at 21 Wellesley Road. We lived there for some time, but were later to move some dozen times to various different camps.

Norman was always being sent around the country on courses – I recall P.T. instruction courses and some gunnery. He obviously kept fit, even if he didn't play much sport. He played no squash at all and very occasionally hockey. I also recall a flying course in Scotland amongst many others. We saw little of each other. Norman would ring me from time to time saying that he was now in a different location (we knew that the rules forbade us from mentioning exactly where he might be) on a course, or on some task, and that he expected to be there for a month or whatever. Even when he returned he didn't like to tell me about it. He got no pleasure from discussing what he or others were doing, and he remained to the end of his life disinclined to talk about his war service, like many of that generation. Neither I nor the boys were able to draw from him even the branch of the Army he served in."

During the war Norman had very limited opportunity for sport. He played hockey as a guest player in the early part of the war for Guildford, alongside Jack Gregory another English international, helping the club to win the 1940 London Six-a-Side Tournament. There were a number of inter-services games, of which only a few results were recorded for posterity. One which did feature in post-war summaries was the first game of the wartime inter-services series, in December 1941, in which the Army ran out victors over the RAF at Halton by seven goals to five.

4

ALLHALLOWS 1946–1950

RIGHT: The Sketch magazine in its January 1948 edition pays tribute to a third successive Amateur squash championship win.

WEST COUNTRY LIFE

Whither a fledgling schoolmaster? A fitness regime; discipline in the Allhallows classroom.

After demob from war service Norman was quick to pick up the threads of his sporting life. He had kept reasonably fit and healthy, and was ready to find release from the long years of deprivation through the medium of competitive sport. When he had last played serious sport, in 1939, he had been a raw 21 year old with the world at his feet. In 1946, when organised sport re-established itself in England, he was a mature 28, uncertain whether his pre-war promise would be fulfilled all those years later.

He set himself the task of finding out. The first step was to take his physical fitness to a higher level. He trained assiduously, road running, working with weights, and playing as much as he could. He had given up rugby when he left school so his winter games were squash and hockey. In the summer months cricket was his first love, with tennis and golf holiday past times. His passion for sport, and his belief that he could achieve success at it, confirmed the plan hatched when he was only 17, that teaching was to be his career.

He applied to a number of public schools, and in August 1945 was offered and accepted a post as master in charge of Geography and History at Allhallows School, near Lyme Regis in Devon, a public school with a good reputation, which took pupils from 11 to 18 years of age. This was a major career decision, not just to enter the teaching profession, a vocation he never lost, but to remove himself from the home counties, the centre of the sporting world, at least for the sports which Norman played.

As we shall see, that Norman overcame this significant handicap to his sporting progress, is perhaps the most remarkable aspect of his success. The daily diet of sport which was then an essential part of the public school curriculum, and the ready availability of facilities for working on fitness, were to prove valuable, but they were no compensation for the lack of

ABOVE: The Allhallows School crest.
Norman taught at the school from 1945 to 1950

regular top class competition that the decision to locate to Devon entailed.

Tony Watson was a pupil at All Hallows when Norman arrived, accompanied by "*a most beautiful wife and a three year-old son, Anthony, who Norman was trying to make into a squash player. I remember this little boy running around the squash court with a specially made cut-down racket.*" War baby Anthony Norman Borrett had been born on 21st March 1942 in a nursing home at Newmarket, where Charles Borrett was the vicar. He and his wife Jean had helped Mullie through the early days of motherhood, whilst Norman was away with the Army.

Tony Watson was a beneficiary of Norman's teaching of History and Geography. "He was, for me at any rate, a very fine teacher. Before he arrived at Allhallows my worst subject, by a long way, was History, my best mark being 6%. In one year he got me up to the point where I got a credit in School Certificate. Geography was the other end of the scale and in School Cert I managed 96%, and I give most of the credit for that to Norman. It was not the case with most masters in those early post-war days but Norman had our total attention in the classroom.

The classrooms had board dusters which were wooden on one side and covered in felt cloth on the reverse, and if thrown they were formidable objects, especially in the hands of a county cricketer...

...Norman had the ability to write on the board with one hand while launching a board-duster, unsighted, with the other hand, with unerring accuracy at the boy who was transgressing - invariably scoring a hit. No doubt this treatment would today be viewed as too aggressive, but it was certainly very efficient and no one complained.

As to his sporting ability little needs to be said: the finest hockey player in the country after the war, and the best squash player in the country after the war. It was such a shame for him that the war intervened in his sporting career at the wrong time.

So in summary a wonderful sportsman (not quite a C. B. Fry) I believe he got five blues at Cambridge; a very fine teacher of Geography and History; with a beautiful wife. What more can one want?"

THE ALLHALLOWS YEARS – SQUASH

*The structure of squash post-war;
the search for West Country competition;
how to fit in two winter sports.*

Competitive squash was a relatively young sport. The game was said to have originated at Harrow School where boys waiting their turn in the rackets court are reputed to have knocked up with a soft ball in a nearby fives court, and the name of 'squash' to have come from the squashy sound of the soft rubber ball as distinct from the click of the hard rackets ball. The game became popular after the First War, when the West End social clubs pioneered the game in London, and in 1922 the Bath Club organised an invitation tournament for them. In the same year the Amateur Championship was first staged, and the Open, for amateurs and professionals, was instituted in 1930.

The game in the schools was given a great stimulus by the creation, in 1925 and 1926, of respectively, the Drysdale Cup for boys under 19, which was to become the unofficial British junior amateur championship, and the Evans Cup, for boys under 18, which was until 1950 a handicap event.

By 1939 the number of courts was still small but the game was becoming increasingly popular beyond its origins in the public schools and the London clubs; men and women working in the cities found that squash offered the opportunity for all the exercise they wanted, cheaply and no matter what the time, the weather or the season. The war hit squash harder than most games as clubs, and particularly schools, found that a return to pre-war growth was hindered by a number of factors: the main problem was the scarcity of courts caused by bomb-damage and change of use – at least one court had become a whisky store; planning restrictions prevented the building of new courts, the shortage of building materials prevented the renovation of damaged courts, travel difficulties caused by petrol shortages limited competitive play, and the fact that a large number of players in the services had scattered across the globe removed many of the better players from the scene, at least temporarily. There were other obstacles: clubs and schools found that it was impossible to obtain balls of the proper consistency, and suffered from a shortage of experienced players or professionals to teach the game. The international development of the game, which had in the 1920s spread to the

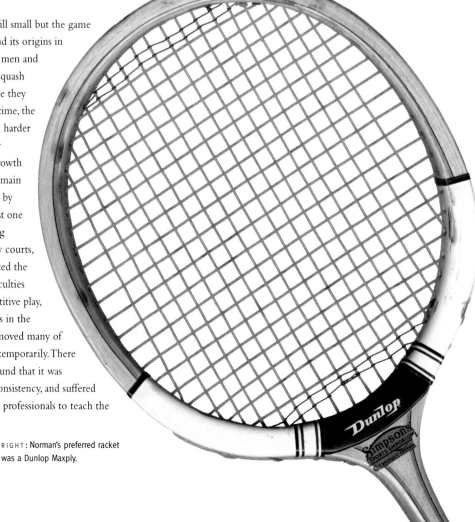

RIGHT: Norman's preferred racket was a Dunlop Maxply.

Dominions and the Colonies, now suffered from currency restrictions on clubs wishing to send teams abroad.

Thus the game struggled to get back on its feet, a financially fragile and still fledgling sport, run by a few devoted enthusiasts. In 1946 and 1947 the SRA initiated a handful of representative matches, mainly in London. Meanwhile the Bath Club and the Cumberland Club led the revival by restoring their respective competitions, the former for the West End social clubs and the latter for those clubs not eligible to compete in the Bath Club Cup and which were situated within twelve miles of Charing Cross. At schools' level the revival of the game may be said to have started earlier with the advent of the Surrey preparatory and public schools tournament at Surbiton Lawn Tennis Club in April 1944. The Drysdale restarted in 1946 and the Evans Cup in 1947.

The competitive structure of the game familiar to squash players today, with national age-group representative matches, a multiplicity of clubs, ladder competitions, and frequent inter-club matches, did not exist. The Bath Club Cup and the Cumberland Cup were the only inter-club competitions. An inter-county championship existed, but it did not involve all counties, and friendly county matches were rare.

Life in Devon was good for Norman and Mullie, and Allhallows was a friendly if somewhat uncompetitive school. The thought process which had caused Norman to become a schoolmaster, that it would give him a better chance to fulfill his sporting ambition than if he had worked, for example, as a stockbroker in the City of London, had not taken into account the difficulties of distance which went hand in hand with the pleasures of Devonian life.

In the early post-war years, as noted earlier, London-based and armed services players had the opportunity to play regular club, and top quality representative matches. From the second post war season, that beginning in the autumn of 1947, when the Bath Club Cup first returned to its pre-war format of a league basis, the players in that league were involved in match play every week. But for a budding champion living in Devon there were no opportunities to play the quality and quantity of squash necessary to raise his game to the top level. To get some appreciation of the diet of squash which top players deemed appropriate only some 15 years later, witness the comments of Framlingham's other squash international old boy, Humphrey Truman. In the 1960s, when Humphrey was playing at the top level, it was his view that he needed to be playing against good opposition five times a week, and three of those would need to go to five games. Without this concentration of competition he felt he would lose match fitness and competitive edge.

Norman, entirely self-taught, practised on his own in the court at Allhallows, occasionally knocking up with boys or colleagues. Tony Watson recalls one such session:

"Norman was wanting to practise for the 1946 Amateur championship. He took me on court and after a long knock-up he said: 'you are two games and eight-love up and it's your serve'. I just could not scramble that single precious point, even though I was not a bad player, later playing at Oxford for a college which went four years unbeaten save by one college."

The opposition which Norman needed was not to be found at hand. Thus from time to time he made the two hour car journey from the school in Rousdon, just west of Lyme Regis, to Torquay to play with Bill Clements, the professional at the Imperial Hotel and a fine player. When Clements emigrated to Rhodesia in 1950 the press tribute was generous:

'At the Imperial Hotel he can claim the advancement of several good players – Michelmore and Haycraft are two instances – as well as the pleasure given to many not destined to reach the heights. The present amateur champion N. F. Borrett would have been in the top flight without any help. But he would be the first to give credit to the constant match practice that he has been able to get only from Clements in accounting for his remarkable ability to dominate the amateur game so completely as he has done for the last four years. I am told they play level and that it is anyone's guess who wins. Not many other professionals with their handicap of teaching beginners could say that.'

In fact Norman never had constant match practice from Clements. Although his chief interest, as recorded in the Pembroke College Who's Who was travel and, as Mullie puts it "he was mad on

cars, particularly his 2 litre MG" *(pictured above)*. Norman did not make the journey to Torquay often, as petrol rationing was a very limiting factor for a four hour round trip.

Even county squash for Devon, in which Norman participated after 1948, did not offer the quality competition he needed. He would rarely play in the inter-county south-western area rounds, only entering the fray if and when Devon had won that section and had reached the next, inter-area, stage. "The focus of my squash season was November to January, after which the hockey pitch was my priority until April. I regretted that in my short squash season I could not find any strong competition for practice." Mullie remembers that "Norman would come home after practising by himself in the Allhallows Convent squash court and complain to me there was no one for him to play against. Perhaps because of this he threw himself into training; day after day, running twenty times round the school hockey pitch, completely dedicated." He eschewed alcohol, save for a glass or two of wine on special occasions. He smoked an occasional pipe. Norman's weight was a mere 9 stones 8 pounds, light for his height of 5 feet 10.5 inches. He made himself one of the fittest men in squash.

…He made himself one of the fittest men in squash.

The first post-war Amateur, December 1946;
squash practice by a PoW;
from Devon to Essex for a county game.

Given his Devonian isolation, it is hardly surprising that it was as a virtual unknown that Norman's entry for the first post-war English Amateur squash rackets championship attracted little interest. A shortage of newsprint also prevented the publicising of the game that pre-war reporting had achieved. As an undergraduate Norman had competed, and looked promising, in the two pre-war Amateurs, but had not got past the third round, and that was eight years ago; also he had not played a competitive squash match since the war.

The SRA was only able to arrange the restoration of the national championships in December of 1946. Played at its traditional pre-war venue of the Lansdowne Club in Berkeley Square, it was, in effect, the amateur championship of the world. As the years went by, the Amateur attracted more overseas players, but in the early post-war years only a few such could compete with the British, who had developed and still dominated the game.

A parallel structure, also under the aegis of the SRA, ran the professional game, which comprised a relatively few players, British teaching professionals for the most part, with a handful of Egyptian and Indian based coaches. They competed in a small number of tournaments, the big event being the British Open Championship, hosted by the Lansdowne Club, which attracted the best professional players in the world. The Khan family, who were to reign over world squash in the 1950s and early 1960s, had not yet emerged on to the wider stage, and the brilliant Egyptian Mahmoud Karim was the early post-war Open master.

The first post-war Amateur commenced on December 2nd 1946, and attracted an entry of 64. Norman had to take time off from Allhallows, as the Christmas holiday did not start until mid-December. As there was no guide to the form of the players, there was no seeding. In the first round Norman played Roger Pulbrook, who as Oxford's captain had been defeated by Yardley in Norman's first Varsity match, and Norman beat him soundly 9-2, 9-4, 9-1. Yardley, one of the top six players in the country pre-war, was not a competitor in the Amateur. His cricket had taken him to Australia for the 1946-47 first post-war English tour, where his performances were such that he staked out a strong claim to captain England after Hammond's retirement, thus depriving the English squash scene of a potential Amateur champion.

Norman's second round opponent, L. M. Minford, a triple Oxford blue, put up a spirited display before going down 9-2, 10-8, 9-7. The Evening Standard reported that Norman...

'had a good chance to come through to the final. He played very skilfully, using all the known shots - but he was inclined to obstruct... The second game had been a severe test of stamina, but so fit is Borrett that, while Minford was wiping his glasses during the one minute spell allowed after each game, Borrett practised shots against the wall.'

In the third round on Friday 6th, Norman comfortably dispatched D. G. Yeats-Brown, whom he had last met in the final of the Kensington Schools squash tournament in January 1936. His quarter-final opponent on Monday 9th was the fancied South African-born but London resident, Dr. Peter Hildick-Smith who had beaten the Suffolk first string, Peter Cadbury, a Cambridge friend of Norman and Mullie, who was to become Timothy's godfather. As a spectacle it was slightly spoilt by the number of lets claimed. The two contestants were of a similar style, with a highly focused will to win and a ruthless determination; in the first round Hildick-Smith had shown his ruthlessness by playing *"heart-breaking squash against F. A. Nunn and did not lose a point in the match."* Norman gave a convincing display in winning the first two games, showing remarkable retrieving powers in the fast rallies. Hildick-Smith then played with greater certainty in winning the third game 9-6, with good use of the side wall, and the fourth game was level all the way. Norman applied all the pace he could, taking the ball as early as possible, and finished the match with a hard-hit cross court shot just above the board, to close out the fourth game and the match, 9-6.

The next day Norman's semi-final opponent was Brian Phillips, one of England's best players, who was to become a good friend. Phillips had spent some years as a German PoW keeping himself fit for squash, spending many hours hitting any object which could act as a ball against a wall. Norman's speed about the court took him to a 9-6, 9-5, lead, when Phillips began to strike some brilliant shots just above the tin to take the third 9-5. As with his win over Hildick-Smith, Norman, having eased off slightly in the third game, had reserves available to raise the pace again to take the fourth game 9-4...

...So at 3pm on Thursday 12th December the unknown Devonian schoolmaster stepped on to court to contest the final of the Amateur.

His opponent was John Gillies, a fine player, capped by England both pre and post-war, who was to emigrate to New Zealand in 1948 amidst press comment that he had probably been robbed by the war of the Amateur championship. Gillies had survived a draining semi-final on the Tuesday, only winning 9-7 in the fifth game. Norman was younger and fitter. His gruelling training on the Devon roads had prepared him well for this showdown, in which his strategy, and his natural inclination, was to rely on his speed and stamina to maintain a killing pace throughout.

The Times noted that '*the match was played at a faster pace than any played before in the tournament and the ball was kept lower over the board. This was expected, for Borrett believes in speed of foot to attack the ball as early as possible, and this quality brings him, weight forward, moving towards the target; and Gillies, who has been the most attractive to watch of all the competitors, relies on varying drop shots from almost any part of the court with fast cross-court strokes with that roll of the wrist that contrives to lend the ball speed off the front wall.*' The reference to the roll of the wrist – putting top spin on the ball – is interesting, as it was the very opposite of Norman's belief, drilled into his students, which was to cut every shot to make the ball die.

The match was something of a disappointment, given Gillies failure to find his best touch. '*But Borrett's skill must not be overlooked. Starting with the freshness which comes from the right amount of tuning up, he forced the pace and kept it up relentlessly throughout. Furthermore he showed intelligent court craft in taking every chance when his opponent was out of position.*' Norman ran out a decisive winner, 9-3, 9-6, 9-3, making the winning point with a precise side-wall nick.

Norman and Mullie went to Frinton, to his parents, after the Amateur, term having ended, and they did not return to Devon until a few days before the start of the Easter term, in the second week of January 1947. Norman had a full teaching schedule at Allhallows and his spare time was largely taken up with coaching squash and hockey. He trained strenuously, but did not play any squash, other than one game, on Monday January 27th, for which he had to take a day off school. He travelled to the eastern suburbs of London to Wanstead, to play top string for Essex against Cambridgeshire in the inter-county championship. He won his match in straight games, and the county duly achieved a 5-0 victory. In late January Norman was interviewed by BBC TV, making a rare foray into the world of squash.

One practice match for the second post-war Amateur – January 1948; a brandy for John Thompson; both the Open and the Amateurs v Professionals clash with hockey.

As the 1947-48 squash season got under way, it was clear that squash was booming. Despite the continuing scarcity of building materials for the repair or construction of courts, there was unprecedented activity in the regions. All the old area championships, except that of the North of England, had been revived, as were many local tournaments. Norman had little opportunity to participate in this revival.

The Open Championship of 1946-47, finally held in the following season on December 17th, was the last one played on the traditional challenge system, all challengers playing a knock-out to determine the man who would meet the holder in the final. The right to challenge Jim Dear had been won, early in 1947, by Mahmoud Karim. The challenge match was then postponed from its March date because Dear was playing then in the British rackets championships. The new date, early in the 1947-48 season, was then changed twice, firstly for an injury to the holder and then for the illness of the challenger. If only such sympathy had been afforded Norman when he sustained his bout of food poisoning just before the Amateur in January 1952 ! The match when finally played, over two legs, went to Karim, 2-0, with the second leg going to a tight fifth game. Gerald Pawle, a leading commentator on the game, writing in the Evening Standard, referred to Karim's having succeeded to the mantle of Amr Bey: '*Once again an Egyptian is virtual champion of the world, and how strange it is that a country boasting only three clubs should twice in a generation have given us such a master of an essentially British game.*'

The Londonderry Cup for Public Schools Old Boys was played for the first time since the war, and won by Harrow, but Framlingham did not enter a team. If the three best OF players were to be available at the same time the team would be a strong one: Norman Borrett, Digby Flowerdew, and, Lieutenant J. D. Molyneux. The latter, who had been in the same squash side as Norman at Framlingham, was fifth string in the Royal Navy side that won the services' championship in mid-December, and Hampshire champion.

The year had but two days to run when Norman finally went on court in a competitive contest. The first ever match between the Executive Committee of the SRA and the Jesters Club was played at the Latymer Court SRC. The sides consisted largely of senior members of both organizations, Norman being invited to play first string for the Jesters against Brian Phillips for the SRA. Played only one week before the Amateur, chief interest centred on the match between these two. Norman won a well-fought game, 9-5, 9-7, 9-5. For him it was an important opportunity for top class practice before the big event. Phillips, in regular practice from his matches in the Bath Club Cup, was given warning of the difficulty he would have of wresting the Amateur championship from the holder.

The Amateur championships for 1947-48 took place at the Lansdowne Club in the first week of January 1948. Two significant changes had been introduced by the SRA. First, the date was altered from its traditional mid-December position to early January, with the beneficial result that schoolmasters and university undergraduates could more easily enter. The presence of the entire Oxford team and two of the Cambridge side gave greater quality to the entry. The second change was the re-introduction of seeding. The fact that only two of the seeds fell by the wayside was a very satisfactory outcome, given the difficulty faced by the SRA committee of judging form so soon after the war, made no easier by the fact that the premier club competition, the Bath Club Cup, was still being played on the league system, with the result, so it was said, that the players taking part lacked competitive incentive.

The early rounds of the Amateur gave Norman an opportunity to get his eye in against some of the leading players. He was given a hard time for over an hour by Peter Kershaw's spoiling tactics in the second round, and his next match, against Samuelson, was described as containing more good strokes in each game than in the whole of the Kershaw match. The fourth round, the quarter-final, pitted Norman against Dr. J. F. Stokes, runner-up to Amr Bey in the Amateur of 1937. Stokes found that Norman's defence, coupled with his much greater speed, denied him the time to produce the skilled shot-making he had displayed in earlier rounds. Roy McKelvie writing in the Daily Express thought '*Stokes played well enough to beat probably any other amateur in England, and in the rallies, often dominated the court. But Borrett's pace was so great, and his power of recovery so good, that he was able to make attacking recovery shots, or winners, from difficult positions.*'

Brian Phillips was Norman's semi-final opponent for the second successive year. The match contained the hardest hitting of the whole championship, as both men sought to win the rallies by sheer speed of stroke; there was only one lob in the entire match. The pace of the game made a certain number of lets inevitable, but the number was not high. Norman, as customary, reached almost everything by virtue of his speed about the court and his anticipation; Phillips soon found that nothing short of a nick would win the point. It says much for Phillips' accuracy that he managed to win so many points in this way. He cut the ball heavily, keeping it low, and scored with some fine cross-court kills.

Phillips was renowned for losing the first game as he took time to warm to the task, but on this evening he started well and was hitting the ball even harder than Norman. The absence of defensive play meant

points were won on short rallies, although some long exchanges occurred in both the first and third games. Norman won by playing an earlier ball than Phillips, so forcing the latter to defend. As the SRA report of the match put it, '*to have to play a defensive game against Borrett is a hopeless task for anyone*'. The match lasted forty minutes, with Norman well in front the whole time except for a period in the middle of the third game '*when he became almost human, and putting several shots into the tin, let Phillips creep up from 1-5 to 6-5.*' A fine straight games victory for the champion put him into good touch for the final, on Monday January 12th, against his pre-war Cambridge colleague J. R. Thompson, who had mastered Seymour-Hayden in the other semi-final with a display of great pace and hard hitting.

Recently Thompson recalled his game plan for the Final: "I had a brandy before the game and then went for it. I was chiefly a rackets player (a modest ssessment by a man who played fine squash for his country), and decided that the best approach was for me to hit the ball hard and keep up the pace."

He maintained this attack in the opening salvoes but could make little impression on Norman, who went from 2-2 to game in eight minutes. The players, both at peak fitness, took no interval and the second game saw Thompson drop his hard hitting policy in favour of a safety first approach, in the hope of forcing Norman into errors by sheer perseverance. The resultant longer rallies played into the champion's hands as Thompson lacked Norman's stamina. Rallies of between 30 and 40 strokes were numerous, and one of 48 took a lot out of both men. At 8-3 down Thompson resorted to the lobbing tactics employed successfully by Kershaw in the earlier round, but to no avail as the game was lost 9-3. Notwithstanding the severe pace of the play, neither player called for an interval after the second game. Thompson's lobbing tactics had more success in the third game, as Norman faltered for once and hit several shots into the tin, putting Thompson in hand at four-all. However Norman gathered himself, raised his game again, and the sheer amount of running Thompson had been forced to endure began to tell. The end came quickly.

The furious pace of the match was reflected in the match time of 34 minutes, half of which was taken up by the second game. The game was played in a good spirit, and the total of eight lets, one to Norman and seven to Thompson, compared favorably with the previous year's final: '*Throughout the championship Borrett was giving his opponents far more room in which to make their shots than he was in the habit of doing last year*'. More on that topic later.

RIGHT: Norman retained his Amateur Squash crown in January 1948

Norman's second title had been achieved without losing a single game. There were only two other players in the field who approached him for speed, but neither could match his ball control. The SRA report concluded '*His form was all the more remarkable in that his scholastic duties in the West Country gave him little opportunity for match practice against the leading amateurs.*' Remarkably, Norman was to play no squash at all for the rest of the year, until December 3rd, when he played the first of three matches to get himself into some sort of touch for the 1949 Amateur.

The logistics of getting from Bristol where he was captaining England at hockey for the first time, against Wales on the Saturday, to Edinburgh on the Monday meant that Norman did not take his place in the first post-war England squash international, against Scotland, on March 15th. Seymour-Hayden, Kershaw, Lassalles, Brian Phillips and Gillies played five singles and, the unique Edinburgh doubles court permitting this innovation, two doubles, all of which went England's way save for one of the doubles games. The Bristol international also prevented him playing in the first knock-out version of the Open Squash Championship, to which nine professionals and seven amateurs were invited, between March 8th and 15th at the Lansdowne Club. Although the date of the Amateur championship had been altered to permit schoolmasters and university men to enter, the dates of the newly structured Open were not so accommodating. The SRA's own report commented that '*the amateurs most unfortunately did not include either the winner or the runner-up in the amateur championship. Both being schoolmasters, they were unable to give up the necessary time*'. Gerald Pawle wrote that '*it is a pity N. F. Borrett is unable to play, for on this season's showing he is the only amateur capable of fully extending Mahmoud or Dear.*'

The new, more 'democratic', knock-out format to the Open of 1947-48 produced a final between the same two players as had emerged the previous year under the old challenge regime. It was won again by Karim, meeting Jim Dear for the fourth time; the general view being that the match provided the finest exhibition of squash since the war. Dear led 3-0 in the fifth game before Karim fought back to 7-3. Dear then rallied, playing many brilliant strokes on the way to 7-all, then 8-7, game-ball and match point. Karim saved that point, but after a long rally was put out and Dear served for the match again. Karim saved it once again and made first one point for 8-8, and then another for 9-8. Dear put him out three times, but could not score and Karim finally got home 10-8, after a 56 minute marathon.

England played Scotland at hockey on April 10th in Inverness, depriving Norman of the chance to play for the Amateurs against the Professionals in the annual squash match at Hampstead Squash Club on Sunday the 11th. Such clashes did not trouble Norman; he accepted them as an inevitable consequence of playing two winter sports.

The Londonderry Cup;
The Amateur January 1949;
Roy Wilson crushed;
Norman loses for the first time since the war;
Jim Dear's heavy racket;
the county championship;
and a first international cap.

The inter-county championship attracted an increased entry in the 1948-49 season as it gained in popularity. Whilst the metropolitan counties were dominant, there were signs of strength in some other counties, especially Hampshire and Norman's county Devon. International play increased, and while England remained much the strongest country, there were signs of a resumption of the global spread of the game which started just before the war.

Squash was becoming ever more popular at all levels, and club and county tournaments grew in number as more players took up the game. The SRA, which was in effect the controlling body for world squash, had moved tentatively into a new era with the announcement that a small office had been secured in the London's West End, and that it had appointed its first full-time secretary, H. E. Hayman.

Despite these healthy signs there remained concerns that the number of players who took part in competitive squash was small compared to the overall number playing socially. One welcome development was the reversion to a league competition format of the Bath Club Cup, the equivalent in squash importance to the county championship in cricket. It was a widely held view that the Bath Club Cup provided the regular weekly match-play which was the training ground for champions and would-be champions.

These developments were only marginally helpful to Norman's search for regular serious competitive play. However it was pleasing to his old school that he was prepared to find time to turn out in the Londonderry Cup. The Old Framlinghamians, on the back of Norman's preparedness to participate, entered the competition for the first time post-war in the autumn of 1948. In December's second round match against the Old Aldenhamians, Norman lost only one point in disposing of his opponent in the top match. The absence of Dr. Digby Flowerdew was compensated by the good form of J. D. Molyneux, who was to play in the Amateur in January 1950, winning easily at second string. Oscar Ford, who had organized the team, and Hinds won at three and four and the only loss was by M. R. Garrard at five.

The structure of squash team matches is such that if you have a banker at first string you need find only two winners out of the remaining four for the team to win the match. The converse of this truism is that when your banker is absent, as was the case in the third round against the Old Tonbridgians later that month, all the strings have to play one higher than their earlier station, and the result is immediately in the balance. Worse luck faced the OFs as apart from Norman, Molyneux and Ford were also unavailable. Tonbridge fielded Brian Phillips at first string, and OF Brian Shelley did not detain him for long. Hinds, Young, Rolfe and M. B. Smith did their best but garnered only one game between them.

BLT&S summed up Framlingham's first season back in the Londonderry in these words: '*Framlingham, facetiously known as the Old Borrettians, aided by the Amateur Champion, and the Navy player J. D. Molyneux, won their first round match in fine style but crashed badly in the next round.*'

Norman was now playing hockey for Somerset, and under that county affiliation played in the West trial on Saturday December 18th. He then drove from Taunton to London on Sunday morning in time to get to the Hurlingham Club for a 4pm squash match for the Jesters against Middlesex. His opponent D. M. Bull, whom he was to play again only three weeks later in the semi-final of the Amateur, gained only seven points in all. Norman's MG was then turned North-East for Frinton.

F. M. Strawson, writing a preview of the Amateur in the BLT&S magazine, thought that the chances of Norman not reaching the final in ten days' time were remote indeed.

'*Should Borrett be deposed, his defeat would indicate a marked recovery in the standard of post-war squash, for by reason of his great speed of stroke and foot, uncanny anticipation, unerring ball control, magnificent fitness and relentless concentration, he has shown himself a most worthy successor in the line of champions initiated in 1922.*'

It was Strawson's view that Norman was '*an amazing man, for he rarely plays more than once or twice a term. On the opening day of the 1948 Olympic Games, in which he captained Britain's hockey team, he told me he had not touched a racket since winning the title early last January. But he is always fit, and a week's intensive practice with leading professionals, combined with his natural aptitude for the game, is sufficient to bring him to the requisite state of efficiency.*' Gerald Pawle expressed similar sentiments in the Daily Telegraph: '*How Borrett maintains his form without preliminary match practice is one of the game's mysteries, but I expect him to win the cup for the third time. He has an intriguing first round match against a player of similar determination in W. H. L. Gordon.*'

For the first time, save for occasional USA team participation before the war, the 1949 Amateur squash championship was other than a purely English competition. Officially nominated players from Ireland, Scotland and Denmark were entered. There was less than universal player approval for the start time of 10 o'clock on Saturday January 1st, but with sixty four entrants an early commencement was necessary.

Norman's timing and side-wall shot making were awry as he lost a game to the dogged W. H. L. Gordon, whose success lay in the manner he slowed the champion down by a judicious mixture of drop shots and lobs. Norman began to warm to the task in rounds two and three, defeating Chalk and G. D. Evans in straight games, for the loss of six and nine points respectively. The game of the quarter-final round was that between him and Roy Wilson, who had only recently returned to squash after an interval of eight years. The latter '*a most promising player*' and '*the dark horse of the tournament*' was expected to give Norman his first trial of strength. Instead the gallery witnessed a devastating exhibition by the champion which settled immediately any doubts as to his form.

BLT&S's correspondent reported that...

> ...'*Borrett can seldom have played so relentlessly against a class opponent who in spite of going all out could not detain him in court for more than 22 minutes nor score more than two points...*

... Borrett is said to have made no more than three mistakes in the course of the match but what was more remarkable was the number of outright winners which he made. Wilson had obviously never come across such speed before and had no reply to it. Borrett gave a good example of his quickness of brain and movement when he fell full length and yet rose in time to cross the court and play the next shot.'

The semi-finals saw victories for old rivals Norman and Brian Phillips. D. M. Bull, who had suffered blistered feet in dispatching J. R. Thompson in the quarter-final in four games, did not keep Norman on court for long. At first he tried to unsettle his opponent with high slow shots down the side walls, a tactic which he soon abandoned. The Times reported that '*it was not until the third game that he (Borrett) made the semblance of a mistake. In side-stepping for position he is as nimble as a matador. His quick hitting is more incisive than that of the others, and he finds the nick at the foot of the side walls more often.*' Bull was given no time to play the delicate drop shots upon which his game was built, and '*like the spectators, looked relieved as the end came in nineteen minutes*'. He had won a total of six points.

The ruthless efficiency of Norman's game continued into the final on Monday January 10th on the famous Bruce court before a packed gallery of 130. Phillips' chance of winning depended on his being able to keep Norman at the back of the court and go for the drops and angles at which he excelled. He was given no opportunity to deploy such tactics as Norman applied relentless power in his returns and maintained an impeccable length. The Times noted that '*Borrett is better than last year at making drop shots off the side walls, and he does this more often. He is also cruelly good at killing the ball down the other side when his opponent is out of position.*'

Norman dominated play from the tee, and Phillips thus spent most of the match behind him. Norman made it plain that he was not going to give an inch when playing a drop shot, and Phillips was obliged to run round him several times. This failure to move away might well have resulted in two penalty points awarded against Norman, but not for the first time the marking was lenient and he escaped punishment. BLT&S' view was that the only thing which marred a good match was Norman not giving enough room to his opponent. '*He is particularly guilty after playing a drop. He comes back in line with the ball, instead of towards the centre.*'

Having made three errors in winning the first game, Norman made only two in the second, as two drops were played into the middle of the tin. Notwithstanding the heavy slice he always applied to his hard-hit drives Norman was not slicing or cutting his drops, but when they came off they were highly effective. The third game saw Norman remorselessly hunt down his man, harrying him into errors he would not make against a lesser opponent. Norman was much the quicker player about the court, hitting more and more winners as the match progressed. Phillips tried to get his game going but was outclassed, gaining a mere eight points in all. Norman's third consecutive championship win saw him lose only one game in six rounds and concede a mere fifty points. The previous year he did not lose a game but gave up seventy five points.

Norman was back at school for the beginning of term on the Wednesday, but felt he could not take a day off as soon as the following Monday, and cried off from the annual Amateurs v Professionals match at Hampstead Squash Club. BLT&S was not happy:

'*By fixing Monday January 17th as the date (for the annual match) it was hoped that the schoolmasters would be able to be present, and while J. R. Thompson thereby played and gave a really great exhibition of squash, it was much regretted that the Amateur Champion was not able to be present.*'

Thompson was a master at Marlborough, and thus a little closer to London than Norman. A week or two later Norman did manage to play one of the professionals he might have played against in the Amateurs v Professionals match, when, in a friendly at Queen's Club, he beat the ex-Open champion, Jim Dear, eight years older than Norman, 9-8 in the fifth game. Dear's legendary status in all racket

games meant that the result of even this friendly contest warranted a mention in the press, together with Dear's opinion that Norman would beat any other professional in the country. Norman played a few times against Dear in practice matches. Dear had an impish sense of humour. After one of these matches, which had gone to five strenuous games Norman, not satisfied with his form, attributed it to too heavy a racket. "Try mine" said Dear. He had been playing with a rackets racket, much heavier than a squash racket.

RIGHT: The draw for the 1948-49 Amateur had Norman at top seed.

The squash inter-county tournament, and the squash international, season fell each year in the February to March period, and Norman played much more squash during this period in 1949 than he had in either of the two previous post-war years. Devon had beaten Gloucestershire and Somerset to win the county South Western area title, and called on Norman to join them for the inter-area stage – the national quarter-final match against Hampshire. Norman duly responded and at Torquay on Saturday, March 12th, he beat Oxford blue M. H. Routh, 9-5, 9-4, 9-3, but the match was lost 3-2, and the county was out of the tournament.

Having been prevented by hockey and then school commitments from playing in the England squash internationals against Ireland in Dublin on Friday February 11th and Denmark in Copenhagen on Tuesday March 8th, Norman finally made his debut in a squash international on Friday March 18th in the game against Scotland at the RAC. Despite being out of practice, he did not take long to beat Peter Harding-Edgar in the first string match for the loss of eight points. Brian Phillips, Hooper, Dagnall and Bull all won as England completed a 5-0 victory without dropping a game.

…Norman finally made his debut in a squash international on Friday March 18th in the game against Scotland at the RAC.

Norman got back home from England's last hockey international of the season, away to Ireland, on Monday 11th. After only three nights with his parents in Frinton, Norman took Mullie and six year old Anthony off on the Thursday to the West Country, to the Cornish Riviera Club at Carlyon Bay in Cornwall. Mullie and Anthony were to have a holiday, and Norman was to play squash over the Easter weekend in the West of England Squash Championship. He had been

THE SQUASH RACKETS ASSOCIATION
The Amateur Squash Rackets Championship, 1948-49

(HOLDER: N. F. BORRETT)

To be played in the Courts of the Lansdowne Club, 6, Fitzmaurice Place, Berkeley Square, London, W.1.

(by kind permission of the Committee of the Club)

from Saturday, January the 1st, to Monday, January the 10th, 1949

FIRST ROUND SATURDAY, Jan. 1st.	SECOND ROUND. MONDAY, Jan. 3rd.	THIRD ROUND. TUESDAY, Jan. 4th.	FOURTH ROUND. THURSDAY, Jan. 6th.	SEMI-FINALS. SATURDAY, Jan. 8th.	FINAL. MONDAY, Jan. 10th.	WINNER.
* 1. N. F. BORRETT ... A	BORRETT					
2. W. H. L. GORDON ... 10.0	9-1, 4-9, 9-4, 9-5. Bruce	BORRETT				
3. D. CHALK B	CHALK 2.0	9-2, 9-4, 9-0	BORRETT			
4. G. R. G. BROWN ... 10.0	9-1, 9-0, 9-3.		9-5, 9-0, 9-4 Bruce			
5. G. NEWTON ... A	PAGE		2.0			
6. F. PAGE ... 10.40	9-3, 9-6, 3-9, 9-2 A	EVANS	Bruce 2.0	BORRETT		
7. R. G. PENDERED B	EVANS 2.0	5-9, 10-8, 9-2, 10-8	Referee: C. L. Stubbs	9-0, 9-1, 9-1		
8. G. D. EVANS .. 10.40	10-9, 4-9, 9-5, 7-9, 9-0.					
* 9. A. W. H. MALLETT A	WILSON					
10. R. B. R. WILSON 11.20	9-4, 5-9, 4-9, 9-2, 9-6 B	WILSON				
11. R. C. DRAYSON B	DRAYSON 2.0	9-7, 9-5, 9-3.	WILSON			
12. C. I. STRINGER 11.20	6-9, 9-6, 2-9, 9-0, 9-2		5-9, 9-2, 9-3, 9-4. A 2.0			
13. R. B. HILL A	ELGOOD				BORRETT	
14. B. C. ELGOOD 12.0	9-3, 9-4, 4-9, 9-2 Bruce	ELGOOD		Bruce 2.30	9-2, 9-1, 9-3.	
15. P. L. RICHARDS-J. TRELEAVEN B	ROUTH 2.45	7-9, 9-3, 9-5, 9-7.		Referee: F. M. Strawson		
16. M. H. ROUTH ... 12.0	9-0, 9-3, 9-6.					
*17. D. M. BULL ... A	BULL					
18. P. C. SAMUELSON .. 12.40	3-9, 4-9, 9-6, 9-2, 9-4 A	BULL				
19. W. O. LANE B	SHERRARD 2.45	9-6, 9-5, 9-3.	BULL			
20. P. SHERRARD 12.40	9-8, 7-9, 9-7, 4-9, 9-6.		9-1, 9-7, 9-2. Bruce			
21. C. J. HOVELL A	HOVELL		2.45			
22. J. P. JOHNSON ... 1.20	9-6, 10-8, 9-3. B	HOVELL	Referee: P. W. Le Gros	BULL		
23. E. J. E. READWIN B	WILSON 2.45	5-9, 7-9, 9-7, 9-4, 9-0.		9-1, 1-9, 9-1, 9-5.		
24. C. J. WILSON 1.20	W.O.					
*25. J. R. THOMPSON ... Bruce	THOMPSON					
26. P. E. HARE .. 2.0	9-5, 9-0, 9-1 Bruce	THOMPSON				
27. D. S. ANDERTON A	DARRAH 3.30	9-2, 9-0, 9-0.	THOMPSON			
28. N. G. DARRAH 2.0	9-6, 9-5, 9-7.		9-4, 9-2, 5-9, 1-9, 9-3. A 2.45			
29. J. S. SOUTER B	SOUTER				Bruce BORRETT	
30. J. B. THOMAS .. 2.0	5-9, 9-6, 0-9, 9-4, 9-7. A	BOYD			5.0 9-2, 9-4, 9-2	
31. D. Y. BOYD ... Bruce	BOYD 3.30	9-3, 1-9, 6-9, 9-2, 9-2			Referee: R. G. de Quetteville	
32. J. A. STEWART 2.40	9-5, 9-4, 7-9, 6-9, 9-5.					
33. D. E. J. HUNT A	BOUSTEAD					
34. R. M. BOUSTEAD ... 2.40	9-1, 9-3, 9-1. B	BOUSTEAD				
35. E. E. HARRISON B	HARRISON 3.30	9-2, 9-4, 9-5.	BOUSTEAD			
36. B. O. SMITH (Denmark) 2.40	9-4, 9-0, 9-0		9-4, 9-4, 9-5. A 3.30			
37. N. W. NICHOLSON ... Bruce	MICHELMORE					
38. J. MICHELMORE .. 3.20	9-6, 9-2, 9-2 Bruce	STOKES	Bruce 3.30	BOUSTEAD		
39. J. R. C. YGLESIAS A	STOKES 4.15	9-5, 10-8, 9-3.	Referee: H. E. Hayman	9-0, 9-2, 9-7.		
*40. J. F. STOKES .. 3.20	10-8, 9-4, 8-10, 9-4.					
41. W. S. M. JAMESON (Ireland) B	JAMESON					
42. T. C. WILKINSON . 3.20	9-3, 9-0, 9-5. A	JAMESON				
43. H. M. MORTIMER B	MORTIMER 4.15	9-7, 9-5, 9-3	JAMESON			
44. P. HARDING-EDGAR (Scotland) 4.0	9-6, 9-7, 9-0.		9-5, 4-9, 9-3, 2-9, 9-5. Bruce 3.30			
45. J. A. PALMER-TOMKINSON A	WISDOM				PHILLIPS	
46. D. WISDOM ... 4.0	9-5, 10-8, 7-9, 9-5 B	HOOPER		Bruce 3.30	5-9, 9-2, 9-5, 9-3.	
47. A. D. P. BRAZIER B	HOOPER 4.15	9-2, 9-5, 9-3.		Referee: H. A. Lascelles		
*48. N. E. HOOPER 4.0	9-0, 9-1, 9-0.					
49. J. T. WILLMOTT ... Bruce	WILLMOTT					
50. R. B. M. KING (Denmark) 4.40	6-9, 7-9, 10-8, 9-3, 9-2 Bruce	GOODACRE				
51. D. I. BURNETT .. A	GOODACRE 5.0	6-9, 5-9, 9-4, 9-6, 9-7	PEAKE			
52. K. GOODACRE 4.40			9-0, 9-3, 9-0. A 4.15			
53. R. PULBROOK B	PULBROOK					
54. W. G. L. ROBBINS 4.40	W.O. A	PEAKE	Bruce 4.15	PHILLIPS		
55. A. G. AITCHISON Bruce	PEAKE 5.0	9-7, 7-9, 9-6, 9-1.	Referee: H. W. Backhouse	5-9, 9-4, 9-3, 9-2		
*56. J. M. PEAKE 5.20	9-4, 9-3, 9-6.					
57. P. J. PHILLIPS A	PHILLIPS					
58. T. F. R. BULKELEY 5.20	W.O. B	DAGNALL				
59. M. T. TURNBULL B	DAGNALL 5.0	5-9, 10-8, 9-10, 9-7, 9-7	PHILLIPS			
60. H. J. A. DAGNALL 5.20	9-3, 9-4, 9-7		6-9, 9-5, 9-7, 9-1. Bruce 4.15			
61. F. M. LANCASTER Bruce	LANCASTER					
62. D. DUGDALE ... 6.0	2-9, 10-8, 5-9, 9-6, 9-2 Bruce	PHILLIPS				
63. D. E. WILLIAMS .. A	PHILLIPS 5.45	9-5, 10-9, 9-5.				
*64. B. C. PHILLIPS ... 6.0	9-2, 9-1, 9-7.					

* Denotes Seeded Player

Any player not ready to play at the time appointed will be scratched unless the steward or stewards present decide otherwise.

Players are required to wear white clothes and white or crêpe soled shoes.

Each match is the best of five games of nine points.

The Dunlop "low-bounding" ball to be used.

Professionals have been appointed markers for all matches, who will act as referees for the first three rounds. L. W. R. Keeble will be in charge of these arrangements. The referees' decisions will be final.

Tickets for seats in the gallery can be obtained from the Secretary of the S.R.A. or, on the days of play, at the entrance to the gallery A limited number of seats for the semi-finals and final will be reserved for competitors. Applications must reach the secretary of the S.R.A. **not later than December the 15th.**

A, B or Bruce against the time of play indicates the Court reserved. The Stewards reserve the right to transfer any Match.

The entrance to the Lansdowne Club Squash Courts is in Fitzmaurice Place.

NOTE:—All communications should be addressed to THE SECRETARY, THE SQUASH RACKETS ASSOCIATION, 25, The Haymarket, London, S.W.1. December, 1948.

J. H. BROAD & Co., Ltd., 8, King Street, Richmond, Surrey.

invited to play hockey for the Tramps in Kent at the Folkestone Hockey Festival; he was a great fan of the Tramps, a side of county and international players whose social skills were regarded as of almost equal importance to their stickwork. The Times, in its preview of the Festival, noted this affiliation: '*England's captain in 1949 is a Tramp. Since the war he has been the one forward reasonably certain of his place in every international match*'.

Norman turned down the Tramps in favour of the squash: "Brian Phillips had been on at me for some time to play in this tournament, which he always enjoyed". It would also give Norman valuable practice for the Open Championship, due to start on the Wednesday after Easter, which he had entered for the first time. Cornwall proved to be a better bet than Folkestone. Norman, Mullie and Anthony enjoyed the brilliant Cornish weather, and Norman got some good practice. The eight man field was not strong, save for Phillips. Norman disposed of his semi-final opponent for the loss of only one point, and was in good form for the final against Phillips. Phillips had won the West of England title on the last two occasions it had been held, in 1939 and 1948, and was by common consent the second best amateur of the day, not having lost a match since the war to any amateur save Norman. Norman gave no favours to his friend as he dominated the first two games, 9-4, 9-4, but then met stiff resistance as Phillips got to game ball in the third, before Norman took the game, and the match, 10-9. Norman's control of the game and his generalship of the court showed what an all-round player he had become.

Norman and the family drove from Carlyon Bay to London on Easter Monday for the 1948-49 Open squash championship on the Wednesday. This was a month later than the year before, a change designed to enable schoolmasters and those from universities to play. On this particular occasion it also enabled the long awaited meeting between the amateur and the professional champions to take place.

In the first round Norman Borrett was drawn against his Olympic hockey colleague and Army squash player John Peake, whom commentators rated as the fastest mover in the game. Norman out-ran and out-hit him, winning 9-3, 9-4, 9-1. Two days later, he raised his game to new levels:

'*In defeating Peake he had been no more than the Borrett of two years ago: a fast, relentless retriever of everything, hitting hard to a length and playing the occasional half drop. Now, against N. E. Hooper, he was the complete player, more so than he had ever shown himself to be before. Angles, straight and diagonal drop shots, reverse angles: all were played and were interspersed with an even more accurate and harder hit drive to a length. No less than three successive rallies were won with a beautifully played and very fast reverse angle, which was clearly as unexpected by Hooper as it was by the*

gallery. This indeed was a true amateur champion, going all out in preparation for the next day's semi-final.'

That semi-final was the most eagerly awaited match of the year. It took place on Saturday April 23rd between the reigning Open and Amateur champions, Karim and Norman, and the winner would lay claim to be '*the greatest player seen in England since the war*'. Only W. E. Clements had extended Karim so far that season, while Jim Dear, Karim's closest rival over the last two years, had to scratch from the tournament. John Oliff in the Daily Telegraph pointed out that Norman had '*never played a match against any of the leading professionals, though in practice with Dear there has been little to choose between them.*' So great was the interest in the match that money could not buy a seat. The press carried a lot of coverage. '*Immediately the draw was known every squash enthusiast tried to obtain tickets. It was the quickest sale of tickets for this game ever known. Borrett is a more rugged type of player. He is heavier in build than Karim, but very quick and agile. He hits the ball a mighty whack and though he possesses every known shot and the knowledge of when to use the right one at the right moment, he gives the impression of employing much more effort than Karim. The Englishman's chief fault is that he tends to obstruct by not moving quickly enough out of the way after he has played his shot. This is quite unintentional but it is a bad habit that must be cured before he meets Karim who is faultless in this respect. I expect Karim will win but not by a wide margin because I expect this to be Karim's hardest match since he became the open squash champion last year.*'

Gerald Pawle wrote of the fascinating discovery he had made six years previously, when he '*saw an unknown Arab professional playing a British game better than I had ever seen it played before.*' ...

...This magician from the Nile, named Mahmoud el Karim, self-taught on the antiquated stone courts of the Gezira Sporting Club, was '*poetry in motion, every lithe movement having an effortless rhythm... he is all fire and beautifully controlled fury... He plays every stroke the game has ever known.*'

The match they produced was a minor classic, with Borrett playing superbly but being comprehensively beaten by a great player at the top of his form who could answer every question Norman posed. Excepting, possibly, the meetings between Karim and J. P. Dear in 1947-48, the popular view was that there had been no better matches since the war than the two semi-finals and the final of this Open.

Brian Phillips in turn played superlative squash in the final, taking the third game and throughout giving Karim as stern a test as he had faced in the two years since he won the Open title.

If Karim established himself as the greatest player seen in England since the war, Norman was viewed as the next best, notwithstanding Phillips' great performance. The Times reported the match in the following terms:

'The first semi, in which Karim beat N. F. Borrett by the surprising score of 9-2, 9-4, 9-0, was of course disappointing to the many who believed Borrett to be so outstanding a player that he could extend the champion. But it served to show that the Egyptian is armed at every point. He had to contend with speed – the game was as fast as one can remember – and if one excepts a period when the court was too small for both of them, Karim was matched and made to do most of the running. We now know the full value of Karim's skill.'

The SRA report put some perspective on what for Norman's supporters must have looked a forlorn scoreline: *'The long awaited meeting between Karim and Borrett resulted in the former winning by three games to love, Borrett winning only six points. To leave that bare statement as the record of the match, however, would be far from accurate. In the first place those three games took thirty-three minutes to play. In the second, many of the rallies were of twenty or thirty strokes. In the previous round Borrett showed he had mastered every stroke in the game: he has always been known for his speed and determination. No matter what he did, however, Karim had an answer to it. Karim's speed, determination and stroke-play were all that little bit better than Borrett's and, when one player at squash is a little better than another, the one is bound to win. That it took Karim as long as thirty three minutes to win, although losing only six points in three games, shows how little that little bit was. That throughout he continued to give an impression of smooth fluent mastery shows what a great player he was.'*

The SRA's end of season report recorded that *'Norman Borrett, the present Amateur Champion, has been the outstanding amateur of the post-war period. It was not until March of this year however that he represented his country at squash (he has played for and captained the England hockey team on several occasions) and having successfully defeated the Scottish first string in the match played at the RAC it was only right and proper that he should be given his colours.*

The SRA is unfortunately unable to pay the travelling expenses of those who represent this country, and England is indeed fortunate in having class amateurs who are in a position to afford the time and money to travel considerable distances to play international squash.'

Two practice games for a fourth Amateur win 1950; a struggle against Seymour-Hayden and problems with Roy Wilson; hockey clashes with the Amateurs v Professionals, the Open, and two internationals; and Devon reach the county final.

Denmark made their first squash tour to England in November 1949. On Friday November 18th Norman played for England in the only international of the Danes' tour, at the Junior Carlton. John Olliff reported in the Daily Telegraph that:

'England's amateur champion every year since the war, N. F. Borrett, although rather short of practice, gave a demonstration of relentless attack which, combined with his clever side-wall play, was altogether too much for the hard-hitting O. Rasmussen, whom he beat for the loss of six points."
Some of Norman's shots were so fierce they *"made even the hardened gallery gasp'.*

Norman had one other game in preparation for the Amateur, for the OF team in the first round of the Londonderry Cup. The team lost to Haileybury. Whilst Norman beat Dr. Stokes 9-5, 9-5, 9-2, the rest of the team all lost: J. D. Molyneux to Alan Fairbairn, Ted Newcombe 10-8 in the fifth, Oscar Ford and M. R. Garrard. The team could have done with the presence of Digby Flowerdew, still playing regular squash in Kenya where he had, earlier in the year, won the Kenya squash championship for the third year running, losing only 22 points in the four rounds, whilst his wife had narrowly lost in the final of the Ladies Championship.

On Tuesday December 13th the SRA celebrated the 21st anniversary of its formation with an evening of exhibition matches, Amateur versus Professional, and a dinner. As Amateur champion Norman would have played M. A. Karim, the Open champion, in a repeat of his epic match in April, but the latter had not yet arrived for his annual visit to England and in any event Norman could not absent himself from Allhallows in the last week of term. Their places at the top of the order were taken by Brian Phillips and Jim Dear.

Norman usually counted on the annual match between the Executive Committee of the SRA and the Jesters Club, this year held on January 3rd, as a good opportunity for practice for the Amateur, which was to take place at the Lansdowne Club from January 7th - 16th. He was however unavailable this time, and would have to rely on the first few rounds of the Amateur to play himself into form. In its preview of the big event The Times wrote: *'Should N. F. Borrett win, which is expected, it will be the fourth time running and he would therefore be an outstanding champion having overcome tolerably strong opposition in a convincing and invariable fashion'.*

In the first round Norman, top-seeded, was drawn against

RIGHT: The magazine Sketch
devoted a full page to the
January 1950 Amateur final.

G. D. Evans, whom he had beaten in the third round the previous year. Norman lost fewer points this time, five in all, and looked to be in good touch. All the accustomed severity was in evidence and the ball was seldom more than a foot above the board throughout the match. Norman concentrated on playing more drops and angles than previously and these tactics, added to his heavily cut length shots, proved too much for Evans. In the second round Norman repeated his very first Amateur championship victory, back in 1946, by beating Roger Pulbrook with ease, for the loss of four points. His third round victory over W. S. M. Jameson was also uncomplicated, six points only being conceded. John Olliff, in the Morning Post, described Jameson as someone who '*can be brilliant against any ordinarily good player, but Borrett, who is perhaps the best amateur the game has yet produced, outclassed him in speed, footwork, and sound basic principles.*'

The fourth round brought a different story as he ran into, literally in some instances, Seymour-Hayden, the Navy champion. It was believed that if Norman had a weakness it was in dealing with lobs, for which the low-beamed courts at Framlingham College were no doubt the origin. Seymour-Hayden exploited this to the full, and for the first time in four years an amateur was able to match Norman point for point. A very close first game to Norman, 9-7, was followed by an equally close second in which he led eight-seven, game-ball, only to be pulled back by his opponent who went on to win 10-8. With the gallery sensing a tight finish Norman began to change the match around. By increasing the pace and playing some very hard hit angles he forced Seymour-Hayden into error, winning the third game 9-0. Although never giving up, Seymour-Hayden could not live with the speed of his opponent, and conceded the fourth game 9-4. In all 32 lets were awarded, an unsatisfactorily large number, although The Times reported the match was played in the very best spirit.

In the semi-final Norman defeated Roy Wilson 9-1, 9-6, 9-6, but it took forty minutes and was a struggle. Wilson was determined to avert a repetition of the merciless defeat he had suffered at Norman's hands in the quarter-final the previous year. The chemistry between the two players was almost bound to produce sparks: the one hot-blooded and the other ice-cool. The sparks were to burst into flame at their next meeting. The two players went at each other from the start. Norman was fortunate not to be penalised for obstruction as his eagerness to press for the dominant position in centre court frequently gave his opponent insufficient room to play his shots. The press took different views of the seriousness of this. The reporter for BLT&S was scathing: '*The referee declined to take any positive action to deal with the persistent crowding and baulking indulged in by the champion. Even when [in the third game] Borrett crowded Wilson to such an extent that Wilson's racket came into contact with that of Borrett so that Wilson's snapped*

into two pieces, a let was all he had as consolation for a broken racket'.

The Daily Telegraph saw it differently: '*The champion was always the master, and beat R. B. R. Wilson, 9-1, 9-6, 9-6. One can only imagine that Wilson had not seen Seymour-Hayden win a game from Borrett in his courageous attempt to dethrone the champion by means of the high lob and the drop. Wilson's battery of low, hard drives made no impression on Borrett, who is about as impressionable as the Sphinx. When Wilson mistimed a*

… *When Wilson mistimed a volley and broke his racket in two across his opponent's shoulder, Borrett picked up the head of the racket and handed it back to him as if it had been his handkerchief.*

volley and broke his racket in two across his opponent's shoulder, Borrett picked up the head of the racket and handed it back to him as if it had been his handkerchief.'

To complete the picture, The Times' report also made no mention of baulking, or indeed of the third game racket incident, confining itself to praising Wilson's noble effort in fighting back from adversity. '*The champion, while never looking like giving way, did occasion doubts of his being in quite such devastating form as he was a year ago.*'

Whichever version one prefers, the common theme is clear: Norman's sang-froid made him a very difficult player for a more temperamental opponent to overcome. The issue of baulking would arise again, later in Norman's story.

Sunday was a rest day so the players had two days respite before they met in the final on the evening of Monday 10th. BLT&S noted with satisfaction that in the final against Dagnall, '*Borrett was giving his opponent more room for his shots than in the previous match. Throughout the match the champion's grave demeanour never deserted him and surely no one has ever more truly earned the title of 'poker face'.* The first two games were a repeat of the semi-final, with Norman conceding an early lead before closing out the game, 9-4, 9-5. Dagnall was up against such a speedy opponent that he was forced to go for the difficult winner, with the result that he gave away many points. The third game

FIRST GAME. BOTH QUITE FRESH.

A WRISTY SHOT BY BORRETT.

ALL EYES ON THE BALL.

BORRETT SHOWS HIS AGILITY

. . AND BACKHAND DRIVE.

DAGNALL BEGINS TO TIRE.

DR. J. C. GREGORY PRESENTS THE CUP.

TOP OF THE SQUASH CLASS

ONLY a ciné camera could do justice to the skill of the players, but these pictures show some moments of the game on January 16, in which N. F. Borrett, a schoolmaster, decisively won the Amateur Squash Rackets Championship for the fourth time running. In three well-fought games at the Lansdowne Club, Mayfair, he beat H. J. A. Dagnall 9—4, 9—5, 10—8. Borrett made sure of the first two games in 22 minutes, but the third was a different story. Dagnall was now very tired, but rallied well, going from 3—1 to 4—3, and having game point in his favour at 8—6. At this critical stage the pace began to tell, and the holder's superior stamina and consistency of play eventually won him the game. Borrett's armoury of shots is not extensive in its variety, but his wristy action and perfect judgment of angle strokes make him an outstanding player. To be champion four times in succession constitutes a record. The nearest to approach it was Amr Bey, now Amr Pasha, Egyptian Ambassador in London, who made two hat-tricks between the years 1931 and 1937.

contained the personal drama of the match as Dagnall showed increasing signs of wear and tear, yet played shot for shot with Norman to lead 8-6. His exhaustion at this stage was painful to watch as Norman increased the pace of the rallies and pulled back to 8-8, at which point Dagnall was a beaten man, the champion going quickly to 10-8 and securing his fourth championship; in doing so he became the first man to capture four successive Amateurs. The Times applauded: '*There is no doubt that the ability that belongs to champions to bring out the very best in a final is Norman Borrett's flair. He is certainly an outstanding champion. It is not as much on variety that he relies as on consistency with the weapons he knows how to command. One of the most prominent in yesterday's final was the half-paced shot off the side-walls very low which is so exhausting for the opponent to retrieve.*'

Norman did not spend long on the Monday evening celebrating his win. He had to get back to Devon as term had just started. He felt that he ought to turn down the invitation to play the following Sunday in the annual Amateurs versus Professionals match. It was being played at the New Grampians in north London; and he had to be back to Allhallows ready for an early classroom start on the Monday. The Times correspondent expressed the no doubt widely-held disappointment: '*It is a great pity that N. F. Borrett, the amateur champion, cannot spare the time to oppose Karim in the top match.*'

On Friday 27th January Norman was travelling again, this time to Cardiff to play for Devon in the inter-area stage of the county championship, the county having won their regional group of matches without his help. He surprisingly lost the first game to the young Welsh international, D. H. Andrews, but then warmed to his task to achieve a victory which helped Devon to a 4-1 win over Glamorgan to reach the county championship semi-final.

Norman decided to miss the England/Ireland squash match at the RAC on Friday February 10th, foregoing the match practice it would have given him for the county championship semi-final against Sussex at Torquay, on Friday February 24th. This latter match evolved into a titanic struggle, four of the five ties going to five games, the exception being at third string where Hubert Doggart beat the Devon county title holder Plum in straight games. Doggart's brother, Peter, at fifth string, defeated Treleaven in the fifth game, In the top match Norman '*a tower of strength to the team*' beat N. E. Hooper 9-5 in the fifth after losing the first two games whilst he found his range. Unusually, he had an attack of cramp in the third and had to leave the court for three minutes, lucky, in the opinion of the SRA reporter, to be allowed back to take the next three games and the match for the loss of only one more point. At second string John Michelmore kept up his record of never having lost an inter-county tie since his first appearance four years earlier, with a grand victory over Dr. Stokes 9-5 in the fifth and

Haycraft, the Oxford blue, scored the vital point at fourth string with a 10-8 fifth game win over T. P. E. Curry, the Olympic runner.

The final against Middlesex at the Cumberland Club on Sunday March 12th was another nail-biter. Middlesex had one supreme piece of luck in that the Home Fleet returned from its spring cruise two days before the match, thus enabling Commander Seymour-Hayden to play first string against Norman, and avoiding the need for each of the lower strings to play higher up the order. This stroke of luck was crucial, for though Seymour-Hayden was swept aside, 9-7, 9-6, 9-1, by Norman, back to his best, and Michelmore maintained his record with a straight games win over England player David Bull, Plum and Treleaven both lost. All depended on the fourth string match where Alan Fairbairn beat Haycraft in a very close encounter. Thus Devon's attempt at a first ever championship came to an end.

Norman was unable to play for England against Scotland in Edinburgh the following Friday, March 17th , due to school duties, and again could not enter for the Open squash championship, which, lasting from Wednesday April 12th to Monday 17th, coincided with the Edgbaston hockey international against Ireland on Saturday 15th. The SRA's report again noted his absence with regret: '*It is a great pity that neither the winner nor the runner-up in the Amateur Championship has entered. Convincing as was his defeat at the hands of the Open Champion last year, there are many who would like to see how Borrett would have fared against some of the other professionals.*' Perhaps an acknowledgement of Norman's commitment to playing for the England hockey team in the middle of the tournament would have dispelled any implication that he was not keen to play, and thus risk losing.

Karim won the Open, for the fourth year running. He also won the Scottish Open a few days before, beating the visiting Australian professional Gordon Watson in the semi-final, and the young Pakistani professional Abdul Bari in the final, both in four games. Bari had reached the final by beating W. E. Clements, Norman's old friend from Torquay. The three month visit to the UK of Karim, Watson and Bari for the Open tournaments and a series of exhibition matches covering as much as ten per cent of all English squash clubs, had created unprecedented interest in the game. It was indeed a pity that Norman did not get to play against any of the three.

Brian Phillips had taken the opportunity in February of a business trip to the States to play in several American squash tournaments, an experience which he recounted in an article for BLT&S. One of his visits had been to the New York University Club, where he found that '*Norman Borrett is remembered as a cute little boy, as are Pat Sherrard and Maurice Baring through their Cambridge tour in 1938. Their photographs still hang in the bar of the University Club and they sure look cute.*'

THE ALLHALLOWS YEARS – HOCKEY

Seeking a club and a county; the Great Freeze; selection for England; internationals in Dublin, Hawarden, and Luton.

The first post-war hockey season started in October 1946. Norman rang around the Devon and Somerset hockey clubs and made contact with Taunton Vale, a well-known Somerset club some 50 miles away. This provided him with regular Saturday afternoon games. A group of the farming members of the hockey club got together to provide Norman with petrol to enable him to get to the games.

Norman received invitations to play occasional matches for wandering clubs, where a better standard of play could usually be expected. The pipe-opener to the season, on the last Saturday of September, was the Bournemouth six-a-sides, and Norman played for the West of England Wanderers. The invitation to play came from R. J. O. Meyer, the Somerset cricketer and later headmaster of Millfield, and the team included two County cricketers apart from Norman, Somerset's E. A. Hann and Essex's R. F. T. Paterson, who had kept wicket for Essex in the Clacton game Norman had played against Notts in August.

Playing on the Somerset County Cricket ground at Taunton, Taunton Vale started their season with a bang. On October 25th they put nine past Bristol, and after only six matches had scored 60 times, Norman's tally being seventeen. One of the games was a demolition of E.S.&A. Robinson by 12–0, of which Norman scored six. '*The last goal was scored by Borrett, a very fine individual effort; taking the ball in the centre of the field by the half-way line he veered across to the right, beating all opposition as it came in his way by sheer stickwork and ball control; he turned in across the centre of the goal, drew the keeper and dribbled the ball into the empty net.*'

He continued to play for the club throughout his time in Devon, enjoying the social side as well as the sport. Whether the less competitive environment served his hockey as well as if he was based in London, which was the fulcrum of English hockey, is doubtful. If he was ever criticised at his peak, it was for a tendency on occasion to hold on to the ball too long. It is tempting to attribute this in part at least to the easy opposition of his early club hockey.

Norman's county affiliation was Essex, the county of his birth and for whom he had played pre-war. He was chosen to play again post-war, at Brentwood on the county cricket ground, against Hertfordshire on November 16th. It was to be one of the more exhausting games in which he ever took part. To quote the Hockey World report: '*The Essex outside left failed to materialise so that Borrett became the complete left flank, scoring once and having numerous shots saved.*' The ten man team gave Herts a good game, but were defeated 5-1.

There could be no clearer demonstration of his boundless energy than the remarkable fact that after the game Norman drove from Essex to home at Allhallows, where he stayed on the Saturday night before driving on Sunday to Taunton for the Somerset county trials; remarkable as much for the effort required to play in two high quality matches, as for the fact that he was appearing for two different counties on consecutive days. He was keen to expedite the switch from Essex to Somerset to reduce his lengthy and costly travelling commitment, and in order to spend less time away from Allhallows.

This two-county weekend represented the most serious test so far of where he stood in post-war hockey. One of seven Taunton Vale players taking part in the trial, he was happy with his performance, as he felt his way back to the faster pace and the higher skill levels of the top players in the country. Although his weekly hockey for Taunton Vale was of good club standard it was not a severe examination. But he was blessed with physical and mental abilities which enabled him to find another gear when necessary. He was fit and athletic. His squash was a help, both in the speed of foot and reflex which it demanded as well as in the familiarity it gave him with performing on the big stage. These physical attributes were complemented by a remarkable mental toughness, determination, and natural confidence, which combined to give him a head start over most of his peers.

Norman had a full teaching schedule at Allhallows and in the Easter term of 1947 his spare time was largely taken up with training and coaching the boys. Save for one game of squash for Essex Norman's own sporting focus in the Lent term was on hockey. Divisional hockey matches were used as preliminary trials by the England selectors, and it was therefore important for Norman to remind the selectors in the first post-war divisional matches, that his skills had not diminished in the eight years since he last pulled on an England shirt.

Although he had now effected the switch in county hockey affiliation from Essex to Somerset, he remained attached to the East for divisional hockey. Thus on Saturday January 11th he played for the East against South at Southgate, the first of the divisional trials. One of his opponents was Frank Jerrey, who had been a pupil at Framlingham a year or two before Norman, and, having previously played for Diss, was now living in Kent, for whom he was a free scoring centre forward. Hockey World's preview of this event highlighted several players whose performance would be keenly observed: '*Borrett, well, is just Borrett and few forwards in the game today*

...Borrett, well, is just Borrett and few forwards in the game today can match him for stickwork...

can match him for stickwork.' East beat South 3-2 and Norman did not disappoint those who had come to see what effect an eight year hiatus would have on his international career. Hockey World's reporter was impressed:

'Having opened the scoring with a well-placed drive, the ubiquitous Borrett was in irrepressible mood, frequently threatening the South goal... He planned and personally led a further East attack and scored with a cleverly lobbed flick. He was completely dominating the game at this stage... The non-stop Borrett was the outstanding forward on the field... if he lost the ball he quickly tackled back and regained it... It may be that in the second half it seemed that at times he hung on to the ball too long, but that could be explained by the fact that (Baylis having been injured) he was the only sound member of the East left wing.'

Two Saturdays later came a second opportunity on the big stage, as East played North at the West Herts Hockey Club's Watford ground in front of over one thousand spectators. Ken Cranston, centre half for the North, was a fine cricketer, and was to play the first of his eight Tests a few months later against the touring South African cricketers. He scored twice from penalty corners as North swept home five goals in a convincing victory. The Times noted that 'Wakeling and Borrett, usually deadly shots, tested Aitken now and again but were far from their best'. The English selectors had however been sufficiently impressed and Norman was picked for Whites against Colours in the English trial at Luton on March 1st.

From late January until mid-March the Great Freeze, the worst winter of the 20th century, had the country in its grip. By mid-February, electricity to industry had been cut off completely, and families were banned from turning on electric fires between 9am and midday or between 2 and 4 in the afternoon. Greyhound racing was banned, the BBC's Third Programme and the new gimmick of television were cut off, newspapers were cut to four pages, and German PoWs were ordered to clear snow from the railways by hand. Allhallows was isolated. Norman did his best to organise some indoor hockey, which provided the only form of exercise the pupils, or Norman, managed during this bleak spell.

The snow, ice and blizzards caused the Luton trial to be postponed. The rearranged fixture having also been lost to the weather it was only a bare week before the first international that the trial finally took place, at Guildford on March 22nd. Eight hundred spectators attended to see the contenders for the first post-war caps. Norman rose to the occasion. Early on he finished a good passing move with a tap-in goal and was soon on the score sheet again after dribbling through the Possibles defence. Combining well with his left wing partner Tony Baylis, Norman took the game to the opponents at every opportunity, as the Probables ran riot. He beat the goalkeeper in

a penalty bully to score his third and just before the end added his fourth goal as Probables won 8-1. The Times enthused: 'Borrett was the outstanding forward on the field. His stickwork and clever passing quite bewildered his opposing half and his tackling back and positioning made many good openings for his side.'...

> ...'Borrett was everywhere and his display left nothing to be desired nor gave the slightest ray of hope to any of his rivals for the inside-left position', was Hockey World's comment on the dominance of his play, but there was some criticism to go with the praise: 'We do think there were a number of occasions when he should have been pulled up for undercutting.'

It caused no surprise when the selectors chose the Probables team en bloc for England's first hockey international since the long war-time interruption, on March 29th against Ireland at Londonbridge Road, Dublin. This meant that Cranston, who had put up a strong display in the Final trial for the Possibles, missed out on the chance of being selected for England at both hockey and cricket in the same year. The England team, six of whom, including the brothers Micky and David Walford, were winning their first cap, boarded the 8.40 p.m. Holyhead train at Euston on Thursday March 27th, reaching Dublin's Royal Hibernian Hotel at breakfast time on the Friday. The Saturday dawned wet and the Irish rain was to continue all day, leaving the pitch heavy, with patches of standing water. Remarkably England 'gave Ireland a lesson in the finer points of the game... their stickwork bearing the hallmark of class and their positional play was well-nigh perfect. That they did not score at least four or five goals was to a very large extent due to the churned-up pitch, which repeatedly held them up.' The Irish Times went on to describe Norman as the man of the match, 'a great inside forward, whose stickwork was a revelation.' The match became a personal battle between Norman and Carroll in the Irish goal, but the latter took the honours as the Irish, quite against the run of play, scraped a 2-1 win with a goal, four minutes from time, following a 30 second England goalmouth scrimmage, 'a miniature rugby scrum in which the rules of the game were impartially ignored by both sides.'

It would be an extraordinary event today if an international sportsman, in any team sport, played club games on the next two days after an international. In 1947 it was relatively commonplace. Showing his love for the game, as well as the enthusiasm and fitness of youth, Norman turned out as a guest for the touring Beckenham Club on the Sunday against the Dublin based Railway Union and on the

Monday against Three Rock Rovers. '*Thanks largely to Norman Borrett Beckenham did much better on the Sunday than in their game the morning before, winning 4-3, and their 'guest artists' played well again on the Monday.*' The stamina of those guest players must have been tested by the typically generous Irish hospitality they suffered on both evenings.

The festive nature of that weekend was a mere warm-up for the Easter festival weekend which immediately followed. The premier festival, of the dozen or so traditional events, was held at Folkestone, and it was there that Norman headed with the Tramps. The usual late-night refreshment was avoided by Norman as, unusually, the Sunday festival highlight game was a full international, England against France. This experiment provoked some press controversy, but the game itself was deemed a success as France were beaten 2-1 in a very fast and hard game. Norman had one goal disallowed, scored another with a flick, and earned journalistic plaudits: '*Borrett played brilliantly and was the best forward on the field*'.

Southgate was the venue for the South versus East divisional match, the next weekend on April 12th. Even though the international season was well under way this was still regarded as an international trial. Norman, Mullie and Anthony were staying at Frinton with his parents for the school holiday so his car journey to North London was, by Allhallows standards, an easy one. Not so the following Saturday's match – a trip to North Wales, to Hawarden, family seat of the Gladstone family, for the season's second international, against the Welsh. The letter from the H.A.'s match secretary instructed the team to meet at Euston Station on Friday 18th, to catch the 5.05 p.m. rain to Chester, where they would stay the night before being transported to Hawarden on the Saturday morning. "Don't forget to bring your own towel and soap" was a reminder that rationing was in effect and even international players had to make do.

It was the first time the two countries had played each other since Norman's debut at the Oval in March 1939, and it was the first time the Gladstone Playing Fields at Hawarden had hosted an international hockey match. The press predicted that Wales' chances depended on how their defence could handle the Borrett/Baylis wing threat. On the sloping Flintshire pitch, Norman '*although more closely marked than he has been in previous internationals this season, was outstanding in the English forward line, and G. A. Baylis on the left wing, responded to the promptings of his partner in his usual proficient manner.*' Wales were thus denied their first ever win over England, who were good value for their 3-1 victory. At the post-match dinner in Chester, Norman, as was his wont, passed his menu card round the table for signatures. A few of the players added comments: Tony Baylis wrote: "Oh Norman, how lovely to play with you again. We'll give Scotland colossal stick." Micky Walford's contribution was more light-hearted:

"I do hope you do a bit of training before next Saturday." Under Norman's own signature appeared the words, written by a fellow player, "The Menace".

The next Saturday, April 26th, saw the team assemble at St. Pancras for the 11.10 a.m. train to Luton, with "lunch at the George Hotel Luton at 12.30", perhaps not much time for digestion before the 2.45 bully-off. There were 2,000 spectators at Wardown Park, and they witnessed a brilliant display of goalkeeping by the Scottish keeper Brodie which must have helped win him his Great Britain Olympic place the following season. The Times: '*For the remainder of the half, and incidentally of the game, it was a case of brilliant saves by Brodie from the English forwards, but his most spectacular effort was when he saved a full-blooded drive from Borrett high up with outstretched hand.*' Norman's left wing partner was Osborn, replacing the injured Baylis, and the understanding that the latter had developed with Norman was badly missed. This left Norman to carry the brunt of the attack, which he did well. England's single, winning, goal came ten minutes after the start '*a typical Borrett effort from a lightning volley off a free-hit taken by centre-half Self, hit so quickly the goalkeeper probably never saw the ball*'.

Norman returned with the rest of the team to London on the Sunday morning but from there instead of returning to Frinton he took the train to Weymouth. Mullie and Anthony had gone ahead of him to see Mullie's father, William, who had recently arrived from Rio de Janeiro. William's father hailed from Weymouth, and two of William's brothers still lived there. After some 40 years in Rio, he had finally decided to retire; a six month holiday in England to see his brothers, his daughter, and his son-in-law Norman, was the first step in a retirement plan which would see him go to live in Canada. Neither Norman nor Mullie had seen him since his last visit, just before war broke out, and just before their engagement.

In his Hockey World September retrospect of the 1946-47 hockey season the leading hockey commentator R. L. Hollands made Norman Borrett the success of the season:

'*Borrett was outstanding last season. He first played for England in 1939 and despite lack of first class practice during the war has improved considerably since then. His greatest assets at present are an astonishing quickness of eye, and of foot to follow what the eye sees, assets which in squash racquets have helped to make him amateur champion. In hockey they have made him dangerous for being that half-stride before the rest which so often gives possession of the ball and time for independent action.*'

Hollands could however see areas for improvement: '*He needs now to develop a greater variety of method, to rely less upon the art of dribbling, at which he is not yet a D. S. Milford, and more upon the constructive possibilities of the combined passing movement, to the variations of which there is no end.*'

Taunton Vale; Wanderers v Occasionals; Dublin for Easter; Bristol, Old Trafford and Inverness internationals; Olympic training weekends.

Stuart MacGregor joined Allhallows in September 1947, aged 11, and, like Tony Watson, was impressed by the disciplinary regime of the Geography master, although it appears that in the time that had elapsed since Watson's time Norman's aim had changed :

"I remember his Geography classes vividly, with the row of wooden board dusters and an arsenal of chalk lined up on his desk. These missiles were fired with great accuracy just over the heads of any miscreants. He also kept a bucket of water at the front of the class into which one's head was plunged for any extreme folly. MacGregor adds, superfluously, "I don't think these would be allowed today."

Hockey was played in the Easter term and Norman taught a number of admiring boys. Tony Watson felt that hockey was, at that time, Norman's best game: '*He could flick the ball from one corner post to the post on the half way line opposite.*'

Norman had returned to his hockey with an eagerness at the beginning of the 1947/48 season. Apart from striving for selection for the international matches in March and April, there was the added spice of the competition for Great Britain's hockey team for the London Olympics in the summer of 1948. He continued to play for Taunton Vale, who had attracted further players of note, including the young Tony Robinson, a future stalwart of the English side. Unsure of Norman's availability, the East selectors sought to persuade him to continue to journey right across the country by naming him in an early East trial staged at the Cambridge University hockey ground on December 6th. He played, having told the selectors that if picked (as indeed he was) for the East side for the divisional matches, he would have to decline their invitation, pending a decision on his qualification, by residence, to play for the West.

On December 18th, school term having just ended, Norman was invited to play for Cambridge University Wanderers in their annual match against the old foe in the shape of the Oxford University Occasionals. This match at Beckenham was a good run-out for the forthcoming divisional trials, both sides containing national and county players. Cambridge won 6-0, with Norman scoring the first and last goals.

January saw the hockey season moving in to the divisional period. Norman's West qualification having been confirmed, his first game for them was, ironically, against his old colleagues in the East on January 24th. A rare example of a man picked to play for both sides. R. L. Hollands was at the Devon County Cricket ground at Exeter to watch. He reported that the game '*produced the best hockey I have seen since the war*', the West winning 3-1, with Norman outstanding: '*Although he did not score he played better than in some of which he has scored more than once, showing a variety of method which has not always been apparent in his game.*' Norman had evidently read Hollands' plea in Hockey World's September summary of the past season for greater variety in his game.

Great Crosby, Liverpool was the venue for the West's next divisional game, on February 14th. The North won by the odd goal in three. For those players contending for international recognition, the divisionals led on to the England trials. Hockey World's preview of the international season spoke of '*A real dearth of forwards of international standard; this was obvious last season and nothing that has happened since gives us reason to believe that the situation has been relieved. Barring sudden loss of form, N. F. Borrett is practically assured of his place at inside-left in the England forward line.*'

Two days after the Liverpool game, Norman received his invitation from the HA to captain the Whites against the Colours in the first England trial at Brentwood on February 28th. The heavy surface did not make for good hockey and The Times was not over-impressed with the game, nor with the Whites performance as they achieved a narrow win: '*N. F. Borrett is a player who could never be left out of a side, but on Saturday he was wandering about far too much.*' The Observer shared that view: '*Borrett accomplished wonders on the difficult ground, but was inclined to get out of place too much and at times was too individual.*'

The selectors chose the entire Whites team as the Probables for the second trial the following Saturday, March 6th, at Beckenham, where Norman, at inside left, made an unarguable case for inclusion in the national team, laying on one goal and scoring another with the best shot of the game from a very narrow angle, as Probables beat Possibles 4-2. He was duly chosen for the season's first international, against Wales.

Leslie Rowan had decided to retire from international hockey at the end of the 1946-47 season; he had first played for England in 1929, and retired after 31 caps, for the last 11 of which he had been captain. The selectors made Norman captain, at the age of 30 but with only eight caps to his name. He was an obvious choice, an outstandingly good player, confident, by nature a leader, with a burning desire not to be beaten. His players, like anyone else of his acquaintance, found that the initial daunting experience of playing under him proved merely a testing ground. If they measured up as a player, but more importantly as a person, they would soon find the forbidding aspect disappearing to reveal an engaging warmth and humour. The role of the captain was greater than it would become in the later years of team managers and team coaches. Norman took this responsibility in his stride and indeed thrived on it.

The Wales match at Bristol on March 13th resulted in a 6-2 win for England, the newly appointed captain scoring twice. He was the outstanding English forward, '*whose every movement threatened disaster for Wales*', as his delightfully precise passing opened up the Welsh defence time and again.

The Irish Hockey Union's grounds in Dublin hosted the Dublin Easter Hockey Festival over the last weekend in March. The Travellers Club, made up largely of past and present Oxbridge players, was one of the 14 teams which took part. As at all Easter festivals the social side predominated, but for Norman the hockey was the reason for his being there. Three games in four days was just what he needed to keep fit and in practice, in summer-like weather.

Norman was back in Frinton, it being school holiday time, on the Tuesday morning. He had only three days with Mullie, Anthony and his parents before he was off again, on Friday, by train to Euston to meet the rest of the England team on the 6pm train to Manchester for England's next hockey game. Ireland were the opponents at Old Trafford, the famous cricket ground, the first occasion it had been used for a men's hockey match. Years later Norman smiled as he recollected the horrified look on the face of the groundsman watching England goalkeeper Aitken digging his boot into the sacred cricketing turf, to give him his mid-circle bearings of the goalposts behind him. The turf provided a perfect pitch for the free-flowing hockey which England produced. '*None of the Irish forwards possessed the constructive ability of the England captain and inside-left Norman Borrett whose passing in this game was first class*'. Norman made several openings for his wing partner Jimmy Greene, and both England goals came from their moves. But the Irish yet again proved tenacious, pulling back England's two goal lead with a penalty bully goal in the dying minutes to secure a 2-2 draw. The Times expressed the opinion that chief credit in the forward line must be given to Borrett, '*who played one of the best games of his career. His passing, stickwork, and above all his tackling back, were a source of continual anxiety to the Irish defence, and had one or two of the other forwards shown the same energy, England might well have put the issue beyond doubt before the interval*.'

A number of the Irish team, including their excellent outside right Stan de Lacy, had played in the Dublin Easter Festival and Norman renewed acquaintance with them at the post match dinner at the Manchester Reform Club. He was clearly in relaxed mood during his captain's after dinner speech, praising Ireland's five year unbeaten run and asserting, in a reference to the fact that Ireland's captain and centre half, the Reverend S. S. Fleming, was an ordained minister, that "the Irish team had no need of God's help."

It was a disappointment to all, Norman included, that England could only achieve another draw, 1-1, in their last home nations international of the season, against a spirited Scottish team at Inverness on April 10th, the England forwards this time not playing to their potential and the side in general lacking confidence. Following a tour of the countryside around Inverness on the Sunday morning by their hosts, the team caught the 3.10 p.m. train to London, which arrived at Euston at 6.50 a.m. on the Monday morning. It had been a long weekend.

Hockey World's summary of the international season concluded that England had failed to accept '*a magnificent opportunity to head the table*', having achieved a convincing win over Wales and having led Ireland 2-0 at half time. '*Scotland were very successful, losing only to Ireland. The best performance was their holding England to a draw at Inverness. Perhaps the long train journey didn't help the English XI. (It is understood that there is no foundation for the rumour that the Scotland and England match will be played at Land's End next season !).*'

The post brought exciting news later that week in a letter, dated April 13th:...

> … '*Dear Sir,*
> *You have been selected as one of the team of 18 players to represent Great Britain in the Olympic Games. The first hockey matches will be played on Saturday July 31st and the Final will be played at Wembley on Thursday August 12th. The team will be accommodated at Uxbridge from Tuesday July 27th to Saturday August 14th.*'

The letter requested a reply within seven days as to availability, and completion of the 'self-measurement form', for official team clothing. Norman duly advised of his 15" collar size, his size 9 shoes, 38" chest, and that his hat size was 7 for the (somewhat surprising) team beret. Norman showed his interest in matters sartorial by adding, in respect of the plain blazer, "I would prefer, if it is allowed, a double-breasted blazer, with an allowance in the making for two 9" vents, on either side, to be put in later after the Games."

As a warm-up for the Olympics, the Royal Belgian Hockey Association invited England to play an end of season hockey international, after the home nations series, in Brussels on April 24th. The three day trip was a great experience for the English team, the first time the players had travelled overseas since the war. The Belgians, for whom the match represented '*le sommet de la saison du hockey Belge*', went out of their way to provide hospitality for their visitors, and the

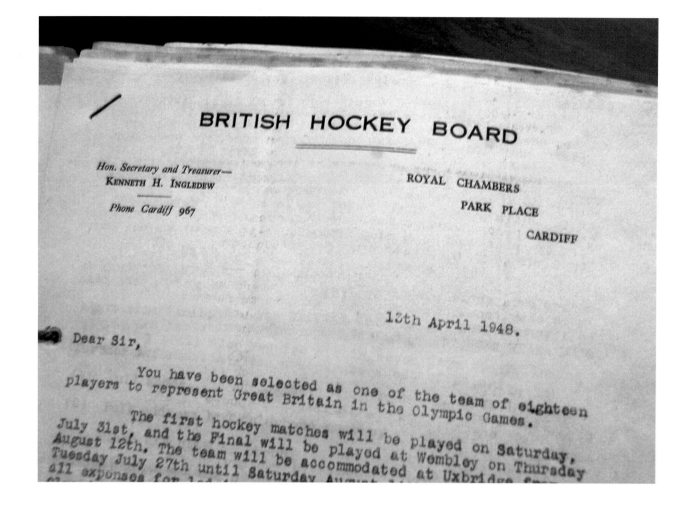

ABOVE: The treasured invitation to participate in the London Olympics

local press filled many column inches previewing the match. The last time the teams had met was April 1938, when England had crushed their visitors 7-1 at Worthing, and there were many references to the need to restore Belgian pride. Pen pictures of the English team included this mention of Norman Borrett:

'*C'est un joueur extremement intelligent et pratiquant un jeu constructif. Son dribbling est remarquable. C'est un maitre d'ecole, Borrett est champion d'Angleterre au squash racket (sic).*'

The match took place before some 6,000 spectators at the capital's soccer stadium. The Belgians adapted far better to the bumpy ground and deserved their 2-2 draw. In the first few minutes Norman won a penalty bully but then flicked the ball over the bar. In the second half Belgium took the lead but a goal from Norman spared England's blushes. Norman began his after dinner speech with an assurance that he would not be speaking in French, "as the Belgian captain would be quite unable to translate it into anything understandable by his colleagues".

The pupils at Allhallows knew when they returned for the summer term of the news of Norman's selection for the Great Britain hockey squad and excitement built throughout the term, as 'Sir' left school for each succeeding GB practice weekend. As the Games were to be held in the school summer holidays a number of the pupils looked forward to joining the crowds at Wembley to cheer on their hero.

The country, and the Government, got behind the Olympic effort. The athletes would do their own training, but they needed the best

diet. On May 29th Norman, and the rest of the Britain's Games entrants, were advised by letter from the Ministry of Food that their ration allowances had been raised to match the special scale which would be available to all visiting competitors at their respective Olympic camps. Provided they returned the extra coupons as soon as they were eliminated from the Games, each entrant was entitled to receive special amounts of Fats, Cheese and Sugar, and additional Meat and Milk.

The hockey training weekends took place in May (London), June (Weston-super-Mare) and July (Park Royal, London). Norman was ill and missed the Park Royal weekend, but the team did not appear to miss him as they crushed a combined Oxford and Cambridge side 8-1, the English centre forward Adlard, who had last played for England in 1938, scoring five brilliant goals. The Times reported that '*the training and tactics developed during the past months under the combined management of Colonel George Grimston, (who was later to become secretary of Sussex County Cricket Club) and C. E. Newham showed the Olympic side to be a machine-like combination. The forwards combined very well indeed and the defence had a perfect understanding with one another. The game was one of the best seen for years.*'

Norman was fit again for the final training weekend two weeks later. This was hosted by Thorpeness Country Club in Essex, and lasted from Saturday July 24th to Tuesday 27th, whence the squad took the train back to Liverpool Street and thence to the British Olympic camp at Uxbridge where they would stay until the hockey final on August 12th. The programme sent to the squad players shows that the Thorpeness weekend started in traditional manner:

Saturday 24th July 1948
1900 Cocktail Party in the Blue Room.
Dress Blazer and Grey Flannels.
1945 Dinner.
2100 Dance.

As the squad were not to be accompanied by their wives one can only suppose that the ladies of Thorpeness Country Club generously acted as dancing partners. The players were instructed in the clothing they were to wear, and when, and of course in their appearance: "Please ensure you have your hair cut before 24th July." After training, lunch, and a team photograph, a match was played against an Eastern Counties side, including Norfolk County OF Frank Jerrey.

The Indian team which defeated Norman's Great Britain side in the final had as its centre forward a brilliant young stick player, Balbir Singh, playing in the first of his three Olympics, in all of which he won gold. He scored two of India's four goals against GB in London,

and in Helsinki all three of the goals which defeated GB in the semi-final, and five of the six which India put past Holland in the final. Now living in Vancouver, he recalls the 1948 final with great clarity, sixty years on:

"It was a thrilling experience to represent India, in its first Olympics as an independent nation. When Britain won the Olympic gold medal in 1908 and 1920, India did not participate in either of the two Games. Later, when India won gold medals in the following three Olympics at Amsterdam 1928, Los Angeles 1932 and Berlin 1936, Britain did not field a team in all three. It was at the London Olympics in 1948 that the two countries met for the first time in the Olympic games.

In order to acclimatise, we left for London a full two weeks before the start of Games. Sir John Bennett, pre-independence Punjab Police Chief and President Punjab Hockey Association, was present at

BELOW: The full Great Britain squad for the Olympic tournament, with those in playing kit ready for the first match. Norman in the centre of the front row row, with Micky Walford front left.

ABOVE:
The silver medal.

the Indian team with loud chants of, 'Well done India - a beautiful goal - score one more'. The fourth goal in the second half made some of them shout, 'Come on India - make it half a dozen'.

War-ravaged England was just beginning to re-emerge. The Britons were in a phase of reconstruction and yet did an excellent job of organising the 1948 London Games at such a short notice. Those were the days of strict rationing in England. Disciplined as they always are, Britons never took more than what was necessary for each person, yet there was no dearth of food in our Olympic kitchens.

Our experiences at London made us change our opinion about the Britons. We found that they were not as stern and ruthless as they were in India as rulers, but considerate and friendly people. Many Londoners used to compete with one another to invite us to their homes for meals, a cup of tea or coffee and for taking a few pictures with us. The pleasant memories of those visits still linger.

In April 2005, I was among the Sikh hockey players who attended the Vaisakhi Festival in Trafalgar Square and joined Londoners in supporting London's bid for the 2012 Olympic Games. London won the bid. I am sure the organisation of the Games will be better than all previous Olympics and I look forward to them."

Living in the camp for over two weeks, Norman managed, like all other competitors, to watch various athletics and other events. He and Mullie were at the Opening Ceremony on July 29th, when 80,000 people saw the flame lit.

Norman was required to attend a number of functions, including, on the opening day, a reception hosted by World Sports at the Savoy Hotel at 6.30 and another given by the HA at the Trocadero at 8.30 for which he had to don morning dress. Perhaps the most glamorous was a reception at Buckingham Palace; the King had invited nine members of the British Olympic team to attend. Norman's luck was in because hockey was drawn out of the hat as one of the nine sports who would send a representative, and he was selected as the hockey player.

Brian Rosen, and his brother Anthony Rosen, were two OFs who attended the Olympics:

"My brother Tony and I watched almost every event at these Olympics. It was long before the days of mass television and I am sure that a lot of people in the country did not even know they were taking place. The performances that I particularly remember of course, 60 plus years later, are those of Fanny Blankers-Koen and Emil

London airport, along with members of the Olympic Reception Committee, to receive the Indian hockey team. Sir John was especially delighted about my inclusion in the Indian team, as it was at his instance that I had originally been 'press-ganged" into the Punjab Police, to represent their hockey team. He hugged me - a possibility that may never have arisen in British India. He was sporting enough to give us a couple of valuable tips, which proved beneficial when we played on the heavy and slow hockey pitches in England.

The fact that Britain and India, Olympic Champions from separate Olympics, entered the final at London surprised no one. The Wembley stadium was full to capacity. The then Princess Elizabeth, present British Queen, was Guest of Honour. The majority of spectators in the stadium that day expected Great Britain to win.

As soon as the match commenced, the incessant deafening cheers backing Great Britain rent the sky. The voice of a few Indians present there was buried under the loud chants of home crowds. The soccer semi-final a day before and a light drizzle at night had turned the pitch heavier and our task rather difficult. How we played and won by 4-0 is already a part of history. The purpose of this write-up is simply to remember some pleasant memories, which throw light on the sportsmanship and character of the Britons.

What surprised us was that with each subsequent goal we scored against Great Britain, a sizeable segment of British fans started backing

Zatopek. Of course my brother and I, both former pupils at Framlingham, watched the hockey final at Wembley with great interest and were very disappointed that India won; it rained slightly during the game and some of the Indian players removed their boots which may have given them a slight advantage - but not four goals. I came to know Norman Borrett, the English captain, fairly well, firstly as a fellow Old Framlinghamian and parent of sons at Brandeston and Framlingham, and years later when I was teaching at the prep school whilst Norman was still teaching at Framlingham. He hobbled around (having had both hips replaced) but still had a great deal of respect from staff and pupils."

Whilst Norman remained disappointed at the fact that GB had not done better he did derive some satisfaction from the numerous congratulatory messages he received after the Games had ended. Sammy Saville, old England player and selector, expressed his appreciation for Norman's "great effort to make the Games a success. The team did awfully well to reach the final and I am grateful to you for all you did." Team Manager George Grimston wrote to express his thanks "for all your loyal help and support which made things so easy and pleasant", and Leslie Rowan, from whom Norman had taken over the captaincy of England in 1948, wrote to say "you and your team have done all and more than the most optimistic expected. More important you have put hockey back to its rightful place as a major – and best – sport; and in days to come I think we shall all look back to your Olympic team as a landmark and the start of a revival. I yelled myself hoarse on the day – but you were up against something which no team I have ever seen could have beaten."

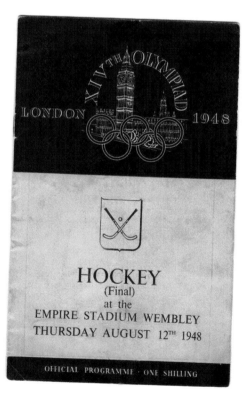

XIV TH OLYMPIAD
LONDON 1948

HOCKEY
(Final)
at the
EMPIRE STADIUM WEMBLEY
THURSDAY AUGUST 12TH 1948

OFFICIAL PROGRAMME · ONE SHILLING

A win and a loss for Great Britain in Amsterdam; Home Countries internationals in Scarborough, Abergavenny and Dublin; the Irish take England to the Guinness brewery, and win.

The 1948-49 hockey season began for Norman with a couple of games for Taunton Vale as preparation for two post-Olympic matches, arranged by the GB selectors. Two weeks before the fixtures Norman received a letter from Kenneth Ingledew, chairman of the GB selectors, hoping he would understand that "to satisfy all parties we ought to take this opportunity of emphasizing that it is a British team and not an English one. As you – an Englishman – captained the team in the Olympics, we feel that it would be better if on this occasion it was captained by a Scot. We are therefore offering the job to Robin Lindsay."

The two matches proved to be Norman's last two GB games: on Saturday October 16th at the Wagener Stadium in Amsterdam against the Netherlands, the Olympic bronze medal winners and, the next day against France. The Dutch won well, 4-1, with '*Borrett, Adlard and Griffiths being the most dangerous in attack*', but the British were disappointing and disappointed. The side felt only partially redeemed by their convincing win the next day over the French 6-0. In the seven matches Norman had played for GB he had scored 10 goals - a scoring rate per game of 1.43. Others have scored more goals for GB but never beaten this average per match.

From the heady heights of Great Britain hockey Norman returned to as much club hockey as he could fit in, for Taunton Vale, enjoying the competition and the camaderie of that less pressured environment. Stuart MacGregor recalls seeing him play for the club against the Allhallows School 1st XI: "I was bewildered by his speed and skill, which was wonderful to watch. He was not the master in charge of hockey, surprisingly, but must have had a big influence on the team because the school produced at that time some very good players, including Bill Luff who played for Scotland, Owen Rowlands who played for Wales, and Mike Ray-Hills an Army, Southgate and Middlesex player, all of whom were in the 1948-49 sides. Mike Ray-Hills appeared with Norman in the coaching photographs in Norman's 1950 book, written and photographed whilst he was at Allhallows. Mike remained firm friends with Norman, sent his son Simon to Framlingham and took an HA team to the College for many years, in which I played a few times."

Norman's Christmas holiday in Frinton was as usual interrupted for a visit to Beckenham for the Cambridge University Wanderers traditional Christmas game against Oxford University Occasionals. Norman scored a fine individual goal in a 3-3 draw. On his return to the Essex coast, it was back to daily runs along the seafront, maintaining his fitness for the Amateur squash championship, which was to start on New Year's Day.

Two weeks after his third consecutive Amateur victory, the 1949 divisional hockey competition began with the West hosting and beating Combined Services 4-1 at Swindon. A week later, West were again in action at Evesham against Midlands on February 5th, this time losing 3-1. Then there was county hockey; Canford School was the venue for Somerset's match against Dorset on February 19th. Micky Walford, playing for Dorset, was a master at Sherborne but found no home advantage for his team as Norman led Somerset to a 7-1 crushing of their neighbours.

R. L. Hollands in his preview of the first English hockey trial at Rugby School on Saturday February 26th, whilst welcoming the emergence of Holmes as centre forward for the senior side, expressed some concern about his inside left: '*the man who undoubtedly could make the openings for Holmes is Borrett, but he has recently become preoccupied with the defensive aspect of an inside forward's job, tackling back so far and so persistently that his team seems to have one too many half-backs and not enough forwards. I hope Borrett will discard this*

... I hope Borrett will discard this safety-first method and show what a fine attacking player he can be, not only scoring goals himself but clearing the way for others to score...

safety-first method and show what a fine attacking player he can be, not only scoring goals himself but clearing the way for others to score.'

Hollands' fears were confounded as Holmes, Norman, and his left wing partner, Jimmy Greene, were the outstanding forwards for the senior side in a 3-1 win. The best performer on the junior side was the Oxford University full back Denys Carnill, who well merited his selection for the final trial at Dean Close School in Cheltenham on March 5th, a match played in a snowstorm so that after half time, with nearly an inch of snow on the pitch, a red cricket ball had to be used. Norman scored in a six goal win for the Probables. The Times felt that Carnill was '*most unlucky to be passed over*' after the game for selection for the first international, and that '*N. F. Borrett, who was not at his best in the early trials, seems to have regained his old form, most of the winners' goals*

coming from his openings.'

The selectors retained Norman as captain of the England hockey team for the three spring internationals. On March 12th Scotland were the visitors at Scarborough Cricket ground where 2,500 spectators saw a game which remained fast and fairly furious for the whole 70 minutes. England held the upper hand for most of the match but the Scottish defence was steadfast. Dann, at outside-right for the home team, sustained a deep cut to the forehead early on and went to hospital, only returning to the pitch for the last few minutes. There were no substitutes permitted in those days and England struggled to overcome the numerical imbalance. Borrett and Greene linked well on the left, and Borrett's stickwork twice took him clean through the Scottish ranks but to no avail. Commenting on the 0-0 draw, Hollands saw the Borrett/Greene combination as the best on display, but again had reservations to express: '*Both did some very clever things but one does feel about this pair that for some reason or another they are missing greatness. It may be that it is because each has a tendency to be individualistic in his game*'.

The next international, against Wales at Abergavenny on March 26th, presented Norman's team with a chance to redeem themselves in the eyes of the spectators. The Welsh were swamped 7-0, and Norman scored a hat trick, one from a short corner with '*a terrific shot which hit a full-back on its way to the goal. At inside-left Borrett was in great form, his stickwork being of a high order indeed. But for all that there were times when he did hang on to the ball too long. With two such grand players as Borrett and Greene forming the left-wing why is that wing not more dangerous than it is? Perhaps over-use of the through pass: let us see more short passing and a willingness to interchange positions*'. Other press comment was equally critical of Norman's holding the ball too much and failing to bring his inside right into the game: '*A great improvement in tactics will have to be made if England hope to win (against Ireland in their next match).'*

The previews of the Irish match on April 9th in Dublin anticipated that England would give their hosts a close match, and there was a risk of Ireland losing its remarkable record of winning 14 and drawing one of the 15 games with the home countries since 1937. The Irish Hockey Union did their patriotic best, arranging for the English team to start their visit, on the Friday, with a tour of the Arthur Guinness brewery followed by a four course lunch, and on match day, to be taken to the parliament building to meet the Taoiseach.

The Irish Times considered that England had discarded a lot of rather dead wood from the team which had drawn with them in 1948, but had retained some experience both in the defence and in the forward line, which '*leans rather heavily upon the individual genius of N. F. Borrett*'. In the event Ireland won a thrilling match 3-2, cheered on by 5,000 spectators. England threw everything they had at the Irish defence in the last quarter hour in an attempt to level the scores, but to no avail: '*Fletcher, Holmes and Borrett earned full marks, playing better than at any other time in the season*', was Hockey World's view, but R. L. Hollands in the Daily Telegraph commented that '*Borrett scored England's first goal, but was not at his best.*'

Irish hospitality continued after the game, with a dinner at the team hotel followed by the Pembroke Wanderers HC dance. On the Sunday the team was invited to an IHU cocktail party at 1130. As their train did not leave Dublin for Euston (via Holyhead) until 7.20 pm there was also time for a tour around Dublin that afternoon. It was a weary party that reached Euston at 6.35 am on Monday, and Norman finally reached Frinton to join Mullie for the school holidays in time for lunch.

Hollands' end of season summary for Hockey World concluded that France, Belgium, and particularly Holland, were improving and that the England's problem was a lack of punch. He did not go so far as to suggest the remedy of using the goal-scoring skills of Norman at centre forward. That was not to surface until the following year.

* * * * * * * * *

New beginnings: fatherhood, authorship, the Triple Crown, and a return to Framlingham.

Norman's 1950 hockey season had started late, as he missed both the West hockey trial and the first divisional match through squash commitments. Apart from English hockey's two trial matches, international practices were rare, as were training camps, blackboard planning, inspirational talks and the other trappings of the 21st century sporting scene. Norman was thus free to switch codes at a moment's notice, being his own coach, chauffeur, motivator and exchequer.

He did play in West's second match, against the North on Saturday February 4th at Hereford. '*Free of the demands of squash N.F.Borrett took over at inside-left after missing the South game. In the West's three-two win he scored all three goals, and, with Fletcher, was outstanding*'.

His county hockey season began with a game for Somerset on Saturday February 18th at Glastonbury against a Dorset side, containing Micky Walford and Frank Hopkinson, which was intent on avenging the 7-1 drubbing they had received from Somerset the year before. Norman was always a thorn in Dorset's flesh, but Somerset could not repeat last year's heroics and the result was a 3-3 draw.

Sunday February 26th saw Norman driving to Bournemouth with a heavily pregnant Mullie as passenger. Mullie had decided,

somewhat unusually, to accompany him, as she planned to visit friends in Bournemouth, the town where she had spent many holidays in her youth. Her plans were interrupted however when she realized, mid-journey, that birth was imminent: "Norman told me not to worry - he would drop me off at the hospital, in Bournemouth, declaring, as if he were an expert on the subject: "It's just like shelling peas, darling, nothing to worry about!' At that point I put my foot down and told him I had booked to have the baby in my local hospital at Lyme Regis, and that was where we must now go." Norman got the message and course was immediately altered for Lyme Regis. By the time we got there the baby's head was already beginning to show. Once Norman was sure I was all right he kissed me goodbye and set off again, with the 7 year old Anthony, for his hockey match, which, I recall, he won." Mark Timothy Borrett was born just after 3pm that afternoon. Mullie laughs as she tells the story:...

…"Life with Norman could not be described as all smooth sailing, but when I married him I already knew that sport was to be his life and so I knew what I was getting into. If it made him happy, which it did, then I was happy".

Norman had not been picked for the first English hockey trial on 4th March at Guildford, as the selectors rang the changes with a view to bringing fresh blood to an England team whose performances the previous season - a draw with Scotland, a 7-0 thrashing of Wales, and a narrow 3-2 loss to Ireland - had been disappointing. Norman was brought in for the final trial, playing for the Probables against the Possibles, at West Herts Hockey Club on March 11th. Not long into the game a penalty corner gave Norman the chance to produce '*one of his uncommon but deadly cannon balls. It crossed the goal line unchallenged at about Adam's apple height.*' He scored a second goal as the Probables won the game 4-3.

For the season's opening international against Wales, at Bournemouth on March 25th, the selectors proceeded with their plan to bring in fresh blood, bringing in no fewer than seven new caps, including Denys Carnill at right back, and recalling as goalkeeper the 37 year old J. B. Evans, whose previous 16 caps had all been won pre-war. Norman Borrett, Micky Walford and Frank Reynolds were the only survivors from the team which had ended the previous season. Importantly the selectors also took the view that the leadership of needed changing, and the captaincy was switched from Norman to Walford.

The Daily Telegraph implied that Norman's place was not as guaranteed as it used to be: '*The problem of what to do with two almost equally-fancied good inside lefts, was solved by turning one of them, Geoffrey Stocks, into a centre forward.*' The Times' correspondent thought that '*as Norman Borrett was such a past master in stickwork and the making of openings, the selectors would do well to try him at centre-forward instead of Stocks.*' Hockey World's view was that England possessed 'a definite superiority at inside-left where the incomparable N. F. Borrett will be playing'.

Wales were beaten soundly 4–0, Stocks impressively scoring three times. The Times reported Norman as '*showing his usual clever stickwork as he made many good openings*' although their correspondent stuck to his earlier theme: '*One can't help thinking that the selectors might have experimented a step farther at half-time by trying Borrett at centre-forward and Stocks at inside-left.*' Hockey World's commentator thought that '*Borrett did many good things, but at times did seem too slow in passing the ball.*'

Good Friday fell on April 7th, and Norman played three games for a strong Tramps side in the Folkestone Festival, playing also for the Festival XI against the visiting Dutch club side. The following Saturday, April 15th, the match of the season took place at Edgbaston cricket ground as England hosted the champions Ireland. To equal the hospitality which the Irish had shown England the year before would be difficult, but the HA tried hard; perhaps the Friday visit to Bournville was not quite the same as the Arthur Guinness brewery trip, but the Saturday tour of Aston Villa Football Club and lunch there with the directors, before being greeted at Edgbaston by no less a personage than the Deputy Mayor of Birmingham, might have interested some of the Irish players. There was the customary after match dinner, at the Midland Hotel, where Micky Walford took Norman's place in proposing the health of the Irish team, and on the Sunday a drinks party at the Priory Lawn Tennis Club followed – for the Irish team only – by a visit to the Birmingham Police HQ.

The match programme, price 6d, spotlighted the rival captains, England's right-half Micky Walford's profile revealing his astonishing sporting versatility: a triple blue at Oxford in hockey, cricket and rugby football; county cricket and hockey for Somerset; and eleven England hockey caps. R. L. Hollands was pessimistic after all the selectorial changes, bemoaning the fact that '*it has been the failing of all English teams since the war that they looked winners everywhere except in front of goal.*' But these fears were to prove groundless as the English finally triumphed, for the first time since 1936, over their Irish bogeymen 3–2, Norman opening the scoring with a penalty corner shot '*nearly as straight and hard as Matheson's (a beautiful hitter) for Ireland.*'

The last of the home countries internationals, on April 22nd, was held at Aberdeen. Despite getting off the sleeper train from London only at 7.15 on the morning of the match, England overwhelmed Scotland 5–2, thereby winning the triple crown and regaining the championship which they last held in 1936. The following Saturday saw the England team fall to earth in Amsterdam, comfortably losing their first match against Holland since the war by 3–0.

During the Easter term Norman had received a letter from the Framlingham headmaster Kirkman, asking him if he would be interested in returning to the College to teach and to run the games in due course. Norman and Mullie did not take long to agree that this was a fine opportunity to move back to his alma mater, and to be near to his parents' home in Frinton: "For squash and hockey Devon was even further from the centre of things than Framlingham. It also gave me an opportunity to be involved in coaching the boys. I was delighted to return." Norman was duly engaged to start work in September 1950.

During 1949 and 1950 Norman spent his spare time at Allhallows, of which there was not a great deal,

TO IMPROVE YOUR HOCKEY

MR. NORMAN BORRETT, now a schoolmaster, played hockey for Cambridge University against Oxford in 1938 and 1939, and while still at Cambridge was "capped" for England. He has represented England in every international match since the war and was England's captain in the 1948 and 1949 matches.

A book on hockey by an exponent of Mr. Borrett's calibre has an obvious appeal and, after reading his "Improving Your Hockey" (Faber and Faber, 10s. 6d.), it is equally obvious that he has achieved his aim of producing a book which will help the average club and school player to better his game.

There are excellent photographic illustrations as well as diagrams which make the tactical moves of players easy to understand.

writing a book, "Improving Your Hockey". It was published by Faber & Faber, and sold as an instructional guide 'for all classes of players', from school beginners to more experienced club players. The technique of the various strokes, positional play, diagrams of tactical moves, and the art of captaincy are all covered in an easy, readable style, enhanced by a series of photographs, many taken at Allhallows featuring Norman in action, assisted by Allhallows pupil Mike Ray-Hills.

Good behaviour, a matter about which Norman Borrett was a stickler, makes frequent appearances:

> '*On the field the captain should see that his team plays in a sporting manner. He should be quick in stopping any of those incidents which can ruin a game, such as a player losing his temper or disputing an umpire's decision, however bad it may be.*

HITTING THE BALL
Left: Top of the backlift. Note the position of the wrists and the open face of the stick
Centre: Moment of contact. The face of the stick is upright
Right: Follow through and finish of stroke. The stick is pointing in the desired direction of the hit

Plates 11, 12 & 13

There is one other side to a captain's duties. This is the social side, and it is by no means the least important as far as his club is concerned. The popularity of his club will depend not only on the sporting manner in which its members play the game but also on how well they look after their opponents… He should make a special point of thanking (the umpires) and making sure they are invited to tea, and are not allowed to drift away forgotten'.

The author was ahead of his time in dealing not only with how practice is best achieved but also the importance of diet. He concedes, however, the individual nature of this topic: '*Heavy food is best avoided, although I have known a player eat nearly a pound of steak followed by a 'golden' pudding before an international match, and play a grand game afterwards'.* Discreetly, Norman could not, years later, recall the name of the hungry Army captain who played against Ireland.

The book was favourably reviewed across the sporting press, and it sold well. It is still worth a read, notwithstanding the significant changes which have taken place in the playing surface, stick construction, rules and tactics over the last fifty years. OF David Boulton was one of many who found practical value in the book in later years:

"Norman's book on hockey coaching, tactics and the like was very helpful. I used it to some good effect in improving the performance of my Technical College team, although never of course to the standards of the very good College XIs produced by Norman in 1950s with the likes of Mayhew and Porter playing".

David Barker, an England indoor international, who succeeded Norman as Head of Geography and as master in charge of hockey, considers that while the modern game is tactically different to some of the ploys described in the book, many of the techniques remain relevant today and the book was in many respects ahead of its time. There is a signed copy in the College's Library. David was struck by Norman's description of the various roles of captaincy, roles at which he believes Norman himself excelled:

'On a captain largely depends not only the success of a team, but also the spirit in which his team plays the game… he must be able to rally his side, and instil in them that fighting spirit which will not admit defeat and will turn a losing position into a winning one… he will need to be tactful and something of a psychologist. … A captain must take the lead not only on the field of play but also in coaching his team and preparing them for matches… a captain should see that his team plays in a sporting manner…'

ABOVE: 'Hitting the ball'. A photo from Norman's 1950 instructional book, Improving Your Hockey.

THE ALLHALLOWS YEARS – CRICKET

Essex call again;
a chance meeting in Devon;
five centuries for Seaton;
Devon county debut;
and a record stand.

Norman's post-war summer holidays were spent, at least for a part of the time, with friends and family in Frinton. The family beach hut was in frequent use, but Norman needed serious sport as well as family fun. Over the years he was to play occasionally for the MCC and for the Gentlemen of Essex in matches around East Anglia, and he maintained his connection with Frinton cricket, playing in several games every summer holiday. The annual derby game against Clacton on 10th August 1946 was played in cold and windy conditions. Norman, batting at number three, was dismissed for two runs by Arnold Quick, Clacton's Essex county player, whose four wickets helped dismiss the home team for a mere 112. But then came Frinton's turn. Norman, opening the bowling with his left arm spin, ran through Clacton, taking 8-38 in twelve overs as the visitors were dismissed for 56.

This and similar club cricket exploits were noticed by the county selectors. The following week was Clacton's Essex County cricket week, one of the traditional county festival weeks.

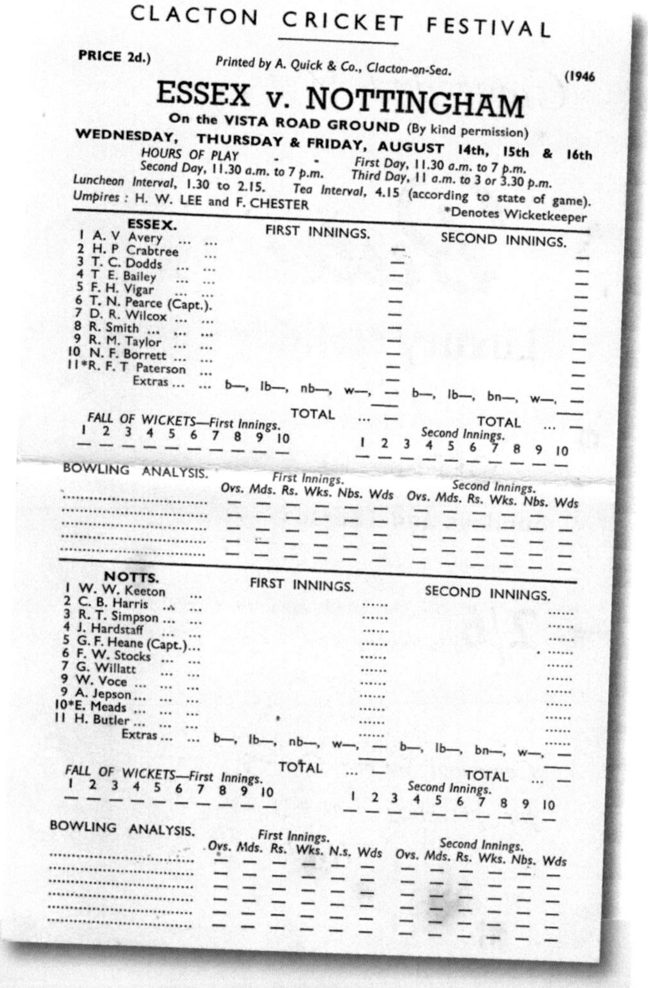
CLACTON CRICKET FESTIVAL

PRICE 2d.) Printed by A. Quick & Co., Clacton-on-Sea. (1946

ESSEX v. NOTTINGHAM

On the VISTA ROAD GROUND (By kind permission)

WEDNESDAY, THURSDAY & FRIDAY, AUGUST 14th, 15th & 16th

HOURS OF PLAY - - First Day, 11.30 a.m. to 7 p.m.
Second Day, 11.30 a.m. to 7 p.m. Third Day, 11 a.m. to 3 or 3.30 p.m.
Luncheon Interval, 1.30 to 2.15. Tea Interval, 4.15 (according to state of game).
Umpires : H. W. LEE and F. CHESTER *Denotes Wicketkeeper

ESSEX.	FIRST INNINGS.		SECOND INNINGS.	
1 A. V Avery		—		—
2 H. P Crabtree ...		—		—
3 T. C. Dodds		—		—
4 T E. Bailey		—		—
5 F. H. Vigar		—		—
6 T. N. Pearce (Capt.).		—		—
7 D. R. Wilcox		—		—
8 R. Smith		—		—
9 R. M. Taylor		—		—
10 N. F. Borrett		—		—
11*R. F. T Paterson ...		—		—
Extras	b—, lb—, nb—, w—,	—	b—, lb—, bn—, w—,	—
	TOTAL ...	—	TOTAL ...	—

FALL OF WICKETS—First Innings. 1 2 3 4 5 6 7 8 9 10 — Second Innings. 1 2 3 4 5 6 7 8 9 10

BOWLING ANALYSIS.

	First Innings. Ovs.	Mds.	Rs.	Wks.	Nbs.	Wds	Second Innings. Ovs.	Mds.	Rs.	Wks.	Nbs.	Wds
....	—	—	—	—	—	—	—	—	—	—	—	—
....	—	—	—	—	—	—	—	—	—	—	—	—
....	—	—	—	—	—	—	—	—	—	—	—	—
....	—	—	—	—	—	—	—	—	—	—	—	—
....	—	—	—	—	—	—	—	—	—	—	—	—

NOTTS.	FIRST INNINGS.		SECOND INNINGS.	
1 W. W. Keeton ...		......		......
2 C. B. Harris		......		......
3 R. T. Simpson		......		......
4 J. Hardstaff		......		......
5 G. F. Heane (Capt.)...		......		......
6 F. W. Stocks		......		......
7 G. Willatt		......		......
9 W. Voce		......		......
9 A. Jepson		......		......
10*E. Meads		......		......
11 H. Butler		......		......
Extras	b—, lb—, nb—, w—,	—	b—, lb—, bn—, w—,	—
	TOTAL ...	—	TOTAL ...	—

FALL OF WICKETS—First Innings. 1 2 3 4 5 6 7 8 9 10 — Second Innings. 1 2 3 4 5 6 7 8 9 10

BOWLING ANALYSIS.

	First Innings. Ovs.	Mds.	Rs.	Wks.	N.s.	Wds	Second Innings. Ovs.	Mds.	Rs.	Wks.	Nbs.	Wds
....	—	—	—	—	—	—	—	—	—	—	—	—
....	—	—	—	—	—	—	—	—	—	—	—	—
....	—	—	—	—	—	—	—	—	—	—	—	—
....	—	—	—	—	—	—	—	—	—	—	—	—
....	—	—	—	—	—	—	—	—	—	—	—	—
....	—	—	—	—	—	—	—	—	—	—	—	—

BELOW: T. N. Pearce leads out the Essex XI against Notts, at Clacton, August 1946. Norman is fifth from left, Ray Smith, sixth and Trevor Bailey eighth.

On Wednesday 14th August, Peter Smith the England and Essex leg spinner, being unavailable, Norman was selected to play his first game for Essex in seven years. He was picked as a bowler, against Nottinghamshire in the county championship. Frank Vigar and the captain Tom Pearce, fellow Frintonian cricketers, were also in the team, so Norman was made welcome in the dressing room. The Vista Road Recreation Ground was not far from the Borrett residence at Frinton, and Mullie brought Anthony along to watch.

With Keeton and Harris opening with a stand of 196, Notts reached 363. Norman was brought on just before lunch with the score 152 for none. He bowled steadily and returned the respectable analysis of none for 38 from eleven overs, despite being struck for two sixes by Bill Voce. Harry Crabtree and Sonny Avery put together an opening stand of 189 to give Essex first innings lead, Norman, on the scorecard at number ten, not being called upon. Second time around Notts were routed for 149 by some accurate fast bowling by Ray Smith and Trevor Bailey who took all ten between them. Norman caught Reg Simpson, the England batsman, off Smith, and Heane off Bailey, and bowled three overs for four runs. Essex, needing 149 to win had time only to make 14, Norman opening the innings, being seven not out.

It was to be Norman's third and last game for the county. He was picked for Essex Second XI to play Surrey Seconds at Chelmsford two weeks later, and batting at seven made the third highest score of 18 in a total of 246, against an attack including both Lock and Laker. Surrey were bowled out for 96 and following on made 295 for 6 wickets. Norman bowled six wicketless overs in the first innings and 20 overs, taking 1-67, in the second.

The following summer, whilst practising squash by himself at the Allhallows Convent squash club, Norman's Devon County cricket career was born. Norman Humphries, who lived near Allhallows, a useful squash player but also, more pertinently, the captain of Devon County Cricket Club, arrived one evening to play squash at the Convent to find a stranger, whom he didn't realise was Norman Borrett, changing. He asked the unknown man if he would like a game. The offer was accepted and they played, during the course of which Humphries realised he had unwittingly taken on the Amateur champion. Norman Borrett, having soundly defeated and thanked Humphries, then apologized for not sharing a drink with him, as he "would like to stay on court for a while to get in some serious practice"! Before departing, Humphries persuaded Norman to play cricket for Devon. The two were to become good friends and three years later Humphries became Tim's godfather.

Cricket for Norman was more than just a recreational break before the serious sports of winter. He loved the game and sought to play it to the highest level possible. The weather that summer of 1947 was made for cricket, and particularly for batsmen. Denis Compton and Bill Edrich broke all Middlesex records as they each scored over 3,000 runs. Meanwhile in Devon Norman found he too could do little wrong at the batting crease, scoring five consecutive centuries for Seaton Cricket Club, for whom he played on Saturdays during the summer term. Tony Watson, on leave from the Army, also played for Seaton, and for East Devon: "I went in at number three and Norman batted at four. He invariably got to his century before I had reached my fifty, if I got that far." Norman's annus mirabilis for Seaton ended with him at the top of both the batting and the bowling averages.

Norman's first match for the county was against the Royal Navy at Devonport on August 30th. That same day at Lord's, before 60,000 people over the three days, Denis Compton began the game for Middlesex against Lancashire in which he was to score the seventeenth century of his own annus mirabilis, establishing a record which will never be beaten. The Navy batted first and made 361, Norman taking 4-79. In Devon's reply of 343 Norman contributed an elegant 63, and when the Navy went in again they were bowled out for a paltry 75, Norman claiming 5-34. Devon knocked off the 94 required for victory for the loss of two wickets.

For Norman the Devonport game, before a few score of enthusiasts, represented a highly satisfactory beginning to an association with Devon county cricket club that was to last twelve years. He had no regrets at not having had more opportunities to play for his native Essex, although it is interesting now to speculate as to the career he might have had there if his brilliant Seaton successes of 1947 had instead taken place for Frinton under the noses of the Essex selectors.

His debut for Devon in the Minor County championship was delayed until 1949, as his summer holiday of 1948 was taken up with the Olympics, but thereafter he played every summer, save for 1951 and 1955, when he was away on South African hockey and squash tours.

In 1948, amidst the excitement of the build-up to the Olympic games, Norman found relaxation in his summer Saturday cricket with Seaton, although he had taken on another burden there. He had, at the club's annual meeting in March, been elected to captain the club in the coming season 'until the end of July owing to the unavoidable absence of the captain Mr Hart and the illness of the vice captain Mr Grant.' Captaincy on the field was no issue for Norman, who enjoyed being in charge, but he was glad that the club's administrative strength helped ensure his off-field duties were limited.

The next season Norman turned out for Seaton, freed of his temporary captaincy burden the year before. He batted 10 times, scoring almost 600 runs at 97.33, topping the average, and he was

N. F. Borrett (Devon) adds his signature to the bat presented to Tavistock Cricket Club by Mrs. A. T. Goss, wife of the president, to mark the centenary of the club.

LEFT: Playing for Devon in Tavistock C.C.'s Centenary celebration match, August 1949.

second in the bowling, taking 19 wickets at 15.31. When the holidays arrived, he played for the Allhallows Old Boys in the school's cricket week, a practice he continued until the mid-1950s, as a warm-up for his Devon cricket. Stuart MacGregor played in some of those games; his main recollection is not just of Norman's batting but of the fact that as a bowler he spun the ball a lot.

Norman played for Devon throughout August, fitting in eight two-day Minor Counties Championship matches.

In only his second match he made a considerable impact, on August 5th and 6th against Dorset at Paignton, sharing an unbroken stand of 262 with Troman as Devon amassed 407 for three declared, Norman ending with 134 not out. The stand remains, 63 years on, a Devon record for the 4th wicket.

One week later in his fourth match, on a good pitch at Instow, Oxfordshire bowled out Devon for a paltry 97, Norman being out for 7, forcing Devon to follow on. Devon's wicket-keeper Stuart Mountford recalls Norman's determination to make amends for the poor display: 'He said to me he was going to score a century in the second innings. I didn't believe him. Sure enough he made a gritty 103 out of 234.'

In his next match Norman scored 73 not out, out of 193, and 109 out of 223, against Kent II at Torquay. Derek Ufton, a Charlton

> ... He said to me he was going to score a century in the second innings. I didn't believe him. Sure enough he made a gritty 103...

Athletic and England soccer player, made a century for Kent, whose opening bat was Dick Mayes, later a Suffolk player and a Wolverstone Hall schoolmaster. Norman was given 21 overs in the first innings, clean bowling a 16 year old Tonbridge schoolboy called Colin Cowdrey for 10. In his final match, against Gloucestershire II, he scored a pugnacious 87.

At the end of a season in which he had scored 661 runs in 14 innings at 60.09, finishing second in the Devon and sixth in the national Minor Counties averages, and taken 13 wickets in 148 overs of left arm spin at 32 apiece, he was, unsurprisingly, awarded his county cap. The Cricketer Annual wrote; '*In his first season with the county, that great games player, N. F. Borrett, played some fine innings.*' Despite his success, and the batting successes of other batsmen, Devon did not manage a win, and the county's application to become a member of the First Class Counties Championship in 1951 was turned down. If the application had been successful Norman, and others within the team, would have been unable to participate in full-time cricket, but no doubt might, as so many other amateurs did, have continued to play during the summer holiday period.

1950 had started with welcome news from the secretary of the MCC, that Norman, 'having been proposed by B. K. Castor Esq, and seconded by G. M. Louden Esq', had been elected a Member of MCC. Castor was a distinguished cricket administrator, having been the secretary of Surrey Cricket Club after his stint at Essex. MCC membership brought Norman great pleasure over the next 50 years, in the last two decades of which he could always be found by his friends at major matches sitting in his reserved seat in front of the pavilion.

Norman's cricket in 1950 was a mixed bag of success and failure. He had had a good summer with Seaton but in the Minor County Championship Devon suffered from the poor August weather as five of their season's total of fourteen matches were abandoned. Norman only batted five times in his six matches for Devon, scoring a mere 64 runs. He was glad to have had the chance in these matches to see, at close quarters, an old Cambridge acquaintance, 'Podge' Brodhurst, who opened the batting for Gloucestershire II, and to observe the brilliant stroke-making of England player Harold Gimblett batting for a Somerset County eleven. In the last match of the season against Surrey II at Exeter, Norman faced a testing spell of off spin from Eric Bedser, and had scored a patient unbeaten 32 out of 71 for 3 when rain intervened to prevent any further play in the match.

At the end of the 1950 summer term Norman, Mullie, Anthony and baby Timothy said goodbye to Allhallows after five happy years and headed for Framlingham where Norman would teach Geography and, in the early years, English. He was to stay for thirty years.

5

FRAMLINGHAM REVISITED

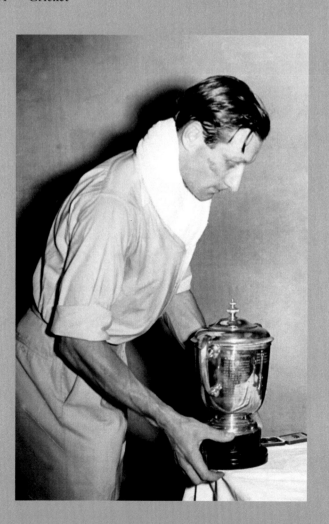

SQUASH – THE SUFFOLK YEARS

The explosion felt around the squash world.

'On Thursday November 9th 1950 there occurred at Lord's an 'explosion', the blast of which will be felt in all the world of squash, for Norman Borrett, four times and reigning amateur champion, and undefeated by an amateur since the war, was beaten by Dr. G. P. Hildick-Smith in the Bath Club Cup match between the RAC and the MCC. Borrett, a schoolmaster, formerly in Devonshire, is now at Framlingham College in Suffolk and was making his first appearance in the Bath Club Cup.

One of the many phenomenal points about Norman Borrett's play is his ability to play well without previous match practice. Year after year he comes to the Amateur Championship with only a few practice games with Clements behind him and yet almost in his first match gives of his best. This time he tempted Providence once too often. It was his first serious game of the season and one is left once more admiring the skill and fitness which enables him to produce such good form in the circumstances.

But let us not detract from the skill shown by Hildick-Smith in achieving what no other amateur has done. He played cleverly and after the second game slowed the play down with skilful lobs, tempting Borrett to snatch at his overhead shots. In addition Hildick-Smith scored several points from well-disguised cross court drops. There were many brilliant rallies just as there were many rallies won by unworthy shots, all of which is typical of early season play.

Borrett has been known to baulk, particularly when under pressure, but he gave one of the cleanest displays in this match and only on one occasion in over an hour might he be said to have merited a penalty point against him. He has been regarded as a ruthless player but in Hildick-Smith he met his match in this respect, for the latter did not hesitate to exact the physical as well as the arithmetical penalty on one or two occasions when he found Borrett between the ball and the front wall.

... It will certainly whet the appetite for a return match between these two. Should it occur, as it may, in the final of the Amateur Championship, we venture to think that there may well be a different result, but that it will provide the finest exhibition of amateur squash seen in this country since the war, there is no doubt whatever.'

Thus BLT&S, an organ not normally given to dramatic language, told the story of Norman's first defeat by an amateur since the war, 9-7, 3-9, 9-4, 3-9, 3-9. It is interesting to observe the accuracy of the prediction that the two players would next meet in the final of the Amateur, and the accuracy of the predicted result, if not the over-excited anticipation of the highest quality of play.

Norman had never had the chance to play any top quality club squash during his years at Allhallows, and he was interested in seeing whether, now living within 100 miles of London, he could get to play London mid-week squash. The MCC, a club which he had joined to play cricket, was delighted to have the Amateur champion play for them at squash, in the Bath Cup. The question would be whether he could fit the necessary travelling time from Suffolk to London into his College timetable. Headmaster Kirkman knew he had a rare talent in his Common Room, but was not always prepared to accept his new master's request for occasional dispensation. In the event, even with the MG to take him door to door, to get to MCC's courts in St. John's Wood for a home match starting at 6 pm Norman still had to excuse himself from College duties at 3 pm, drive like the wind, change in a hurry, play his match, watch his team mates play, snatch a sandwich, and retrace his steps to Framlingham, arriving there just before midnight.

So the experiment lasted only for two games, the loss to Hildick-Smith and a straight-forward win one week later against Lt. Col. Maud of the Bath Club team. Norman's place for the remainder of the Bath Cup season was taken by his old Cambridge captain, Norman Yardley. The defeat by Hildick-Smith, whilst only in a club match, was a turning point in his squash career. Although the South African had been playing a great deal of squash over the previous six weeks, and Norman none at all, the champion had been proved to be mortal, and his future opponents would know that they did have a chance to topple him where none had previously existed. Whilst he was not to lose again for over a year, he now knew that the easy mastery would not be his gift for much longer.

As a comment on Hildick-Smith's fitness, it is noteworthy that he played, and won, two five set matches on the Saturday, two days after defeating Norman, the first for Middlesex against Lt. Col Maud of the Army, and a mere 3 hours later against Dugdale for the Jesters versus Yorkshire.

On the first day of that Autumn term Norman was in the Framlingham College squash court, playing for fun and for exercise, and coaching the boys; *"No one asked me to take over responsibility for College squash, but I just did so"* was Norman's explanation of his role. He found the courts quite unchanged from the days, before the war, when he last played in them. Post-war austerity had put on hold the plans to upgrade the courts built in 1931.

Neil Joy was already a pupil at Framlingham College when the new master joined. He watched Norman coaching a highly rated prospect:

"Norman took the then school squash captain, Chris Ford, who was no mean player, under his wing for some intensive tuition. Being a keen player myself, I watched their first encounter with some amazement. Norman, in his Cambridge Blue sweater, stood on the tee in the centre of the court, and hardly left it for the half-hour they played. Chris, on the other hand went round and round the court like the proverbial bluebottle, and lost the match 5-0, each game being 9-7.

… Chris, on the other hand went round and round the court like the proverbial bluebottle, and lost the match 5-0…

This score line might suggest to the reader that the apprentice was close to beating the master, until it is revealed that he was in receipt of a seven point handicap in each game. By the end of the term, Norman was no longer wearing his sweater and was seen to have to move around quite rapidly to make his returns. He also managed to reduce the handicap advantage Norman was prepared to give him."

Gerald Garnett was another pupil observer of these games: "Ford was certainly one of the best squash players the College had produced. He won all his matches against county players from Suffolk and Norfolk and was the only winner in the match against the Jesters. He was a full county player while at the College. In the end of term College v Masters match, Ford was pitted against Norman. It was said that, before going on court, Norman told Ford that he was intending to play 'all out' against him so that Ford should get an idea of how good (or otherwise) he himself was as a schoolboy player. They duly played and Norman won 9-0, 9-1, 9-0. Ford went on to win the Junior South of England championship at Hove SRC in January 1952 and played county squash."

The OF squash team seized upon Norman's presence at the College to get him to play in the Londonderry Cup. On December 12th the team won their second round match at the St. George's Hospital courts, beating the Old Aldenhamians by three matches to two, Norman and the Newcombe brothers winning, whilst J. P. Davey, the Suffolk county player, and R. A. Quinlan lost.

In the third round, the OFs were without their saviour and were unceremoniously dumped out of the tournament by a very strong Lancing side consisting entirely of internationals and county players led by Roy Wilson. OFs E. E. Newcombe, Quinlan, G. T. Edge, W. Shipley, and Brian Shelley did not manage a game between them.

A Fifth Amateur Championship after a bruising semi-final.

Norman ran the country lanes of Framlingham over Christmas and the New Year getting fit for the great test of his squash year, the Amateur. His only practice opportunity before the big event was the annual fixture between the Executive Committee of the SRA against the Jesters on Wednesday January 3rd at Hampstead Squash Club. Playing top string he beat his old rival Brian Phillips in straight games, 9-6, 10-8, and 9-4. The two sides then dined together as guests of the SRA, who also entertained the touring side from Heliopolis Club in Alexandria. BLT&S's reporter noted, with his usual elegance, the absence of one great Egyptian squash player: "Alas, his diplomatic duties prevented the attendance of His Excellency Amr Pasha, the greatest champion of them all, but few more sporting and delightful visitors could be possible whatever their fortune on the court under strange conditions may be, than this team of his compatriots." As Amr Bey, the Egyptian Ambassador had won the Amateur a record six times pre-war.

On Friday January 5th the 1951 Amateur started, with Norman as top seed. The presence of the Egyptian touring team as well as players from Belgium, Canada and Iran ensured that the event maintained its international status. The largest-ever number of entrants, 104, meant an increase in the size of the qualifying tournament, played on the preceding Wednesday and Thursday, from which ten players went through to the main event.

Norman's progress through the early rounds was straightforward, with an initial victory over qualifier Peter Robinson costing only five points; then a walkover from W. S. M. Jameson, followed by a win over the young qualifier and future star Mike Perkins for the loss of eight points. In the quarter final Norman played Alan Fairbairn, of Middlesex, later to rise to the very top of the game, but here unseeded. Fairbairn was a fine sportsman, whose cricketing debut for Middlesex in 1947 created a stir as he scored a century in each of his first two matches. He had put out the last year's runner-up, Dagnall, in a 55 minute struggle in the third round and was clearly in top form. He put up a tremendous fight against the Amateur champion, and ran him to three close games, Norman winning 9-6, 9-7, 9-4. There was much talk after the game of Norman having lost speed.

The second seeded Hildick-Smith in his quarter-final did not allow Commander Seymour-Hayden to play his natural game, setting a tremendous pace and maintaining it throughout, causing The Times correspondent to comment: *'how like N. F. Borrett he is in this way'*. The Daily Telegraph, commenting on the loser's propensity to obstruct,

" "

… many times when the Commander stood in front of him, as if peering out to sea for enemy submarines, the South African hit him in the stern at point-blank range.

opined that he '*does himself a disservice by his habit of ordering the marker to record his objections to the marker's decisions in addition to making everyone feel thoroughly uncomfortable.*' Some sections of the press now rated Hildick-Smith as favourite to take the title.

Norman's semi-final against Roy Wilson, one of the most improved players in the game, was not a good advertisement for the sport. As this match represented Norman's greatest test during his Amateur reign, it is worth examining in some detail the way the press saw the encounter.

Gerald Pawle, writing in the Sunday Times, was clear in his condemnation of the match: '*Since the war there have been exhibitions in first-class squash rackets which have caused grave misgivings about the future of the game. I have seen nothing however to equal incidents in yesterday's semi-final, and if championship squash is to degenerate into warfare of this kind it is a sorry prospect indeed. Borrett has a reputation as a very determined player, but he was not the chief offender here. From the middle of the second game right up to the closing rallies Wilson adopted flagrantly aggressive tactics, doubly deplorable because, as he was playing so well at times, they were obviously unnecessary. The champion was plainly disconcerted, but this does not tell the whole story. The Borrett of other years would never have floundered so sadly in adversity as he did for long periods in this match.*

He looked stale. Gone was the deadly accuracy with which he has always killed the ball across the court; gone was the confident touch with the drop shot; and by comparison with other years he seemed almost leaden footed, though he did make one miraculous recovery after falling full length.'

The Manchester Guardian described the match as '*a distasteful one, for Wilson appeared to be so over-excited that he frequently crowded*

noted that '*many times when the Commander stood in front of him, as if peering out to sea for enemy submarines, the South African hit him in the stern at point-blank range.*'

Seymour-Hayden did not court popularity. He had not been impressive in his first round match against Mohtadi. BLT&S

his man, did not draw away properly from his shots and twice hit Borrett after his shot had been made. Throughout an embarrassing match Borrett's behaviour was exemplary.'

The Daily Star spoke even plainer: '*No games champion of this country has been subject to so many ill-mannered and unprovoked attacks as Norman Borrett, who defends his Amateur squash rackets title against Peter Hildick-Smith tonight. Because Borrett earned a reputation for crowding his opponent when first he won the title in 1946, there are players who are under the impression – quite wrongly – that he still does so. I recall P. Kershaw and W. H. L. Gordon using aggressive tactics against the champion in previous championships and they have now been followed by Roy Wilson of Surrey. Wilson is a very good player, but has still to learn that bad manners and temperament neither win matches nor championships. Had he played calmly and properly he might well have beaten Borrett.*'

Roy McKelvie in his Daily Mail column wrote: '*Following his much criticised display against squash champion, Norman Borrett, Roy Wilson, 26, of Surrey, apologized to the referee, J. F. Stokes. Said Borrett after winning the amateur title for the fifth successive year: "I thank all those who have made this*

RIGHT: Amateur champion for a record fifth time running, January 1951.

C.P.P. 2

N.F. BORRETT (Holder)

Norman established a mental superiority in the deciding game, pressing ahead after a number of lets, finally taking the game 9-4 and the match in just over one hour of extremely hard work.

Waiting for him in the final was Hildick-Smith, who had been unfortunate in having not had a semi-final contest, as an influenza-stricken Brian Phillips had been obliged to give him a walk over. The rose-tinted anticipation of the BLT&S's November article that the players would produce a classic was not borne out. Ruthlessness was matched with ruthlessness, and the 'backside drive' was much in evidence, but play was fair and hard.

In the first game Norman was hauled back after creating an early lead and lagged behind 4-6 before going through to win the game to six. After Hildick-Smith, playing brilliantly, led 6-0 in the second game, Norman stubbornly fought

agonizing championship enjoyable." '

Wilson played brilliant squash in the first game, hitting the ball hard and to such a length that Norman was powerless. Wilson finished the game at 9-1 by driving the ball hard into the fleshy part of Norman's back on finding Norman between him and the front wall. Wilson carried this form into the second game, as the champion, for the first time in the championship since the war, found himself in the role of defender. Wilson, leading 7-5 in the second, at last began to make errors, and amid great excitement Norman fought back to win the game 9-7. In the third, Norman's old weakness overhead was in evidence and Wilson raced to game at 9-1, Norman continuing to make unaccustomed errors. Norman then raised his effort in the fourth game, and at 3-2 Wilson cracked, twice missing the ball entirely and now looking a worried man. Norman went serenely to game at 9-2, and there were few who now doubted his ability to win.

back to 4-8. Hildick-Smith then committed the cardinal sin of serving out of court at 8-4 and Norman seized his chance, increasing the pace and winning the game 10-8, showing what extraordinary tenacity he possessed. The third game was an anti-climax, a 9-1 formality, Hildick-Smith's spirit and stamina having been broken, and Norman had won his fifth successive championship. The loser was disappointed at his below-par performance, but for the winner there could be nothing but praise as he raised his game far above that of the earlier rounds. All four living ex-champions were in the gallery at the final, and Norman was proud to receive the cup from H. E. Amr Bey Pasha.

BLT&S felt that '*merely to record that Norman Borrett won the Amateur Championship for the fifth year in succession does not do justice to a tournament which differed widely from its three predecessors. For Borrett is almost in the veteran class and there were others, knocking at the door, who were expected to offer a more potent challenge than in any year since the war.*

ABOVE: January 1951: after his toughest Ameteur yet, Norman receives the trophy from former champion Amr Bey.

Indeed, Borrett was barely favourite and his form in the early rounds seemed to bear out the assertion of those who held that Borrett had had his day. His victory then was all the more meritorious and in it we saw him display qualities on which he had not previously had to call.'

Six days after the Amateur, on Sunday January 21st, Norman was able for the first time to lead the Amateurs against the Professionals at the New Grampians Club. The professionals were captained by Jim Dear, who played at first string against Norman. The Times reported:

'N. F. Borrett set the seal on a distinguished career by beating J. P. Dear in the top match by 9-10, 9-3, 9-7, 9-2. Here it should be said that these encounters are always friendly and, with nothing accruing from the results, are for the benefit of spectators, of whom there were a great many.'

Freed from the cares of defending his championship, Norman showed himself as a far more versatile stroke-player than he would reveal in intense match-play, and the match was played in a delightful spirit. Dear, the professional at Queen's Club, was a master of the game, having thrice been runner-up to Amr Bey in the Open Championship in 1935 to 1937, before winning the event on Amr Bey's retirement in 1938. He lost the title in 1947 to Karim, who again defeated him in the 1948 final.

Dear was now 41 years old and was facing the fit amateur champion, eight years his junior, for the first time. He had also been concentrating on rackets in view of his impending defence of his world title, and thus had managed little squash practice. It was a splendid match, full of first class squash at a great pace. Dear soon went 2-7 down in the first game, but thereafter played some delightful squash, causing excitement in the packed gallery by winning that game after twice being game point down. After that Norman raised the pace, as he was always capable of doing against any class of opponent, and took the last three games. Dear retained his world rackets title which he had held since 1947, defeating J. H. Pawle over two legs. He announced his retirement from championship play afterwards, thus ending a remarkable career of international dominance in three sports - squash, rackets and real tennis.

The match between the two second strings is of interest. Hildick-Smith played the Pakistani Hashim Khan, in his first public appearance in England, who was to become the dominant force in world squash over the next 10 years. Hashim astonished the gallery with his unconventional grip, his amazing speed of foot and stroke, and his deadly drop-shot. He delighted everyone with his persistent cheerfulness, applauding hugely when his opponent played a good shot. Hildick-Smith put up a great fight before losing 3-1.

Norman regretted the fact that Hashim did not play top string in this fixture: "My one regret in squash was that I never got to play Hashim". Norman was at that time clearly superior to Hildick-Smith, and it is tempting to speculate if Norman would have given the famous Pathan a close game.

The question as to which county Norman would decide to represent at squash was a matter that featured in the press. Suffolk SRA, in their annual report, were full of eager anticipation: "*We are hoping that next season we may be able to call upon the services of the amateur champion, Norman Borrett, who is now a master at his old school Framlingham, if he can be persuaded to play for us*". In the event Norman retained his Devon squash affiliation, and continued with that county until he retired. On January 27th Devon played in the quarter-final, inter-area stage of the county squash championship. Devon had again won their group – the south-western area – with easy victories over Somerset and Gloucestershire; hopes were entertained that with the amateur champion joining the team for the quarter-final stage, greater success awaited. The press saw some unusual glamour in the contest:

'*Two of the greatest all-rounders in sport will clash in the Sussex v Devon*

MARCH . 1951

Amateurs v. Professionals

The teams photographed before the match. Standing (left to right): A. W. H. Mallett, G. W. T. Atkins, A. H. Fairbairn, L. W. R. Keeble, J. R. Thompson, E. S. Hawes, W. E. J. Gordon, R. B. R. Wilson, D. R. Bocquet, Seated: C. Read (marker), Hashim Khan, N. F. Borrett, J. P. Dear, G. Hildick-Smith, D. R. Butcher (marker).

inter-counties squash championship quarter-final at Middleton-on-Sea this weekend. Hubert Doggart, England and Sussex cricketer and Corinthian Casuals footballer, and Norman Borrett, amateur squash champion, England hockey captain and Devon county cricketer. Borrett's first appearance of the season has caused some surprise for he left that county for a teaching appointment at his old school Framlingham College, Suffolk. But he is still eligible for Devon and hopes to take them a stage further than last year when they were runners-up for the title. Borrett is in a class of his own as far as squash amateurs are concerned, and only last weekend gained a great win over Jim Dear, former Open champion, when helping the Amateurs beat the Professionals'.

66 99

... Borrett is in a class of his own as far as squash amateurs are concerned...

Devonian hopes were dashed on the visit to Middleton-on-Sea where, despite Norman winning a stern four game battle at top string against N. E. Hooper, all the other Sussex players, Dr. Stokes, Bretton Priestley, and the Doggart brothers, beat their Devon counterparts for a 4-1 win for the home side. Sussex duly went on to win the championship.

BELOW: Mahmoud El Karim, all supple stoke play and finesse, and Hashim Khan, 'the fastest runner ever in a court, who can strike the ball like a thunderclap.'

England's two squash internationals of the year, against Ireland in Dublin and Scotland at the RAC, on Friday nights in February and March, were won without the loss of a tie. Norman, who would have played at first string, was unavailable for the first due to teaching commitments and the second because it would have meant him getting from the RAC to Northampton for the English hockey trial the next day – a very risky undertaking, particularly for one who was keen to consolidate his place in the first hockey international.

Norman opted not to compete in the Open Squash Championship at the Lansdowne on April 4th, falling as it did right between the Wales and Ireland hockey internationals. The SRA's annual review noted that '*once again it was disappointing that the amateur champion was unable to enter*'. A new name, which was to bestride the international squash scene for the next decade and more, was engraved on the trophy: Hashim Khan had won the UK Professional Championship in March, beating his cousin Abdul Bari in the final. In his first Open, seeded second to Karim, he ran out the winner, for the first of six consecutive titles, beating Karim, who had won the event for the previous four years but who was sadly far from fit and unable to give of his best, 9-5, 9-0, 9-0.

A Sixth Amateur Championship?
Signs of vulnerability;
a return match with Karim;
first signs of arthritis; Hashim Khan;
the quarter-finals of the Londonderry.

Norman's pre-Christmas preparation for the defence of his Amateur squash title consisted, apart from his usual diet of endless running around the College grounds, of five squash matches, one rugby match, a few Saturday hockey matches for Norwich Grasshoppers, and three representative hockey games. He would have played one more squash game, the first ever match between England and Wales in late November, but College duties prevented his making the Thursday night trip to Cardiff.

The preparation did not go well, as his squash revealed for the first time a vulnerability, raising the question of whether his remarkable powers were on the wane. The first evidence arose in his first game of the season, in October, when he played for the Jesters against his old University. Cambridge's fifth string that day was David Sheppard, already an England Test cricketer, and later to become Bishop of Liverpool. Norman's opponent, Peter Robinson, was a promising player, later to be capped by England, but who had been swept aside by Norman in the Amateur in January. Frank Strawson, chairman of the Jesters and an ex-international squash player, commented on this Cambridge match two months later, when previewing the forthcoming Amateur Championship in BLT&S, under the headline 'Borrett Again?':

'The 1952 British Amateur Squash Rackets Championships opens at the Lansdowne Club London on Friday January 4th and the final is to be played on Monday evening January 14th. It is 30 years since the event was first held – at Lords... The favourite must be the champion of the last five years Norman Borrett... He is a schoolmaster and his form before Christmas is never really known, not even to himself, as he rarely plays before the end of term. He did turn out for the Jesters against Cambridge in October, when he lost the first two games to the Varsity captain, P. M. H. Robinson. But Borrett sportingly played under the double handicap of a heavy cold and a swollen ankle, of which he said little, though nursing it for an important hockey match. He never looked like losing and when he did turn on the heat he won with convincing ease. The holder has that hallmark of all champions – the ability to pull out that little bit extra in times of stress – and in the absence of evidence that he has suffered any measurable decline, he must surely be considered to have a good chance of winning once again.'

The old adage that one should not believe everything one reads in the press applies to this passage. A recent conversation with Peter Robinson reveals that far from Norman playing under not one but

two health handicaps, he was in fact fit and well, but merely short of match practice, a point he stressed to Peter before the game. At two games to love and 5-4 up, Peter stopped playing when Norman lost a shoe, threw it, to great hilarity, into the gallery and played on. Norman then argued against Peter's perfectly reasonable request for a let, on the grounds that he, Norman, had played on so no let should be granted. The marker, overawed by the Amateur champion's insistence, awarded the point to Norman, who having at last broken Peter Robinson's spell, ran away with the next three games. The latter recently summed up Norman as a player: "He was not unfair, and nor was he a baulker, but, as my experience shows, he was tough, ruthless and highly competitive; he would not ask for a let if one got in the way - he would drive the ball into his opponent's back. And he would expect the same treatment himself. He was fast and fit, but also a stroke maker who hit the ball very hard. His focus on speed and fitness meant he was later compared to Jonah Barrington, but I would say he was more akin to Broomfield and Lyon than to Jonah, who did not have Norman's firepower."

The second match was also at Cambridge, a few weeks later against Geoffrey Atkins, a treble blue, who had come down that summer. Atkins recently recalled the game clearly: "It was an exhibition match. It was the only time I ever played Norman; he was a legend in the game and I was nervous. But he was charming on the court and let me win." Atkins' modesty disguises the fact that this was a wonderful win for him. Norman never let anyone win, and it seems very doubtful if he altered this philosophy on this one occasion. Humphrey Truman agrees: "In my view Norman would have been trying to win, but no doubt if the game had been played in the Amateur championship, the result would in all likelihood have been different." It was only the second time Norman had lost to an amateur since the war.

...It was only the second time Norman had lost to an amateur since the war.

Norman played in November and December for the OFs, in the second and third rounds of the Londonderry Cup, but was not kept on court long enough to gain much practice, failing to grant a single point to P. M. Johns of Mill Hill, and only four points to M. E. Ash of Canford. For these matches the side was strengthened by the return to the UK of Digby Flowerdew. Flowerdew was still a good player. He had won the prestigious West of England championship in 1936, had been seeded in the Amateur pre-war, twice reaching the semi-final, in 37/38 and 38/39, and had played regularly for Surrey. After the war, he had worked in Africa and had been champion of Kenya for the same years, 1946 to 1950, as Norman had been British champion. Given a bye into the second round, the OFs beat Mill Hill 4-1, and Canford by the same margin.

Norman's form had been poor against Robinson and Atkins, so it was important that he should perform well in a fully competitive match. The opportunity for this arose two days before the Amateur, when he had his annual outing, playing for one side or the other, in the match between the SRA's Executive Committee side and the Jesters. On two of the last four such matches he had been paired with, and beaten, his old rival, Brian Phillips, and this time the two met again, in the top string match. But this time Norman lost. He conceded the first game 9-6, fought back to take the second 9-5, but then subsided 9-1, 9-0 in the next two. The effect of what proved to be food poisoning was just beginning to take hold. The following day he was not at all well, and took the difficult decision to withdraw from the Amateur late on the eve of the championship.

It was thus, in that unsatisfactory manner, that he gave up what was taken by many to be a certainty of extending his record of consecutive wins from five to six. John Horry, writing in BLT&S, was in little doubt as to the importance of Norman's misfortune: '*The Amateur Championship opened sensationally when it became known that Norman Borrett, five times champion, had scratched owing to suspected food poisoning... His form in winning practice games and friendly matches prior to the championship had not been impressive, but with Borrett that counted for little and he would have been a brave man who wagered large sums against Borrett's sixth win.*'

The Times viewed the news with mixed emotions: '*This year's event has been marred to an extent by the last minute scratching of the holder N. F. Borrett because of illness. This has however some compensation in that the championship is now more open than previously, for Borrett has won the title for no fewer than five years in succession*'. The Daily Telegraph's article began:

'*It was as though a car had moved off without its driver when the Amateur began at the Lansdowne Club yesterday. N. Borrett who has held the title every year since the war was a non-starter, laid low with suspected food poisoning.*'

In Norman's absence Peter Hildick-Smith, last year's runner-up, became the firm favourite. He duly proved himself the best player in the field and took the title, being extended only by Seymour-Hayden in the semi-finals. Brian Phillips, suffering from bad blistering, could not produce his best in the final, thus missing what was to be his last

chance of becoming champion. There was, BLT&S noted, a lurking regret at Norman Borrett's absence: '*Hildick-Smith's method is similar to Borrett's in that he sets up a tremendous pace and maintains it. Considering Borrett's absence the final was surprisingly fast.*

A curious similarity exists between these two in their attitude towards the game. In court both appear excessively poker-faced and grim, although Hildick-Smith on occasion is wont to smile with real pleasure at an especially good shot by his opponent accompanying this with a characteristic method of applauding by hitting his left hand with the face of the racket. Both, off court, are far from grim and full of impish humour. Hildick-Smith would no doubt have preferred to win the championship by beating Borrett if only to reverse the bad trouncing which Borrett gave him in the final in 1950, but once Borrett was forced to withdraw, Hildick-Smith had only Seymour-Hayden to overcome.'

One Old Framlinghamian did play in the Amateur, Dr. Digby Flowerdew, for the first time since reaching the semi-final in the 1938-39 event. He was a popular figure, and the press were disappointed at his failure to go far in the tournament.

Roy McKelvie writing in the Daily Mail on January 15th reported that '*Less than an hour after winning the British Amateur Squash championship last night, South African Dr. Hildick-Smith, 32 year old*

... He got food poisoning at a Christmas party with last night's championship runner-up, Brian Phillips... "I couldn't play in the championships – I was nobbled", joked Borrett...

specialist in children's medicine, went to the cocktail party of his squash club – the Jesters – at the RAF club in Piccadilly... Friendly joke of the evening was against Norman Borrett who had been undefeated champion for the past five years. He got food poisoning at a Christmas party with last night's championship runner-up, Brian Phillips, 31 year old Lloyd's insurance man. 'I couldn't play in the championships – I was nobbled', joked Borrett.'

The bout of food poisoning had evidently been severe, but Norman was recovered sufficiently in seven days time to take Mullie to the first SRA Ball at the Hyde Park Hotel on Thursday January 10th. Impatient for activity, he then played two days later in the first round of the divisional hockey tournament for East against Midlands,

episode, nor in regular practice, having played no more than the two OF games, plus the collapse against Brian Phillips, in two months.

In the event the expectations came to naught as Hashim withdrew injured, and Norman instead played Karim, with all the Professionals moving up a string. BLT&S recalled the match between the two top strings: '*It is nearly three years since Karim and Borrett last met, when in the semi-final of the Open Karim lost only six points. Borrett's play has probably receded since then – certainly his form has been poor this year, and lacking the practice of the amateur championship, he is not in fighting trim. Yet the shots were still there and so was the agile brain controlling them. What then of Karim in that he allowed Borrett twice as many points as in their last meeting? Karim is the older man by several years and it did appear that he had slowed down a little. Only he knows whether in this friendly match he was 'flat-out'. Whatever the reasons the result was a delightful match with none of the tension associated with a championship and if Karim put down more balls than we expect of him, it did not make any difference to his all-round superiority which was not sufficient to prevent the match from being a fine exhibition of squash at its best.'*

Given Norman's complete lack of competitive practice his performance was outstanding, and raised doubt in the minds of those who had believed that the illness which had caused his withdrawal from the Amateur had in fact saved him from losing his crown to one of the pretenders to the throne - Hildick-Smith, Phillips, Seymour-Hayden, and Atkins, who were the top four seeds in Norman's absence. The Times correspondent was impressed with Norman's game:

'*Karim defeated Borrett 9-5, 9-5, 9-3 in what was generally agreed as the finest example of the game seen so far this season. Karim, who was far below form last year through reasons of health, is now happily at his best again and it was therefore a fine performance by Borrett, not in full practice, to win almost half the points recorded by his opponent. Karim made a brilliant start but later on when Borrett set up an attack in his characteristic forceful way he resorted to intelligent defence, lobbing to prolong the rallies.*'

and did well, although seen to be suffering from the effects of his illness. He resumed training and hoped to be fit enough to perform well in the Amateurs against Professionals squash match at the New Grampians on Sunday January 20th.

This contest was eagerly awaited by the squash world, for it pitted Norman against Hashim, and Hildick-Smith against M. A. Karim, perhaps the four best players in the world. Hashim, visiting the UK only for the second time, was both the Open and the Professional champion, whilst Karim was the holder of the Dunlop Professional championship. The SRA selectors, picking the Amateurs team, evidently believed Norman should still be rated above Hildick-Smith, placing Norman at top string, with the new Amateur champion at second, even though Norman was lacking match practice. Brian Phillips was chosen as third string and Seymour-Hayden as fourth. The match against Hashim was the one Norman had been waiting for. Hashim's style, endless retrieving and boundless energy, was quite different from Karim's, all supple stroke play and finesse; Norman felt that his own speed of foot and shot would stand him a better chance against Hashim than against the Egyptian. Norman ignored the fact that he was neither at his fittest three weeks after the food poisoning

A fortnight later, playing hockey for the East on February 2nd, Norman suffered what was probably the first attack of arthritis in his hip. He was unsure what the pain was, but was sufficiently concerned to decide to withdraw from England's squash international against Ireland at the RAC on February 8th. An England side of Phillips, Seymour-Hayden, Fairbairn, Wilson and Atkins did not concede a game in a whitewash of the Irish.

Norman was more upset to miss Devon's squash match against Middlesex in the first round of the county championship, inter-area stage, February 10th. Devon had again won the South–West area title, without Norman's participation, and hoped to continue their run with a win over a strong Middlesex side. The result would turn on the game between the top strings: an eagerly awaited instalment in the Borrett versus Hildick-Smith series. As Norman was unfit and Hildick-Smith was unable to make the journey, Middlesex's ability to produce the better reserve at fifth string gave them the tie 3-2. Norman was keeping his injury quiet; Gerald Pawle in the Sunday Times was in the dark: '*the county championship promised to produce the amateur squash match of the season when Middlesex played Devon, and many people have asked me for the result of the first string set, in which the new amateur champion should have met his predecessor Norman Borrett. Strange to relate neither found it possible to turn out, and Seymour-Hayden led Middlesex to victory*.'

Two weeks later Norman was fit again, and led the OF squash team on February 22nd in a crucially important match in the Londonderry Cup, a competition described by Gerald Pawle as '*perhaps the season's most enjoyable squash rackets team event*'. The OFs had, by virtue of an easy draw, got through to the quarter final, where they met Cranleigh. Pawle believed that with Norman and '*the popular 30s championship player Digby Flowerdew*' in the side the OFs would reach the semi-final for the first time.

Playing a young Old Cranleighans side containing three county players, OF hopes lay in winning at first and second string and hoping for a third victory somewhere in the bottom three stings. Norman, as expected, got the team off to a good start by beating David Vaughan, a useful county player who was to become Amateur Veterans champion in 1972. It was Norman's first match since his splendid struggle against Karim on January 20th and he was given a close game before winning 9-6, 10-8, 9-5. Then Mike Dobson and Brian Shelley were beaten in three close games. 2-1 to Cranleigh and the OFs had to win both the last two ties. Ted Newcombe at four and Flowerdew at two traded games with their opponents, before both went down in the fifth game 9-6 and 10-8 respectively: a 4-1 defeat which could so easily have been a 3-2 win. Cranleigh went on to lose in the semi-final 4-1 to Winchester, who in turn lost 3-2 to Haileybury in the final.

Norman declined the invitation to play squash for England against Scotland at Edinburgh on Friday March 14th, as it was the day before the final England hockey trial. The Open Squash Championship, scheduled for April 2nd to 7th, also clashed with hockey – in this case

England's match against France in Boulogne on the 6th. Norman opted, as he always did, to play in the hockey international.

Hashim Khan from Pakistan and Karim from Egypt had come to England in February for two months, taking in the Scottish Open, the Dunlop Open Professional Tournament and finally the Open Championship in April, Hashim winning all three tournaments at the first attempt. As international travel became easier, the best players in the world were homing in on the major British professional tournaments, confirming Britain's position as the home of squash.

In the Dunlop, Hashim and Karim, acknowledged as the best two players in the world, had contested a wrestling match, in which one penalty point and 20 conceded lets gave a clear picture of the crowding tactics adopted by both players. In the Open, the two were again seeded one and two. Norman would have been seeded third behind them. In his place Hildick-Smith became third seed and could manage only four semi-final points from Hashim; Brian Phillips, the fourth seed, did rather better in his semi-final with nine points off Karim. In the final, the two masters adopted a more open style of play but still gave up fourteen lets, nine in favour of Karim, as their speed of foot brought them into frequent near-contact. The speed of the play was such that Karim suffered stomach cramp in the second game and lost the third, and the match, to love, Hashim finishing him off with a stroke peculiarly his own – a forehand smash at a shoulder high ball which found the nick on the left hand wall. Hashim's attitude on court continued to gain him many admirers. BLT&S' perception was that '*His most important characteristic is neither his speed nor his skill, but the obvious zest and enjoyment which he brings to the game. His smile of delight is as broad and apparently as genuine when he is truly beaten by a good stroke as when he retrieves the apparently impossible*'.

There was little doubt that no first class player could go into the court with much hope of beating or even taking a game from Karim, who was in a class of his own. But in a yet higher class was Hashim, now clearly the best player in the world.

Norman, on College vacation, was in the gallery at the RAC in April to watch Chris Ford play in the Drysdale Cup. The SRA yearbook's schools report on Framlingham notes that Ford had shown considerable improvement during the year: '*Although he won all his school matches and the South of England Junior Championship, he was disappointing in the Drysdale Cup*'. This was a harsh indictment for a player who reached the quarter-final only to lose there to the fifteen year old Haileyburian wunderkind Nigel Broomfield, who was to become one of England's greatest players. Norman was the author of the Framlingham paragraph in that yearbook, and his comment shows how he occasionally found it difficult to accept that others could not achieve what he himself could have achieved.

Retirement from championship play;
the new Amateur champion's no cigarette
training regime;
England internationals in Cardiff and Dublin;
Devon reach the county championship final.

The beginning of the College academic year in September 1952 brought a new crop of squash players competing for places in the school team, and in the school and house championships. The general standard of play at the College was now showing the benefit of Norman's tuition over the previous two years. The team of Keith Mackenzie, Ian Foster, Jasper Garnham, David Mead and Alan Brooks won seven out of the ten matches played. Norman arranged for both Mackenzie and Foster to enter the Drysdale Cup in the following Easter holiday.

Norman practised with the team and kept himself as fit as ever. The ache in his hip was however becoming more frequent, particularly after exercise. He consulted a distinguished Harley Street orthopaedic surgeon, Bill Tucker, who diagnosed that the condition was not, as had been suspected, muscular rheumatism, but the early stages of arthritis, the condition from which his mother had suffered for many years. An irony was that Norman possessed great bone density, and remarkably never suffered any broken bone.

A decision had to be taken: to retire from sport or to carry on and risk making the condition worse. He was too young to stop doing what he loved. Perhaps he could carry on but take things more carefully. He wanted to continue to play hockey as long as he could, so he would reduce the squash he played by retiring from tournament play. The Amateur demanded six games in 10 days, and the Open only a little less. He would continue to play one-off matches, internationals, county games and occasional representative matches, and still try to be competitive. There was one other factor which affected his decision. Even before the 1951 Amateur, seeking to get into shape, both physical and mental, to win the event for the fifth time, he found that the killer instinct was becoming just a little elusive...

...He told Roy McKelvie, who quoted him in the Daily Mail, that he "now finds it difficult to work up 'a hate' in the court."

Having thought through the pluses and the minuses, Norman took the decision that he would not, for the first time since the war, send in his entry form for the Amateur by the closing date, Monday November 24th.

Norman played his only squash game of the pre-Christmas season on November 19th. He led the Jesters at Cambridge against the University side which was in the final furlong of its preparation for the annual battle with Oxford. Unsurprisingly, he took time to find his touch, but it was rare for him to lose a game in doing so. He defeated the Cambridge captain D. A. Swales, 9-10, 9-2, 9-7, 9-4.

He was not able to make the date for the OFs' Londonderry Cup match against Lancing, one of the strongest sides, on December 3rd. The side therefore had a new look, with recent leavers Chris Ford and Humphrey Truman coming in at the top and bottom of the order, and Michael Evans playing for the first time. Ford had done well during the season, playing for Essex at the end of November in a friendly against Cambridgeshire and winning at fifth string. He also did well in the tie against Lancing to take Roy Wilson, six weeks before he was the runner up in the Amateur, to 10-9 in the second game of a straight games defeat. Ford continued to play good squash for several years. His life was cut tragically short when he was killed in a car accident in 1972, aged 39. Michael Evans at second string, the Newcombe brothers at three and four, and young Humphrey Truman at five all lost.

As he was not going to play in the Amateur Norman decided not to take part in his usual pre-tournament practice in the annual contest between the Executive Committee of the SRA and the Jesters, on December 29th. The 1953 Amateur began on January 2nd, BLT&S regretting '*the disappearance from the entries…of two who have the best record in the game since the war – N. F. Borrett and B. C. Phillips...*

…Borrett, winner for five successive years, is still a comparatively young man but he is suffering from trouble in one of his legs which would make it imprudent to risk the strain of several hard matches. It is too early to know whether this is a temporary or permanent retirement but the championship is the poorer for his absence.'

The Sunday Times reported that 'Borrett, temporarily out of the game through trouble with his hip, is deprived again of his chance of equalling the record of Amr Bey in winning the title half a dozen times.'

The event was won by Alan Fairbairn, who having put out the holder Hildick-Smith in the quarter-final, then beat Seymour-Hayden in the semi, and a nervous Roy Wilson, 3 games to one, in the final. The Times correspondent wrote: '*There must always be a regret that N. F. Borrett, the outstanding Amateur champion since the war, has not been able to enter*'.

BLT&S carried an interesting interview with the two finalists, entitled How They Trained. As an insight into the difference in approach to physical training in those days as compared with today, it makes fascinating reading: '*Alan Fairbairn, asked how he had trained to*

*defend his championship title, stated that
he gave up smoking and drinking spirits on
1st November. He did no running and
relied on his squash matches, which
averaged nearly three a week, to keep him
fit. He did not go especially early to bed. In
the great final match he wore a pair of
shoes which were slightly too small for him
and on the following day his feet were 'in
ribbons' and he could scarcely get a shoe on.*

*Roy Wilson stated that last year he
trained up to the hilt and was convinced
that this was worth quite four points a game
to his opponent. Accordingly he did no
special training this year, and no running.
He cut out drinking spirits but drank beer
and especially Guinness. He does not smoke
cigarettes and cut out cigars but allowed
himself an occasional pipe. He started the
championship under-trained and virtually
relied on the early matches to bring him up
to the pink of condition by the time he
reached the final. His one "must" is early to
bed – 10 to 12 hours every night.'*

Norman's approach, not just in
the run-up to a tournament, was far
more ascetic, and his pre-tournament
training considerably tougher; but in
his case he did not have the advantage of averaging three games of
squash per week. In his case he averaged one a month at best.
Humphrey Truman's approach, already quoted earlier, was similar to
Fairbairn's: "I needed, to stay match fit, to play five times a week, and
for three of those matches to go to five games."

Norman's decision to reduce his squash commitments was
severely tested during the first three months of 1953, which produced
an unusually heavy series of squash (and hockey) matches. He still
greatly enjoyed the change from one sport to the other, even if he was
finding the wear and tear of the volume of games now taking a toll.
After playing hockey for the Schoolmasters against Sandhurst on
January 7th, he suffered an attack of inflammation in the hip. It was
painful but it did not prevent him from accompanying Mullie to the
Hyde Park Hotel the next night for the SRA/WSRA annual ball,
where they joined the party of Peter Hildick-Smith and his fiancée,
celebrating their engagement.

The hip condition, which he chose to describe to the press as
simply "trouble with his hip", was however bad enough to put him
out of the first East divisional match on January 10th. He had
recovered in time to captain England in the second squash
international played against Wales, at Cardiff on Friday January 16th,
and to attend the Welsh rugby international the next day, as guests of
the Welsh SRA. Fairbairn, having just defeated Wilson in the final of
the Amateur, played at first string and Wilson at two, with
Seymour-Hayden and Hooper at four and five. Norman played at
three, winning 9-1, 9-1, 9-4, as all the England players won in
straight games.

Norman missed the Amateurs versus Professionals squash match at
the Lansdowne on Sunday 25th, as he was captaining the East hockey
team against the West at Swindon the day before.

Devon had again progressed through their South-Western area
matches to reach the inter-area stage when they always called on
Norman to join the team. The area first round, or national
quarter-final, match was at Wanstead against Essex on Saturday
February 7th. For Norman this was the nearest thing to a home

match; the MG had only to cover 90 miles to the court. He played Michael Lyon, Jeremy Lyon's older brother, and he won comfortably. Haycraft, who in the earlier rounds had filled the role of top string, played at two and just overcame John Forder in the fifth game. Michelmore, Plum and Etherington-Wilson each won their games, the latter against John Taylorson at fifth string. Michael Lyon recalls that match 55 years later: "Norman had taken the game to a different level with his focus on taking an early ball, the cut he applied to every shot, and his speed around the court. Like Jonah Barrington a generation later, he changed the way the game was played." Michael was struck by the man as well as the player. "Norman did not know me, a much younger man, from Adam, but immediately offered me a lift home in his car. It was a long journey and from our chat I formed the impression of a very decent, unassuming, human being".

The following week Norman took three days leave from the College for two squash matches. The death of King George VI in 1952 had been marked by the creation of a memorial fund. The SRA supported this with a series of exhibition matches on the Noel Bruce court at the Lansdowne on Wednesday February 11th at 5.30pm. Norman got away from Framlingham early and was in the West End by 5pm. The main event on the programme was a match between the Open champion of the last two years, Hashim Khan, and the Amateur champion of the last two years, Alan Fairbairn. Hashim won in five games, with Fairbairn having the great advantage of American scoring (every point he won was to score in his favour, including those when Hashim was serving). Norman's match was a doubles. Whilst he was pleased to support the charitable aspect of the evening, he found the game a difficult one. It was not a situation in which he could play his normal game; that is, to win.

Norman's second squash match of the week was as captain of England against Ireland in Dublin on Friday 13th. Having stayed in London on the Wednesday night, and spent the next day in London, Norman and the rest of the England squash team caught the 8.45pm train from Euston to Dublin via the Holyhead-Dun Laoghaire ferry. The train got in to Dublin at 7.23 on the Friday morning, so the team were glad of some time to rest at their Dublin hotel in preparation for the match at 4.45 that afternoon. Although selected as third string, Norman played at two, Fairbairn having dropped out at the last moment. Ireland performed better than ever before in third fixture, Wilson dropping a game at number one and Nevill Hooper losing at number four to G. P. Jackson, the Irish triple international. The Irish press said that '*the most impressive of the visiting team was N. F. Borrett, who outplayed a plucky opponent in J. P. McHale by an exhibition of driving to a perfect length. Once Borrett had the attacking position there was no answer to*

... Once Borrett had the attacking position there was no answer to his blinding pace, and he made virtually no errors...

his blinding pace, and he made virtually no errors, McHale earning each of his five points by hard running.' Hooper became the first England player to lose a tie in any match since the war, although the sweating court made something of a lottery of the angles.

The inter-county championship semi-final between Devon and Hertfordshire took place at Torquay on Sunday February 22nd. The MG had a long journey to this game, Norman arriving pretty exhausted on the Saturday evening at the Imperial Hotel. It must have been one of the longest drives ever undertaken by a man wanting to play an hour's squash. It started in Norwich shortly after he had come off the Eaton Park pitch following a 5-0 defeat for his team, Suffolk, by Norfolk, a game in which he was described as the outstanding player on the pitch.

On arrival at the famous old hotel, the venue of his post-war pre-Amateur championship practice matches against Bill Clements, the resident professional, Norman had to change into a dinner jacket for the pre-match dinner and dance for both teams, hosted by the Devon president Mr H. G. Michelmore. Devon survived this hospitality better than their opponents, winning the match 4-1. It was perhaps unsurprising that Norman found the first two games of his match against top string Tony Mallett a stern test, before winning 9-5, 8-10, 9-4, 9-0. Haycraft and John Michelmore pulled off fifth game victories, Pellew won in three and Plum lost in five. Hertfordshire badly missed Geoffrey Atkins, their top string, England squash international and Amateur Rackets champion, who was, with J. R. Thompson and D. S. Milford, on a five week tour of the USA and Canada with the British rackets team.

The next weekend the final of the inter-county squash championship was played at the Bath Club. Norman was hopeful that at last Devon would find glory, but it was not to be, as they were defeated by Sussex, winners for the third successive year and the ninth time in the seventeen year history of the competition. Devon were runners-up for the second time in four years, but it might all have been different. The Doggart brothers, Peter and Hubert, played first and each won in straight games. Pellew, fourth string for Devon, then beat Bretton Priestley in five tight games to reduce the margin. Haycraft then played John Barrington and went to 6-1 up in the fifth game. With Norman due next on court against Hooper, whom he was expected to beat, things were looking good for the Devonians, but Barrington played above himself and pulled the fifth game out of the fire 9-7. The tie now being beyond Devon's reach, and as Norman was anxious to rest his hip, it was agreed that the top match would be left unplayed.

Norman was unavailable for the third match in the international squash series, against Scotland at the RAC, on Friday March 20th, as he was captaining England against the Rest in the final England hockey trial the following day at Evesham. In his absence the England five, although winning 4-1, suffered the indignity of losing a tie, for only the second time ever, when Norman's Devon colleague C. B. Haycraft lost on debut, 9-7 in the fifth to C. N. Campbell.

Hashim Khan was seeded top and Mahmoud Karim second in the Open squash championships which took place at the Lansdowne Club from March 25th to 30th, with the two top amateurs Fairbairn and Wilson at three and four. Norman was captaining England in the first hockey international of the season on the Saturday of the tournament, the 28th, and even if he had changed his mind about no longer playing championship squash, could not have taken part. Hashim, in his book on squash, reveals that he would not have been able to play in the final, which he won, as was usually the case, against his younger brother Azam, if it had not been for the treatment - an injection and some medicine - given to him by fellow competitor Dr. Peter Hildick-Smith.

Gerald Pawle, writing a review of the squash scene for a London magazine, drew attention to the strange incongruity of the best players in the world descending on London to play in the Open, at the Lansdowne Club, home of big match squash, where a mere 150 spectators could view each contest. '*An ace professional like Hashim Khan will win less than £200 if he scoops the pool with all three major professional titles. After paying for his travelling expenses and his board and lodging while training here for many weeks before the championships start, he is substantially out of pocket. Most professionals from abroad have to rely on private backing, and when Mahmoud el Karim first came here from Egypt, it was King Farouk who made the trip possible.*

As for the 'shamateur' in squash, he does not exist. All through the season, from October to April, the best amateurs are in constant demand all over the country. There are league and cup matches; the County Championship, which may take the Londoner to Devon or Lancashire; various area championships, national tournaments; and the international fixtures which may mean a journey of hundreds of miles for half an hour's appearance on the court. The expense of it all comes from their own pockets; I remember a journey to Copenhagen a few seasons ago, when England's team had to find some £250 between them to represent their country against Denmark.

As squash has attracted an ever-widening public, tension on big occasions is much greater than it was. This puts a premium on match temperament. Norman Borrett, the England hockey player who won the Amateur Championship at squash five years in succession after the war, was not a classic stroke player, but he had an ice-cold brain, and in any championship his relentless concentration turned the scales time and again in his favour. Borrett was a squash rackets machine. But the man who really revolutionised the game was Amr Bey, until recently Egypt's Ambassador in London. Before he became interested in it, squash had followed rather unadventurously in the pattern of real rackets, which is played with a hard ball in a much larger court. Then the young Egyptian, practising for hours on end, and all the year round, created an entirely new range of stroke and tactics.

Six times he won the British championship, and, when he retired unbeaten, another of his countrymen, Mahmoud el Karim, monopolised the major world titles for several years. Today his mantle has passed to a stocky, balding Pakistani who will soon be electrifying us with his fantastic speed and control of the small ball, which moves like lightning in the torrid atmosphere of a crowd-encircled court. Hashim Khan is the 'Iron Man' of squash rackets. Apparently tireless, he is the fastest runner ever in a court. He can strike the ball one moment like a thunderclap, and a moment later stroke it for the softest of winners with magical certainty.'

The Open saw some brilliant squash. Sadly an injury to Karim during his win over Hildick-Smith, meant he had to give a walk-over to Safirullah. There was a career best performance from Roy Wilson, beating first Bari and then Safirullah to reach the final. Hashim, his opponent, had permitted his brother Azam to win two of the first four games of their semi-final before demolishing him in the fifth. Wilson put up a great display against Hashim in the final, winning the second game and stretching the champion throughout. The second game contained a number of long rallies, one of which lasted fifty strokes during which Hashim had to return at least a dozen strokes by Wilson which would have been winners against any normal player.

Norman was at the RAC Club on April 21st to watch the two members of the College squash team who had entered for the Drysdale Cup. Keith Mackenzie had to scratch because of injury but Ian Foster played, losing in the second round. The event was won by Jeremy Lyon of Lancing who beat the holder Nigel Broomfield in the final. This result was reversed in the Evans Cup, as Broomfield achieved the second of his remarkable four wins. Norman had high hopes for the future of English squash from what he had seen at the Drysdale, and at the Evans Cup at Surbiton in April where Jeremy Lyon had retained his title. Lancing also won the Under 16 title through David Jude. Norman was right. Less than ten years later Lyon, Jude and Humphrey Truman, members of the Wanstead squash team which won the Cumberland Cup, would all play for England. A new era had begun, both in the professional game and in the national game.

Autumn 1953 retirement from hockey on Bill Tucker's advice; but what about squash? A trip to Paris.

Fourteen years and 30 caps after he was first selected for England Norman was finally forced to call time on his hockey career. A second visit to Harley Street, one year after the first, to see Bill Tucker, had persuaded him that to continue would only make his condition worse. However he declined to accept Tucker's advice to retire also from squash, refusing to deprive himself totally of his enjoyment in playing sport. Although he had given up tournament play in the Autumn of 1952, he had since then established what he felt was a workable schedule of matches: "At least I can keep playing squash to a reasonable level."

The 1953/4 season began for Norman on November 9th, with a repeat of the previous year's trip to Cambridge, as captain of the Jesters team to play against his old university. The university captain and first string, John Partridge, had earlier in the month taken two games off Seymour-Hayden and one off Roy Wilson and was in good form. Norman however found his touch immediately and, despite turning an ankle over, dispatched Partridge 9-4, 9-1, 9-7.

Norman had accepted an invitation from the SRA president, Captain Palmer-Tomkinson, to represent the SRA against the Jesters three days later in the inaugural Frank Strawson memorial match. The ten players chosen were intended to be the country's best, and the concept of the fixture was to show off the best aspects of the game. Norman's ankle sprain was worse than he had initially thought, but he was determined to turn out in this special match. With only the one competitive match to his name so far that season, he was presented with a seemingly impossible task in being placed, quite unjustifiably, ahead of Wilson who played second string, against the Jesters top string, the amateur champion Alan Fairbairn, who was in regular match practice. The BLT&S reporter takes up the story:

'Of the ten players in the match, eight had been seeded in recent amateur championships and this match probably represented the greatest gathering of stars ever seen in any one match. The meeting between the present amateur champion, A. Fairbairn and the ex-champion, N. F. Borrett was eagerly awaited for these two had not met since the amateur championship nearly three years ago when Borrett won 3-0. Unfortunately Borrett sprained his ankle a few days before the match. He sportingly went into court and at first seemed little troubled. Playing beautifully crisp shots, never more than one inch above the tin, he almost overwhelmed Fairbairn and obtained a lead of 7-0. But once the present champion had got his machine-like game going smoothly there was a different story and thereafter Fairbairn scored 24 points to his opponent's 3. It was plain that Borrett was in trouble with his ankle and with Fairbairn finding his deadly touch for drops the match was becoming a massacre. As the Jesters

had already won, there was little point in risking further injury – Borrett wisely accepted advice to retire. He plays little match squash nowadays but many will cherish the memory of those beautiful strokes in the first game.'

With Norman losing 9-7, 0-9, 1-9 (retired), Hooper losing to Phillips, Peter Doggart to Thompson, and Dagnall to Turnbull, the only win for the SRA was that of Roy Wilson over Seymour-Hayden.

The ankle was mended by November 27th when the Old Framlinghamians' opening effort in the Londonderry was again led by Norman. He won his tie against David Blake of the Old Aldenhamians 9-3, 9-2, 9-3; with Chris Ford at two, Michael Evans at four, and Keith Mackenzie at five all winning, and Ted Newcombe at three being the only loser, the OFs won 4-1. Michael Evans, playing only his second match in the team, recalls the pressure the other members of the team felt from Norman's presence in the side:

"I never saw Norman playing at his best as I did two years National Service which took me out of the London squash circle. It was not until I joined Lillywhites in 1951 that I came back to the game, playing for Queens Club in the Bath Cup and for the Escorts. I met up with Norman again through the OF participation in the Londonderry. By then Norman was not quite the force of earlier days, but still very formidable...

> …*It was plain that Borrett was in trouble with his ankle and with Fairbairn finding his deadly touch for drops the match was becoming a massacre.*

...The second time I played in the Londonderry Cup, under Norman's captaincy, I had the embarrassment of serving out of court on match point, under my captain's eagle eye. This mortification is something I have never been allowed to forget, as Norman invariably greets me with: 'Ah, the only chap I've ever known who serves out of court on match point'".

In the second round, on December 4th, the OFs lost to the Old Haileyburians 4-1, Chris Ford, Michael Evans and Ian Foster losing in straight games, and Humphrey Truman winning at fourth string 10-8 in the fifth game. Norman was at the last minute unable to get away from Framlingham and was forced to scratch against Alan Fairbairn – a match he would almost certainly have lost.

The next Friday, the 11th, Norman did get away from College after lunch, for a 5pm squash international at the Lansdowne Club, captaining England in the match against the touring Netherlands team. England put out its strongest side, Fairbairn, Wilson, Borrett, Seymour-Hayden, and Brian Phillips, not wishing to be impolite to their visitors, whose first match against England this was. They outclassed the Dutch, winning 5-0 without dropping a game. Norman got little satisfaction from his game against Blom, in which he conceded six points. Lance Tingay in the Daily Telegraph thought there was no point in describing the games in any detail but '*it was pleasing nonetheless to see the former Amateur champion, N. F. Borrett, the greatest of the post-war holders of the title, in action again. Borrett, even when not in championship trim, as he has not been for the last year or two, still gave the impression of ruthless dash about the court, an impression of overwhelming force and speed which Blom, of all those present, must have felt in full measure.*' The hosts clearly performed well at the post-match dinner at the Mayfair Hotel, for the Dutch manager, in writing to Henry Hayman of the SRA, said how his team were proud "to have encountered the strongest team in the world! And not only in the court – but out of it – that team gave us a reception we will never forget."

Norman found that whilst he would seize up afterwards, he could last out a match. There were significant differences in the effect on his hips of squash and hockey. Squash required more hip movement but it was a game where it was rare to be on court longer than 45 minutes, and it demanded explosive bursts of short distance movement. Hockey on the other hand was a 70 minute affair and called for virtually continuous longer distance running. He was happy to retain the discipline he had imposed on himself that he would not play in tournaments calling for several consecutive games. His days of competing in the Amateur were behind him. This did not concern him: "I had won each of those I played in. Perhaps my appetite had dimmed somewhat".

The 1954 Amateur started on New Year's Day. Gerald Pawle in the Sunday Times thought that Alan Fairbairn would face a hard struggle to retain his title. '*Gone are the days when one player – Norman Borrett – dominated the scene and the only point at issue was the margin of the champion's success.*' Fairbairn did win the championship, beating Roy Wilson for the second year running, in a great final, not so much for the quality of the squash, but for the sheer guts displayed by Fairbairn in coming through to win after a match of some 85 minutes. Nerves did not play such a major part on Wilson's play as the year before, and, as BLT&S saw it, '*it was only in the closing stages that one sensed that*

Wilson had cracked mentally rather than physically... There were too many lets and here Wilson was the chief offender, fourteen lets being given against him not to mention two penalty points, compared to three lets against Fairbairn, and Wilson must be criticised for not getting away from his drop shots, particularly in the forehand corner.' Wilson led 7-3 in the fifth game and looked a winner all over, but was then beaten by a man who would not give up.

For the England squash selectors it was not important that Norman had not taken part in the Amateur, the premier test of the current abilities of the country's leading amateur players, for the last two years. One week into the Amateur, on Thursday January 8th, Norman received three stereotyped letters from Henry Hayman, SRA secretary. The first was for the season's first international, the second was an invitation to play for the Amateurs against the Professionals on Sunday the 24th, and the third was to play in Paris in late February in a combined squash and real tennis match against the Paris Club de Jeu de Paume, the players having to bear their own fares. Norman was pleased with all the invitations, which fitted neatly into his strategy of playing good occasional, non-tournament, squash. He accepted all three.

The letter concerning the international gave no details: "I have now been instructed by the selection committee to issue a firm invitation to you to play for England against Wales on Friday next, the 15th. I shall be grateful if you will confirm by return that you will be able to do so." It was not until five days later, only two days before the event, that details were provided, in a second letter, confirming the identity of the two teams, the venue, the Naval and Military Club, and the timing: the players were invited to tea at 4.30 pm before the 5.30 pm game, and to dinner in the regimental dining room after the match at 7.30 pm for 8.00 pm. "The cost of dinner and drinks (within reason!) will be borne by the SRA, but any drinks ordered after rising from the table should be paid for personally."

These calls to sporting arms for one's country were always couched in terms which brooked no refusal. This one did however contain a 'perk', even if a qualified one: "Tickets for the match at Twickenham on Saturday, for which, I am afraid, you will be required to pay, are available."

England again put out their strongest side, Norman playing one string lower than in the Netherlands game, at four, behind Fairbairn, Wilson and Seymour-Hayden, with Brian Phillips at fifth string. Norman was in ruthless mood, not permitting D. O. Bartlett a single point. BLT&S sympathised with the loser: '*Borrett's score against Bartlett does less than justice to the latter. He played well, but Borrett played with the ruthless majesty that won him five amateur championships and Bartlett's task was hopeless*'.

The next weekend, Sunday January 24th, Norman was captain of the Amateurs team which took on the Professionals at the Lansdowne Club. The SRA charged 15 shillings for the best seats, and seven and

ENGLAND v. IRELAND, 1953-54
12.2.54. AT THE ROYAL AUTOMOBILE CLUB. England won by 5 ties to 0.

S.G. 236278

G.P. JACKSON (Ireland) v. N.F. BORRETT (England) (captain).
N.F. Borrett won 8.10, 9.6, 9.3, 9.2.

sixpence for side standing. Fairbairn at first string lost to a masterly Hashim Khan in straight games, while Wilson at two scored a noteworthy victory over Karim three-love. BLT&S felt there was 'a sadness about this notable victory, Karim showing all his old lithe grace and beautiful ease of stroke, frequently countering Wilson's speed and well-played drops and angles with even better shots, yet there was not quite the same effortless precision and he seemed slower than before.' At third string Seymour-Hayden played the game of his career in disposing of Roshan Khan, professional champion of Pakistan, in five long games over an hour and ten minutes, to give the Amateurs the match 4-3. Norman played fourth string against the Junior Carlton professional Abdul Bari, the first of the famous Khan dynasty to gain a professional teaching post in Britain, and who had regained the form which enabled him very nearly to beat Karim five years before. For the first half of the opening game the contest was very close, Norman showing all his old skill and, according to BLT&S, '*if anything, more versatility of stroke play than when he was amateur champion. Then he turned his ankle over and, although far from immobile, was unable to move as quickly as usual and certainly not quickly enough to compete with Bari's pace.*' Bari won 9-4, 9-1, 9-3.

This burst of squash activity for Norman continued with a match at the RAC in London, for the third home countries international, against Ireland, on the evening of February 12th. England duly won the tie, their sixth successive victory over Ireland. Lance Tingay in the Daily Telegraph was in jingoistic mood: '*England stands today at amateur squash where she did in most other sports 50 years ago and can teach the rest of the world a lesson. In 30 years the only defeat has been in the United States, where the game is different. Yet Ireland might without injustice have got one rubber last night. Guy Jackson, an Oxford Blue and a fine exponent of lawn tennis and real tennis, came closest to getting one against Norman Borrett, the former Amateur champion. With Borrett lacking some of his old sting, Jackson made the most of his chances. He salvaged the first game by a hairsbreadth after trailing 1-5, but the rest of the match was one of diminishing Irish returns.*'

Fairbairn, Wilson, Seymour-Hayden and Phillips all won in straight games. Norman played at four, having strapped his suspect ankle, and the game he dropped was his first in international matches. He and Jackson knew each other well: Jackson had played against Norman at hockey, as an inside forward, both for Oxford University Occasionals in the annual Christmas match, but also for Ireland.

On the Saturday, Norman went to Twickenham at the SRA's invitation, and his expense, for the England v Ireland rugby game. He motored down to Torquay after the rugby and stayed at the Imperial. On the Sunday afternoon he led Devon to a 4-1 win over Glamorgan in the quarter-finals of the inter-county championship, Devon having yet again, and without his help, won their area to qualify for the quarters. He played the Irish international D. J. O'Brien and won 9-1, 9-5, 9-3.

The friendly match in Paris, over the weekend of February 27th and 28th, against the Societe Sportive de Jeu de Paume et de Racquets was a most enjoyable event. This mixture of sport and socializing comprised a 3-string squash fixture and a 2-string real tennis match, on the Saturday morning, a visit to the France v New Zealand rugby on the Saturday afternoon, dinner on the Friday and Saturday evenings at the invitation of their French hosts, and a return home on the Sunday. The players were billeted at the homes of their hosts and were royally entertained. For Norman there was the particular pleasure of spending time with his old friend and 1937 Cambridge squash captain, Maurice Baring, who played in the real tennis fixture. Norman's

BELOW: Norman travelled thousands of miles for his sport, and occasionally persuaded Mullie to come too.

squash game was close, and he only just won in four close games, 9-10, 10-8, 10-8, 9-1, at first string against Robin Lees, the RAF champion then resident in France.

The inter-county championship semi-finals took place on March 6th, Devon playing old rivals Sussex away from home. Norman could not get away from College. His absence from the Devon line-up was critical, coupled as it was with the loss, to a Californian university scholarship, of Colin Haycraft, Devon's number two player. Sussex won 5-0 and went on to defeat Surrey in the final to secure a fourth consecutive inter-county title.

The arrangements for away international squash matches were financially more complicated than for home fixtures. Norman's invitation letter for the last match in the series, against Scotland on Friday March 19th at the Edinburgh Sports Club 'probably starting at 5 p.m.' was mostly taken up with the travel arrangements: "I have provisionally booked third class sleepers on the 10.35 p.m. train from King's Cross on the night of Thursday, the 18th. The SRA will pay the travelling expenses. The Scottish SRA has offered to put up the bachelors, permanent or 'temporary', but players accompanied by their wives will have to stay in a hotel at their own expense, I am afraid."

The 'perk' this time appeared to be unqualified: "It is usual for the Scottish SRA to provide tickets for the Calcutta Cup match on the Saturday and I expect they will do so again."

England again put out a strong team, with Norman played at fourth string, behind Fairbairn, Wilson and Seymour-Hayden, with Dick Hawkey replacing Phillips at five in his first match for England after a period of knocking on the door. Norman defeated C. N. Campbell for the loss of six points and, as expected, England won 5-0, only Wilson dropping a game. Norman did get to the rugby, and the Scots were beaten there too, 13-3.

The squash season ended with the Drysdale Cup at the RAC on April 5th. Norman was there to see Humphrey Truman play. Humphrey did not disgrace himself, following Chris Ford's example by losing in the quarter-final to Nigel Broomfield, who went on to beat Jeremy Lyon in the final. The season had seen a broadening of the

game's frontiers. Apart from the arrival of another member of the Khan clan, Roshan, there had been the Dutch team's tour of England, while Wales had visited Scandinavia and beaten both Sweden and Denmark. This increased international activity was part of the SRA's plan to raise the standard of play in the weaker countries, the success of which was shown a few years later when Peter Gerlow from Denmark became the first overseas-based winner of the Drysdale Cup in 1960 and 1961. It had also been the first season in which Norman had played in all the international matches. This was for the first time possible, due to the fact that he no longer played hockey for England and was thus available for squash selection. He showed that although he could no longer dominate his compatriots he could still beat all but the top two or three in the country.

* * * * * * * * *

Less squash; heavy defeats to Fairbairn and Safirullah; success in the Londonderry; and Suffolk champion

The 1954-5 season saw Norman play only four matches, plus two for the OFs in the Londonderry. The second Frank Strawson Memorial squash match, which pitched the SRA against the Jesters, took place on Armistice Day. All five of the England team who had played in two of the three internationals the previous season were involved, but the two best of these, Fairbairn and Wilson, were playing at one and two for the SRA, whilst the other three, Norman, Seymour-Hayden and Brian Phillips, were at one, two and three for the Jesters. For Norman and Seymour-Hayden this was a tough assignment, particularly for Norman whose first game of the season this was, and who logically should have played at two, behind Seymour-Hayden.

'Fairbairn the current champion beat N. F. Borrett, many times champion in the past, 9-4, 9-0, 9-0. Not only was there five years age difference but Borrett was clearly not fit enough for a game as fast as this. Nonetheless there were glimpses in the first game of the pace which Borrett used to be able to set up, a pace which other amateurs could not live with. As it was, once Fairbairn had drawn ahead to win the first game, there was only one in it, and the champion looked to be as quick and consistent as ever'.

The Jesters won 3-2, their three victories coming at three,

four and five. Seymour-Hayden was beaten 3-1 by Wilson, whose squash was continuing to improve. Norman, asked in later life why he put himself through this, losing to players who could not live with him when he was fitter and younger, gave the simple response: "I loved the game; I couldn't give it up."

Two weeks later he played his second game of the season, this time for England against Wales in Cardiff on November 25th, the eve of the Welsh Championship. Wales were led by D. B. Hughes, the outstanding player to play for Wales since they entered the international scene. England did not put out its strongest team, neither Fairbairn nor Wilson being available. Seymour-Hayden this time played at one, above Norman at two, and lost a close encounter with Hughes, who thereby reversed the result of their contests the previous season, in the finals of both the Welsh and Midlands championships. Hughes thus made history by recording the first ever victory for Wales in a tie against England. Norman defeated R.Butterworth at two, not without some difficulty, 10-8, 9-8, 9-5. Hawkey at three and John Barrington at five won easily but and Peter Doggart dropped a game before beating Needham.

Norman's availability for the Londonderry Cup, played in London one week later, meant a lot to the OFs, who were thus able to turn out a good side. With Norman playing the top match, and Hinds at two, the side had a strong tail, with John Davey, the Suffolk county player, at three, Humphrey Truman at four and Michael Evans at five. This side comfortably beat the Old Stoics to reach the fourth round, when they lost a close match to the Old Salopians 3-2, Norman and Evans winning but Hinds, Davey and Truman losing.

Norman was in London for SRA Executive Committee meetings during the Amateur in early January and saw some of the play. Seymour-Hayden reached the semi-final for the fourth successive year, losing to Wilson in a game where there were too many lets: as BLT&S commented 'this often happens in games in which Seymour-Hayden plays, but on this occasion there were twice as many lets given against Wilson as against his opponent.' Fairbairn tamed the young Army champion Mike Perkins in the other semi-final. A very long, 80 minute, final, which made great physical demands on both players, saw Wilson deservedly achieve his ambition of winning the championship after twice being runner-up. Fairbairn later announced his retirement from championship squash, but, taking his lead from Norman, was to play for England for some years to come.

Norman did not play in the other two squash internationals against Scotland and Ireland, and was far from match fit when, on February 22nd he was telephoned by Henry Hayman at the SRA, and asked to take the place of the ill Alan Fairbairn in a British team to play an Overseas Professional Team, in a memorial match in aid of the widow of Abdul Bari. Bari had died of a brain thrombosis at the age of 33, only eighteen months after his appointment as professional at the Junior Carlton, where he had established such mastery of the court that he was able to beat his redoubtable cousin Hashim there.

Norman had played and lost to Bari in the Amateurs against Professionals match only one year before, and was happy to participate in this event, which would raise some funds for Bari's widow and 2 year old child. Norman had four days in which to get some practice, in the cold open-backed Framlingham courts against the boys, and against Martin Irving, the College French teacher who had played his first inter-county match for Suffolk that winter. But these conditions were very foreign to the hot-house and the fast ball of the Bruce Court at the Lansdowne Club. In younger days, a fitter Norman could make that dramatic transition easily, but not now. He was defeated in straight games by Safirullah of Pakistan, a brother-in-law of Hashim Khan, and father of Mohibullah Khan, later a British Open champion.

The Overseas side was a remarkable one. Hashim himself played at one, with his nephew Roshan at two, his brother Azam at three, and at five, Jamal Din, not one of the Khan clan, five times Open Veteran champion from 1968. Hashim had won the British Open for six consecutive years from 1950, then lost it to Roshan in 1956 before regaining it from Azam the following year. Azam then took over, winning the event for the next four years.

From those heady heights, Norman returned to the grass roots. On Sunday March 20th, the final of the Suffolk closed squash championship took place at Ipswich Squash Club. He had never entered this tournament before and he was curious to see how he would perform. In fact he went rapidly through the early rounds and did not take long over the final, beating Brian Belle, Suffolk county cricket captain, Oxford double blue, and former holder of the county squash title, 9-0, 9-1, 9-0.

Devon had won the South-Western area section of the inter-county squash tournament, and faced Sussex in the inter-area round. Norman was not able to get away from school duties to play and Devon lost 5-0. His squash career was easing to a close. Or so everyone thought.

HOCKEY – THE SUFFOLK YEARS

Norwich Grasshoppers; Suffolk; the East;
England captaincy restored;
joint Home Countries champions.

Shortly after moving to Framlingham in the summer of 1950 Norman joined Norwich Grasshoppers, Norfolk's top club, where two other OFs, Frank Jerrey and Gerald Mitchell played. He played whenever he could, but his attendance was inevitably confined to the pre-Christmas period due to his Easter term College and international commitments. He found that part-time club hockey wasn't fair on anyone and he retired from the club after two half-seasons in 1950 and 1951.

The goal Norman set himself every autumn was to build his fitness so that by the time of the Amateur squash championships, in the first week of January, both his speed and his stamina would be highly tuned. Just as in the Allhallows days, he had little or no opportunity for competitive squash matches so the fitness regime comprised daily running, squash practice usually by himself, hockey dribbling and shooting by himself, and occasional hockey matches for the Grasshoppers and other teams. Term ended on December 16th 1950, enabling Norman to play a mid-week game of hockey on December 20th for Cambridge University Wanderers against Oxford University Occasionals in the annual clash at Beckenham. The sides included 10 international players. The Daily Telegraph was struck by Norman's speed: '*Though the pitch was slow and slippery he dribbled fast enough to beat his man and his passing made openings for others.*' Norman showed brilliant stickwork and scored one of the best goals of the game in a 4-3 Light Blue victory. Three days later Norman had to turn down an interesting invitation to play for the Schoolmasters side which played Tulse Hill in a revival of this popular pre-war fixture. Some great names did manage to turn out, including David Milford.

In his first Framlingham Easter term Norman managed to fit in six hockey matches, twice for the East, once for the HA and for Suffolk, and the two England trials. Having applied to the East and to Suffolk to reverse his affiliation to the West and to Somerset, he was then unable to play in the East hockey trial on January 13th, as it clashed with the Amateur squash championship. The East selectors, delighted that he had rejoined the fold, were unconcerned at this and picked him for the first divisional match, against the South at Folkestone on February 3rd. The Evening Standard, which followed hockey closely, predicted that the game would be the best of all the season's divisional matches. '*One man who could swing the fortunes of the*

match more than most is Norman Borrett, back now with the East, where he won his spurs as a Cambridge undergraduate, after a spell with the West. In the Occasionals – Wanderers match, I saw him carve gaps in a defence of much the same standing as the South's. Tomorrow he may do the same again. Alternatively, if in the mood which sometimes takes him to play 'fourth-half' he could lose the game for the East. Three halves are enough; four forwards are not.'

Norman proved to be in his most attacking mood. '*Borrett and Forster stood out as the most constructive forwards on the field. Borrett was at his very best and gave both his wing player, Hudson, and Holmes in the centre, many perfect passes which should have been turned to account.*' Three days later Norman was in South West London, playing for the Hockey Association against the touring South African Universities team at Motspur Park. He was in good shooting form, scoring five times as the HA demolished their young opponents 9-1.

Norman's third game, East's match against North at Lincoln on February 17th was abandoned for an unplayable pitch after 20 minutes' play, and his fourth was five days later for Suffolk against Norfolk at Eaton Park, Norwich. He scored the first two goals for his new county. '*Much of the Suffolk danger lay in Borrett's scheming but he was quietened if not entirely curtailed by Self*', the Norfolk centre half and England player, and Norfolk proceeded to a fine 4-3 win.

The Times, looking forward to the first English hockey trial on March 3rd at Felsted School, put forward a number of player permutations for each position, until it reached the inside left berth where "*N. F. Borrett is, of course, a certainty.*" The Felsted game was of interest to Norman for a number of reasons. He had played against the School there several times when he was a boy at Framlingham; and he would be visiting the school regularly over the coming years in his new capacity as Framlingham's hockey coach. He did not know then that John Cockett would join Felsted as a teacher after graduating from Cambridge. At inside left for the senior side, Norman scored in a 4-3 win. This put him in to the final trial two Saturdays later at Northampton, playing for England, whilst Cockett, who had played well, was selected to oppose him, at right half for the Rest.

Norman '*an automatic choice [for the first international] at inside left, was at his best*' at Northampton, scoring twice as the English XI beat the Rest 6-1. '*On both sides the half back play was excellent, with Cockett, who was opposed to Borrett and Wootton, the English left wing, the most prominent on the field. Even so, the artistry and fine positioning of Walford, his opposite number on the England side, gained him preference over Cockett who is an international player in the making'.*

The school holidays were as always a busy period for Norman, with the three home countries internationals and, this year, one additional game against Sussex. The first hockey international, on March 31st, saw England, captained by Micky Walford, achieve a clear, but not altogether convincing, 4-1 win over the Welsh at Hawarden. Norman scored the second goal after working his way through the defence, from a pass by Forster, and tricking the keeper as he came out. In the second half the passing of the English inside forwards *'had the Welsh defence repeatedly in a tangle.'* The Times thought the Welsh deserved a better result for their spirit. *'Special mention must be made of P. G. Clark, at centre half, and J. P. Taylor, in the forward line.'* Norman, as usual, passed his dinner menu card round the teams after the meal, and under the signature of J.P. Taylor is written "Thanks for the lesson".

Norman was at Hove county cricket ground on April 7th playing for H.L.Lewis' XI against Sussex, and one week later was heading for Dublin for England's match against the Ireland side. The Times commented that *'much will depend on N.F. Borrett at inside-left, who is playing as well as ever this season. If however matters are not going well for England by half-time it might well pay to experiment with Borrett at centre-forward. With his fine stickwork and good tackling back he should make an ideal centre-forward.'* The result, a 1-1 draw was a fair result, the Irish putting up their usual spirited display. Norman *'worked tremendously hard',* and Walford did not adopt The Times' suggestion of moving him during the game from inside left to the middle of the attack. The Times believed that England's half back line failed to assert itself and generally was *'not up to its usually high standard.'* The selectors were of the same opinion and took decisive action, dropping captain and right half Micky Walford, and centre half Ledger for the forthcoming Scottish match. John Cockett, still at Cambridge, was awarded his first cap in place of Walford.

On the following Saturday, April 21st, England played their final match in the home nations series against Scotland at the Lever Brothers ground at Port Sunlight, Cheshire. The pen portraits of the players in the sixpenny programme included this for Norman, who was restored to the captaincy in Walford's absence: *'A phenomenal figure both on the squash court and the hockey field. His play has that indefinable something, made of application, genius and sheer magic. Schoolmaster and hockey author. Played 20 times for England.'*

Perhaps the restoration of the captaincy spurred him on, for as the Evening Standard reported, under the headline 'Borrett

leads England win', *'England had an inspired leader in N.F. Borrett, the captain of Suffolk, who at left inner was a constant danger to the Scotland defence. Time after time he split the defence open with his astute moves.'* The victory by four goals to two, with Norman contributing one, made England joint champions with Ireland. Cockett's debut was a success, and he was, in the view of The Times, one of the best half backs on the field. So began a career which would include 37 England and 18 GB caps.

John Cockett was in many ways similar to Norman as a multi-talented sportsman, Cambridge double blue in hockey and cricket, eight first class cricket matches for Cambridge and 80 Minor County games for Bucks, a natural at all games and an East Anglian schoolmaster. He recalls his first impressions of Norman:

"I first came across him when he was captain of England hockey and I wondered who this forthright, stern, commanding figure was, who liked to hog the ball at inside left (my cross-pass from right half was popular if he was in position!). A daunting experience for the first game or two. He did not suffer fools gladly and could present a forbidding face until one got to know him - thereafter he was great fun with a strong sense of humour. He was quite a different person with those who were a bit nervous of him and with those who knew him well enough to pull his leg, which he enjoyed enormously. He was such a talented performer at any round ball game he played, not many have equalled his versatility."

Over the Whitsun weekend in mid-May, the Hockey Association marked the 1951 Festival of Britain with an international tournament at Twickenham Rugby Union ground. Three matches were played, and the event culminated in a black tie dinner for the four men's teams and the Scottish and English ladies' teams. In their first match on the Saturday England, with the same side which had played so well against Scotland, were poor in losing to Belgium by the only goal of the game. Whilst the ground was not a good hockey surface, England did not perform. The Times correspondent commented that *'almost without exception each and every one of the English defence was obsessed with the idea that Borrett was the only forward on the field and with increasing regularity clearances, many of them half topped from lack of practice, went in Borrett's direction. They were invariably intercepted by Goossens the dominant Belgian centre-half.'* Monday's 3-2 loss to Holland showed England in a

ABOVE: England v Scotland April 21st 1951. Scottish keeper Stewart saves from England centre forward Campbell, with Norman mid-goalmouth.

better light and on Tuesday, in an easier match and on a better surface at St. Mary's Hospital ground, Teddington, England dispatched France 5-0 with Norman, who captained the side in all three games, scoring four.

R. L. Hollands' end of season critique of the England XI of 1951 identified as the weak point, *'unmistakably, and rather surprisingly, the half-back line'*, a surprise because in 1950 Walford and Robinson had been the making of the side. Walford however never quite touched his best form in 1951. As for the forward line, only once did they all strike form together; *'N. F. Borrett (Suffolk) who has retained his form and fitness wonderfully well over the twelve years he has played for England, showed himself once again a thoughtful and constructive forward. Unfortunately both for him and for England, his abilities in this direction are too well known, with the result that he is invariably the object of too many passes from his own defence and becomes in consequence a target on which the opposition concentrate, with crippling results for the forward line as a whole.'*

The HA wrote to a number of players during early April, to enquire if they were able to participate in a British Hockey Board tour of South Africa, from July 31st until September 18th, encompassing 14 or 15 matches in Rhodesia and the Union. Each player would need to contribute £50 to the cost of the tour, plus £12 for the cost of his equipment. As the team would be put up in private houses, the only additional cost would be a player's own incidental expenses, which would not need to exceed £10. The letter ended, after requesting a prompt response as to availability and ability to pay the sum of £62, with the bizarre request that the player should also advise:

'(3) Your age and playing experience, giving particulars of school or college, and occupation; and (4) In what positions you are able to play.'

Norman promptly replied, indicating his willingness to go. He had never been to Africa and was delighted at the prospect. The squad of 17 which was then selected comprised four Englishmen - Norman, as vice captain, Derek Day the goalkeeper, Peter Smith the newly capped full back, and Neil Forster the Cambridge inside forward; six Irish led by Stan de Lacy, the right winger who would captain the party; four Scots and three Welsh.

BELOW: The sun shone
in Frinton whilst Norman
was in South Africa.
Queen Magazine.

Great Britain and Ireland hockey tour to South Africa 1951.

At the end of the College summer term, the family's usual routine was for Mullie and the boys to head for her in-laws at Frinton whilst Norman went to Devon for the month of August, where he would play half a dozen games for Devon in the Minor County cricket championship. But in 1951 hockey occupied Norman for most of the College summer holidays. As soon as the term ended, he travelled to London to be fitted for his blazer and the other kit required for the tour to South Africa. His kit would be packed into his personal travel case, now smartly emblazoned with two bands in the team colours, painted on at his request by Brian Ivory, top artist at the College at the time. "Norman seemed pleased enough. I still have his signature in my autograph book."

In the last week of July the hockey tourists set off on the long air journey from London to Rhodesia. On arrival at the capital, Salisbury, the team transferred to Bulawayo and, in a pipe-opener to the tour, played the Rhodesian national side. The hosts put up fierce resistance against the British-Irish team's superior stickwork and tactics before succumbing 2-0, Norman scoring from a long corner. Still finding their land legs, the team lost their second match 2-3 to a Rhodesia Junior XI, but made amends by beating the national team again 4-0.

On August 11th the tourists played their opening game in South Africa, against Griqualand West / Bechuanaland, winning 3-0, the first goal coming from Norman as he picked up on the run a centre from de Lacy on the right wing. The team then drew with Western Province in Cape Town, Norman scoring the only goal. The first Test against South Africa was played at Hartley Vale, Cape Town, on August 18th, just two weeks into the tour. A goal down early on, the team struggled and, though Norman broke through

> 'beat the defence on his own with a brilliant swerving run and a shot the goalkeeper never saw.'

more than once, his shots were well saved. However, two goals in the second half put the tourists on top and the match was won 3-1 with a goal from Norman who 'beat the defence on his own with a brilliant swerving run and a shot the goalkeeper never saw'.

Having beaten Eastern Province at Port Elizabeth 3-0, with Norman scoring the final goal 'after swerving his way through the

Below: Mrs. Borrett with her seventeen-month-old son, Timothy, on the beach at Frinton

Province defence by brilliant dribbling' the British Irish combination then drove North to Queenstown to play Border. Their first experience of a gravel pitch unsettled the team and they were 3-1 down at half time, the goal having come from Norman's conversion of a penalty bully. In the second half the better stickwork and control of the two insides, Norman and Neil Forster, both of whom scored, enabled pride to be salvaged in a remarkable 5-5 draw.

Back at Port Elizabeth, Norman opened the scoring in the second Test against South Africa, with an opportunist goal from close range. The equaliser came from South Africa's centre forward Peter Winslow, later to become a South African Test cricketer, and the two goalkeepers saw plenty of action as neither team was able to score again. The tourists then travelled a long way North to Pretoria for the game against Transvaal; a good grass pitch was to the liking of GB&I who got well on top, winning 3-1, with goals from Walker and Norman against one from Winslow. It was then back to the coast for the third Test, in Durban, where the home goalkeeper Clarke played a decisive part in South Africa's 2-1 victory, making many fine saves, including one in the second half from one of Norman's short corners which looked a goal all the way. Winslow scored both goals for the hosts.

BELOW: The GB&I hockey tourists leave for South Africa, July 1951. Vice captain Norman extreme right, Captain Stan de Lacy two to his right.

Peter Smith, the England full-back, saw Norman in a different light on the tour: "On tour with the British Isles side, of which he was vice captain, I discovered that there was another side to Norman; whilst he was enormously self-confident, which gave him a slightly arrogant air, he had a very humorous and friendly side when he was not competing, and we struck up a friendship which lasted until he died. I found him great company, and kind, but on the field nothing was going to stop him! He and I were 'billeted' together quite a lot, and he was always much admired, and liked, by our hosts – particularly our hostesses! Norman's behaviour was always impeccable and, unlike the rest of us, he consumed only a little alcohol.

Norman only knew one way to play a game, and that was flat out; I never saw him take it easy. One example of this was when we played the Durban Test against South Africa. Norman had been challenged to a game of squash by Bill Clements, the English professional based in Torquay with whom he had played in England before each Amateur Championship. Unfortunately Clements never turned up and, since there was quite a gallery to watch the

...he made mince-meat of me... I hardly scored a point in the one set we played.

match, Norman 'demanded' that I go on court with him since, as he said, 'all these folk have come to see me play!' Foolishly I accepted the challenge and I do not believe he would have played any harder had it been the final of the Amateur; he made mince-meat of me and even asked 'what do you think you're playing for?'! I hardly scored a point in the one set we played."

The South African Squash Championships took place in Johannesburg in August. The squash press had some months earlier carried the story that Norman was hoping to play in the Championships whilst on the British hockey tour. It did not happen. If it had, it would have been some feat, even by Norman's unusual appetite for non-stop sport.

A good grass surface at Bloemfontein against Orange Free State again suited GB&I and the forwards moved and linked well. Walker scored in the first half and Norman from a penalty bully in the second to secure a 2-0 win. At the same venue, the next match was a very close affair against S.A. Universities ending in a 2-2 draw. The heavy travel schedule began to take its toll as the team moved on to Pietermaritzburg where they lost 2-0 to Natal.

The last game of the tour was on Saturday September 15th at Johannesburg where the fourth and final Test was held. A tight game was fought out to a 1-1 draw, but GB&I would have won had they been able to put away even one of the many penalty corners awarded to them. Norman, as the chief penalty striker, found it difficult to penetrate the home team's defensive screen of three men in the goal and the centre half just two yards in front of the keeper. Post tour analysis focused on this inability of the tourists to score from penalty corners, notably in the four Tests when only one goal resulted from no less than 42 penalty corner awards. Two reasons were put forward – the tight S.A. defence and the very strict application of the 'sticks' law. Seven weeks after their departure, the team regained UK soil on Tuesday September 18th, having travelled some 12,000 miles and played 15 matches including four Tests, winning seven matches with five drawn and three lost.

The Test series had been drawn, with one win each and two draws. The team had had to face a number of difficulties

> Seven weeks after their departure, the team regained UK soil on Tuesday September 18th, having travelled some 12,000 miles and played 15 matches including four Tests, winning seven matches with five drawn and three lost.

on top of the inevitable lack of cohesion in a team comprising players from four countries: they faced unfamiliar surfaces and altitudes, most of the pitches being harder and faster than UK ones, and the local interpretation of the obstruction rule proved to be lenient by UK standards. The injuries suffered by de Lacy, Thomas and Theobald, all forwards, meant that Norman, at the age of almost 34, played in virtually every game, and was the chief goal scorer with 11 of the 32 goals scored. Hockey News' review of the tour picked out full-backs Peter Smith and

George O'Hara, wing-half P. G. Clark and forwards Borrett, Forster and Davidson as the outstanding players. Norman and his colleagues had been treated to marvellous hospitality wherever they went, had experienced some of Africa's most compelling sights, and made many friends. Norman was to revisit some of those friends four years later when he led the British squash team to South Africa.

The team's England goalkeeper, Derek Day, 14 times capped by England between 1951 and 1953, felt that he got to know Norman better during the tour:

"I had just played my first season in the England team, in which Norman was very much the 'senior pro', being, apart from Micky Walford, the only England survivor from the 1948 GB Olympic side. We were given very generous hospitality by the South Africans, and we travelled a lot by train and coach, so there were good opportunities to get to know one's team-mates. Norman was very fit, playing in most of the games, and although beginning to slow up a little, remained a fine player. He was a good tourist, joining in everything, with many stories to tell, and was always cheerful. Despite the aura which surrounded him as a remarkable sportsman – a real Corinthian – he mixed in with everyone."

C. J. Kaplan, a member of the South African hockey selection committee, and the man who played fifth string for the South African squash side that played four Tests against Norman's touring team in 1955, wrote a review of the hockey tour for Hockey News. He concluded that hockey was in better health in South Africa than had been expected; to have drawn the Test series had perhaps been a trifle fortunate, but the provinces had also done well, defeating the tourists once and drawing with them three times. Kaplan was complimentary about the play of both Peter Smith - 'I do not know of a better attacking full-back' - and of Norman Borrett: 'Between the two 25s the British and Irish forwards were, on balance, perhaps superior to the South Africans. Borrett, their inside-left, who captains England, is a great player. He has made a deep study of the game (his recently published book should be read by all players), he works tirelessly, his stickwork and ball control is a joy, and he made countless openings for his fellow forwards.'

A week late for what was only his second winter term as a master at Framlingham, Norman got down to hard work in his Geography and English classes, getting to know the new year's pupils.

A famous drop goal;
John Conroy knocks at the door;
captain of the Triple Crown winners;
but no ticket to Helsinki

In the autumn run-up to the 1952 Amateur Squash championship, Norman kept himself fit with his usual running programme, augmented by three squash matches, a hockey match in Scotland, a rugby game at the College, and his two customary hockey games in London just before Christmas.

The hockey match came only three weeks into the term, in Edinburgh. Norman had obtained his headmaster's permission to travel to Scotland to attend the Scottish Hockey Association celebration of its golden jubilee with two matches on November 3rd; the first between an England and Wales combination versus Scotland and Ireland; the other between Scotland and Holland. No fewer than 10 of the 16 players who had toured South Africa featured in the first match and the tourists exchanged reminiscences and photographs. The press identified Norman and Neil Forster as the two outstanding forwards for the Anglo Welsh side, as they won 3-1. Following the match a jubilee dinner was held. The players had to purchase their own tickets for the dinner, but were evidently not likely to over-imbibe: *'Tickets including wine (limited) 25 shillings.'* This was arguably at odds with the invitation, in the Scottish HA's welcoming letter addressed to the players, *'to drink deep of the hospitality offered to you by the Association.'*

On December 1st Norman played his first game of rugby since before the war. The College versus the Old Framlinghamians rugby match was always keenly anticipated by the pupils, who looked forward to seeing familiar recent leavers in the OF line-up. Almost all of those selected were regularly playing good club rugby and they tended to be in their late teens or twenties. During Saturday morning lessons on the day of the match, rumour had it that one of the Old Boys had withdrawn through illness and, as it had not apparently proved possible to find a last minute replacement, Mr. Borrett, the English and Geography master, had agreed to step in.

The College was alive with expectancy as to how he would deal with the full weight of fifteen lusty schoolboys intent on making him, a 34 year old who had not played, or even coached, rugby for some 12 years, suffer in the way all schoolboys wish to see their teachers suffer. Rugby was not a sport for which "Sir" was famous. It was, however, their sport and they were going to show him.

In those days, it was obligatory for the entire school to watch all home 1st XV rugby matches, but the touchlines that December day were even more packed than usual. Norman played at full back, attempting to afford himself some protection ahead of the Amateur Squash Championship in only one month's time. In the opening minutes the Old Boys, having the heavier pack, won a scrum and the ball went down the three quarter line. Norman broke into the line at great speed and, showing a clean pair of heels to the College defence, touched down in the corner. More was to come. The Old Boys were awarded a succession of penalties and, being unfamiliar with the individual skills of some of his team, the OF captain selected a number of different kickers to convert the penalties into points. All failed. When a further penalty was awarded the captain was clearly unsure to whom to entrust the goal attempt. A general chorus broke out around the ground of 'give it to Borrett', and the captain did as he was bid.

The penalty was perhaps five yards short of the half-way line, some forty yards out, near the touch-line. The previous, unsuccessful, penalty-takers had place-kicked, as usual. Not Norman. Wearing his lightweight hockey boots rather than the heavier rugby boots designed to aid kicking, he took the ball in his hands, looked up towards the distant posts, trotted forward three or four paces and let fly with a drop kick. The touchlines cheered madly as the heavy leather ball sailed over the bar. The College side, suitably deflated, lost the match to the OFs 22-12.

On the following Monday, when the drop goal was still being discussed, Norman took his usual Geography class with one of the junior forms, first lesson after lunch. Gerald Garnett was in that class: "One of the braver pupils drew on the blackboard in brief outline a diminutive match-stick man drop-kicking a rugby ball over the posts, seemingly miles away. Upon their hero's arrival the boys stood up, as was the custom in those well-mannered days, and then resumed their seats. Norman espied the blackboard cartoon, turned to the class with the sharpest of looks and demanded to know who had done it. 'I did, sir' came the artist's reply. 'Rub it off' commanded Norman, tossing him the blackboard cleaner. The apparent severity he would adopt at moments such as this enabled him to keep control, whether in the classroom or on the sports field, but the twinkle in his eye gave away his true feelings".

A number of the pupils who watched that game speak of

his having hurt his leg, or perhaps more significantly his hip, in dropping that goal. One such was Norman Mayhew: "I believe this one kick had a lasting and accelerated effect on his right hip and probably curtailed his sporting life by some years."

The pre-Christmas hockey contest between Cambridge University Wanderers and Oxford University Occasionals was a good run out, amongst strong company. Norman was the chief instigator of the Wanderers' best movements and according to The Times showed '*all his old cleverness.*' Two days later he was at Tulse Hill for the annual game for the Schoolmasters against the host club. This resulted in a 4-1 victory for the teachers, made possible by a stream of through passes from Norman to his winger and by '*a typical Borrett goal*' as he dribbled clean through the Tulse Hill defence and slipped the ball past the keeper to settle the result.

The teams contained a number of distinguished sportsmen, including John Cockett at right-half for the Masters, now at Felsted, and John Dewes, the Cambridge and England cricketer, at left-back for Tulse Hill.

The food poisoning at the turn of the year which forced Norman to scratch from the Amateur squash took a lot out of him, and he was not at his best when resuming hockey activity on January 12th, for the East against Midlands. East were beaten 6-4 and although he was, in the eyes of The Times reporter, seen still to be suffering from the effects of the illness, Norman scored the goal of the game in the second half: having gained possession near the circle, he sold a dummy, dribbled past two defenders to the back line, and beat the goalkeeper at close quarters with a flick shot, an '*effort which alone merited a share of the spoils for the East*'.

He worked hard on regaining strength, and on January 20th played his tremendous squash match against Karim in the annual Amateurs v Professionals tie. It was Olympic year and he was keen to make the Olympic hockey team for a second time. He increased his runs in the roads around the College, sometimes with a stick and ball which he would rebound off the verge into his path, and sometimes running with the boys in the squash or hockey teams. Mullie remembers Norman's hockey pitch routine for training: "he'd run slowly across the goal line and then tear up the side lines. And I'd say: 'You'll do something to that heart of yours' and he'd say: 'I've always done this.'"

During the term he frequently played for spells in College 1st XI hockey practices, admonishing players as they fell out of position, and driving them on to greater endeavour. Norman Mayhew, who was then in the Colts side, also remembers seeing Norman practising dribbling and shooting by himself on the Back; "What was remarkable was his ability to play international hockey without the benefit of regular club hockey. Another who was able to do this was John Cockett of Felsted."

Ian Foster recollects the remarkable level of stamina Norman possessed: "The First XI devised a bet that after our hockey practices on the Back, Norman could not beat us running around the perimeter of the pitch. The handicap which he was given was that as he finished each lap, another of us, fresh, would start against him. We put our best runner as last man, in the hope that Norman would have tired by then and would lose the bet. We were of course all pretty fit, but we never won the bet."

Another of the many pupils at the College who were keen on sport was John Edwards. Having first encountered Norman at the age of 11 in late July 1948 when he had been taken by his father to watch GB Hockey's pre-Olympic practice match at Thorpeness, he was greatly excited when the legendary OF joined the staff. John was soon to become "one of those who had the benefit of being subject to the Borrett style of discipline, being chased round the hockey pitch and being whacked up the backside if we were either not quick or agile enough, in my case both, to the accompaniment of 'get a move on boy'."

On February 2nd when East met West at the West Herts ground at Watford, Norman found himself playing against Micky Walford, who had announced his retirement from international hockey at the beginning of the season, saying: "I realised last year I was getting slower. I have also lost the urge to train hard and practice, which is essential, particularly as I can never start playing till the end of January." Micky played at right half for the West in this match and was thus opposed by Norman and Hudson, who proved to be the best wing pair on the pitch and who gave him a very difficult time. West defeated East by 4-3 with a penalty bully goal in the last few minutes.

The pre-Olympics fitness programme had however received a severe jolt. Norman felt an ache in his right hip during this match, and the joint stiffened up afterwards. He was worried about it, but, suspecting it might be something serious, decided not to reveal the real injury, describing it as a torn muscle in his leg. He had nearly a month, until the first England hockey trial on March 1st, to let the hip settle down. He decided he would not play hockey or squash in the meantime, and he immediately withdrew from the Irish squash international on February 8th, and, with great regret, from the Devon county squash inter-area match against Middlesex. The hip appeared to be better within two weeks and caused him no difficulty in playing squash for the OFs in their big Londonderry Cup match in the last week of February. He knew he could play in the hockey trial.

After some years of urging from a number of the hockey commentators, led by R. L. Hollands, the selectors experimented in that trial, at the Leys School, Cambridge, by picking Norman at centre forward rather than inside left. Given that his stickwork and shooting were generally better than any of the alternative choices it was not, for the selectors, a great gamble.

But for Norman this was a worrying time: he was 34 years old, having to hide a hip condition, keen to play in another Olympics, and John Conroy was snapping at his heels for the inside left berth. Could he continue to perform?

The selectors puzzled a number of observers by excluding both Hudson, who had done well as Norman's wing partner in the two East games, and Cockett from either of the teams, whilst giving another chance at right half to Micky Walford, who had been persuaded to put his retirement on hold. As the match unfolded Norman's worries receded: the hip felt fine and he did well, scoring a goal and initiating many neat moves. 4–1 down with 15 minutes to go, the senior side scored three times as the clever stickwork of Norman and Conroy opened up the junior side's defence.

The date of the second, and final, English trial at Reading on March 15th represented a clash for Norman – on the evening of Friday 14th England were to play a squash international against Scotland in Edinburgh. For Norman the squash match was of considerably less consequence than a trial crucial to his chances of retaining his place in the hockey side. He had again been chosen in the middle of the attack, captaining the England XI against the Rest. Cockett was restored at right half and Hudson at left wing, with Conroy now at inside left in the junior side, the Rest. The trial gave few answers to the selectors' questions, the Rest winning 1–0, with Norman shooting well but failing to score. Conroy was transferred at half time to the England side alongside Norman but played less well there than he had in the first half alongside Cooke. Norman could feel Conroy's breath on his neck.

John Conroy was a player of a similar style to Norman,

with brilliant stickwork. It seemed unlikely that the two of them could readily fit into the same side. There was a degree of rivalry between them, the old dog keeping the young pup from usurpation of the leading role in the kennel. Norman was a master of the through pass. A tale, no doubt apocryphal, has it that Conroy was selected to play in an important game, where the selectors would be present, at left wing, outside Norman at inside left; Conroy spent a fruitless afternoon chasing after Norman's through passes but they always beat him to the goal line. The scandalous suggestion was made that when Norman was later asked by the selectors what he thought of the young Conroy, he opined that Conroy wasn't quick enough, thus ensuring that the young pretender had to wait a little longer to launch his distinguished international career...

...Norman had again felt his hip in the Final Trial. One of the England selectors noted him limping as he left the field and asked if he was all right. Norman replied that he was fine: "I am just suffering from blisters."

Norman was due to captain Suffolk against Lincolnshire the week after the trial, but withdrew in order to give his hip further recuperation time. It had settled down by the next weekend, March 29th, when England were to play Wales at Bristol in the first international.

The international selectors were faced with the same difficult decision as in 1951, of how to accommodate two fine inside lefts. Then it had been Borrett and Stocks; now it was Borrett and Conroy. The dilemma was made worse by the fact that Cooke at centre forward was at least as effective as Norman in that position. In the event the selectors decided to retain Cooke in the middle and to play Norman at inside left, thus dropping Conroy. As The Times neatly put it: '*Conroy is unlucky not to get a place in the side, but Borrett could not be left out.*'

England struggled at Bristol in the first half, playing with driving snow in their faces. Norman gave England the lead after 20 minutes, finishing off a clever move with a good goal. After half time, the three English insides played some fine hockey and dominated the Welsh. Hockey News saw Norman playing '*much more as a forward and much less as a half back*' in this game. In the second half he completed his hat-trick. '*No captain can do better than give his side encouragement by example.' The view of R. L. Hollands was that 'Borrett not only made openings, but was up in the circle to exploit them, and there are three goals to his name to prove it.'* Hollands had fine words also for Carnill who *'was in such a mood of magnificence that he not only answered for the sins of others, but would have played the Welshmen quite adequately on his own.'* Cooke scored two additional goals as England opened their 1952 campaign with a crushing 5-0 victory. The selectors made a significant change for the next match, against France, finding a place and a first cap, for Conroy, at left wing.

Comben Longstaff, the HA's Hon.Match Secretary, raised an International XI to play a memorial match in honour of the late President of the Bacchanalians at Edgbaston, the day after the Welsh match. Most of the England team played but Norman, quietly wanting to rest the hip, withdrew and John Conroy took his place.

The French match, at Boulogne, was won with a good display by 2-0, with Conroy readily justifying the award of his cap. He was to go on to win 32 caps over the next 8 years. The weather was "ghastly" (one of Norman's favourite words) and the 'hard tennis court' surface disturbed the rhythm the team had developed on grass. Carnill excelled again at right back and Fletcher at inside right was the pick of the forwards. Norman's after dinner speech was delivered in French, written on Framlingham College notepaper, and in rough translation read as follows:

Norman's French had evidently impressed his hosts, for the following weekend, at the Easter Hockey Festival at Lowestoft, he was asked by Racing Club de France to turn out for them on the Saturday, injuries on the Friday having left them two men short.

The English selectors kept the same team for the Irish match at Park Royal, White City, on April 19th save that Peter Smith came in at right back for Jones. Previewing the game The Times believed that *'Conroy is too clever a player to be left out of any side and there appears no reason why he should not be a success on the wing with Borrett as his partner.'* England's selectors evidently believed in a grand plan to lull the visitors into a false sense of homeliness, by playing the match at the Guinness Sports Ground in Park Royal, and by arranging the pre-match lunch to be hosted at the ground by Messrs Guinness.

The grand plan succeeded, as before a crowd of some 5,000 spectators and on a perfect pitch, England posted the largest score achieved against Ireland since 1931, winning 5-1, thanks to the good combination of their forwards and Conroy's two individual strikes in the later stages to put the game beyond the visitors. Apart from Conroy's two, Button, Cooke and Fletcher scored one each. Maurice Kittrell, later to become a skilful England inside forward, was an excited teenage spectator:

"Norman Borrett's sporting reputation was an inspiration to any schoolboy: a leading squash player, a cricketer of county

"I am going to speak to you in French, which will, I am well aware, be a considerable shock to the English who are present, and actually to me as well. Perhaps, my French friends, you might even so understand a little of what I am going to say. But before demonstrating to you my formidable knowledge of your language, I would first of all wish to thank you in the name of the English team for the warmth of your welcome. You have been truly friendly and we have tasted with pleasure every moment since our arrival. The match this afternoon was a great joy for everyone. This type of pitch is different from that which we have at home, but we found it very good. I wish to thank again the umpires and also the Club de l'Inquetiere, M. Blanchet, and the French Hockey Federation for everything that they have done. Now I ask the English team to drink to your health."

standard, and a hockey player who any young aspiring player wanted to emulate. So when I, as a keen young hockey player, heard that Norman was to play for England against Ireland at Park Royal, I knew that this was an opportunity not to be missed to see a master at work. His entrance on to the pitch was like the entrance of a Roman gladiator. There was an air of self-assurance, not arrogance, about this lithe athletic figure, carrying a clutch of sticks, one of which he immediately placed behind the Irish goal. 'Why has he done that?' I enquired of my neighbour, a seasoned player. 'That's his short corner stick' was the response; 'he strikes the ball like a rocket.'

When the game started I watched in awe as he fetched and carried and made passes which dissected the Irish defence. It was a lesson to all budding inside forwards. Short corners came and went and each time play was held up while Norman retrieved his special stick. Unfortunately he had an off day and although the shots were struck with great power – indeed rocket-like – none found the mark. Nevertheless I went home that day elated and encouraged."

Needing a win to capture the Triple Crown, England travelled to the Singer Recreation Ground at Clydebank, Glasgow on April 26th for the season's last international.

They achieved the required victory in style, by a margin of 7–0, giving England the remarkable scoreline for the season's three matches of 17 goals for and only one against. The Daily Telegraph attributed the success to Norman: 'N. F. Borrett, as against Wales, was the chief architect of victory". The Sunday Times reported that 'the feature of the match was the brilliant form of Borrett, who made the openings for five of the goals. Conroy also did well and these two were the best wing on the field'. R. L. Hollands'

view was that 'England's captain, N. F. Borrett, had recovered his touch today, and his passing was the foundation upon which others built their successful game.' Two goals each came from the three insides, Borrett, Cooke and Fletcher, and one from Conroy. The win marked the most successful season for years for Norman's team.

Just before England's first international of the season, against Wales on March 29th, the Olympic selectors announced the names of six players they had invited to take part in the forthcoming Olympic trials: the two English full backs, Carnill and Smith; the English left half, Robinson; the Welsh goalkeeper and centre half, Dadds and Clark; and the Scottish centre forward or left wing Davison. R. L. Hollands, writing in Hockey News, was critical of the selectors timing; by picking players without waiting to see how they performed in the home internationals they gave the impression that the six were in a category of their own, and created the potential to embarrass national selectors if they should want to drop any of the players named. He pointed out it would have been much better to have adopted the 1948 selectors' procedure of not announcing any names until after the last home international of the season: 'I hope no more names will be made public until the internationals are over and the full list of those to undergo training can be published.'

Within two weeks the selectors compounded their error by announcing five more names: the Welsh right wing, Saunders-Griffiths; the English right half, John Cockett; and three English inside forwards, Cooke, Conroy and Fletcher. Hockey News pointed out that the eleven names so far announced formed a complete team in their normal playing positions.

The GB selectors met again on April 19th, the day after the England v Ireland match, to pick the remaining 14 squad members and the GB team to play Holland on May 4th. These selections were therefore made before England's match against Scotland which was won 7–0. The names they announced caused some surprise as they included six English players who were not internationals, two of whom were selected for the GB match against Holland. The squad now consisted of all the members of the current English team, save for Norman, Schad the centre half, and Button the right wing.

The selectors then watched England's 7–0 win over Scotland, in which Norman excelled, and it may be that this influenced them to call up Norman on May 28th to take the place of one of the three members of the chosen 25 who had indicated they were unable to accept the invitation. But they stuck with the GB team they had already chosen to play

LEFT: England v Scotland April 26th 1952, Singer Recreation Ground, Clydebank. Top: Norman attacking the circle from inside left and Below: about to flick at an apprehensive goalkeeper.

extra ginger into them, especially at the start."

S. H. Saville, Olympic selector and former England captain, speaking at the AGM of the HA on July 18th confirmed the selectoral philosophy which had been adopted: "I wish that all the players who paid a shilling to the Olympic Fund could have seen the young British XI play and beat Holland in Amsterdam. It was their performance on that occasion that made me believe that the standard of hockey was on the upgrade. We have gone in for youth and speed in the selection of players for the Olympic trials."

Twelve nations entered the Helsinki Olympic hockey tournament. Eight of these were placed in the preliminary round, whilst the other four, being seeded, went into the first round to meet the four winners of the

Holland, in which only Conroy of England's Triple Crown winning forward line played, and the gamble paid off handsomely with a stunning 5-4 win. This success showed that speed and determination could form the basis of a good side and could throw a more mature team off balance.

The 25 man squad assembled at Lilleshall on Friday May 9th for the first training weekend, and again on May 24th. At that point 16 of the squad of 25 were chosen to travel to Helsinki. Norman was disappointed to be one of those left out, but he could see that the enthusiasm of the youthful party had turned them into a team with an exciting potential. He attended the third weekend's training but with the other eight was excused from the fourth one. Robert Fison, the team manager, added a longhand post script to his letter thanking Norman for his efforts at the three weekends: "Many thanks for your letter with which I agree. I will do my best to put some

preliminary round. The four seeds were the four semi-finalists from the 1948 Olympiad, India, GB, Pakistan and Netherlands. GB beat Belgium in the first round, which was in effect the quarter final, but lost to India 3-1 in the semis. India crushed Holland 6-1 in the final, and in the third/fourth place final GB defeated Pakistan 2-1 to take the bronze medal. The GB line up for first two games saw Nugent at inside left and Conroy outside him. In the third match Conroy replaced Nugent, who had suffered a thigh strain, and his place on the left wing went to the young Welshman Taylor. The only other change was that Derek Day, the goalkeeper, stood down from the bronze medal match to give a chance to his reserve, Welshman Gordon Dadds.

The radical difference in approach between the Olympic selectors and their England counterparts was highlighted by the choices the latter made in the home international series the following year. Nugent was not chosen for either of the 1953

English trials, and was never selected for England. Tony Nunn, who had never been selected for an English trial prior to the Olympics, played for GB in all three of the Helsinki games and was one of the stars of the team. Yet in the next domestic season he was not picked for England, who instead chose a debutant, Ivens, for all the internationals. Nunn was finally given his chance by England in 1954 but was then brutally discarded after just two games. Norman, on the other hand, having been rejected by the Olympic selectors, was chosen by England in 1953 as both inside left and captain.

There is no doubt that Norman, at 34 years of age, had lost some of his speed over the last year or so, not helped by the slowly worsening hip condition, and did not fit the Olympic selectors' desire to model their team on youth and speed. Who is to say if his constructive skills, so well demonstrated for England in the Triple Crown winning season just past, would have enabled GB to do better? As doing better would have meant beating the all-conquering Indian team, the answer must be in the negative.

Peter Smith puts the view of a fellow England player: "Playing for England in 1952 and 1953 it became obvious to all that Norman was losing his speed but never his enthusiasm and will to win, and I found out from Mullie how much he suffered for a few days after a hard game, and that he was hardly able to climb a flight of stairs; this, of course, meant that he was unable to train between games, something which must have bothered him a lot. When we were in South Africa in 1951 he was way ahead of us as far as fitness was concerned, having run for miles and miles most days at Framlingham for several weeks before our tour.

He was not picked for the 1952 Olympics, though I think he was a better player than the uncapped player who took his place, but it may have been a risk to take him knowing how arthritis was beginning to affect him so badly. It was typical of Norman to go on playing hockey against his doctor's advice, though he did have the sense to stop playing squash."

An interesting footnote to GB's Helsinki hockey story occurred in July 2010. After years of campaigning by Tony Nunn and others, replica bronze medals were presented to Sir Derek Day and Neil Nugent. They had drawn the two short straws when, the day after the final, GB's manager Robert Fison had had to devise a method of choosing which two players of his squad of 13 were to miss out on medals, which under the Olympic rules of the day could only be given to the eleven who played in the medal match.

Hip trouble;
Hamlet without the Prince;
bereavement;
a last hockey international;
Bill Tucker tolls the bell;
and retirement from hockey.

Norman's autumn hockey began in late October 1952 with two games in one weekend. On Saturday 25th at Brentwood, an hour down the A12 for the fast driver, he played in a 9-1 victory for an invitational side over the local club in celebration of their 50th anniversary. He then sang for his supper by proposing the toast to the Club at the Jubilee Dinner. Amongst those present were two other Old Framlinghamians, one of the founder members of the Brentwood Club, L. Liell, and Colonel N. R. Salew, the first, and until Norman Borrett, the only other, hockey international from the College, whose solitary cap was achieved playing at inside right, for Wales against England in 1932.

Having returned late to Framlingham Norman was off again the next morning to Felixstowe for the final Suffolk trial. His hip was stiff after the game the day before, but he did well. The East Anglian Daily Times on the Monday captioned their photograph of him as *'the Suffolk captain, who played his usual inspiring game in the county trials in spite of a leg injury.'*

Suffolk's first county match was the following weekend when they played local rivals Essex at Bury St.Edmunds.

❝❞

...most of the credit for this splendid achievement ...must go to Norman Borrett...

Suffolk won 3-2, their first win over Essex since well before the war, a *'phenomenon'* of a result according to the EADT. The paper wrote that *'most of the credit for this splendid achievement, and it was an achievement because Essex were fielding a particularly strong team, including two East men and Irish international D. Goggin from South Essex, must go to Norman Borrett. For 20 minutes before the game he lectured his men and worked out enterprising forward movements.* Two goals down at half time, another parley from Borrett during the break produced the desired effect, Suffolk equalising and then scoring the winning goal in the final minute of the match.'

Norman was not called upon to play in the East Trial at Cambridge on November 15th nor the Final Trial at Southend on December 6th - his place was assured in the side for the first divisional match on January 10th. He did manage a game for the East against his old University on November 23th. The annual hockey match between Cambridge University Wanderers and Oxford University Occasionals was played on December 18th at Beckenham, and Norman's presence in the Wanderers side was keenly anticipated by The Times: 'Borrett is usually at his best on the Beckenham ground'. This time the Oxford side was far the stronger and won 3-0. 'The only Wanderers forward to play up to form was Borrett, who worked tremendously hard and made many good openings.'

Two days later the other traditional Christmas game took place, at a muddy Tulse Hill, where the home side entertained the Schoolmasters XI. Carnill, Cockett, Borrett, Robinson and Fletcher were current or recent internationals, but a goal from the Olympian Nugent in the last few minutes cancelled out goals from Norman and Fletcher, and took Tulse Hill to a 3-2 victory.

The New Year got off to a bad start when, having played hockey for the Schoolmasters against Sandhurst on January 7th, Norman suffered an attack of inflammation to the hip and was unable to captain the East hockey team against Combined Services on January 10th. The press noted that he would be missed, particularly in the taking of penalty corners, where his fierce shooting was always a major threat.

On the following Friday, January 23rd, the Tramps Hockey Club, founded in 1928 as a side which played on Sundays and on tour, with players of county and international standard, celebrated its silver jubilee with a dinner at the Kingsley Hotel in London. Norman drove there in the MG. He was a social animal and made considerable efforts to stay in touch with friends and colleagues from his Suffolk fastness. He found himself at the dinner amongst many old friends, including several who had made their name in more than one sport: Freddie Brown, David Milford, Micky Walford and Norman Yardley. He stayed in London that night and was on the road early on Saturday heading West. By 2.30 he was on the pitch at Swindon Hockey Club playing for the East against his old division, the West.

Hockey News had previewed the game in the light of Norman's return from injury: 'Borrett's methods are well known to the rest of the East forwards and his skill in placing the ball should mean still more chances for Ivens, Peake and Hudson to show their scoring power.' Having gone a goal down, the East were lifted by Norman winning, and scoring from, a penalty bully. He was always in the picture, and went on to score twice more as East

ran out 5-2 winners. It was a long drive from Swindon to Framlingham, and Mullie had to help him out of the car when he arrived home at 9 p.m. He had one more hockey match to play before the first English trial, on February 21st, a county game at Eaton Park, Norwich, where Norfolk trounced Suffolk 5-0, the heaviest defeat Norman had ever suffered. As captain of the losing team it was little consolation that he was described as the outstanding player on the pitch.

R. L. Hollands, writing in Hockey News in February, speculated as to the selectors' choices for the first England hockey trial at Charterhouse School on March 7th. He pointed out that although ten of last season's winning England team were available, a number of new players were contenders, including the Olympic team members Nunn, Norris and Nugent. He named the thirty players from whom he thought the trial teams were likely to be drawn. Norman's name was not amongst them: perhaps Hollands felt that the selectors would go along with their Olympic counterparts and write off Norman as too old and lacking pace. In the event Norman was picked, as captain of the senior side, the Whites. Hollands expressed disappointment that Conroy was still being used on the wing (outside Norman) and that Neil Forster was again ignored as an inside forward. On the day Norman and Conroy combined well on the left flank and their side ran out 5-1 winners, with two goals from Norman, two from Norris in the middle, and one from Conroy...

> ...Hollands thought the trial 'a little unreal, for the England captain, N. F. Borrett was away ill, and we all knew that Hamlet without the Prince was unthinkable.'

Norman told the England squash selectors he could not play in the third match in the international squash series, against Scotland at the RAC, on Friday March 20th, as he was captaining England against the Rest in the final England hockey trial the following day at Evesham. As it transpired, Norman suffered an attack of 'flu on that Friday evening and he had to cry off from the hockey trial the next day. Hollands thought the trial 'a little unreal, for the England captain, N. F. Borrett was away ill, and we all knew that Hamlet without the Prince was unthinkable.'

But the trial proved to be a success with the senior side winning 5-0, and the same reporter gave high praise to John Conroy: 'Borrett himself could not have played better than did

Conroy, who took his place at inside left.' However the selectors (the English ones at least) were still believers in the Borrett magic, and selected Norman as inside left and captain for the first international, on March 28th, against Wales at Newport. They could not discard Conroy after his trial performance, but had also to accommodate Norman; so they picked Conroy as centre forward. This evoked some concern: *'Whether two such clever stick players as Borrett and Conroy, bunched together in the centre, are liable to slow up the attack remains to be seen'*. In the event a hat-trick from Conroy gave England a 4-2 victory, but the fears were to an extent borne out - against hard tackling-back by the Welsh insides the English attack did bunch and slow up. R. L. Hollands saw the game this way:

'Conroy is the constructive rather than the dashing type, the designer rather than the destroyer. So too are the other insides Fletcher and Borrett. The result was an over-elaboration of method, too much manoeuvring and not enough drive, so that attacks gave the impression of a blackboard exercise rather than a serious and determined attempt to score goals...Fletcher and Borrett were seriously hampered and passes were all too often given and received standing still, or nearly so.' In the second half *'the forwards dillied and dallied, holding the ball in one place till every gap had closed and every man was marked down.'*

For the next, Scottish, international, the selectors sought to inject pace into the middle of the attack by switching Conroy to outside left and bringing in the Olympian Norris at centre forward for his first cap. Hockey News thought that Norris' arrival would bring much-needed life to the attack, *'but the whole forward line need to get the March wind in their hair, and a roaring, raging wind at that, if they hope to win any more matches.'*

At this moment a family tragedy occurred. 82 year old Walter Borrett had fallen seriously ill at the end of March, and Norman cancelled his Easter trip with the Tramps Hockey Club to the Hague Hockey Festival to be with his father at Landermere. The family were together there when on Good Friday, April 3rd, Walter died. His widow Alice, his brother-in-law Robert Beard, Norman, Mullie, Anthony and Timothy, Norman's brother Charles, his wife Jean, and children Andrew, Elizabeth and Mary, together with many friends, gathered at Frinton Parish Church on the Tuesday after Easter. Walter was buried in the cemetery at his old home town of Barking, near his Dagenham farm. Alice continued to live at Landermere until she died in 1964.

Norman could be forgiven for not being in the most focused frame of mind as he lined up at Guildford Hockey Club a mere four days after the funeral, on April 10th, for the international against Scotland. England, who had beaten the

Scots 7-0 in Glasgow the previous year, were disappointing before 4,000 spectators as Scotland held their southern rivals to a 3-3 draw, after England had led 2-0.

The Daily Telegraph headlined its report *'England's slow and dull hockey'*. The paper blamed some *'methodical and ill-timed passing by the English inside forwards' as* a contributory cause to the result, although The Times accepted that the insides *'were only allowed to give occasional glimpses of real combination by the quick and relentless tackling of the Scottish defence'*. Hollands was again critical: *'But the champions' movements were both obvious and slow for which N.F. Borrett must answer as captain, inside left and director of the attack. No one knows better how to split a defence open than this great forward, who was making his thirtieth appearance for England. But on this occasion the light and life had gone out of him, the effect perhaps of a recent illness. He neglected his wing man Conroy, probably the most dangerous of our forwards, using instead the cross-pass to the inside-right with monotonous and mechanical regularity.'*

The selectors reacted to this performance by taking drastic measures. They discarded Norman, replacing him with Conroy, for the first time playing inside left. Denys Carnill, winning his 15th cap, took over the captaincy from left back.

There were two international matches left that season. The team played much better all round in Dublin the following week, as Ireland were well beaten 3-1. At the cricket ground at Trent Bridge, Nottingham, England then entertained the Netherlands, one of the strongest sides in world hockey, and gained a creditable 1-1 draw. Conroy was named by Hockey News as Player of the Year, having featured at centre forward, outside left and inside left for his country in successive matches - *'probably a unique experience'*.

Norman was not picked again, the selectors no doubt taking the logical position that once having taken the major step of dropping him there was little sense in bringing back a 36 year-old, even one who had been such a pivotal figure in the national team. Since his debut 14 years before in 1939 he had played 30 times for his country, 11 of them as captain. He had scored 26 goals for England, including three international hat-tricks; he scored three goals against Wales in a 7-0 win in 1949, four against France in a 5-0 win in 1951, and a further three against Wales in a 5-0 win in 1952. Of his seven appearances for Great Britain, he had been captain in all of them, scoring 12 goals.

Norman was, surprisingly perhaps to those who perceived him as driven by an inexhaustible desire to compete, phlegmatic at the news of his demotion. He had known, from the moment the previous summer when the GB selectors had decided to leave him out of the team for the Olympics, and from the increasing effect of the hip problem, that he would not hold on to his England place for much longer.

In late 1953 the Evening News, noting the end of Norman's international hockey career, drew attention to *'the long period that three men, the Reverend C. S. Marcon, D. S. Milford and Borrett occupied the inside-left position in the English side. Starting in 1913 Marcon played 20 times for England. Milford who came to the front in the late twenties and still plays first-class rackets, followed with 25, and Borrett 30 between 1939 and 1953. Together they totalled 75 caps in 40 years, of which ten were occupied by wars. That means they tied up the inside-left position for at least two out of every three internationals in the period, longer by far than any other three players have occupied any other one position.'* Interestingly this record becomes even more impressive if one adds to it John Conroy's reign, in succession to Borrett: he was to win a total of 32 caps in a career which ran from 1952-1960, usually in Norman's old position but also at inside right.

R. L. Hollands, in the Sunday Times of December 27th noted that Norman was an uncertain starter for the final East trial at St. Albans, *'owing to a troublesome hip condition.'* In fact Norman had already told the East selectors that he would have to turn down their invitation to play in the trial, and on the day of the trial, January 2nd 1954, The Times carried the news that *'Borrett is understood to be giving up serious hockey because of muscular rheumatism.'* He had again visited Bill Tucker, the Harley Street osteopath specializing in hips, and had been told that it was not sensible to continue playing with his arthritis (The Times was incorrect), which could only worsen with vigorous exercise. Norman had known since Tucker's diagnosis the previous autumn that he was on borrowed time,

> *...He had again visited Bill Tucker, the Harley Street osteopath specializing in hips... it was not sensible to continue playing with his arthritis, which could only worsen with vigorous exercise.*

so the advice was no surprise and he readily took the decision to retire completely from hockey.

Hockey News carried an article under the heading *'No caps for them this year'* announcing that *'P. D.R. Smith and N. F. Borrett, both of whom represented England last year, will not play in any of the trials or internationals this year. Smith, who recently accepted a new business appointment, will not be available. Borrett withdrew from the recent East trial because of a troublesome hip condition.'*

Retired from the game which he loved at the age of 36 Norman had no regrets. He had travelled widely, led Britain in an Olympiad, captained his country many times, and met and enjoyed the company of a host of interesting people, all as a result of a certain skill at the game. The Vice-Presidency of the Hockey Association, Presidency of the Eastern Counties Hockey Association and of the Travellers Club, involvement with the Tramps, Cambridge University Wanderers, Essex, The East, a role as an England selector, all these and other accolades and commitments awaited him. He would never retire from an involvement in the game.

Tony Nunn, who played at outside right in the Great Britain hockey team at the Helsinki Olympics, recalls the Travellers Club days:

"Norman was one of the great hockey inside forwards. My first memories of him are of the consummate skill that he expected all others to embrace, especially those on the wing outside him! He was very much the 'senior citizen' when I first played with and against him. He was never slow to express his feelings on and off the pitch.

I subsequently got to know Norman as a friend and colleague when we were members of the Travellers Hockey Club on tours at home and abroad. After the onset of his arthritic problems, (and I remember him umpiring a Travellers tour match in Holland when he had terrible arthritis and could hardly walk) he always supported and umpired and subsequently became a very active and popular President of the Travellers, encouraging both old and young. He was a great tourist and ambassador in those amateur days when one had as many personal friends in the opposition team as on one's own.

His skills would certainly have withstood the demands of the modern professional hockey approach but I have my doubts as to whether Norman would have wished (or allowed himself) to be 'managed' from the touchline as the players are today. He was a natural at hockey, squash and indeed all sports."

As to where Norman was ranked amongst the best of English hockey players, it is interesting to see the views of an international who played centre forward, both pre and post-war, for England, Lt. Col. R.J. Dickinson. Writing to Hockey News from Singapore in January 1953, on the subject of the unsatisfactory nature of the penalty bully, he recalled Norman's failure to convert one against the Indian goalkeeper in the 48 Final. "In the 1948 Olympic Games, one of the finest forwards England has produced, failed to win a penalty bully against Pinto, the Indian goalkeeper."

Maurice Kittrell's view was that "If the war years had not intervened, Norman's reputation would have been bigger still. I have no doubt that had he played on today's artificial pitches his skills would have developed to an even greater level – he would have ranked with the very best of the modern vintage. His reputation as a hockey player, a competitor of the highest level, and an all-round sportsman, is second to none."

It has been said that Norman was to hockey what Bobby Moore was to soccer many years later: a player with the capacity to take a broad view of a match; a strategist with the gift of assimilating information quickly and then acting upon it.

England's right back during Norman's latter years, who later captained the side, Peter Smith, first saw him playing at a Hockey Festival at Weston Super Mare in about 1947 when Peter happened to be there for the Easter weekend: "My recollection is that he ran about a great deal and was very vociferous! I next saw him when I was amongst the crowd at Wembley in 1948 when he captained the GB side against India in the final, though I have no specific memories of his playing. Probably the next year I clashed (on the field) with him was at the Easter Festival in Folkestone without at first realising who he was, and thinking what a hard player he was as he ploughed straight into me rather than going round me!

When I played in the England trials in 1950 I thought Norman was a bit of a bully, particularly when he kept telling me to pass the ball to him, though he was not the one for me to do so according to the book! I realised then that he was very experienced, slightly 'over the top', but still a very forceful player who was more determined than any player I had met."

Denys Carnill, capped for England 45 times between 1950 and 1960, and for Great Britain 27 times, and Norman's successor as England captain, knew Norman very well, having played many times with and against him: "He was a superb player; marvellous eye, could stop anything and he had an innate feel for the game, the gift of having lots of space around him. He was pretty determined too, not at all a dirty player, but a hard one. As a person he was not everyone's cup of tea: he

…he didn't suffer fools gladly and he wasn't afraid to speak his mind. I liked him enormously and admired him hugely.

didn't suffer fools gladly and he wasn't afraid to speak his mind, I liked him enormously and admired him hugely.

As is well known, he was one of the outstanding sportsmen of his age: hockey, cricket, squash, tennis etc etc. Norman was really good. Why Norman was not chosen for Helsinki, I don't know. I do know that the selectors were more or less obliged to have one or two Welsh and one or two Scottish players in the squad, and it's not inconceivable that Norman had got across the odd selector, but I just don't know. It certainly was true that latterly he was losing a bit of speed."

The Times looked forward to the pre-Christmas annual hockey game on December 18th between the Schoolmasters and Tulse Hill, in which both sides would contain a number of internationals: *'One can be sure that N. F. Borrett still retains much of his old skill'*. Sadly, the lateness of the school holidays meant that Norman and a number of other masters had to drop out at the last minute. He thus missed his chance to play his one game of hockey that winter.

He played occasional games over the next two or three years, when the old urge was too strong to resist. Norman Mayhew recollects one such venture: "I was conscripted in the Spring of 1956 by Norman to play with him against Saxmundham for Framlingham Town on a Sunday afternoon. He was then 38. Not his usual standard of game but he enjoyed it." Robin Manning, an Old Greshamian who played for Ipswich Hockey Club in the 1950s, played against Norman in one of those Framlingham Town games: "he was inside left and I was his opposing inside right. He certainly was a forceful player – if you got in his way he would run straight through you. I got to know him pretty well when I visited the College to play squash for Diss and for Norfolk. A great man."

Mayhew also remembers how, two years later in 1958, "the afternoon after my participation in Cambridge's heavy defeat by Oxford, he appeared in my rooms in St. John's to see what had gone wrong: an example of how he was prepared to help those with lesser abilities than his."

CRICKET – THE SUFFOLK YEARS

*Devon cricket – The Bishop speaks;
the dilemma for College umpires;
ambidextrous bowling.*

In his first summer term at Framlingham, 1951, Norman ran the Colts and helped out Walter Winstanley, the College's Senior Master, with coaching the first XI. One of the main school matches was that against Culford School. Norman, whose ability to spot talent was proved many times over the years, took the view that Ian Foster, a talented but erratic College opening bowler, showed promise but needed to be motivated to concentrate his talent into wicket-taking. 60 years later Foster remembers it well:

"Norman told me that if I could take six wickets in the Culford match he and his wife Mullie would invite me to their home for dinner, complete with wines and port. The big day came, and I came on to bowl. It proved to be one of those days. My first delivery attracted ironic applause around the ground as it hit the sight-screen behind the batsman almost on the full toss. But concentrating furiously I settled down and eventually took my six wickets.

True to his word Norman and Mullie prepared a memorable dinner for me later that week, after which I staggered as quietly as I could back into College in a desperate effort not to wake any one in authority, else we would all have been in big trouble."

The only cricket Norman managed to fit in during that term was local Suffolk club cricket for Campsea Ashe and a couple of games for the Quilibets, a scratch team run by Walter Winstanley. In the Quilibets match against the College, '*a deplorable affair*' according to the College magazine, Ken Mayhew, who had played for Norfolk in 1947 and 1948, took 5-2, and Norman 5-17, as the College were dismissed for 19. One month later, he scored 122 not out in a total of 156 for 7 when his own eleven played a match against the College. The magazine was less critical this time: '*A pleasant domestic brawl in which Mr. Borrett gave a very instructive demonstration not only of hitting out but of calling and running between the wickets*'.

There was no Devon cricket as Norman's summer holiday was taken up by the GB & Ireland hockey tour to South Africa.

Norman played for the Old Boys of Allhallows in their 1952 cricket week and then for Devon in all nine of their August matches, batting on 12 occasions. He was keen to re-establish himself after missing the 1951 season, and particularly to field at cover-point, to prove to himself that his

hip, which had begun to trouble him early in 1952, would not prevent him playing a full part in the side. In his 12 innings he scored two fifties, and although he averaged only 23, Wisden noted, in its review of the season, that Norman's return

E. Cooper (left) and N. F. Borrett going out after lunch to bat for Devon against Berkshire at the County Ground, Exeter, yesterday.

ABOVE: Norman going out to bat after lunch, Devon v Berkshire at Exeter, August 1st 1952.

had strengthened the Devon batting. He bowled a lot of overs, 99, but captured only four wickets at a high cost.

The first of his 50s was against Dorset at Weymouth, where he struck 69 as Devon took a big lead. Dropped when he had scored five, he drove, cut, and pulled powerfully, as he raced to his fifty in only 38 minutes, hitting two sixes and eight fours, putting on 98 in 70 minutes with his partner Bloy. Deryck Fairclough, Devon stalwart and later captain, remembers that playing for Dorset that day was the Reverend Jessop, son of the mighty England hitter Gilbert Jessop, and himself a fast scorer, known within cricketing circles as 'the Bishop'. "Norman was struck on the pad by the ball and a solitary appeal for LBW was heard from the Bishop, fielding a long way from the action at deep extra cover. An immediate response from crease to extra cover was forthcoming: 'No wonder they dissolved the bloody monasteries!'."

Deryck recalls Norman's sense of fun. "As a useful orthodox left arm bowler he would, in less serious games with the umpire standing up close to the stumps, slip in an unannounced good right-arm delivery: this would cause confusion, but not all batsmen or umpires noticed."

From Weymouth, Devon's four-match tour continued to Oxford, where Norman's bright 25 was insufficient to prevent Oxfordshire

…An immediate response from crease to extra cover was forthcoming: 'No wonder they dissolved the bloody monasteries!'

obtaining a first innings win, then to Newbury to play the return match with Berkshire, and finally to Guildford to take on Surrey II. Norman made a duck in this, the first of two games against Surrey II, who included England players Subba Row and Barrington, the latter making 157. Norman's highest score of the season, a hard-hitting 76 including two sixes and 12 fours, was made in the return match, an innings ended by a catch in the slips off Peter Loader, shortly to become an England fast bowler.

During the early 1950s, Norman Borrett played in a number of cricket matches on the College cricket ground, the Back, sometimes running his own XI or playing for the Quilibets, and on occasion for the OFs. These matches were always watched by a large number of college pupils interested in seeing what their schoolmaster would do. One such pupil was Gerald Garnett, who recalls umpiring a match, on the Back, involving Campsea Ashe and one other local village. Norman was playing for Campsea Ashe and in due course came in to bat. Gerald takes up the story:

"The bowler was a large local man who had been trundling the ball down with some success. His third ball to Norman wrapped him loudly on the pads and probably had him plumb LBW. A huge appeal went up and Norman did what all sensible batsmen do in that situation – he moved immediately away from the crease and gave me an unnerving stare with his piercing blue eyes. It all happened in a flash, of course, and I, faced with a predicament for which I was quite unprepared, gave him 'not out'. It was the bowler's turn to fix me with a stare, accompanied, as he walked back to his mark, by what was clearly sotto voce Suffolk invective.

Hoping that the bowler would restore propriety by bowling Norman before he had scored many more, I was obliged to retire for supper before evening prep. I ate my meal quickly and, with others, returned to the scene of my crime only to find the gravity of my offence made worse by the large number of runs Norman had scored in my absence, and his continued dominance as he struck the ball to all parts of the ground. It was only years later that I felt able to forgive myself on learning the story of W. G. Grace's reaction to being given out almost immediately lbw. 'Not so' said the great man to the umpire, 'the crowd have come to watch me bat - not to see you give me out'."

Even in domestic school cricket Norman was, as always, competitive, and liked to put on a show for watching pupils. In a remarkable match in June 1953, the College XI, captained by

Ian Foster,' *played Norman Borrett and ten other Quilibets under his captaincy*'. Norman took 8-53 and scored 62 not out, two thirds of the Quilibets total of 103-8. The College magazine reported:

'Apart from the notable fact that Bromage stumped five, this was just as much a one man show as the above suggests. The captain bowled unchanged and the only wicket he failed to take was run out. When his side's score was 50 for 8 with half an hour to go, and two 2nd XI performers to come, he took complete charge, Wyncoll, who played his thankless part most efficiently, contributing 2 of the last 53 runs.'

The death of his father, closely followed by the ending of his international hockey career and the worsening of his arthritis, meant that for Norman 1953 was not a year he wished to remember. He had left his squash career at the top level behind him the previous year, and his competitive hockey days were now numbered. But his passion for sport meant that he simply dismissed from his mind any maudlin thoughts of giving in to what seemed to be a steady deterioration in his mobility.

He would throw himself instead into his cricket. It was a game, in those days, which was much gentler on the body. As a bowler his slow left arm spin required only six leisurely steps to the bowling crease; as a batsman he had always relied on timing rather than force, and when he did not find the boundary, he could readily manage the twenty yard laps to the far end; and, importantly, he could still, with occasional difficulty, bend well enough to field at cover point. He determined to continue to play Minor County cricket for as long as he was of value to the county. If he would have to reduce the need for running between the wickets by hitting more boundaries, so be it.

His annual Devon sojourn was almost always taken alone, and he would afterwards join the family for a week or perhaps two at Frinton. But this year he needed to spend more time with the family, and he told Devon he would only play in six of the ten August games.

The Western News predicted at the end of July that *'Devon's team has a bigger potential than any of the preceding post-war sides. It is sound in batting, dangerous in bowling, and ought to be the strongest Devon has fielded since the war. There can be few complaints about the batting. Humphries, Fairclough, Cooper, Parker and Borrett are amongst the best players in the county. In bowling the accent is on a pace attack, with Coldwell, Atkinson, and Cole. The spinners in the side are Dean, Borrett, and Kinnersley while Parker and Fairclough have all round ability.'* His bowling was little used, his 31 overs producing four wickets for 112, but he had a fine time with the bat, playing several splendid innings, averaging 38, with 305 runs in 10 innings, and ending second in the

Mr. and Mrs. Norman Borrett were having a family holiday with their sons, Andrew, Anthony and Timothy, who had just returned to the beach hut for tea

"He was an attractive century-making batsman, and a slow left-arm bowler who could also be persuaded into serving up right arm off spinners. As an outstandingly agile cover-point, if playing against a side which did not know him, he would throw in right-handed to the keeper until there was a chance of a run-out, when he would revert to his more powerful left-handed throw. He had a strong sense of humour, and I think he enjoyed his cricket with us – as we enjoyed his presence. He was a tough competitor, and wanted to win. With his level of achievement is that any surprise?"

Cole's reference to Norman's ambidextrousness as a bowler is also recalled by wicket-keeper Stuart Mountford: "I had not kept to Norman before, when, in a county match, he warned me as we crossed between overs, to watch out for the fourth ball of his next over. I was intrigued. He bowled three balls with his usual slow left-arm spin and then, without telling either the batsman, or more importantly the umpire, delivered the fourth as a medium pace right arm seamer."

* * * * * * * * *

The Oval: the Minor Counties Challenge Match 1954

In 1954 Norman played occasional cricket for local village side Campsea Ashe. On one memorable occasion, playing alongside his old hockey opponent and fellow OF Frank Jerrey, he scored a century in 90 minutes, ending 145 not out, in a great win over Felixstowe. He also turned out for the OFs in their win over the Old Ipswichians at Thorpeness in July, scoring 64 out of the OFs' 158, before repairing to Devon, where he played in seven matches.

His opening match, on July 30th and 31st, was against Berkshire at the County Ground, Exeter. Berkshire having been bowled out for 221, with Peter May's brother, John, only contributing seven, Devon were 110 for three when Norman joined his friend Norman Humphries in the middle. They put on 38 together in 33 minutes by the end of the first day's play, Norman having struck 29 of them. On the final day he took his score to 78 as Devon reached 320 for 5 declared. Berkshire's

county batting averages.

In the first match, against Berkshire, Norman was 25 not out when Devon won by 8 wickets. In the next fixture Dorset were the opponents at Seaton, and on a green wicket bowlers were in the ascendancy as Devon won the toss, batted and struggled at 13 for 3. Norman saved Devon's face, batting at number five, with seven different partners, scoring an attractive 50 out of a total of 109, contributing to a remarkable victory. Having won their first four games, by August 12th the local papers carried rare headlines: '*Devon Top of the Minor Counties" – How long ago did that happen?*'

Norman's highest knock of the season was 71 out of a Devon total of 242 made against Berkshire at Newbury on August 14th, but the game ended disappointingly in a two wicket defeat. In the last match of the season Norman made 20 in the first innings against Surrey II, for whom Ken Barrington took 6 wickets, including that of Norman, with his leg spin; Surrey took a big lead when Mickey Stewart scored 126 and Barrington 84, and then bowled out Devon for 124, Norman top scoring with 40. Devon had slipped after their good start to the season and finished 10th out of 26. Nevertheless Wisden described the season as '*Devon's most successful for several years. N. H. Humphries, although unable to play in some matches, again batted excellently, and N. F. Borrett also played several fine innings.*'

Derek Cole, who played many times for Devon alongside Norman, and was later to become president of the county club, recalls Norman as an exceptional all-rounder:

openers could not be separated and, when most of the afternoon was lost to rain, the game ended in a first innings win for Devon.

The following match, on August 2nd, saw Devon in their first innings take 330 for eight off the Dorsetshire attack at the Seaton ground on which he had made those five club centuries in 1947. Norman added 116 for the fourth wicket with Derek Cole, and earned plaudits from The Western Morning News: *'Borrett, master of all the bowlers, played another grand innings, full of perfectly-timed drives and pulls with the odd stylish late cut. He stayed an hour and a half for 61…. The usually aggressive Borrett opened quietly, but soon proceeded to administer the severest chastisement to the bowlers. He went on to his half-century in sparkling style'*. Dorset were bowled out for 118 and 207, to give Devon a win by an innings and 5 runs.

The Devon team continued to perform well above their presumed station, and ended the season with 3 outright wins, 4 wins on first innings, losing one on first innings and having one no result. This left them runners up in the championship to Surrey II, and thereby entitled to challenge Surrey to a deciding match. The challenge was duly made and the match arranged for September 13th, 14th, and 15th at the Oval. Surrey's star-studded 1st XI

had just won the County Championship title for the third year running, and their Second XI inevitably contained a number of fine players with County Championship experience, including Fletcher, Brazier, Pretlove and Roy Swetman, later to become an England wicket-keeper.

In a game in which rain prevented a definite result, Devon excelled themselves by restricting Surrey II to 236, thanks in part to the bowling of the Len Coldwell, whose last match this was before he joined Worcestershire the following season, with whom he won his first England cap in 1962. Devon succeeded in overhauling Surrey's score with minutes of the extra half-hour to spare. Norman justified the decision of Framlingham's headmaster to permit him time off to play, with an important batting performance. Batting at five, he shared the decisive stand of 107 with Fairclough, scored in only 75 minutes, and ended second highest scorer with 42.

Despite winning the match on first innings only, a part-win permissible at the time, their failure to pull off a complete victory meant that Devon, as challengers, had failed to dislodge Surrey II as champions. Worse still, by a fluke of the Minor County rules, which required that points they earned from their first innings win in the Challenge Match had to be added to their season's total, the season's average thus recalculated meant that the county dropped from second to fourth in the final table. This unintended consequence was corrected shortly by a rule change to prevent any future repetition of this unfairness, and Devon were uniquely granted a unanimous vote of sympathy by all their competitor counties at the Minor Counties Association AGM in December. Norman's Devon season saw him come second in the batting averages with 220 runs in six innings at an average of 36.66. His bowling was not called upon.

BELOW: September 13th 1954. The Devon team who defeated Surrey II at the Oval, on 1st innings. Future England player Len Coldwell is 3rd from left, back row.

This card does not necessarily include the fall of the last wicket

Surrey County Cricket Club
KENNINGTON OVAL

3D.

Minor Counties Challenge Match
SURREY II v. DEVON
Monday, September 13th, 1954 (3 Day Match)

SURREY II	First Innings		Second Innings
1 Fletcher, D. G. W.	b Atkinson	22	
2 A. H. Brown	c Fairclough, b Coldwell	23	
3 Pratt, R. C. E.	b Atkinson	0	
4 Brazier, A. F	c Mountford, b Atkinson	95	
5 J. F Pretlove	c Mountford, b Fairclough	10	
6 Tindall, R. A. E.	b Fairclough	3	
7 Pratt, D. E.	b Fairclough	8	
Swetman, R.	st Mountford, b Fairclough	17	
9 Cox, D. F	not out	40	
*10 V J Ransom	not out	5	
11 Kelleher, H. R. A.			

B3 , l-b6 , w , n-b4 13   B , l-b , w , n-b ....

Innings dec.——

Total (8 wkts.) 236   Total............

FALL OF THE WICKETS
1—50	2—50	3—51	4—95	5—105	6—125	7—168	8—213	9—	10—
1—	2—	3—	4—	5—	6—	7—	8—	9—	10—

BOWLING ANALYSIS	First Innings						Second Innings					
	O.	M.	R.	W	Wd.	N.b.	O.	M.	R.	W	Wd.	N.b.
Coldwell	25	10	56	1		2						
Cole	3	2	1	0								
Parker	14	5	22	0								
Atkinson	21	6	59	3								
Dean	11	1	39	0		2						
Fairclough	18	4	46	4								

Score-Board Indicators. For the convenience of the public during FIRST CLASS MATCHES, indicators have been installed on both Score-Boards, from which fieldsmen will be easily identified by lighted numbers corresponding to those on the score-cards. Letter S—Substitute.

DEVON	First Innings		Second Innings
1 H. D. Fairclough	c Kelleher, b Pratt D.	117	
S. J Cray	c Swetman, b Kelleher	25	
6 D. H. Cole	c Tindall, b Pratt R.	8	
4 N. C. F Bloy	st Swetman, b Pratt D.	2	
5 N. F Borrett	c Cox, b Tindall	42	
*7 G. W Parker	not out	27	
8 P Atkinson	b Pretlove	0	
9 T. A. Dean	not out	9	
‡10 S. J. Mountford			
11 L. J. Coldwell			
3 E. Cooper			

B4 , l-b1 , w , n-b3 8   B , l-b , w , n-b ....

Total (6 wkts.) 238   Total............

FALL OF THE WICKETS
1—34	2—58	3—64	4—171	5—206	6—207	7—	8—	9—	10—
1—	2—	3—	4—	5—	6—	7—	8—	9—	10—

BOWLING ANALYSIS	First Innings						Second Innings					
	O.	M.	R.	W	Wd.	N.b.	O.	M.	R.	W	Wd.	N.b.
Cox	22	7	51	0		1						
Kelleher	19	7	38	1								
Pratt (R.C.E.)	16	8	29	1								
Pratt (D.E.)	15	5	45	2								
Ransom	8	4	9	0		2						
Tindall	7	0	29	1								
Pretlove	10.5	3	29	1								

*Captain   ‡Wkt.-keeper   Toss won by SURREY II

Umpires—L. W Martin & A. E. D. Smith   RESULT—Match Drawn

HOURS OF PLAY—
1st Day 11.30—6.30 Lunch 1.30   2nd Day 11—6.30 Lunch 1.15   3rd Day 11—4.30 or 5.0 Lunch 1.15

Printed on the ground by the Surrey County Cricket Club Printing Department

Local Suffolk cricket;
Devon cricket – 7 sixes in a century and top
of the batting averages;
David Larter.

In 1955 Norman managed several games of cricket in the Framlingham area. He was able to bowl more than he had in recent Devon cricket, and showed his worth in the annual match for the OFs against their great rivals, the Old Ipswichians, with 6-64. Norman Mayhew remembers Norman as a "thoroughly talented batsman; I played with him for the Quilibets against Framlingham Town when he scored a very belligerent century. In cricket matches against the boys he would bamboozle us with his ability to bowl equally well with either arm and with spin or medium pace."

Tom Elliott, a pupil of the College, encountered the ambidextrous bowling at close quarters:

"In the summer term of 1955, when I should have been revising for my A levels, I often umpired the evening fixtures of the Quilibets Cricket Club for which Norman regularly played. One evening he opened the bowling, and on handing me his sweater drawled 'Hmm Elliott, shall I bowl left or right arm tonight?' As I had only seen him bowl left arm, I naturally said that I should like him to bowl right arm, privately harbouring the unkind thought of watching his bowling being knocked all around the ground. Well, without any particular help from me, he proceeded to take eight wickets for not very many and, as I recall, had a hand in the other two dismissals".

Norman missed his Devon season, again because he was touring South Africa, this time for squash. Derek Fairclough had a clear recollection of how Norman got his place on this tour: "In the pavilion prior to a game versus Surrey II Norman read in the paper that he had not been selected for the England team to visit South Africa. He was furious and stormed out of the dressing room to telephone the chairman of the selectors to ask the reason why. At this time he said he would play each member of the selected team and beat them. This he duly did and went to South Africa."

It is a wonderfully romantic story but sadly just doesn't fit the facts, which are that although the idea of a tour was mooted as early as June 1954, it was not confirmed until February 1955 when the selectors first wrote to various players asking if they would be available to tour in August that year. Devon did not play Surrey II in the 1954 season, other than at the Oval in the Challenge Match in September. There is no record of Norman playing those with whom he was competing for a place. And yet Fairclough's recollection was so sure…

Local cricket matches were not of much value to a minor county cricketer seeking form, but they were fun and Norman took them as seriously as was appropriate. The College Masters' XI games presented some difficulty in this area. There were few masters who could play to club standard, and there were not many opponents in the Suffolk village teams who would appreciate being made to look foolish. Norman's unusual ability to bowl with either hand was often utilized to inject fun, and to amuse himself, when he felt the match situation needed something different. He knew when to take the game lightly, showing off to the crowd of pupils who always gathered to watch him play, and when to extend himself. Occasionally, the mix would be difficult to achieve.

David Boulton, then a pupil of the College, recalls one such occasion in the summer of 1956: "As a day boy for most of the time I was at the College, my father being the Framlingham station master for British Rail from 1947 to 1956, I saw the College from a different perspective. One of my leisure activities in the summer term was playing evening cricket for Saxtead, alongside David Larter and David Moss who were also at the College at the time. One of the fixtures we enjoyed was playing against the College Masters' XI on the Back in an evening match. As I recall we dismissed the Masters for a respectable total, and then they proceeded to get rid of us quite cheaply under conditions that were getting quite gloomy. When I came in to bat, low down the order,

…he switched to left-handed tweakers with his arm coming round the edge of the sightscreen out of the murk. What chance did I have?

Norman was bowling from the swimming-pool end, right-handed, but when I came in he switched to left-handed tweakers with his arm coming round the edge of the sightscreen out of the murk. What chance did I have? Norman's skill, and his masterly gamesmanship, was too much for me. But perhaps my performance had some merit, as the next summer term Norman agreed, somewhat begrudgingly, that I could play for the 3rd XI, provided that I batted at number eleven."

Along with the rest of the cricket-viewing public Norman was glued to the television in the last week of July 1956 as 'Laker's Match' unfolded at Old Trafford, the Australians subsiding at the hands of the Surrey off spinner as he took 19 of their 20 wickets. The dry weather broke a few hours after the last wicket fell and the rain caused not a ball to be bowled the following day in any of the first class matches. But hot, dry conditions returned immediately and Norman's first county game of the season, at Torquay against Berkshire on August 3rd and 4th was played in good weather. Norman took three Berkshire wickets in the second innings to leave Devon with 181 to win in 2 hours 13 minutes, but none of the Devon batsmen survived long, Norman included, and they slumped to an 83 run defeat.

Devon's cricket presented a different face two days later, when they took on local rivals Dorset at Instow. Micky Walford, who had from 1947 to 1953 scored over 5000 runs for Somerset in the County Championship, a school teacher at Sherborne, playing, like Norman, in his school holidays, was opening the batting for Dorset, who also had Ray Dovey, the former Kent off spinner, to carry the brunt of the bowling. Captaining the team in place of the injured Fairclough, Norman won the toss and batted. The Western Morning News summed up the innings in these words:

'It was Norman Borrett's day in the Minor Counties championship yesterday. Playing his best knock of the season he carried his team to a commanding position. It was splendid forcing cricket as he raced to his century in 103 minutes. (After lunch) the breezy Borrett produced a highly entertaining afternoon's cricket. He hit seven towering sixes – six of them off the right-arm slows of former Oxford Blue David Jowett – and might have been out two or three times before reaching his century. Always ready to take a chance he had a grand innings richly flavoured with mighty drives and slices of luck. But he deserved his good fortune for Borrett is a batsman who really hits the ball.'

So the story goes, on receiving the congratulations of the rest of his team after this knock Norman responded with characteristic blunt banter: "If any of you lot could bat, I would have made a lot more". On the second and final day, the two captains exchanged declarations, only for the match to peter out to a draw. *'Only a fighting innings by Norman Borrett saved Devon from collapse. He was kept severely in check this time and occupied over an hour in scoring 44, but he had again held the Devon innings*

together.' Norman gave himself only one over in the first and two overs in the second Dorset innings. The newspaper noted that *'there was a good holiday crowd and receipts totalled about £60.'*

For Norman the Instow pitch was a happy hunting ground: he had also scored a century there on his first visit seven years earlier. Straight from this game, the Devon side journeyed to Plymouth to play Cornwall on August 9th. Norman was the backbone of Devon's first innings, scoring 74 not out of a total of only 162. In the second innings he was 28 not out as the game ended in a draw, he and Cole holding out against the Cornish seam bowlers, who included the England rugby full-back Roger Hosen.

Devon's three match summer tour then commenced with the return match against Micky Walford's Dorset at Weymouth. Norman's good form continued as he made 44 not out. Oxfordshire were the next opponents, at Oxford Sports Club, a game umpired by Jack O'Connor of Essex, the man who had scored a century in Norman's 1937 Essex debut match and who, in Norman's phrase, "wouldn't run when I called him for a sharp single", thus ending Norman's innings. The third match was against Berkshire at Reading, where Devon scored 98 for 3, with Norman at the crease, when rain washed away all further play.

Norman did not play in Devon's remaining four matches as he had promised to get home to Frinton to join the family for the last fortnight of their holiday, before the new term began in the first week of September. His shortened season had been a great success. He had headed the batting averages with 313 runs in 9 innings at 52.16, being the only Devonian to score a century that year, and had bowled more than in his last, blank, summer of 1954, with 53 overs producing 4-118 at a respectable 29.50. His batting touch remained with him in the couple of games he played for Frinton upon his return from Devon. Batting at three in a cold wet Sunday match against Mistley, he little guessed at the extraordinary denouement the game would have. Having scored 44 out of Frinton's 94 for 9 declared, Norman then took nine wickets for 33, including a hat-trick, as Mistley were dismissed for 93, one run short. The following Saturday he scored 42 out of 165 for 8 declared, before taking two wickets for 44 as Dovercourt were bowled out for 88.

The summer term of 1957 was the last at the College for the finest cricketer the College had known. Suffolk-born David Larter joined the school in 1951; by the time he left he had developed a formidable reputation as a bowler whose pace and lift, from a six feet seven and a half inch frame, created considerable apprehension amongst both schoolboy and local

SEND OFF FOR AUSTRALIA: David Larter (left), the Northamptonshire and former Suffolk cricketer, was entertained by his old school, Framlingham College yesterday, prior to his departure for Australia with the M.C.C. team. David, who left Framlingham five years ago, is pictured signing autographs. Watching are two of his old games masters, Mr. H. L. Baly and Mr. N. F. Borrett, who helped start him on his cricketing career.

club players. He went on to play for Suffolk, Northamptonshire and England, in a career terminated early through injury. In his ten Tests he took 37 wickets at 25.42. He was, both at Framlingham and afterwards, no batsman, as his statistics show: he scored less runs than wickets taken, both in Tests (37 against 16) and in all first class games (666 against 639). The 1957 college cricket team coached by Norman Borrett was notable not only for the presence of Larter but also of two other future internationals in Norman Porter, twelve times a Scotland hockey cap, and Andrew Hancock, an England rugby player and scorer of a memorable last minute try at Twickenham to save the 1965 Calcutta Cup match against Scotland.

The summer vacation saw Norman again play nine innings for Devon. He was not at his best as a batsman, scoring 128 runs with a highest of 48. He had a good season however with the ball, ending with eight wickets at 14.25 each. All eight were taken in his first match of the season, against Berkshire at Torquay, including the best bowling of his minor county career, 6-28 from 14.4 overs. One of the batsmen he did not dismiss was Peter Smith, his England hockey colleague. The first ball of what was to prove Norman's last over bowled the batsman, the second was a dot ball, the third had the new batsman LBW, and with his fourth ball Norman finished off the innings by bowling the number eleven. In the same match he notched his highest score of the season, an innings of 48 which included eight fours and a five, and which the local paper praised as *'a welcome breath of fresh air to a day of generally stodgy batting against bowling which was mostly well on top.'*

Norman opted in 1958 for a short spell in Devon, five matches ending on August 16th, the Exeter and Seaton home fixtures, followed by the three match tour to Dorset, Oxfordshire and Berkshire. He was in fine form and again topped the batting averages, assisted by four not outs in his six innings, with 222 runs at an average of 111.

Micky Walford was again in the Dorset team for the Devon match on August 11th at Wimborne. He was to have a good season, playing in eight of the twelve Dorset fixtures and averaging nearly forty with the bat, including a knock of 157 not out against Berkshire. However, in the Devon match he was first out for a duck as his side were bowled out for 62. Devon in reply amassed 291 for four declared, Norman hitting a season-best 74 not out, as Devon won on first innings.

From Wimborne, Devon went on to Banbury to play Oxfordshire, and from there to Reading to play Berkshire on August 15th as another round of Minor County cricket matches began around the country. Whilst Norman was scoring 67 not out to take Devon to an eight wicket victory over Berkshire, not many miles away at Oxford Walford was scoring 64 to help Dorset to beat Oxfordshire; whilst all this was going on, David Larter took 5-72 for Suffolk as they drew with Norfolk at Felixstowe.

On leaving the College in July Larter had been invited to play four games for Suffolk. He did well, on two occasions taking five wickets in an innings, and at the season's end was signed by Northamptonshire. Norman congratulated the former pupil and encouraged him to work hard at the game, and to build up his fitness. Norman saw that the willowy youngster was going to have to improve his strength and stamina to withstand the rigours of daily fast bowling through a long summer.

* * * * * * * * *

The last West Country Tour; employing John Harris; and retirement from Devon Cricket

In 1959 the summer term at the College kept Norman busy coaching the first XI. He did manage to fit in a few games for local sides, taking it gently as the arthritis increased its grip. August saw him as always in the West country, staying in the Exeter hotel which had become his Devon cricket base over the years.

He struggled to find form in the first three matches, at Torquay against Berkshire, at Falmouth against Cornwall, and at Exeter against Somerset 11. His hip was not good, and his fielding was a painful matter, even at slip, where he had had to move from his usual cover-point position.

Somerset's right arm opening bowler, John Harris, remembers Norman coming out to bat in the Exeter game: "When we saw this 41 year-old man hobbling out to the wicket, we thought Devon must be really struggling to put out a strong side. He scored only a few runs in each innings."

John Harris had first played for Somerset in a second XI match in 1951 when he was just 15 and in May 1952 he made his first class debut, three months after his 16th birthday, against Glamorgan, for whom Alan Watkins scored 84. The schoolboy prodigy was however to struggle to fulfil this potential as an adult. After National Service in the army, during which he played successfully for Northern Command, he found on his return to the Somerset staff that he had only limited opportunities to play for the full county side. In all he played 15 County Championship matches and 52 Second XI and Minor County matches.

One of the highlights of his career was taking 3 for 59 against the visiting West Indian side in 1957, for whom Sobers scored a century, including having Everton Weekes caught and bowled, and scoring a brave 16 not out against the pace of Gilchrist and Hall. In 1959 he twice improved his best bowling analysis with 3-35 against Kent and 3-29 against Worcestershire. But he suffered a split elbow on the right arm (he batted left handed but bowled right handed) when struck by a short ball from England and Middlesex fast bowler Alan Moss, and there was concern that he would not fully recover from this setback.

He was therefore already contemplating his future when, after play in the Exeter game, Norman enquired as to whether he was interested in a school coaching job. It was agreed that they would talk again during the return fixture at Taunton the following week.

Devon's tour went on to Plymouth, where in the return match against Cornwall at Peverell Park, Devon ran up a massive 362 for 7 declared, former Somerset cricketer Roy Smith scoring 150 and Norman an elegant 83. On a good wicket and under hot sun, the two added 171 for the third wicket, Smith hitting 15 fours and Norman 12. Devon won on first innings. After Plymouth it was on to Taunton for the return match against Somerset II at county headquarters on August 7th and 8th. It was David Shepherd's first game for Devon. He played 51 times for them until in 1965 he was signed by Gloucestershire, for whom he played for 14 years before becoming one of cricket's most popular Test match umpires.

At Taunton Norman continued where he had left off

" *...We saw what he was all about, a fine stroke-maker who picked off the bowling for numerous boundaries, so the fact that he could hardly run any singles made little difference.*

against Cornwall, top-scoring with a fluent 37 in the first innings and 45 in the second with some powerful driving and pulling. John Harris saw what the hobbling 41 year old could do: "We saw what he was all about, a fine stroke-maker who picked off the bowling for numerous boundaries, so the fact that he could hardly run any singles made little difference.

As arranged we met after play. Norman bought me a beer and we talked about the possibility of my becoming the cricket coach and groundsman at Framlingham. I immediately liked him as a decent, straightforward man. He subsequently wrote to me advising that the job was available if I was interested. I later gathered that Headmaster Porter had accepted Norman's argument that College cricket would benefit from a cricket professional, the first to be employed since Phil Mead in the immediate pre-war period. I rang him and agreed to come to Suffolk for an interview. I stayed the night in the school sanatorium and was given a good look around the College by Norman, who then drove me back to Ipswich station after the visit. I took the job, and started work at the College in May 1960.

I was given a 5 year professional contract with Suffolk and had great fun playing twice each summer holiday for them until I left the College in 1964. Although I loved Norman I had great difficulty in relating to the bursar, who was formally my employer. As an example, when I asked the bursar if I could take on a milk round at 5 a.m., before my day's work at the College, in order to supplement my rather meagre earnings, he turned me down, but thanks to Norman, he was persuaded to agree.

I enjoyed coaching the College Eleven, and have happy memories of those days. After I had put the team through their paces at my first fielding practice Norman told me, to my surprise, that some of the Eleven had complained that it was too strenuous for them, and that he would take the practices

RIGHT: Norman's 1959 retirement from Minor County cricket is noted in Wisden.

rounder to ... ...

Norfolk, captained for the first ...
former Middlesex and England batsman who returned to play ...
his native shire after retiring from first-class cricket, had their most
successful season since 1939. The professional, E. G. Witherden,
also enjoyed an outstanding summer, scoring over 1,000 runs in
ten matches and hitting three centuries.

Devon's policy of bringing on promising youngsters was a
decided success and seven who were tried performed creditably,
particularly in the field. The county sustained a heavy blow through
an injury to N. F. Borrett, who had been a consistently good player
for many years.

J. A. R. Oliver completed his twenty-fourth year with

Oxford
North
Lincol
Leices
Shrop
Berks
Chesh
Corn
Cuml

from then on. I played for the Common Room side in their occasional evening matches against local villages. In an early one of these we had a portly gentleman fielding at slip who dived and caught an astonishing catch. Norman, fielding alongside him at slip, laughed so much as he too dived, that he slipped a disc and had to be carried off the field. I remember well in one of those games running to field a ball, on the main College ground, the Back, running back towards the boundary edge. As I picked up the ball I heard one of the Eleven, John Bonner, saying in a loud voice 'this is the chap who insists we throw the ball in just over the bails'. Thank goodness I succeeded in doing just that."

John's easy-going personality made him a popular and successful coach at the College, and later a well-regarded first class umpire for 20 years. He was close to Test level, umpiring a number of England Under 19 Tests, and in 2000 being chosen as the reserve umpire for the England v Zimbabwe Test and as the television replay umpire for the Nat West Final, both at Lords.

Norman's decision to seek a coach for the College was made when his own mobility was rapidly declining. Devon captain Deryck Fairclough: "My last memory of Norman is of him playing against Somerset II at Taunton. Not a happy memory I'm afraid. It was obvious he was in great pain and discomfort with his hip when in the field, but he was adamant that I should not have him substituted. It was saddening to see a once outstanding fielder barely able to bend to pick up the ball. This was probably the beginning of the end."

It was indeed the end. The following week, Devon's tour was due to go on to Oxford, Berkshire and Dorset; Norman took the view that he was a liability to the team in the field, and he told Fairclough he would have to pull out of the rest of the tour. The Western Morning News announced 'a late withdrawal from Devon's three match cricket tour is Norman Borrett who is suffering from arthritis'. Thus his Devon career ended, as the condition which had forced him to abandon first serious hockey and then squash, now claimed his cricket. He had been suffering for a long time, refusing to discuss it with his cricket colleagues but, as Fairclough's story reveals, not fooling any of them. His fitness had always been a source of pride to him, and he was only prepared to admit defeat to the disease

when he knew his fielding was letting down his team.

He had ended on a high, batting as well as ever, nine innings for 222 runs, at an average of 27.75. He had only bowled on one occasion, 14 overs of spin for a miserly 13 runs. The nature of cricket, with its leisurely pace and its focus on style and timing, had permitted him to continue to perform, without feeling he was letting down his team mates, almost until his 42nd birthday. In those days it was possible, and was indeed a widespread practice even in the first class game, for a captain to be able to hide an immobile fielder in the field, and Norman had, with his sharp eye and speed of reaction, taken numerous catches for his side at slip. His last match epitomized the problem; he could have continued in this vein, scoring runs and taking a few wickets, but in the field he was immobilized.

His retirement was described in Wisden as 'a heavy blow to the county… for he had been a consistently good player for many years.' His Devon career, over ten years - missing out 1951 and 1955 when he was touring South Africa - involved 56 matches and saw him total 2,408 runs in 80 innings at 37.05, with four centuries and a highest score of 134 not out. His bowling produced 35 wickets at an average of 32.80. His retirement left a void in the Devon set-up both as cricketer and team member - "a wonderful man", in the view of Devon stalwart Stuart Mountford.

Deryck Fairclough could see why Norman was such a successful sportsman, and for some, a difficult colleague: "There was never an element of self-doubt in his make-up and he truly relished a challenge. Not often did Mullie accompany him to matches and Norman, although sociable, rarely lingered at the bar at the end of the day. He appeared to want to get back home as soon as decently possible - as did I."

CLASSROOM AND COMMON ROOM

LEFT: The Hawks Club
tie and the suede
chukka boots – regular
features of the Borrett
wardrobe.

As a teacher, Norman, whose specialist subjects were Geography and English, took O and A level forms. He was different from his Common Room colleagues in every particular. He was disciplinarian, humorous, a hard task master meticulous in completing the syllabus, and human. His confidence was demonstrated by his choice of clothes. A snappy dresser, he favoured a hounds tooth sports jacket with leather-patched elbows, a Hawks Club tie, sharply creased grey flannels or cavalry twill trousers, bright yellow socks and a succession of fashionable suede chukka boots.

Even his delivery of the Grace, which the master on duty had to deliver to a packed dining hall before school meals, was different. "Benedictus Benedicat" (may the Blessed One bless us) in that clear, high tenor voice, always sent a frisson around the hall as he delivered it whilst still on the move towards the high table.

Douglas Thomson had a high regard for Norman's ability to teach Geography: "With one year to go before 'O' levels it was realised that I had not a hope of achieving a pass in Latin. I was accordingly put in a class in which Norman did the two year Geography course in one year. I was thus able to add the subject to my meagre total. Whilst I too was delighted to receive his sports coaching I am also very grateful to him for teaching me enough to scrape into the sixth form."

Most of the pupils who studied Geography under Norman recall the topography and geology of France with unusual clarity. This, according to Norman Porter, was due to the close focus the teacher brought to the topic of the wine-growing regions of the country.

Norman Mayhew thought Norman's teaching made O Level Geography "interesting and successful for me.

❝❞

…Without his help and interest I would not have ventured to Cambridge, and in that respect his influence on my life was immense.

Although he did not suffer fools gladly, those that made the effort were given huge encouragement. Without his help and interest I would not have ventured to Cambridge, and in that respect his influence on my life was immense."

Whilst he was well regarded by his pupils for the effectiveness of his teaching, he could sometimes struggle to inspire a class of boys who had greater interest in their forthcoming weekend than in exploring the byways of Academe. In such circumstances Norman would on occasion resort to an injection of humour. Brian Smith, Past President of the SOF, remembers one such occasion and its surprising sequel: "It was indeed a challenging experience. Somehow the class found itself having to read Treasure Island as part of Norman's quite fruitless attempt to introduce his class to the joys of literature. Norman, I felt, was just as bored as we all were with Treasure Island but, being a long-suffering English teacher, he did have a wicked sense of humour. Something, he must have thought, has to be done to spice the reading. There is, after all, a limit to how many 'Aha Jim Lads' anyone should be prepared to shout. Then suddenly, one day - salvation! That passage had been reached when the pirates burst into song with 'Yo Ho Ho and a bottle of rum,' and 'Lillibulero'.

I can't recall the little creep who perked up enough to raise his hand and ask, 'Sir? Please Sir, what's Lillibulero?' "Ah!" replied Norman, It's a great tune.' Sensing a good skive coming on, another equally odious creep asked how it went. At this point, Norman's sense of humour kicked in. 'Which boy plays the piano?' he enquired, stroking his sideburns. 'Smith, sir, Smith plays the piano.' God, I hated that boy. Smith didn't play the piano, he massacred it, it was the bone of contention of a lifetime that my parents had insisted that I had music lessons at all. 'No sir. Sorry sir, I don't play the piano.' The Borrett lowered his head and looked me laser-like between the eyes, 'But are you taking lessons boy?' 'Yes sir.' 'Then by next week you will play Lillibulero to the entire class.'

I rushed to Eric Copperwheat, the music teacher and choirmaster, who told me he hadn't got a copy of the tune. Great! Off to the Borrett. 'Sorry sir, no copy.' I was totally relaxed, monkeys had flown from my shoulders. But then Mr Copperwheat announced to me, three days before the week was up, that through the good offices of the Borrett, a copy of the music had been procured. How nice! Every spare minute of every day to the dreaded countdown I bored my fingers with that dreadful piece of music. I've hated that music ever since. Every time I hear it I feel nauseous. Practice. Practice.

The dreadful day dawned. Maybe the Borrett was ill? Perhaps he's had to go somewhere? No, as jaunty as you like, he swooped into the lesson with the over-zealous eagerness of a man whose fitness was never in question. But, joy upon joy, we've passed three quarters of the lesson and nothing's been mentioned. The odious little creeps haven't reminded him. I've got away with it. The Borrett's looking at his watch. The bell's about to ring. 'Well boys, that's about wrapped it up for today... except for Smith's rendition of Lillibulero for which little performance we are all agog, are we not boys?' Shrieks of approval. I hated everyone in the classroom with a passion. I found myself moving to the piano as if to my execution. The prospect of hanging concentrated my mind wonderfully but did little for my finger-brain coordination. I lumbered through it. I punished the class by putting up a truly awful performance. The Borrett winced. 'Want a bit more time, do you Smith?' 'No sir. That's it.' 'No it's not Smith, we look forward to a repeat performance next week and to perfection.' And, I'm pleased to report, it was.

Postscript: Some forty-odd years later Norman Borrett nearly ran me over with his car outside the Crown hotel in Framlingham. He looked up and smiled. 'Sorry about that.' he said, 'I wasn't thinking. Can't get that bloody Lillibulero tune out of my head!' I was astonished. Yes, he had remembered both it and me!"

Whilst he would be prepared to let a classroom laugh at one of its own number, he understood that the quid pro quo was to that he had to take the occasional ribbing from the boys. Dr. Bob Fox was one who did that:

"One of Norman's favourite expressions was 'Good Lord'. I remember being in a school play – Agatha Christie's Ten Little Niggers – and I dressed my character in clothes I thought were

❝❞

...On entering the stage my first words were: 'Good Lord', in the voice we all used to mimic Norman. There was a burst of laughter from the school audience.

similar to those Norman would wear. I also stuck fluff to my cheeks in imitation of the tufts of cheek hair Norman affected. On entering the stage my first words were: 'Good Lord', in the voice we all used to mimic Norman. There was a burst of laughter from the school audience. I am glad to say Norman laughed, sitting amongst the audience. He knew I was mimicking him, but he had broad enough shoulders not to be affronted. He was a great asset to the school."

The ability to remember faces and names was acute. Allhallows former pupil Stuart MacGregor recalls: "Although he was at the school a reasonably short time, if he met any Old Boys much later he would remember them. I was only taught by him for a couple of years, but when I bumped into him at various hockey occasions or at Lord's he always remembered me, my name, and all about my father and his profession".

David Carr, who was at the College in the 1970s, tells a similar story: "My father Ken told me that in the early years of the 21st century (when Norman was into his 80s) Ken was umpiring a Gentlemen of Essex cricket match on the Back, the main College ground. During the tea interval, he saw Norman crossing the Back, and thought to approach him to introduce himself. Before he could say anything Norman said: 'No need to tell me – father of captain 1974'. This was probably twenty years after either of us had last seen Norman."

In the classroom, Norman's classes were models of quietness, except on those occasions when Walter Winstanley would have to complain that he could not hear himself teach for the noise of community singing emanating from Norman's classroom next door. Norman believed in a strict code of conduct and that it should be enforced when necessary by caning. Caning, or 'tanning' in College argot, using any implement from a shoe to a hockey stick, had been the accepted form of punishment for a range of misdemeanours in Norman's time as a pre-war pupil. It was still in use on his return as a teacher, until it was abandoned in the 1970s. Framlingham, like most independent boarding schools of the time, operated this system of rough justice, which to the 21st century reader will appear barbaric, without it seems turning its proponents into savages.

John Birt, a pupil in the late 50s and early 60s, and later a Gurkha officer, recalls the occasions when his unruly classroom behaviour led to his being required by Norman "to fetch Willie", the legendary instrument of punishment, which in his memory was a cricket bat, but most recollect it as a hockey stick, which Norman kept in his study for the chastisement of wrong-doers. Traditionally the miscreant was required to fetch the implement himself, to the mirth of his classmates. Norman had the rare gift of mixing humour with discipline, so that all the stories surrounding Willie involve an outcome which was not so bad after all, and illustrate that Norman's bark was far worse than his bite, although it could still be some bark. John's story is a good example: "I will always remember being walloped in class by Norman using Willie, the cricket bat, and then signing it after the event, to general amusement!"

Graham Walsh is one of those OFs to recall the dreaded command to 'fetch Willie, boy': "One day a boy in my class duly fetched Willie, and in addition also brought a pillow. We all laughed, and to his credit, so did Norman". Gentler admonitions would be accompanied by a twinkle in the eye and spiced with Norman's regular threat: "You wait till I see Mother". The incident would be quickly forgotten; Norman did not harbour grudges.

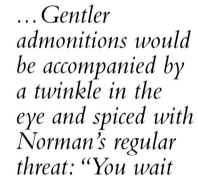

…Gentler admonitions would be accompanied by a twinkle in the eye and spiced with Norman's regular threat: "You wait till I see Mother"…

As a schoolmaster sportsman and a coach to many, with a powerful personality, Norman inevitably assumed role model status to generations of young people, and many of those who have contributed to this memoir have happily expressed their deep affection for the man. But for some, pupils and adults, his confident, direct manner and occasionally caustic wit was uncomfortable. Those traits which in sport made him a winner, were not always curbed in a social setting. Thus the confidence in his own talents could on occasion become a tendency to favour his own view over that of others, and the unshakable will to win could lead his impartiality astray, as John Cockett's story of Norman umpiring a College match exemplifies. The analytical side of his intellect was highly developed - in the sporting context he could see more quickly and easily than

others the consequence of a particular shot or stroke. This could mean the slowness of an ordinary mortal to absorb advice could be an irritant and he did not always succeed in hiding that feeling. The unswerving determination not to give in and to give absolutely everything of himself to the cause could become bloody-mindedness, and could lead him to criticise those who appeared to him to be less committed.

Examples of these failings are provided by Clive Smith and John Saul. Clive, later to become a stylish batsman in the College XI, was in 1955 in the school choir, and in the colts XI, coached by Norman. Clive was nervous when he plucked up courage to inform Norman that he would be unable to attend the next practice game, because he was going on the choir outing. "Everybody within a hundred yards of the nets was advised by Mr. Borrett of what I had just told him, and much laughter at my expense ensued. I was only in the choir for a short time and I loved sport, so there had to be a good reason why I was going on the outing, bur Mr Borrett did not ask me. Had he done so I would have been able to tell him that it was a trip to Cobbolds Brewery in Ipswich - clearly a visit many boys would have envied!"

John recalls Norman's treatment of a fellow pupil, a fine athlete who, having won his hockey colours the previous season, declined to play for the hockey team in favour of appearing at a County Athletics event. Norman told him, in front of others, that he would never play hockey for the school again. An unkind reaction from one who himself had had to make so many choices between competing sports events.

On the other side of the coin, Norman could be, and usually was, caring and considerate, but he didn't like to make it public. A number of pupils were entertained to dinner at the Readery at the end of their last term. Not all members of staff would take this sort of trouble, and the lasting affection felt by many OFs for Mullie and Norman was in no small measure due to similar discreet gestures of hospitality.

Walter Winstanley, second master of the College and a pillar of the Common Room for many years, although a great supporter and a respecter of Norman's achievements, was also an occasional critic of the caustic nature of Norman's wit, being heard to refer to the Readery as 'the Rudery'. Norman had lived in different circles from his pupils and many of his Common Room colleagues, and in recounting the names of people he had met in his sporting encounters, he was thought by some to be a name-dropper. But this apparent conceit disguised a modesty which meant he could rarely be persuaded to talk about his past.

In many ways he was a surprisingly private person. In the words of Norman Porter at Norman Borrett's memorial service: "Yes, he was self-assured, confident, dominant even, but he was never self-promoting. If he knew what was going on in this chapel today he would have said: 'What on earth are you making all this fuss about? Don't fuss.' He hated fuss."

Norman's preparedness to speak his mind, what Norman Porter called his 'verbal bravado', and the views he held of the merit of some of his Common Room colleagues, did occasionally cause trouble. When in 1966 Norman, housemaster of Stradbroke, his old house, was appointed Second Master on the retirement of Walter Winstanley, he caused something of a Common Room revolt. John Saul recalls his father, Tom, who was at the time President of the SOF and, for the period of his presidency, ex officio a governor of the College, telling him of the upset caused by Norman's appointment, which promoted him over the heads of at least six teachers who had been at the College well before Norman's arrival. The Governors received a letter signed by a number of staff expressing their disappointment at the appointment. All the signatories were then spoken to by the Governors, and the appointment was then confirmed. Norman's performance in his new role won over some at least of his critics.

When asked late in life if he would have liked to have been headmaster, Norman expressed some disappointment at not being invited: "I would like to have been given the chance. I think I might have made a go of it." Martin Irving, Head of French, and a senior member of that 1966 Common Room, did not think Norman would have made a good Headmaster: "His straightforward style came across as rather bossy, and the Common Room did not care to be told so directly what was right and what was wrong. When, unknowingly, way back in 1950 when he first became a member of the Common Room, Norman had assumed the chair regarded as the regular seat of the Chaplain Rupert Kneese, and thus he got off to a poor start in some eyes."

But Martin, making no reference to the Common Room near-revolt of 1966, went on: "I never had any problem with Norman; I was always struck by his habitual cheerfulness: he was often in pain but never complained or let it get him down. To me he was a man of old-fashioned values and simple tastes – as just one example he never bothered to spend much money on his house. He wasn't at all showy." Martin became a friend of Norman, regularly playing squash with him on the College courts (and playing together in the same Suffolk side). The two shared an interest in fun, as the bicycle races between them down the main stone staircase in College testified.

The First SRA Overseas Tour for 30 years – South Africa 1955

Norman did not play in any of Devon's minor county cricket championship matches in 1955, as the summer vacation was taken up with a Great Britain squash tour to South Africa, captained by Norman. The idea of a first overseas tour by an SRA team for thirty years had been proposed by the South African SRA in June 1954. By February 1955 the idea had become reality and the SRA in London wrote to Norman and a number of other players to ascertain their availability for a tour to the Union and Rhodesia, with "twenty-four 'playing days', including four Test matches and the South African championships, and seven free days". The letter asked what sum up to £400 each player might be able to raise to defray the total tour cost.

By May, the tour was confirmed and the SRA finalised its efforts to raise the best available team, the SRASA having requested the strongest possible side. The May edition of the Wanderers Club, Johannesburg, magazine, made the South African view clear:

'It is disappointing to learn that neither of the two English Amateur finalists are available. Fairbairn has announced his retirement from competitive squash and Roy Wilson is too tied up by family and business affairs to find time for the trip, notwithstanding the most pressing exhortations. It had been the SRASA's intention that, unless one of these two were available, they would not favour the tour this year, as the Association was under the impression that Fairbairn and Wilson were on a level far above the rest of British players. This assertion however brought a spirited denial from official quarters in England, who have indicated that there is little to choose between their top players and that both Wilson and Fairbairn have been beaten or considerably extended many times.'

Norman Borrett's selection as captain of the team was received, in Britain, with surprise, particularly in the light of the South African concerns. His arthritis was a public fact but he had always kept the worsening nature of the hip trouble to himself, and it was rather his lack of top quality match practice that raised eyebrows amongst squash commentators contemplating a strenuous 14 match tour. He had not played in the Amateur for four years, and although he had continued to be selected by England for the domestic internationals he was no longer the top dog: in the 1952-53 season he had played at third string in the national side, and at fourth string in the 1953-54 season, behind Fairbairn, Wilson and

Seymour-Hayden. In 1954-55 his gradual withdrawal from the game continued, as he played only once for England and in only five other matches. His first ever venture into the Suffolk Championship in March, which he won, was driven entirely by his need to get in some match practice before the South African tour.

Press scepticism of Norman's participation in the tour subsided when it was then revealed that the SRASA had specifically asked for Norman to be included in the party, he having made such a favourable impression during the British and Irish hockey tour in 1951. As BLT&S reported: 'the South Africans are particularly keen to welcome Norman Borrett whom many of them met when he captained (sic) the British hockey team which toured the Union in 1951. Borrett's name is a legend wherever squash is played and even if he is well past his best, he still retains much of the old fire which brought him a run of five Amateur championships in the finals of which he did not lose a single game'.

Norman knew, deep down, that his acceptance of the invitation to go on a gruelling tour was a gamble: it would be the equivalent of several consecutive tournaments, a physical commitment which he had foresworn three years before. Norman's problem was that the old urge to compete again, in a country whose people he liked, was just too strong for him to resist. He persuaded himself that he could last the course and not let the side down.

The five-man GB team was described in BLT&S, with great generosity to the older players, as 'a nice blend of maturity and youth'. The reality was that the three senior members, and Norman in particular, were not the players they once were. The two other veterans, apart from 37 year old Norman, were

…Norman's problem was that the old urge to compete again… …just too strong for him to resist. He persuaded himself that he could last the course and not let the side down.

Brian Phillips, 39, twelve times an England cap, 'whose greatest misfortune was to reach his peak when Borrett was supreme - he is probably the best player never to have won the Amateur', and the newly appointed Naval and Air Attaché at the British Embassy in Madrid, Commander Alan Seymour-Hayden, 37, fifteen times an England international, 'like Phillips, verging on the veteran stage, and unlikely now to win the Amateur crown for which he has been for years such a notable contender'. The two younger members of the party were both up-and-coming Army players, Lieutenant Ian de Sales la Terriere, 24, the Scottish champion with five Scottish caps, and Lieutenant (later Brigadier) Mike Perkins, the 1955 Amateur semi-finalist. The team was to be accommodated at the main clubs of the cities where they would be playing, the Salisbury Club, the Rand Club at Johannesburg, the City Club in Cape Town, and the Port Elizabeth Club, and the SRASA made arrangements for them to be made temporary members of those clubs for the duration of their stay.

Fulfilling his captaincy role, Norman wrote to each of the players in early June, from Framlingham: "This is really to get in touch with you about the SRA tour to S. Africa. I am so glad that you have been chosen to go – heartiest congratulations. It should be great fun and I'm sure that you will enjoy it.

As regards the tour, I feel that we must be absolutely fit and in first class touch with the game before we leave England. They will be expecting great things out there, so we must go all out to win every match. As the first match is just after our arrival, we cannot afford to be out of touch. Naturally you know best how you prefer to get fit, and I would suggest that you play as often as you can before we leave, especially in July. I do not know what opportunities you have for playing squash where you are, but if you are near a court, practice on one's own I find is well worth while, especially if you move about quickly when playing your shots. If you get up to London, I'm sure that Brian Phillips would love to play you, and if you find yourself near here I will welcome a game. I shall be only too pleased to put you up if you would like to come and stay for a few days to have a 'work-out'."

The South African squash community excelled themselves to raise funds to cover the air fares and the expenses of the British squad through provincial levies, club donations, and individual contributions. They had, however, only been able to fund a team of five players, which was bound to put a real strain on the five to survive the testing itinerary, quite apart from the risk of injury. So there was a collective sigh of relief when the news came through, as late as July 6th, that a group of City of London businessmen had funded a reserve, sixth, player, Dick Hawkey, 32 year-old schoolmaster at Merchant Taylors and capped by England four times.

On Saturday August 6th the team met for a dinner hosted by the chairman of the SRA at the Union Club in London's West End. ..

> ...A five course meal, accompanied by Batard Montrachet 1950 and Chateau Leoville Poyferre 1943, was perhaps not what Norman had had in mind as ideal preparation for a tough tour. The event did, however, provide a useful opportunity for players and officials to meet, some for the first time, and in the words of Norman's tour report, "allowed the side to have a few words together before meeting at the airport". In that manner was the strategy for the first SRA tour abroad in 30 years established and debated.

The team flew out on Monday August 8th, on a South African Airways Constellation flight, tourist class. At the Frankfurt stop-over the team ran into the last British Wimbledon tennis champion, Fred Perry, who, in his broad American accent, told them that if he had known about the tour, he would have fixed them up with some sports clothes. At Rome Seymour-Hayden joined the party. On disembarkation at Livingstone, the party checked in to the Victoria Falls Hotel, and rid themselves of some of their economy-class cramp with a long walk around the spectacular Falls, with sunshine on their backs and spray from the cataracts in their eyes. The 24 hour break from travelling was welcome, but the hard work was about to start. Within three hours of touch-down on the 10th at Salisbury, where the team were met by Norman's old friend

Bill Clements, who had left his coaching job at the Imperial Hotel Torquay in 1950 to emigrate to Rhodesia, the six travellers attended the first drinks party of the tour.

Although the next day was a day off, the team followed a visit to the tobacco market with squash practice at the Salisbury Sports Club courts. On the 12th the Governor General of Southern Rhodesia entertained the team to lunch, prior to the first match of the tour at 5pm in which the tourists overcame any digestive problems in beating a combined Northern and Southern Rhodesian team by six matches to nil. The following day, the side visited the tobacco auctions, took a boat trip on Lake McIlwaine, and played Mashonaland, winning convincingly 5-0. The team then travelled to Bulawayo, where the Governor General again looked after them, arranging a climb to the top of the Matopos, to see the Matabeleland burial place of Cecil Rhodes. The match against Combined Rhodesias at 4pm on August 15th was also won 5-0, Norman winning for the third time in straight games.

The team played exhibition matches against each other at the Bulawayo courts the next day. This was a useful exercise for two reasons: to gain familiarity with the difficulties of playing the game on the plateau at 5,000 feet, and to provide a yardstick for the order in which the team would play the forthcoming Test Match. Norman looked very fit, showing no sign of his hip problem, and was in good touch as he beat Seymour-Haydon 9-3 in the fifth; Perkins beat Phillips in five, and la Terriere overcame Hawkey in four games.

On August 17th the team flew to Johannesburg, three days before the first Test. Observing that the team in practice played in a style foreign to the South Africans, making their strokes very late and disguising them well, the Rand Daily Mail predicted that the contest would be between the South Africans' fitness and the visitors' deceptiveness. The 19th saw the first match of the South African leg of the tour. Although the team whitewashed a Transvaal B side at the famous Wanderers Club, there were signs that the next day's First Test was going to be a difficult proposition, as each of the GB side dropped one game and la Terriere dropped two. Norman rested himself from this game in favour of Hawkey.

Local interest in the tour was big, and growing. The day before the First Test, Norman was interviewed by the Rand Daily Mail. The interview contains some revealing passages and is reproduced here in full:

'Six of the most energetic fellows I've seen in a long while flew in from England the day before yesterday to do battle on

BELOW: August 8th 1955. The GB team, Hawkey, la Terriere, Norman, Perkins and Phillips, board the plane for South Africa.

the squash courts of the Union. After limbering up against a Transvaal second string at the Wanderers Club this evening, they will play the first of four Tests against South Africa tomorrow night, and take it from me we'll do mighty well to hold them.

I met Norman Borrett, the tall, sinewy skipper of the British team, over a quiet pint of ale, and he advised me that this is the first representative outfit to journey this far overseas in 30 years. "We play internationals against Wales, Scotland and Ireland every year" he explained, "and we also play in France, Holland, Denmark and Sweden. So far we haven't played in Canada or in the United States. There of course the rules are a bit different and they use a narrower court, a harder ball, and a slightly heavier racket".

Norman, who paid his first visit to South Africa in 1951 as captain (sic) of a British hockey team, is a formidable opponent on a squash court. He was British champion for five consecutive years before retiring undefeated.

"Why did I retire?" he asked. "Well, after five years, being the champion loses much of its novelty." At 37, Norman refers to himself as a "vintage mode" on a squash court. Living in the countryside as he does, he plays but seldom. "The secret of good squash is physical fitness, concentration, and a degree of low cunning" he advised. "I find it unnecessary to practice frequently, but when I do go on a court I prefer to play alone rather than against an easy opponent. It doesn't do your game any good to do battle with a lesser man." Norman is a Geography master at Framlingham College, in Suffolk. "That's probably why they selected me as captain", he told me. "With my knowledge of geography it's pretty unlikely that we'll get lost".'

The First Test on Saturday August 20th, one week into the tour, took place at the Wanderers. Seats in the gallery had been allocated to clubs and had been sold out long before the day. 500 people crammed in, eager to see how far squash in their sports-mad country had progressed, as the best of their nation were judged by their success against the representatives of GB, the home of squash.

Norman took the decision to play himself at first string, where he found South Africa's top player Brian Callaghan too strong for him, losing 4-9, 4-9, 9-6, 5-9. This decision occasioned surprise in the British press. BLT&S commented 'Norman Borrett…has been out of serious squash for some years now and unless the South African air has rejuvenated him, would hardly expect in this country at any rate to beat any of his younger team mates'. That criticism was entirely valid from afar, where on the evidence of the 1954-55 English squash season, Norman would have been ranked below all his touring colleagues save for Phillips and perhaps Hawkey. But the tour produced different considerations, which called for the players to adapt to unfamiliar conditions of climate, altitude, and fitness. And the results of the other players did not suggest they would have done better: at second string, Seymour-Haydon, whom Norman had beaten

only four days earlier, had also lost, to Callaghan's brother Denis, in straight games. Phillips at four and Perkins at five had lost to Barnes and Kaplan respectively, both in five games, and the only winner was third string la Terriere, over Jarvis. The team had not had much time to acclimatise to the altitude, but probably also suffered from a lack of appreciation of the high standard of play of their opponents. The team drew no comfort from the Lions' rugby defeat at Newlands the same day but national pride was lifted somewhat by the news of England's Fifth Test cricket victory over South Africa at the Oval.

The tour moved to quite different playing conditions, to the coast at Durban in Natal on Monday August 22nd, and the next day exhibition matches were played at the Natal Command and Air Force Clubs. Based on the result of these matches Norman announced, on the Tuesday evening, the teams for both the provincial match, versus Natal on the Wednesday and for the Second Test on the Friday. Against Natal Norman put la Terriere at first string and Seymour-Haydon at second, with Norman playing at third, Phillips at fourth and Perkins at fifth. Natal did not provide as strong a challenge as had been hoped and were beaten 6-0, Norman dropping only seven points in beating Hugh Bull at third string.

For the Test Norman altered the order from the Natal game, in a tactical move, designed to reverse the result of the First Test, promoting himself to first string, with la Terriere and Seymour-Haydon at two and three, and Phillips and Perkins at four and five. Whilst the order could be justified by the results of the practice games which the players had contested against each other, it was unlikely that Norman was playing better than la Terriere. In the event, Norman could not find his touch with his drop shots, and found the South African captain Brian Callaghan's lobs difficult to handle, losing in straight games. Both la Terriere and Seymour-Haydon won tough matches in five and four games. With Phillips reversing his First Test result by beating Tony Barnes, the reinstated amateur previously a professional coach in Putney, in straight games, and Perkins winning the most exciting game of the lot, defeating Cecil Kaplan in five hard games, the match was won 4-1. This win, at sea level, caused hopes to rise that the Johannesburg result had been an early tour one-off blemish.

As captain, Norman was player, organizer, selector, baggage master, speech maker, and writer of the post-tour report in the SRA handbook. He passed the speech-making duty around the team members, ensuring he didn't tire them with having always to listen to him as well as giving them, particularly the two younger players, welcome speaking experience. At the post-Test reception for the teams the day after the Durban match, it was Norman's turn. He was an easy, relaxed, speaker, paying tribute to the organisers and to the defeated opponents, and summarising the history of squash in South Africa. He said that from what he had seen, the South Africans had no reason to fear any other amateur side in the world. They had some very fine players.

From Durban the team flew to Port Elizabeth where, apart from visiting the wild elephants of Addo Park, going on a 550 mile tour of the scenic garden route, playing exhibition matches, attending a cocktail party at Paul Prosser's home, and a dinner dance, all in a single day, they played two provincial matches against Eastern Province on the Port Elizabeth Club courts, winning both 6-0. The matches were at least an opportunity to draw a form line through the performances of Norman and la Terriere, who had yet to play each other on tour. They each played Paul Prosser, the Eastern Province top player, Norman playing brilliantly to win in straight games whilst la Terriere dropped one game.

The team's hosts were as welcoming as in every other city, the players being taken to a snake park, ostrich farms, the Kango caves, and yet more drinks parties. On Wednesday August 31st, Norman's fifteenth wedding anniversary was celebrated by flying to Cape Town, the venue for the important Third Test. For the provincial match against Western Province on Friday, the day before the Test, Norman stood down for the second time and Hawkey played the fifth of his eight matches, coming in at fifth string with the others all moving up one from the order in which they had played the Second Test. The match was won 5-0.

So to the big match.

Norman later explained the reason for their optimism about this fixture: "We were hoping for another Test win at sea level, as we were fully aware of the strength of this South African team in their Johannesburg courts." That strength lay in the locals' ability to play in the thin air of the high plateau. Mike Perkins gives an interesting example of the severity of this. "In 1958 I toured South Africa with the Jesters and played Denis Callaghan at the Wanderers. Denis, a highly experienced player in that thin air, had to take oxygen during the match, and that was after the first game!"

For the Test Norman promoted la Terriere to top string, and played himself at two. Both of them lost, the Callaghan brothers proving just how good they were. Norman's effort,

losing 10-9, 9-0, 10-8, was painful not only on his hip but on the feet, which were badly blistered. Seymour-Hayden at three and Perkins at five both won in four games, but Phillips disappointingly lost his fourth string match against Barnes, putting him 2-1 down in their mini-series, and the team's sea-level hopes were confounded as the match was lost 3-2. Everything now depended on the last Test in two weeks' time. "We realised that we should have to improve to have a chance of levelling the series. Before the Test there were the South African championships which we hoped would give us considerable practice in the Wanderers courts".

After five days in Cape Town and a fortnight on the coast, the team returned, for the last leg of the tour, to Johannesburg, landing en route at Kimberley for a view of the Big Hole diamond excavation. Immediately on arrival at Jan Smuts airport the hospitality resumed: the team was taken to Springs in the eastern end of the Rand for lunch at the Country Club, and then to watch an inter-province rugby match, before playing exhibition matches; after which they were entertained to dinner by the Mayor.

Ensconced again at Johannesburg's Rand Club, altitude acclimatisation did not seem too much of a problem as the match against Johannesburg SRC was won easily, Norman winning 3-0 at second string. Brian Phillips was later to recall, in his squash coaching book, Norman's comment on sighting opponent Mossy Berman's choice of shorts, which were

…on sighting opponent Mossy Berman's choice of shorts, which were unusually short-cut for the just-above-the-knee style of the day: "Shorts a bit tight under the armpits aren't they, Mossy?"

unusually short-cut for the just-above-the-knee style of the day: "Shorts a bit tight under the armpits aren't they, Mossy?"

The next day, the match against Transvaal, who were represented by the full Test team, provided a worrying portent for the Final Test. Whilst Norman rested his blistered feet before the championships in two days' time, the order of all the strings was changed, to give the tourists a chance to play opponents whom they had not played in the Tests. This did not help the result, which was a 4-1 win to Transvaal. Seymour-Hayden and Perkins each gained only one game from the Callaghans at the top of the order, whilst Phillips lost to Jarvis at three and Hawkey to Barnes at four. La Terriere was the only winner, beating the fifth string Kaplan for the loss of one game. Norman's team, one or two of whom were beginning to feel somewhat jaded after their efforts on and off the court, would have to pick themselves up for the South African championships.

The seeding choices made by the South African SRA for the tournament, which ran from September 8th to14th, were of interest to the debate as to Norman's string selections for the Tests. Brian Callaghan was made top seed, with Ian de Sales la Terriere at two, Norman at three, and Callaghan's brother Denis at four. Norman was an easy winner in an opening round which contained the shock of the tournament – a defeat for Brian Phillips in an erratic five game match with Hugh Bull of Natal. Norman beat Mossy Berman for the loss of only three points in the second round and the other GB players went through easily, having survived the warm hospitality of the City Officials and the Chamber of Mines at lunch that day.

A dinner dance at Ciro's Restaurant Club on Friday ("where we spent many a happy evening" recalls Mike Perkins) may have had some effect on Norman's sharpness the next day, when in the third round he had a terrific battle with Chris Kaplan, the South African Test fifth stringer.

This was the longest match Norman had ever played, lasting an hour and a half, and he was lame after winning 9-6, 0-9, 9-7, 1-9, 9-4, to go into the last eight.

He was joined by Perkins, Seymour- Hayden and by la Terriere, who had defeated Hawkey in four games. The quarter-finals saw Seymour-Hayden play brilliantly to beat top seed Brian Callaghan in straight games, Norman similarly disposing of Lange, whilst Perkins went out in straight games to Denis Callaghan; la Terriere was surprisingly overcome by Roger Jarvis after leading 4-0 in the fifth game.

In the semi-finals, Norman's earlier exertions proved too much for him and he went down to Seymour-Hayden after a stern battle, 8-10, 9-2, 9-1, 9-2. Denis Callaghan beat Jarvis in straight games in the other match, setting up a final between the two finest retrievers in the two teams. In the final

Seymour-Hayden in his turn found the hot conditions and Denis Callaghan's error-free play too much for him and was defeated 9-4, 9-0, 9-1 after an hour's battle. The championships were generally held to be the best ever held in the country, highly competitive and well supported, with regular attendances of over 400 in the galleries.

On the Sunday rest day between the third round and the quarter-finals of the championships, the team played exhibitions at Harry Oppenheimer's private court, before a dinner with the family and a view of the finest diamond collection in the world. On the day after the championships, the team played North Transvaal, winning easily. The fourth and last Test was played the next day, on September 16th, two days before the team departed for Nairobi en route to London.

Whether the cumulative effect of the exhilarating but exhausting tour took its toll, or whether the high altitude did for them, the British lost the match they had to win by 3-2. Seymour-Hayden, promoted to top string after his splendid championship performance, again excelled himself with a win over Brian Callaghan, in a marathon 105 minutes. La Terriere at second string went down in four games to Denis Callaghan, fresh from his national championship triumph, but Norman, playing at three for the first time, produced his best squash of the tour as he defeated Jarvis in four games. Hawkey, taking Phillips' place at fourth string, lost to Barnes in a match he should have won, having led 2-1 and 5-1. The match was poised at 2-all as Perkins took on fifth string Cecil Kaplan, whom he had beaten in the two preceding Tests, but who, as Norman had found in the championships, was in much improved form. Kaplan this time made no mistake and won in straight games, giving South Africa the match 3-2 and the Test series 3-1.

Norman's decision to play himself up the order in the Tests, when in reality he warranted a lower spot, could be said to have been justified in the first Test, as it helped those who, in consequence, played below him to have a better chance of winning, which they failed to take. Similarly, his decision to continue at one in the second Test again produced a benefit for the team, which those below him this time seized. If in the third Test he had again chosen to play at one, instead of at two, Britain might have edged home. His victory at three in the last Test takes the argument neither one way nor the other. The SASRA made him third seed in their championships, only la Terriere of the GB team being seeded higher. Of one thing there can be no doubt: Norman selected the team for each Test in order for the team

RIGHT: Back row: la Terriere, Hawkey and Perkins.
Front row: Phillips, Norman and Seymour-Hayden.

to win. He always wanted to win himself, but he cared less about that than that his side should succeed. His comment, fifty years later, reflected that: "We were struggling to win. I felt that if I played up the order that would increase the chances of the lower strings, and I might also be able to pull off a win or two myself."

After a riotous last night stag dinner given by the South African side at The Wanderers Club, at which the teams exchanged their international ties and gifts, "six spritely figures staggered to the aircraft and reluctantly left the Union", in Mike Perkins' words, at 0700 on September 17th bound for Nairobi.

The Kenya Squash Rackets association did the team proud for the three days of their Nairobi trip, putting them up in private homes. Safaris, parties, tribal dances, a visit to Mau-Mau country and two squash matches, an international and a friendly, all went by in a pleasant blur. The Test, Kenya's first ever, was won 6-0 by GB, with Digby Flowerdew losing at second string for Kenya and Norman winning at third for GB.

Thus ended a tour which across three countries had provided the six players with friendships made and sights seen which would linger long in the memory. As would the effort they had put in, both off and on the court. Perkins had played in all 15 South African tour matches, Seymour-Hayden and la Terriere in 14, Phillips 13, Norman in 12 and Hawkey in 8 including the last Test. Norman's decision to select himself for more matches than Hawkey was an error, as Hawkey was clearly not match-fit when brought into the side for the final Test.

Norman's personal tally in the provincial matches was played eight, won eight, without dropping a game. He did not play in the Transvaal match but played in all four Tests, losing three and winning one. When asked years later how, not having played more than a handful of seriously competitive matches over the preceding 18 months, and with an arthritic hip condition, he had managed to play a remarkable twelve of the fifteen matches, he explained: "I wore a small device strapped around my right thigh and groin, which emitted an electronic pulse. This had been given me by a medical friend in London as a means of keeping the hip joint mobile. It seemed to have some effect, but I was pretty stiff after each match...

...Perhaps I should have stood down more frequently, but I had accepted the invitation to tour, and to captain, and I wasn't going to treat myself as a passenger".

Norman's report in BLT&S's November edition paid due tribute to the South African team:

"And so South Africa won the rubber - and deservedly so. It was close, always enjoyable and on the day they played the better squash. We felt we had no excuses though perhaps there were reasons, such as the fact that the tour came during their season and it took us some time to settle down to serious squash again; also the fact that we played more or less continuously during the tour and any blisters or strains got little respite. It would be wrong to assume that any of our defeats were due to lack of training. It is however important on a trip of this type to accept and enjoy the hospitality offered and the continual round of travelling, official lunches, dinners, long car trips, dances, etc., although all extremely enjoyable cannot in the long run but detract from performances in the squash court against opponents all extremely fit and not being subjected to the same non-stop treatment. Perhaps one day we may have the pleasure of entertaining a South African side over here and watching how and whether they can take the same treatment."

His conclusion to the report summarised the extent of the tour: "During the whole trip we had taken off and landed 24 times, and covered 15,652 miles by air. (Excluding the Rhodesian and Kenyan legs) we had played 15 matches, winning 11 and losing 4 (three Tests and the Transvaal game), and about 10 exhibition matches, plus the South African championships and the occasional friendly or coaching game. It could not have been a more wonderful experience and the team, of very varied interests and professions, was an extremely happy one. Our only regret was the Test results, but on the whole we feel we had done the game some good in the Union and if they have as few regrets over our visit as we have, then it was indeed a success."

The trip, and the publicity it generated, had been

6699

... A direct result of this tour was the internationalisation of the game...

beneficial in popularising the game at large, and the fact that Great Britain had been beaten in the Tests was viewed as no bad thing, as it evidenced a general levelling-up in international standards. Squash was, even ten years after the stultifying effect of the war, still growing up as a sport for the masses, and ventures such as this by those representing the fons et origo of squash bore a huge significance. A direct result of this tour was the internationalisation of the game, as the SRA noted in commenting on the seeding for the Amateur of 1956: '*That only three out of eight seeds should go to home players would have been unthinkable only a few years ago, and that the title should go to Amin, a player from overseas who had never played in this country until a few days before the championship began, was also without precedent.*'

Any doubts harboured by the South African SRA before the tour began had been dispelled: '*The British team not only provided a considerable stimulant to the game in this country but were also an extremely popular side both on and off the courts*'. BLT&S endorsed this, in language which fifty years on shows how the definition of sporting success has altered: '*Our team has won golden opinions for their sporting behaviour both on and off the court and this, we venture to suggest, is far more important than mathematical success*'. These words did not however disguise the general disappointment felt at the loss of the Test series, and the selectors were put on clear notice that future teams should be good enough to win, however successful they might be as ambassadors.

Norman had been a popular captain with his team. Mike Perkins remembers him as a strong character and good leader: "He easily assumed the position of leader of the party but was in no way heavy-handed, and did not push himself forward. If one had a problem Norman was very approachable about it." Mike found, as have others, that Norman's abrupt style could be initially disconcerting, but warmed to him as he got to know him. "Norman wanted to win, and didn't like losing, but he also made it clear that we were there to enjoy ourselves as well. As a player, Norman was a fine stroke player with a fierce will to win and a touch of ruthlessness about him. There were some players who baulked quite often, such as Seymour-Hayden and Wilson, but Norman was not in this league. It should be noted that in those amateur days, pre-referees, gamesmanship was a regular feature of the game. I recall seeing Lt.Colonel Maud, a fine Bath Club Cup player, dropping his handkerchief and kicking it up the court as he bent to pick it up to get an unofficial breather."

One last effort

The British team got back to England on the afternoon of September 22nd. After reuniting with Mullie and the boys, Norman went straight into College on his return, some ten days after the start of term. He had a new headmaster to meet and get to know, Stanley Porter, chosen by the governors to succeed Reginald Kirkman. He and Porter were not close, being chalk and cheese as personalities, but they rubbed along. Their leadership styles were similarly polarised. Some old pupils today express the view that they regarded Norman as effectively the headmaster during the 1960s, he, rather than Porter, influencing behaviour, discipline and pride in the school.

Mullie had, in Norman's absence, taken on the burden of preparing Anthony for his first term at Tonbridge. His prep school had been Brandeston Hall, which he had attended for five years from 1950. Norman and Mullie took the view that it was best for the offspring of a master of a school not to be educated in that school.

With Anthony's move, Geography and English classes to teach, and a squash team to coach, not to mention Mullie and Tim to devote himself to after six weeks away, Norman was busy. He had also to go to London on Thursday September 29th, only a week after returning from Southern Africa, to attend the AGM of the SRA at the Royal Automobile Club. BLT&S recorded that he gave 'an interesting account of the tour and spoke in glowing terms of the wonderful hospitality accorded to the team'.

When Norman took the decision not to enter for the Amateur championship in January 1953, he retired only from championship play. He had continued to play in representative matches and to enjoy international and county squash. He had now to decide if he should retire completely. He was becoming increasingly lame and the recovery time after each match was painful and prolonged. The South African tour had been a great experience, but it had hurt – not surprisingly after a ridiculous 16 games in 5 weeks - and his body was telling him to stop. But then, less than one month after the return to England, there came in the post an invitation. Fison's, the agri-chemical company, had purchased the old Felix Hotel in Felixstowe as their corporate headquarters, but had retained and developed its squash courts. These courts were now the centre of squash in the East of England. It was therefore the obvious place, indeed virtually the only place, to hold the SRA versus East of England match on Saturday October 15th.

The postcard stirred the old urge to compete again. The truth was he looked forward to another go at the sport he loved; he had played well in South Africa, could still win at international level, even if not at the very top of the tree, and the desire had not gone away to "show these fellows I can still play a bit". There was, in addition, the attraction of meeting up with his South African tour colleague and old adversary Brian Phillips, who would be playing top string for the SRA.

For Norman it was his first squash of any sort since Nairobi. Phillips was in slightly better practice, having been playing in the Bath Club Cup; he surprised the gallery, and himself, by winning, unusually for him, the first game. When he went two games up, the end was in sight for Norman. But Norman was not one to turn up just to please the gallery and lose gracefully. He dug deep, finding reserves of energy and speed of foot which belied his lack of fitness and match practice. He levelled the scores at two-all. Phillips did not give up, and fought hard to get himself back into the match. But Norman was tenacity itself and brought off a fine win 5-9, 9-10, 9-3, 9-8, 10-9...

...Mullie recalls the aftermath: "Not for the first time, when Norman arrived home late in the evening he hooted the car horn. I opened the garage door, and Norman drove the car in. He opened the car door, but was rooted, as stiff as a board, to the seat. I had to drag him out of the driver's seat on to the floor, and he was then able to crawl on hands and knees into the house."

It is worth noting that Brian Phillips, a year older than Norman, played the next day, the Sunday, at Ipswich SRC for the SRA against Norfolk and Suffolk. He demonstrated his own remarkable grit and stamina in taking Dick Hawkey to a 10-9 fourth game before losing. When asked who was the best of the amateurs he ever played against, Norman's response was Brian Phillips, although he also had a high regard for Alan Fairbairn.

The story does not end there. Three weeks later, Norman volunteered for more punishment when he accepted the annual invitation to play for the Jesters at the Lansdowne in the Strawson Memorial match. This event, designed for the leading ten amateurs to demonstrate the courtesies as well as the skills of the game to the gallery, started at 5pm on Thursday November 10th and Norman had to leave College after morning school to get to West London in good time. He had anticipated playing fourth string against a player of similar vintage, Tony Mallett, but on arrival in London he was told that the Jesters first two strings, Fairbairn and Phillips, had both dropped out. So Norman found himself promoted to second string and playing against Dick Hawkey. The SRA won the fixture 4-1, with Roy Wilson beating John Barrington, and the 18 year old Nigel Broomfield not giving Peter Robinson any chances. Norman's match with Hawkey was a nail-biter. BLT&S reported the hard battle thus:

'The issue was settled in a rather unsatisfactory match between R. B. Hawkey and N. F. Borrett. This was a battle between the old and the new, and right well did Borrett acquit himself. He is seldom seen in action in London nowadays and his appearances in the previous memorial matches have shown him to be out of practice and out of condition. But today, following on his tour in South Africa, we saw much to remind us of the majestic Borrett of old. Hawkey, on the other hand, was to start with nervous – possibly too keen to win – and was unable to show us his normal shots. Not until Borrett had won the first game and led 7-1 in the second did we suddenly see the real Hawkey who then took ten points in a row and having thereby won the second game, romped away with the third to one. Possibly Hawkey thought that Borrett was done for – at any rate he eased the pressure and Borrett came back at him with a real show of fighting squash. And so it was that Borrett reached 8-3 in the fifth game and all seemed over. Yet by this time Borrett's hip was palpably troubling him and he was limping. We were treated to the unedifying spectacle of 4 lets in successive rallies in 3 of which Hawkey was the appealer. Having eventually saved this protracted match point, Hawkey gradually crept up and after saving a further match point at 8-7, won the match 10-8. The last game produced a dozen lets - sufficient comment on the tension - but it was perhaps a pity that this tie should have been played in a match of this kind.'

Mullie had some sharp words for Norman about his physical state on his return home that evening.

It was now a struggle for Norman to conceal the discomfort which was his constant companion. College pupils, that race of acute observers of any sign of weakness in their schoolmasters, could discern a limp. The schoolboy imitations of their schoolmasters, a daily part of life at boarding school, which usually extended only to mimicry of the idiosyncrasies of voice, now included, in Norman's case, the stiff-hipped gait of a man carrying pain.

One way of showing the boys that he could live normally was to play normally. He took the College squash side into the court for some coaching. He could show them how they should play. He challenged them, all five, to a game, one after the other. Tom Elliott remembers: "It was probably in the autumn of 1955 at a time when Norman was limping quite heavily. My friend and contemporary, Alan Brooks, was captain of squash and he told me that Norman had challenged the whole College team to a match, one after the other. Alan played the first match and took three points off him but the other four members of the team all went down 9-0, 9-0, 9-0".

The garden at the Readery in Castle Street, whence the Borretts had moved on leaving the College property in Albert Road, was in need of some work. There was no shortage of helpers happy to help with the landscaping effort as an alternative to school after-hours duties. Norman regarded such activity as healthy and a sensible use of pupils' spare time. He would sometimes forget to advise his colleagues in the Common Room of this occasional reallocation of pupil labour and did not endear himself to a number of them as a result; but the criticism he thus attracted tended to come from those staff members who would not themselves have been able to interest boys in helping to work their particular garden. One example will suffice. Norman incurred the displeasure of the history master following this exchange with pupil Malcolm Sneath:

… Alan played the first match and took three points off him but the other four members of the team all went down 9-0, 9-0, 9-0…

"Sir, why am I not picked for Thursday's hockey match?" "Because you are taking your History exam that day"; "But I have no chance of passing it, sir"; "Well all right, I'll put you back in". Result: contented pupil, unhappy History master.

The two squash matches Norman had played in the autumn persuaded him – Mullie needed no persuasion – that it was not sensible to continue: he was slowing up and he was dependent on the strapped-on pulse emitting aid to survive the pain of each match. He told the English selectors that he was giving up international play. Their response was to suggest that he should retire after one last game, as captain. Although the proposal was no doubt driven, to a degree, by sentiment, they knew they could rely on his presence to get the best out of the team, that he would make a good speech at the after-match dinner, and he would generally add lustre to the occasion; and indeed that he would be a winner.

His final international was the first of England's season, against Wales, the minnows of international squash, at Hampstead SRC on January 20th 1956. It was fitting that as the old went out, the new came in. Nigel Broomfield, the outstanding schoolboy player of the post-war period having won the under 18 Evans Cup no less than four times and still not yet 19, made his debut for England, playing at second string. Norman, twenty years older than the debutant, played at five, after Roy Wilson, Broomfield, Mohtadi, and Fairbairn. Norman won his last international 9-4, 9-1, 9-6.

His retirement from county squash marked the end of a nine-year run of representing Devon in the county championship. The Devonians had again done well in the inter-county championship, winning the south-western area section, and the selectors felt they might well beat Middlesex in the inter-area round to be played at the Junior Carlton on February 11th, if they could secure Norman's presence at the top of the order. They pleaded with him to see them through the campaign, and he agreed. However there was to be no fairy-tale ending, as on the eve of the match Norman suffered an attack of arthritis and was forced to pull out. Devon lost by four ties to one.

The only exception Norman made from his retirement was to support the OFs in the Londonderry Cup. In the first round, the team, without Norman, had beaten Cranleigh 3-2. In the second round in December, the team beat the Old Foresters 3-2, a good victory remarkable for the fact that for the only time in the Londonderry Cup, Norman lost; John Taylorson, the Essex county player, played a fine game to beat him 9-4 in the fifth game. Truman beat Taylorson's brother,

Evans lost to Essex stalwart Oliver Pollard, but Foster and P. S. Newcombe both won.

> Norman's loss to Taylorson, a good county player but not near the top of the national tree, delivered a decisive message to Norman. He would make the next round of the Londonderry against Tonbridge, for whom his old friend Brian Phillips would be playing, his last match. In the event he was not fit enough to play and the OFs went out of the competition.

When the South African SRA, inspired by Norman's British team tour the previous year, mounted a five week tour of the UK in December, it was inevitable that Norman would want to meet them. But then the Jesters asked if he would play for them in the first match of the tour, on Friday December 28th. The South African Test side had not changed much since the year before, but Denis Callaghan was now first string; Cecil Kaplan had moved up from fifth string to second, a new face, the Rhodesian D. L. Hodgson, was at three, whilst Norman's old acquaintances Jarvis and Barnes were still at four and five. For the first match the tourists put out four of the Test team plus their captain, H.W. P. Whiteley, who had been champion of South Africa seven times before and once after the war. He was now a senior player, but was playing regularly, and Norman did very well to win in the fifth game. This was, finally, his last game.

Whiteley's end of tour report drew comparisons between the playing conditions in South Africa and the UK: "We soon realised that we had to adjust our style of play to suit the slower courts, and… found that we could not capitalise on stamina built up under marathon conditions which is often a feature of match play in South Africa." After this neat summary of the difficulties encountered by Norman's tourists in 1955, another insight followed: "We felt that we perhaps did not do as well in the important international matches as we might have done had there been more opportunities for rest… In fairness however this was much the same treatment as we gave the British touring team… and we can well remember the obvious signs of wear and tear which all members of that team showed before returning to England".

Norman was elected President of the SRA at its annual meeting on December 30th 1980. At the same meeting, Jonah Barrington, the country's top player for 15 years and the current British Champion, was elected a member of the SRA Council.

Bob Morris was secretary of the SRA at the time. He tells an interesting story of how old grudges die hard:

"Early in my time as Secretary of the Squash Racquets Association (SRA) I was alerted one evening to the sudden death of the then President, Major General Roddy Fyler; he had suffered a heart attack whilst returning home by train having spoken at a County Association Squash Dinner. The following morning Vice Presidents were informed, and arrangements were made for an extraordinary meeting of the Vice Presidents to discuss the appointment of a new President. The meeting was held in the Royal Air Force Club and attended (amongst others) by Sir Dennis Truscott, Janet Morgan (President of the WSRA), Roy Wilson, Edward Clowes and Peter Cantlay. None of the then Vice Presidents wished to be considered for the Presidency, and the name of Norman Borrett was put forward – by me, following discreet discussions in advance of the meeting with one of my predecessors – the highly respected John Horry. John had felt that there was no-one with stronger credentials for the position than Norman, and I had therefore anticipated a swift conclusion to the meeting once his name was mentioned. It was not to be. Some of those present had clearly suffered from Norman's robust style of play, and one of the older Vice Presidents claimed that the 'Penalty Stroke' in squash had been introduced to try and deter Norman in particular, but others as well, from striking an opponent with a hard-struck ball when the poor opponent was judged (by Norman) to be in the way!

There were then extended (and fascinating to a young Secretary) discussions about the game as it was played in the post-war era until it was eventually agreed unanimously that Norman Borrett should be invited to become President of the SRA. He accepted and served in that capacity for 10 years. Norman's decade as President was exciting and arguably the one in which greater changes were made in the presentation of squash than any before or since. Transparent courts were developed to permit all-round viewing, and the SRA acquired its own demountable Perspex court which was used in such varied settings as Wembley Conference Centre, Brunel's Old Station in Bristol, Birmingham International Centre and The

ABOVE: The SRA Patron
greets the SRA President.
Jonah Barrington waits at
the end of the line.

Royal Albert Hall - these last two venues being chosen when England hosted the World Individual and Team Squash Championships in 1987.

As President, Norman devoted much time to the presentational aspects of the Association, attending all major finals to award the prizes and invariably attracting lengthy applause from the crowds when announced - together with his achievements in squash - on to the show courts. He chaired Annual General Meetings with authority: much needed at a time when some in the SRA sought to disrupt the balance of its activities in favour of more commercial interests in the game. And he demonstrated what some might have considered to be unusual diplomacy when agreeing in 1990 to stand aside and allow the then WSRA President to be the first President of a newly amalgamated governing body for both men's and women's squash – 'Squash England'."

To mark Norman's appointment as President, Bob's predecessor as Secretary of the SRA, John Horry, wrote an interesting career summary of the new President:

'The long vacations enjoyed make scholastic careers particularly attractive to those games players who have excelled at school and university. It adds to their pleasure if young men after university, return as masters to their old schools where in their last year they were often treated as demi-gods and which they can look back on with pleasure and nostalgia. The immediate post-war years were rich in such examples and the names of Hubert Doggart, Norman Borrett and Dick Hawkey spring readily to mind. Their prowess usually extends to more than one game, and some collect a considerable bag of Blues in the course of their university careers. The war deprived many of them of some of the best years of their sporting lives, and the immediate post-war years at the universities were notable for the older than usual age of the undergraduates, as well as for their maturity at games.

Norman Borrett left Framlingham College in 1936, and immediately made an impact on Cambridge sport obtaining Blues at hockey and squash. Just before the war he was a member of the Cambridge squash team which toured the United States.

After war service in the Army he went schoolmastering to Devon which gave him his cricket qualification to play for that county, although his first appearances were for Essex, the county of his birth. However he soon moved to Framlingham and stayed there as a schoolmaster until his retirement two years ago.

He burst upon the post-war squash scene in 1946 and won the first Amateur Championship after the war with some ease, dropping a game to Peter Hildick-Smith in the quarter-finals and to Brian Phillips in the semi-finals. From then onwards for five years he was supreme. His job in the wilds of Suffolk prevented him from playing much squash in London, and it was said with some truth that every year the first round of the Amateur Championship, played in early January, was often his first competitive squash of the season. He used the early rounds to get his eye in. He also found time to win 12 caps playing squash for his country. His prowess at hockey at which he captained Great Britain in the Olympics often conflicted with his squash. He served on a number of committees of the Hockey Association, the offices of which were across the corridor from the offices of the SRA, and he usually looked in there when visiting the Hockey Association.

Norman had the reputation of being a ruthless player at squash and woe betide a baulker who had the misfortune to get too near him in the course of play. His sporting appearances were curtailed in his later years by that bane of so many sportsmen – an arthritic hip, but surgery has largely conquered this in his case. Now retired from schoolmastering, he has more time to give to the problems of the SRA which can only gain from his sage advice and long experience of the game of squash.'

The topic of baulking was keenly discussed in those days. There were players of this era who transgressed the rules, the referees being less officious than they are today, and obstructers were usually dealt with by being hit by a well-struck ball from behind. Norman gained something of a reputation as a baulker, particularly in failing to move to the side to give his opponent a view of the ball after he had played a drop shot.

John Thompson, a colleague of Norman in the pre-war Cambridge side and his opponent in the final of the 1948 Amateur, offers this view: "Norman was not a deliberate baulker, save when he felt his opponent was not playing fair, and then he would give him some of the same treatment. He was a magnificent striker of the ball and a great athlete with wonderful speed around the court. I never experienced any problem when playing him.

He was clearly the best player in the country for the seven or eight years after the war, when no one could take a game from him, let alone a match. He was supremely fit, made very few mistakes, hit the ball hard and was a good stroke player. He was a very committed competitor. We weren't close friends - I found him a bit brusque - but he was good company.

I put his emergence after the war, at the age of 29, down to the fact that there was no-one of Gandar-Dower's genius - who had been dominant before the war - and to the fact that Norman post-war was fitter, stronger and more confident than pre-war."

Geoffrey Atkins was Amateur, and World, rackets champion, Amateur real tennis champion, and reached the last four of the Amateur Squash championships in 1952, a few months after he became only the second amateur since the war to defeat Norman: He recently opined: "I do not regard Norman as a baulker: if you gave him a fair view of the ball he would do the same to you. The penalty point was not introduced to deter Norman, but to deter Alan Seymour- Hayden, who along with Roy Wilson – and I played them both – were baulkers who deliberately made it difficult for their opponent to get a sight of the ball. I did not like that approach and I don't believe Norman did either and would react against it when he encountered it."

In any analysis of Norman Borrett's greatness as a squash player, unbeaten for years in the domestic game whilst playing a minimum of competitive matches, the standard reached by Hashim and Karim must be the benchmark. Hashim was one year older than Norman, but a later developer, certainly in global terms. Norman's years of supremacy were between 1946 and 1952, when he was last top-seeded in the Amateur at the age of 34. Hashim's dominance was from 1951, when he first won the British Open, until 1957, when he last won it, at the age of 42. Hashim's wonderful continuing health and fitness was in direct contrast to Norman's decline into painful arthritis.

Hashim did not play in the Open Veterans championship, but was still winning the North American Veterans professional title in 1967, aged 52. He played again in England in 1977 in the Open Vintage class, winning the event for four years until his 65th birthday in 1980.

Norman and Hashim shared a deep dislike of being beaten. That they did not play each other is a matter of regret to all lovers of the game for it would have been fascinating to see them contesting a match when Norman was at the height of his powers. His game was based on similar principles to Hashim's, speed of foot and of stroke, as well as a deftness of touch which could change the shot from a drive to a drop shot at the last moment. Norman introduced a previously unknown speed of foot to the post-war game, but Hashim raised that standard even higher, some of his retrieving bordering on the miraculous. Hashim was viewed as having no great variety of shot but his hitting was thunderously hard and to a length, and he could play a deadly drop shot from any part of the court. Norman would not, even at his peak in 1949 or 1950, have beaten Hashim in his prime, but he would have extended him.

One of the reasons for Norman's dominance over all amateur opponents during his five year reign, was his speed about the court. Mike Corby, a gifted squash and hockey international in the 60s and 70s, expressed it in this way: "Norman Borrett brought to the game of squash a level of fitness not previously seen, in the same way twenty years later that Jonah Barrington took the game to another, previously unknown, level of physical endeavour." But just as with Barrington, fleetness of foot and stamina will not make a champion of a player who lacks the racket head control, speed of stroke, the hand-eye coordination, and the mental resilience which are the chief characteristics of the champion squash player. In Norman's case he had all those skills in abundance, plus certain unusually strong personal character traits, notably a ruthlessness, a killer instinct, the desire to win and its twin, a considerable distaste of losing.

Jonah Barrington, then described as the fittest man on earth, began his domination of world squash under the tutelage of Azam Khan, Hashim's younger brother, whom some would argue was a better player than Hashim, but was obliged by Pashtun custom to pay due respect to the older brother. Azam later wrote this revealing insight:

"In 1965 a group of members at the New Grampians squash club, where I was the resident professional (and later became the owner) asked me to coach a young player called

ABOVE: As SRA President, Norman presents the 1966 Open Trophy to Jonah Barrington – with opponent Aftab Jawaid.

Jonah Barrington. At that time, Barrington worked in a mill. He used to come early in the morning to have squash training from me and then left for the mill. Despite this 'hurried' training, I made him ready to challenge for the very next British Open, in 1966. The day before it started, Barrington played a match against me and could take only one point in three games. He was so depressed that he wanted to withdraw from the tournament. But I knew the prevailing standard and encouraged him to go ahead."

The rest is history. Barrington not only won the 1966 Open but went on to win the title five more times. Shortly after winning that first title, he again played against Azam - only to lose in the same manner as before. Remarkably, Barrington was to remain unbeaten by a British player for 15 years. His influence over the game in Britain was immense, as he later became director of excellence and then president of the SRA, being instrumental in promoting the sport, in particular on television.

Jeremy Lyon recalls Barrington telling him: "I knew that if I was still in the match after two hours I would win it." Barrington having shown the squash world the benefit that fitness could bring to one's game, all the top players focused on this aspect in succeeding decades. And in some cases took it to

extremes: an extraordinary example of that is what is believed to be the longest game ever, a titanic struggle played out on a glass-backed court in Chichester, Sussex on March 30th 1983. Play extended over 2 hours 45 minutes and occupied only four games. The first point was won after 7 minutes, and the first game after 71, Gamal Awad having clawed his way back to 9-all from 1-8 down. The rally at 9-all lasted over 300 shots and 8 minutes and ended in a let being awarded. Awad won that game 10-9 but Jahangir Khan, a giant of the game, took the next 3 games to 5, 7 and 2, the last in only 13 minutes. It is suggested that Gamal, who became the professional at Horsham, and died at 49 of heart failure, never fully recovered from that night.

Dick Hawkey, a fellow England international, renowned as an awkward man to beat, viewed Norman as a very fine player. In particular Hawkey recalled the tenacity which Norman displayed on the court: "even when he was well on top he never gave you a point". A graphic illustration of this comes from two old pupils of the College, Ian Foster and Humphrey Truman, who travelled from Suffolk to London to see their squash master play in the Amateur. It was an early round and Norman was playing a relative minnow. The first two games were won by the defending champion to love, and the third game was standing at 8-0 when there was a collision. The minnow claimed a let. Norman did not accept that a let was justified and after considerable discussion with the referee won the argument, to the chagrin of the gallery which was inevitably hoping to see the minnow escape a whitewash.

It was in the strength of his desire to win and the ruthless application of the killer instinct that Norman stood out from the rest. These were amateur days, and single-mindedness in the pursuit of victory such as this was rare at a time when to "lose well" was not only a British, but a general, sporting rule. The ice-cool intensity and purpose which Norman brought to the sport he played would be unremarkable today, but it was then. He was what is now described as professionally minded, in an amateur world.

… These were amateur days, and single-mindedness in the pursuit of victory such as this was rare at a time when to "lose well" was not only a British, but a general, sporting rule…

It is worth pointing out that of all those who saw him play and who have contributed to this memoir, none has suggested that within the hard man lay any unsporting instincts. He was ruthless: he would hit the ball hard into the back of an opponent who got between him and the front wall, but he expected the same treatment when the roles were reversed; he did not like baulking, but he would react in kind when he encountered it. He was quite capable of a certain amount of gamesmanship, but of the sort imagined by Stephen Potter, which would rarely amount to more than occasionally letting his opponent knock up on his own before entering the court for the first point, or remaining in court between games, practising shots, whilst his wilting opponent gasped for breath outside court.

When Norman joined the teaching staff

at Framlingham in September 1950, the two College squash courts, on which Norman had learnt his squash in the 1930s, were still open at the gallery to the winter air and were still a foot shorter and two feet lower than normal size; but as Norman had clearly overcome – if not thrived upon – these problems, the pupils saw no reason to doubt their own ability to reach a proper standard in the game. And indeed, just as it had been those twenty years before, an outstanding pupil emerged that very term, notwithstanding the idiosyncrasies of the courts.

In the winter of 1951, fifteen year old Humphrey Truman, at the College from 1949 to 1952, played second string to Chris Ford in the squash team. He also captained the tennis team the following summer, when the College VI lost to U.C.S. Hampstead in the final of the national schools tournament, the Glanvill Cup, and reached the semi-final of the public schools version, the Youll Cup. These successes led to Truman's selection for the Boys XII All England Club representative side.

Humphrey's recollection of Norman's influence on his squash career is unexpected: "He hardly ever played squash with me or coached me at Framlingham, but we did play a lot of tennis together." Norman was no slouch at tennis and having accumulated sufficient points in East Anglian tournaments was invited (but declined) to play at Wimbledon in the Championships, but he was not in Humphrey's league.

Norman's approach to coaching squash was to start with the grip and the essence of every stroke: 'Hit the ball as if you were knocking the head off a daisy with a stick', demonstrated by a snap of the wrist. Every shot was to be cut hard in this manner. Norman had spent hundreds of hours, at Cambridge, at Allhallows, and at Framlingham practising on his own. The methods he had developed were passed on for the pupil to practise on his own: the clinging drive down the side-wall ('don't hit cross-court until you have worked the opponent up and down the side-walls and got him out of position'), the drop-shot from mid-court to pull the opponent up to the front of court, and, for practice only, the lofted shot into the front wall near the right hand angle so that the ball came back at the right height for a volleyed kill above the tin. All were explained and then demonstrated, by Norman playing against the pupil, or against two pupils at once – a popular practice variation – or, in later years, by Norman entering the court from the gallery. It was those entrances which left the strongest

BELOW: At 49 years of age, Dunlop still rated Norman 'a special player', warranting free restringing of two of his Maxply rackets.

ADVICE NOTE

DUNLOP SPORTS COMPANY LTD.

WALTHAM ABBEY · ESSEX · TEL · WALTHAM CROSS 27741
ANSAFONE : WALTHAM CROSS 23018

(2)

Dunlop Sports Co Ltd.,
Free Supplies to Pros & Special
Players,
Waltham Abbey,   (Tax as Trade)

2824/25.

DELIVERY NOTE NUMBER

ACCOUNT No.	BRANDING
48001	

035371

CUSTOMER ORDER No.	
22.	

26/10/66

CODE	QTY.	/12	DESCRIPTION	01	02	03	04	05	06	07	08	09	10	11	12	13	14	S/S IND
~~516021~~			~~SQUASH RACKET.~~ ~~RESTRING NO.1~~															
516021	2		SQUASH RACKET. RESTRING NO.1															2
				3														
				4														
				5														
				6														
				7														
				8														

CONSIGNED TO:
(if different from above)

MR · N F Barrett
Framlingham College.
Framlingham.
Suffolk

CARRIAGE
£   s.   d.

CARTONS	PARCELS	SACKS	PER	PACKER	CHECKED

impression on the pupil as Norman took the racket and, still wearing his heavy overcoat, played the shot in question, an inch above the tin.

If his enthusiasm, speed and anticipation in the most serious of competitive matches sometimes led to accusations of crowding an opponent, he only taught proper court manners and courtesies. Whilst as a player he might sometimes not have followed his own teaching, he always taught his pupils to give room to his opponent and not to baulk. In one College match, the College first string, having on several occasions backed his opponent into the backhand corner before playing, at the last moment, a forehand drop shot into the opposite, forehand, court, was told by a spectator that it was plain to see that he had been taught by Norman: a strange criticism of what is a perfectly legitimate manoeuvre, there being nothing illegal about putting one's opponent into a disadvantaged position by delaying one's shot in this way, but a story which demonstrates the reputation Norman achieved in some quarters.

Norman worked hard to develop the game at the College. In his first few years he would regularly turn out in squash kit and play the College first five, one after the other, not conceding any points even to the youngest of the team. His coaching showed early dividends. On April 18th 1951 the College second string, Keith Mackenzie, did well in the Drysdale Cup, reaching the third round. The College squash team had played more matches over the two winter terms than was usual, Norman having already used his influence to obtain fixtures against club and county sides, as well as the revival of a pre-war fixture with Lancing College, where the squash master, Sam Jagger, was an old acquaintance. The only other school match was against Felsted. In that first season the College team won only four of its seven matches, despite the presence of the two outstanding post-war talents in Chris Ford and young Humphrey Truman.

A bonus for the side occurred during the Easter holidays. The SRA's report tells the story: '*A match was played at the Hague during the hockey XI's tour in Holland and drawn three-all. This was probably the first squash match ever played by a school abroad*'.

Mike Garnett saw him teach the boys squash in 1953/54. "He was beginning to limp but that didn't make any difference as he dominated the tee shouting 'you must gain the centre of the court if you want to win.' " He would also play two of the team at a time, holding that central position in the court, from where the game can be dictated, even by a player who takes

> *... Norman limped into the court, seized the pupil's racket, and played a shot of breath-taking finality: whether a drop shot of great delicacy from the back court or a ferocious cross shot just above the tin, all the while clad in a heavy overcoat. ...*

only one step to left or right to retrieve. As occasional light relief he would play left-handed, his ambidexterity representing for the observer an unnecessary addition to the God-given talent he had been already. He would on occasion teach the hard way, as Colin Micklewright recalls: "The first time Norman got me to play a practice game with him, he moved me all round the court until I became stranded at the front of the court with him behind me; he drilled the ball into my lower back (bruised for days after) with this admonishment: "Never get caught in mid-court like that boy if you want to become a good squash player." What a man! But he taught me a lot, including getting me through my Geography A Level - no doubt because I was scared of that sawn-off hockey stick!"

As the years went by and Norman became more lame, these coaching sessions consisted less of his changing into squash kit to play full games against the members of the team and increasingly of his coaching from the gallery, from where he would call a halt to the play before entering the court to demonstrate a particular shot or a positional manoeuvre. In those days there was no back to the court above the out line, so that the gallery was open to the elements and spectators tended to be fully clothed against the cold. Thus when Norman would stop the play to demonstrate a shot, the pupil's astonishment was all the greater as Norman limped into the court, seized the pupil's racket, and played a shot of breath-taking finality: whether a drop shot of great delicacy from the back court or a ferocious cross shot just above the tin, all the while clad in a heavy overcoat.

Simon Molyneux, the son of Commander Molyneux who had played many times for the Navy pre and post-war, and who himself played squash and hockey for the Navy, was one of those astonished pupils in the mid-1960s: "I recall one day when, coaching at squash, he was clearly frustrated by my inability to keep the ball low. He hobbled into the court, took my racket, and amazed us by driving the ball time and time again just above the tin: 'Like this, boy'."

By the 1960s the College team was playing some sixteen matches spread over the Christmas and Easter terms. Fixtures arranged by him included the Suffolk air force bases at Wattisham and Martlesham, Ipswich and Colchester squash clubs, Cambridge University and the main East Anglian schools. Most of these teams were played both home and away. The players in the team always looked forward to the away matches, representing as they did a rare opportunity to see the outside world, and to taste the forbidden fruit, in particular in its Tollemache bitter formulation. Chris Milner-Moore was a member of the successful squash team of the early 1960s, and recalls the fun which the team had, thanks to the relaxed manner in which Norman ran the side. "He permitted us to drink a beer, or even two, at supper at our away matches. I was fond of him and owed him a lot for the enjoyment I got from the game over many years." Chris played at the top of the order for Suffolk from the age of 17 to 50.

Bob Fox recalls Norman coaching him for the College squash team in the late 1960s, "standing in the middle of the court with me running in all directions trying to get the ball back. At the end of our session he had won every point - pretty amazing given how limited his ability to move."

Norman was prepared to treat his team members as adults, as long as they were sensible. His pupils, thus given an insight into an adult world, knew where the boundary lines were. Budding stars who failed to respect those boundaries were no longer selected. Norman was popular with pupils in the teams of all sports for this reason. He gave them the feeling they were being given some trust, some freedom of action in a world which was in every other sphere closely supervised. The privilege of being treated in this way depended on two things. Good performance on the court, field or pitch was a given, although Norman was prepared to forgive a player's lapses if his effort and his attitude was good; this leads to the second point. Behaviour was deemed as important, if not more so, than performance. A stickler for the old-fashioned virtues of politeness, respect for elders, and personal integrity, Norman had a reputation for intolerance where failings in these areas were observed.

Norman was good at keeping in touch with the success of his existing and former pupils. It helped that he was often in London in his role as a member of the SRA committee. In January 1959 he saw Humphrey Truman put out Pickering, the Yorkshire champion, in the second round of the Amateur, before succumbing in the third round. Humphrey was then experiencing his best season so far in senior squash. He won the Wanstead club title, was runner-up in the Middlesex championship, and played in the Bath Club Cup for Queen's Club. He won the 1959 RAF championships at both squash and lawn tennis, and at squash won both his ties for Essex as his county beat Hertfordshire and Suffolk, the latter including another Old Framlinghamian in John Davey, to win the Eastern area. In the inter-area rounds Essex won again and reached the final. There they lost 5-0 to a Surrey side containing internationals Denis Hughes, Roy Wilson and Mike Perkins.

He was later to go on to greater success, winning the South of England championship, being capped for England, and seeded eighth in the Amateur, an event in which he once led the fine Egyptian player, Amin, twice a winner of the championships, two games to love until in his own words "the spell was broken". Humphrey subsequently took over from Norman the mantle of leading the OF side in the Londonderry Cup and also led the OF tennis team in the d'Abernon Cup.

He became the only post-war sportsman to play both squash and tennis for England. At tennis his forte was in doubles, in which he played in the Wimbledon Championships many times, in partnership with Keith Collar, reaching the last sixteen, and then with Davis Cup player Gerry Oakley, with whom he made the last eight. In the mixed he partnered his sister Christine, three times a ladies singles' semi-finalist and runner-up in 1961. As a busy chartered accountant working in his father's firm, Humphrey sometimes had difficulty getting away from work in good time, even for important tennis matches. Sister Christine's usual good humour was absent when in July 1959 Humphrey arrived only just in time for the quarter-final of the Wimbledon mixed doubles, against Rod Laver and Darlene Hard, hot and out of breath. Christine was not impressed to be told that his train from the City had broken down three miles away and he had had to run from there, carrying his kit.

Christine never won a Wimbledon title, but she might have done in the mixed, were it not for her unswerving loyalty to Humphrey. Rod Laver recently reminded her that she was the only girl who had ever turned him down, when she had said she would play in the mixed with Humphrey rather than with him.

Another, younger, Framlinghamian showed some promise at the game in 1959. Norman broke his Christmas holiday in Framlingham early in January to support Stephen Sayer, who at 14 had reached the final of the Evans British Open Under 16 championship. Norman arrived only three minutes late at the Junior Carlton Club courts but nearly missed the contest, as Sharif Khan, seventh son of the great Hashim Khan, and a Millfield pupil, needed only 15 minutes to take the title. This example of Norman's support for his pupils was entirely typical, and endeared him to parents and boys alike.

One of the reasons that Martin Pearse went to the College in 1959 was that his father had, pre-war, been in the top eight squash players in the country and, knowing Norman well, sent his son to the College. Martin was a fine player at school, but has achieved greater fame in later life, playing for England at squash at various age groups, over 45, 55 and 60, and being runner-up in both the British and the World Over 60s championships in 2006: "Norman instilled in me the desire to try 110%, never ever to give up, and to make life as difficult as possible for one's opponent. When I was a pro I did just that, but have in older age mellowed somewhat!"

One of the best squash coaching books was produced in February 1960. Written by Brian Phillips, the foreword was contributed by Norman, writing from Framlingham College:

"When Brian Phillips asked me to write a Foreword to his book I was naturally, in his phraseology, 'tickled pink'! Having kept the Amateur Championship crown from him for several years, the time had obviously come when I could help him, although as I write, I am wondering whether this will prove to be the case! Of course I readily agreed, for Brian has been not only a great opponent of mine but a friend as well.

That last remark shows what a true sportsman he is, because his disappointment must have been great at not attaining that place on which he had set his heart. Lesser men would have been tempted to be the opposite of friendly. Surely one of the pleasures of playing any game is meeting people and enjoying their company.

As a player Brian Phillips was one of the best never to have won the Amateur Championship. He has spent many hours in a squash court against many types of players, and there is no doubt that he has studied the game widely and intelligently. He has also put in hours of thought and service for the good of the game as a member of various committees of the Squash Rackets Association, the governing body of squash rackets in the world. What he has to say therefore on playing the game, on the rules of the game, and on squash rackets clubs in various parts of the country and the world, should be most helpful to all keen players, and they can rest assured that the author has a great knowledge of what he is writing.

I find the book easy to read and most amusing in places. Squash rackets players would do well to read it carefully and use it for reference before practising or playing matches."

Norman was a strong believer that sport is character-forming. For him the way in which the sportsman or woman, young or old, conducted himself or herself on the court or on the pitch was of paramount importance. He may himself have played hard, from time to time baulking an awkward player on the squash court, or running through an obstructing defender on the hockey pitch, but he never disputed a referee's call or raised his voice, even under provocation.

He was a shrewd judge of character and would select players, both pupils and adults, whom he knew would perform when the heat was on, in preference to those with technically superior skills. And he would, sometimes to the annoyance of teachers of lesser vision, insist on promoting young talent into the school's first team.

This focus on good behaviour and character was typical of the boarding school ethos of the time. It is surprising that not all members of the Common Room were firm exemplars of it during the years of his influence in that body. Norman was, mostly, loyal to his fellow teachers but his forthright nature sometimes made it difficult for him to restrain his frustration with increasingly liberal approaches to issues of discipline and conduct.

John Cockett's multiple sports talent did not extend to the very top in squash:

"We were also opposing masters in charge of squash, and gave a demonstration (or rather he did) after the school match, which consisted of me running like the proverbial blue-bottomed fly and him standing in the middle shouting 'run, boy, run!' Long after his retirement from the game he was still a phenomenon. No wonder the poor chap could hardly walk in later life."

Squash matches started at six in the evening. It was not until nine, after squash club sausages and mash and a pint of bitter, that Norman, and whichever Common Room colleague he had prevailed upon to share the transport burden, would herd their charges into the cars for the journey back to College across the dark Suffolk countryside. The prized places were those in Norman's car, first because he drove an Aston Martin DB4, and second because his driving style was an extension of his personality – fast and decisive. Norman's image was of course enhanced by his car, at least in the eyes of the pupils. Most of them were typical lovers of fast cars, and as John Birt puts it, "the Aston Martin, and thus the man who drove it, were so cool in the eyes of us mere teenagers." OF Andrew Wright was in the cricket and hockey teams which involved away matches against Felsted, and he recalls: "Transport to these fixtures in the Aston was popular, not least because of the tales the boys could later tell their friends back at the College of doing 100 mph, plus, on the only piece of dual carriageway on the A12."

To put one's car at the disposal of the College in this way was probably not viewed in the Common Room as a significant sacrifice until one particular evening. Norman was steering three of his team homeward when he spied a pheasant on the verge of the country lane. Exclaiming "Supper for tomorrow night!" he swung the car expertly across the lane and neatly executed the bird. The College second string player that evening was asked to pick up the corpse whilst Norman prepared the boot for the booty. The hapless boy did as he was bid and got back into the front seat as Norman began to move the car from its position on the verge. Sadly, the boy had failed to close the door as the car began to reverse and, with a horrendously expensive noise, the door was wrenched away from its pillar. Norman showed his experience of overcoming stressful sporting moments by driving home without uttering more than a few words of encouragement to the chastened second string, who, to his surprise, lived happily ever after.

The Aston Martin would give forth a throaty roar when the accelerator was depressed, as it frequently was. Norman occasionally forgot this attribute as he parked the car outside the front door of the College on return from late night duty with the squash team; summoned the next day to attend upon the Head, Norman was advised that his car noise had awoken Geography teacher and complainant Percy Clarke at 10.30 pm. Norman's opinion of both Messrs Clarke and Porter did not improve as a result.

In 1968 Norman relinquished responsibility for College squash after 18 years in charge, to John Maulden, one year before the two new courts were to be installed. Scores of pupils had learned from Norman how to turn an opportunity for exercise into a competitive sport which would give them satisfaction for many a long year. Some went on to high achievement, whilst others played county and club squash; but most simply absorbed the right way to play and how to give of one's best.

Norman's record as the only Old Framlinghamian to win the Suffolk squash championship was equalled in 1974 by Chris Milner-Moore, much to Norman's pleasure, as he knew well both

Chris and his father Rex. Other College squash news, and the changing times they represented, were however not all to Norman's liking. That year, the College squash team played against Suffolk Ladies. The magazine reported this milestone thus:

'Versus Suffolk Ladies - won 4-1 (in the nicest possible way). The discovery by the Second Master that the deputy College captain in the last match of the term had been beaten by a lady was indeed a moving occasion'.

For Norman, changing times did not mean that the traditional way of doing things should be abandoned. Outsiders could be forgiven for not being aware of this characteristic. As a spectator at a Suffolk County squash match in the College courts, Norman was asked by a County official, impressed by the presence of the English squash legend, if he would like to umpire one of the matches. Having no truck with the subtleties of the latest obstruction rules, confining himself to basics, and rejecting a multitude of passionate appeals from the players, Norman incurred the unbridled wrath of the County management.

Whilst Norman had given up responsibility for College squash, he retained interest and influence. Graham Walsh, who was to play Division One national squash in Sussex, expressed the debt he owed Norman for teaching him squash and thus helping him embark on 30 years of fun and camaraderie in the game: "I was practising on the then new courts in the winter of 1976, hammering the ball up and down the side wall. I did not realise I was being watched by Norman, standing above me in the gallery. He shouted down to me: 'not like that boy - wait a moment'. He limped on to the court, took my racket, and, scooping up the ball, volleyed it straight into the front wall forehand nick. As any squash player will confirm - an exceptionally difficult shot".

Brian Phillips describes the nick shot in his book: *'A nick is the result of making the ball bounce absolutely in the angle which the floor makes with the wall, striking both wall and floor simultaneously. 'Half-nick' means that the side wall has been touched just before the floor. Norman Borrett, G. P. Hildick-Smith, G. W. T. Atkins, I. C. de Sales la Terriere and N. H. R. A. Broomfield have all demonstrated this stroke in the course of their matches, and at an even greater pace the fabulous Khan family are at it all the time. To see Hashim Khan deliberately aiming at the dead nick across the court – sure in the knowledge that he will hit it more often than not - is one of the great moments of modern squash. There is no answer to the dead nick.'*

Norman hadn't played a competitive match for over 20 years when he stepped on to Walsh's court and hit that nick.

COACHING THE BOYS – HOCKEY

Norman was a thinking player,
whose quick mind enabled him to identify
immediately the weaknesses in the opposing team,
the moment when to change the direction of
attack, the time when to make a through-pass or to
move the ball cross-field. He was a clear and fluent
writer about the game, as his two books testify and,
after retiring as a player, a good speaker about it.

In 1954 he was approached by the publishers
of the Lonsdale Library to take the lead on
producing the hockey title in their series of books
designed to be a guide to the playing of different
sports. This was to become the twenty-first in the
series. Norman was happy to take on the
responsibility, and in the school holidays of the
summer and winter in 1954 wrote 11 of the 15
chapters, and the introduction to the other
contributors, Denys Carnill, John Evans and Peggy
Lodge, who wrote chapters on full-back play,
goalkeeping, and the women's game. As the
publishers of 'Hockey' put it in on the fly-leaf,
"The authors are all players of great experience
and their names are known everywhere. Norman
Borrett, for instance, is perhaps the greatest
exponent of the game this country has produced."
Norman's interest in the history of the game is
shown in his chapter on the subject, starting from
the Greek bas-relief of the fifth century B.C.,
unearthed in Athens in 1922, which showed a form
of hockey. The book was published in 1955, and
like its 1950 predecessor, found its way on to the
shelves of schools, public libraries and hockey clubs.

He was therefore a natural coach. To impart his
knowledge to others, and in particular to the
College pupils, gave Norman great pleasure. His
love of the game, and his innate competitiveness, made him a
passionate and committed teacher of the game.

Norman's influence on the development of hockey at the
College was significant, taking the work of his predecessors
F. W. Stocks and C. E. Thomas to a different level. From the
pre-war situation in which Club games had made up the bulk of
the fixtures, by the time of Norman's arrival in 1950, with more
schools playing the game, school matches began to make up most
of the fixtures. His connections in the world of hockey brought
fixtures against Suffolk, at full strength, Cambridge University

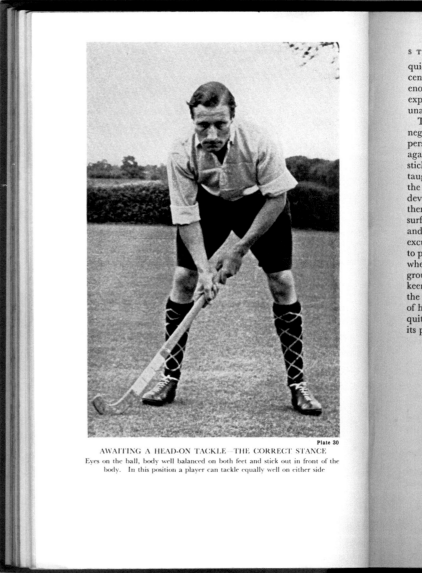

Plate 30

AWAITING A HEAD-ON TACKLE –THE CORRECT STANCE
Eyes on the ball, body well balanced on both feet and stick out in front of the
body. In this position a player can tackle equally well on either side

ABOVE: From Norman's 1954
book "Hockey", 'Awaiting a
head-on tackle'. The
determination is palpable.

Wanderers, Pembroke College,
and Oxford University
Occasionals, thus demanding
that Framlingham be taken
seriously as a hockey school. In the 1950s the 1st XI toured
Holland at Easter to take part in a schools hockey festival, an
event which was supplanted by the Oxford Easter Schools
Festival. Norman persuaded the HA to bring down strong teams
to face the school, and in 1960 he got his friend L.S.E. Jones to
bring a team of internationals and county players to play the

College XI. Internationals Mike Corby, John Deegan and Freddie Scott were three of the well-known names who gave the boys an exhibition of skill which put nine goals past the hapless College goalkeeper, three of which were scored by Ian Foster, OF and Surrey county player.

He was also influential in the development of the England teams of the period. As an England selector Norman watched as many games as he could, to keep up with the form of current players as well as to spot emerging talent. He attended the Bloemendal Easter Hockey Festival in April 1965. Dutch hockey hospitality is legendary but Norman was as always careful, and he had a serious task to perform. Hockey News reported: *'Norman Borrett, an England selector, here with the Travellers, has picked a young English Festival side to play the Dutch Under 22 XI, round which the selectors hope to build the 1968 Olympic side'*. One of those chosen was Richard Oliver, the Felstedian and Oxford University right back, who played for GB in the 1968 and 1972 Olympics and won many caps for England.

Norman Mayhew, whose award in 1958 of a Cambridge hockey blue was celebrated by a College half-holiday, and who went on to play many times for Suffolk and the East, has this view of Norman's coaching:

"It was as a schoolboy hockey coach that Norman was supreme, and it was not until I left that I realized what a thorough tactical knowledge had been imparted by the coaching methods used. In both1955 and 1956, for only half a term did the snow and ice permit outdoor hockey. No matter, we played in the confined space of the very small gym, and our stickwork improved immensely.

When, later, I had the good fortune to play hockey with some very distinguished players, and to partake in some selection duties with Norman, I realized the great respect he commanded among successive generations of players. This was epitomized in 1999 when he was guest of honour at the University Hockey Match sixty years after he was captain of Cambridge."

The style of hockey in the years up to the last decade or two of the 20th century was based on strict positional discipline. Today, there is still a positional structure, whether 4-4-2 or 3-3-3-1, or variations, the difference being that today there is greater flexibility. The old style was exemplified by Norman Borrett, in his coaching at the College, as Norman Mayhew recalls:

"In the middle of a practice match, Norman would tell us

…it opened my eyes to the patterns in the game, something that never left me…

to freeze where we were when he blew his whistle. Then it would be: "Why did you pass there when the pass is covered? That avenue is always open". Or "Why are you not covering that pass? You are out of position". I found this method extremely valuable because it opened my eyes to the patterns in the game, something that never left me. Norman demonstrated the skills to us and we practised them in the gym when the pitch was unfit. I think Norman felt that the spring term was so short and so often severely curtailed by the weather that no opportunity to play a full game should be missed.

It was Norman who converted us all to the Indian stick. There was only one make, Sams. I suspect he was a major influence in introducing them throughout the country."

By the time Norman began teaching hockey at Framlingham in 1950, he had himself switched to the new Indian head style, and was an advocate to the pupils of the version manufactured by Sams, which, by the mid-1950s, had virtually monopolized the marketplace.

Norman Porter went on to play hockey for Scotland. His teacher was a major influence on encouraging him to play hockey: "You didn't realise what you had picked up out of habit – the level of competitive hockey you had played because of the Framlingham fixture list. And go outside the College and suddenly you find yourself being selected for all sorts of different things. The sport was very different in those days: the sticks were long and thin and you had roll-ins rather than hit-ins when the ball went out of play. Many pitches were located either side of cricket pitches and hockey couldn't happen until the cricket season had finished. The goalkeepers were often wicket-keepers and they'd use the same pads - none of this astronaut stuff they have today."

Porter went on to become a schoolmaster himself at Wellington, and later at Woodbridge School. Looking back, he analyses the way in which Norman Borrett influenced not only his hockey career but his decision to become a teacher: "Whiskered cheeks bristling, Norman created an initially intimidating impression. His peerless skills were also intimidating for the tentative learner. Woe betide the hapless left winger (me) who allowed a decent pass to hop over his stick into touch. One never dared venture more than a couple of old-fashioned yards infield. Positional discipline was fiercely ensured. In the pre-global warming 1950s we had severe winters. That cut into fixture lists and our outside practice opportunities. Solution: plenty of runs along the Dennington/ Saxtead roads, hours of inside work in the gym, armed with new-fangled Indian headed sticks. Fitness habits, basic skills duly put in place. Matches were played, when weather conditions allowed, against impressive sounding sides: Suffolk, Cambridge University, Ipswich - and yet our fledgling XIs somehow seemed to cope. And all that seemed routine.

That was, I suppose, the secret. We never knew, while we were at school, just how high was the standard of hockey for which Norman Borrett was grooming us. We were privileged without knowing it. One can only begin to make comparisons once one has moved into the world beyond Framlingham. OF hockey players carried their pedigree with them, and, in large numbers reached the upper echelons of hockey. For me, the discovery came when that timid, goal-shy left winger was instantly deemed good enough to play for St. Andrews University. Somehow I moved infield, started scoring goals, and kept on scoring them. Four years in the university team, Scottish Universities, Scottish Trials. When the chance came, it was in the winter of 1962/3 - a winter similar to the worst of our Suffolk winters. The fitness habit had remained instilled. The skills learned on the Back and in the gym were now instinctive. Come the trials, the stamina lasted better than most - lots of goals in the last session. Selection to play for Scotland. A dozen caps. Something that can never be taken away.

So yes, I owe Norman a great deal. If I were brutally honest, it was probably the chance to play and coach hockey which led me into teaching. Languages were the basis of the job, but the hockey qualifications probably got me the various jobs. They almost certainly determined the direction of my career.

Now, after some 55 years of teaching and coaching the game which has been the sporting love of my life, it is good to have the opportunity to pay due tribute to the man who started it all. It is not an exaggeration to say that my learning of hockey at Fram under the critical eye of the man who was arguably the greatest amateur sportsman of his generation, determined the quality and shape of my professional life. As the advert once had it: 'One never forgets a good teacher'. Thanks, Norman. I do remember where it all started. With you.''

Ben Barringer was a pupil from 1956 to 1961. He too has a strong recollection of Norman as an inspirational hockey master:

"In the Spring of 1958 I was not quite 16 but had been pulled out of the Colts and picked as centre-half for the 1st X1 - a decision that attracted considerable comment and not a little criticism from the School because there were older guys who could have done as well or better than me.

In those days, as many will remember, the team was everything - praise for the individual was almost taboo. The most heroic of tries, goals or boundaries were invariably acknowledged as a team effort and nothing more. Against Felsted at half time we were just ahead; Norman came on to the pitch to give encouragement to his anxious, silent and steaming horseshoe of players. He looked directly at me - his pipe clenched between his teeth - and said, with an imperceptible nod and the briefest hint of a smile, "Well played" and he used my name. I was completely stunned but I guessed what he meant - he was saying we'd both done well - he'd taken a chance on me, I hadn't let him down and he was pleased. I have never and will never forget that moment.

He had that impenetrable aura of supreme self-confidence and the genuine, effortless charisma of a man who knew that he was extraordinary in the true meaning of the word - a man who knew that he had few equals and even fewer masters in what he excelled at. And if that wasn't enough, he seemed to exude a peculiar magnetism irresistible to schoolboys - a subtle irreverence which took nothing, including himself, particularly seriously. He had that casual attitude to discipline and good behaviour possessed only by those rare men who could produce instant obedience just by his presence. He never shouted - merely needing to raise that sharp, clear voice by just a fraction which was always more than enough to achieve the desired effect. He never bothered to rebuke or cajole because he assumed that we all knew what was expected of us and if we weren't prepared to apply the necessary effort then we were of no use to him. He was truly a class act."

In 1963, at the age of 45, Norman underwent an operation to replace his right hip. It was performed at King Edward VIth Hospital by Tony Partridge, whose son Charles was a pupil at the College. Norman claimed that the replacement "must have come from a woman because it makes me walk funny". He was not freed from the effects of the arthritis for long, as his left hip had begun to deteriorate, and it too was replaced in 1969.

But this operation was not successful and it was necessary for further replacements of the left hip in 1985, and finally, when he was 82, in 2000. Both ankles were affected by the hip failures and in the last ten years of his life Norman was not only dependent on two sticks for balance but had to wear specially built-up ankle-high boots for support. The combined effect was to shorten his height by some 5 inches. Denys Carnill recalls Norman being rebuffed by Mullie when he suggested to her that they should use his old hipbone as a door knocker. Mullie provides the somewhat macabre information that Norman kept the bone in his bedside drawer.

ABOVE: Wearing the racoon coat given him by a parent, Norman gets the hockey balls ready for a College match.

As he became less mobile, he amused himself at the start of 1st XI hockey matches on the Back by showing his potential skill at bowls; rolling the match ball from his place on the touchline to stop as nearly as possible to the centre spot. His accuracy was measured by the volume of applause from the pupils present. His hockey coaching, like his squash coaching, moved from playing a full part in the team's practice, fully changed, to a role on the touchline, clothed in the vast raccoon coat given to him by a friend, flat cap and suede chukka boots, from where he would from time to time advance menacingly across the pitch towards the pupil whose performance had failed to rise to the desired heights. "Look, boy, do it like this" as a stick was grabbed and a deft piece of stickwork enacted.

Tony Parsons, a pupil in the 1960s, played hockey for Wales on 43 occasions and twice for Great Britain, scoring 15 goals:

"I am grateful Norman knew enough people to get me into the Welsh set-up as a schoolboy. As a coach at Framlingham his style was akin to a very severe supporter, barking instructions at us across the Back, clad in his vast fur coat, uttering intermittent cries of "Silly boy" and "Don't be soft boy", when mistakes were made. As a parent I used to use those phrases to my two boys!

He knew the game so well that he could give you the structure to follow, the moves to make, the enthusiasm to run and run, and above all else, the desire to win. We all held him in awe because we knew what he had achieved and what he still could do. I recall Norman stopping a practice game to complain we were not shooting straight, and, after instructing our goalkeeper to stand about a foot inside the left-hand post, proceeded to strike the ball time after time into the goal in the gap between the keeper and the post: "Boy, that is how to do it."

He was not above bending the rules of the game to one's advantage, and he showed me a trick or two. Whilst I never saw him play in a match, his reputation was huge, of comparable stature to soccer's Bobby Moore, although I visualised him as more of a Jimmy Greaves, always scoring goals. In my playing career I always thought of Mike Corby and P. J. Wilson as later versions of Norman, in more ways than one.

Norman had an air of arrogance which in later life I realized all top flight sports people have, as a necessary part of their make-up if they are to succeed. Some carry it from the sports field to life in general. But it is not an unpleasant arrogance; it is just knowing that they can do it better than the next person. Norman influenced many boys of which I was just one; we all need mentors like Norman to influence our lives. We were lucky to have someone like Norman and I will ever be grateful".

Simon Molyneux was in the same College XI as Tony Parsons and remembers the same example of Norman showing how to shoot at goal, getting Clive Hedle**y**, the goalkeeper, to stand just inside one of the posts, and then hobbling to the edge of the circle, and proceeding to put several shots straight between Clive and the post. "One could not help but be inspired by demonstrations like that."

Simon goes on to Norman as a personality: "He was not a populist; he spoke his mind too readily for that. Neither did he come across a warm man, but he was hugely respected by everyone and was always the quintessence of fairness.

In retrospect, two things strike me. One is that he rarely mentioned his own extraordinary achievements. The other is that, although he must have been in pain and must have been extremely frustrated by his arthritis, he never complained about it - he just limped around in his enormous brown fur coat. These things show him to have been a steely character, lacking in self-pity.

His coaching style was straightforward – pithy comments mixed with clear direction! He made the sport enjoyable. One simply tried to put into practice what he said, as one knew he was right. His name and his contacts helped the College to get such good sportsmen to come and play against us. I remember playing against a team which included a Pakistan international, who was of course quite an inspiration to us boys."

The description of Norman not coming across as a warm man was the view of many. But, as John Cockett expressed it earlier, he had warmth in abundance once he knew someone well enough to drop the steely exterior. He also had great charm, as many of the parents, particularly the mothers, of his pupils would attest. The air of arrogance which was evident to some was what others viewed as self-confidence. A parallel may be drawn with how Vic Marks, the cricket writer, described the Test cricketer Brian Close: "Close was never arrogant, but I've never encountered a man with such a deep reservoir of self-confidence."

As master in charge of hockey, squash and cricket he was a disciplinarian and was quite intolerant of players whose kit was poorly turned out or who were unpunctual. In particular he would berate any pupil, senior or junior, whose behaviour was disruptive. A man of impeccable manners, he hated failings in that area in others. He also had the ability to scold with a light touch, as John Maulden recalls:

"College centre forward shoots high over the bar from close range. Utters loud expletive. Norman: "Smith, let's keep the good Lord out of this.""

Maulden adds that Norman sometimes did not find words to be necessary: "Opening batsman in explanation on returning to the pavilion after being wrongly given out caught by the wicket-keeper down the leg-side off a short pitched delivery: 'It hit a bunch of keys in my trouser pocket, sir.' Norman: withering stare needing no words."

Bob Fox was captain of the 1st XI hockey for two years in the late 60s. "In those days we rarely if ever lost a game, and I attribute this to the quality of Norman's coaching. He was demanding but fair and was always willing to try out a new strategy or a new player line-up to keep us on our toes."

As an occasional umpire of College hockey matches Norman was unimpressed by pompous umpires, particularly those who might ignore his attempts to make his own always impartial decisions in favour of 'his boys'. John Maulden provides an example:

"Opposition Posh Umpire, with blazer and badge, at the other end of the pitch from Norman, blows his whistle for an offence in the shooting circle right in front of Norman, and in favour of the opposition. Norman, afterwards in the Common Room, incandescent, relates the appalling tale to his colleagues: "…And the ruddy man had white gloves into the bargain".

John Cockett recalls an example of Norman's impartiality in a needle match between his boys from Felsted and Framlingham, umpired by a neutral umpire hired by John Cockett at one end and by Norman at the other:

"The Framlingham right wing lost control of the ball, nudged it forward obviously with his foot and continued on his way right under Norman's nose, with me standing on the touchline immediately behind him. No whistle. I challenged Norman after the game about this incident – to which he replied 'advantage, old boy, advantage'."

Peter Smith's view of Norman's umpiring, at least when not officiating at the College, throws a more favourable light: "After retirement Norman almost became an even nicer person, and became a very good umpire (although he had no time for them as a player!)".

Easter holidays for hockey masters meant the Oxford Hockey Festival, where a number of schoolboys obtained an early feel for university life, staying in different colleges, and playing five or six matches against other schools. Norman always accompanied the side, and looked after the holiday-minded boys with an easy blend of discipline and freedom. There were occasions when Norman would apologise to them for having entered "their" pub by mistake, preferring to let them enjoy themselves without the inhibition of his presence. He would instead seek out his own friends.

John Cockett recalls: "Norman wasn't the world's most magnanimous loser. On occasions at the Oxford Hockey Festival, we would meet up at the pub after the games and I would ask him how his boys had got on. Invariably his reply was; 'God, the goals those fellahs missed'. 'And what was the score, Norman?' 'Oh, we lost 1-0'!"

John Maulden remembers an almost identical conversation, this time in the Common Room on a Monday morning with Norman reporting Saturday's match at Greshams:

Norman: "We were all over them".

Curious member of Common Room: "What was the score Norman?"

Norman: "4-1 to them".

It is said that Norman didn't have time for those pupils who were not good at sport, and to an extent that is true: there are many who fell into that category who did not get on with him. But a distinction should be drawn. As Andrew Wright puts it: "If you were good at a sport but gave no enthusiasm to it, Norman would not bother with you; but if you were no good at a sport yet were keen to do better, Norman would happily spend hours encouraging you."

The fruits of Norman's labours in coaching the College hockey team were evident in the representative honours won during this period by, no doubt amongst many others: Norman Buck for Sussex, Norman Mayhew and Tony Knight for Suffolk and the East, Keith Gray for the East, Derek Moss for Suffolk, Michael Spencer for Warwickshire, Roy Quinlan for the Army and Combined Services, Ian Foster for Surrey and the South, the Wright brothers for Kent, Robin Anderton and Stephen Sayer for Essex, and Hugh Jenner for the Army and England trials; higher achievements fell to full internationals Norman Porter, Tony Parsons, Jim Crosbie; and schoolboy, Under 21 and indoor international Peter White; schoolboy international honours were also won by a number of pupils including Peter Over, Rick Parry, and John Smedley. Norman sometimes found that his efforts to promote the talent he had nurtured were rebuffed. "I thought Mark Creasey was a potential international, and I recommended him for an England Schools trial. In those days they tended to take my word for talent and sure enough he had a letter offering him a trial. He brought it to me and said he didn't think he would bother to accept. I think he was worried it might all turn out to be a bit expensive." The irony of this early financial nervousness would

not have been lost on Creasey when, some thirty years later, he made headlines with his discovery of gold in the Australian outback which netted him a reported £80 million fortune.

In 1978, after 28 years of coaching hockey at the College, Norman retired from the role, handing over to Brian Underwood. He wrote in the College magazine:

"A few years ago I retired from running the cricket after a spell of twenty-five years but continued with the hockey. Now, after an even longer spell, I am giving this up and take the opportunity to say how much fun (and frustration) it has given me to coach the many keen young players who have performed on the Back, and how much pleasure, too, to see that so many have continued to play the game, whether at international or club level after leaving the College. I pay tribute to the groundsmen who have worked so cheerfully to provide good grounds for the game."

Norman became part of the fabric of the College when in 1970 a new tarmacadam hockey and tennis surface at the College, was named 'Borretts' in his honour. A reception for Norman and Mullie in the College Library was followed by a match between Suffolk and the College 1st XI. Ten years later, in March 1980, 'Borretts' was resurfaced with astroturf, becoming The Norman Borrett Ground, the opening ceremony being performed by Humphrey Truman's sister, the Wimbledon tennis finalist Christine Janes, followed by a match between the College 1st XI and England Under 17s.

RIGHT: Keeping a watchful, if somewhat critical eye, on the play, from the touchline – at a College hockey match in 1980.

Following his retirement from minor county cricket, Norman continued to play occasional cricket in and around the College, for the Quilibets, Campsea Ashe, Framlingham Town, and in the less glamorous context of the College Masters' Cricket Club team. His mobility was reduced but the felicitous driving on both sides of the wicket remained to charm those who had never seen him at his best, both club opponents and pupils.

The College Masters team had been the brainchild of teacher Martin Irving, head of the French department. In the words of Bob Gillett, author of 'The Second Sixty Years', the College story from 1925 Irving had, back in 1953:

'…in the course of one afternoon's jaunt, intended to demonstrate the reliability of his motor to a prospective purchaser, arranged matches with Easton CC and Laxfield CC, elected a president (himself), invited Norman Borrett to undertake the captaincy (an invitation which, to the enormous benefit of the team both in efficiency and good humour, he accepted'.

Norman had run College cricket on Walter Winstanley's retirement from that post in 1956. The job of organizing matches, persuading masters to fill in with umpiring duty, arranging the inter-house competition, coaching the First XI, and overseeing the progress of the lower XIs, gave Norman little spare time to play the game himself. He needed practice of some sort for his annual summer holiday minor county matches for Devon.

His practice came through batting and bowling in the 1st XI nets, occasionally bringing along a cricketing acquaintance to provide him, and the boys, with some more serious competition. One such visitor was Jock Livingston, the pugnacious Australian who played for several seasons for Northants, and Norman's left-arm spin gave him a worth-while early season net.

The employment of John Harris in 1959 as coach and groundsman freed Norman from some of the more time-consuming aspects of responsibility for cricket, but he retained a firm grip on things as master in charge, and he would, despite increasing lameness, still occasionally bat, and frequently bowl off a few paces, against the first XI in the nets. These nets were, to half their length, made of all-weather asphalt. Nick Horne, a leg-spinner in the XI from 1959 to 1961, bowled at Norman on several such occasions.

"I had, with the aid of the cricket coach John Harris, learned to bowl a googly. On the rare occasions it pitched, it sometimes even turned. During one net session, after Norman had been belting my leggers to kingdom come for about 20 minutes, I was so fed up with this treatment I risked the first googly I'd ever tried 'in public'. As always, this was even slower and tossed higher than my leg-break, but of course the asphalt nets were bouncy; the ball not merely pitched, but, as Norman shaped to cut, it turned back quite a way, bounced, and ducking his head sharply, in a most un-Borrett like and undignified way, he took it on the shoulder.

He wasn't happy. He stopped batting, looked at the strip, came down the net to me and said 'Horne, what did that hit? Don't tell me you can bowl a googly!' I admitted, without revealing the novelty of what had just occurred, that indeed I could. He said 'Do it again!' I proceeded to bowl several balls that hit the side netting, back-netting on the full, or didn't turn, but eventually I did manage another proper googly. This time he said nothing, just gave me a long stare, then off he went, bat under his arm.

Some ten years later, I visited the College one summer. A cricket match was going on, and I was chatting on the Back with Norman. The conversation ended, and we said our au revoirs. Then, to my surprise, he turned back to me, smiled, gave me the full benefit of those pale blue eyes for several seconds, and said 'Horne, you had me fooled', before finally walking off.

At the time, his remark, out of context, puzzled me. I couldn't think what he meant. However, on reflection, it struck me he could only have been thinking of that 'first public googly' (by miles the most satisfying I bowled in my life). Norman knew how pleased the young Horne had been to have bowled a ball he didn't spot (of course it never happened again), and his comment was an exquisitely dignified way of reminding me of my one little triumph".

Norman Porter, who played for the school at all the major games, describes Norman from the viewpoint of the pupil: "He was remarkable. At cricket he could play left-handed or right-handed as he was ambidextrous, bowling left-hand slow and then suddenly converting to right-hand fast. It was the same at squash, where we used to play against him and he'd take people on two at a time.

It was like the iceberg effect; we knew the top bit of what he'd achieved, but we had no idea of the scope and range of his achievements. We knew he was good but we had no idea he was that good and it was only in later life that we found out how long he was squash champion and what a privilege it had been to be taught by him.. The more I've discovered about him the more

I can see why The Times described him as '*Probably Britain's most talented post-war all-round amateur sportsman*'. He was for us pupils the total embodiment of the Corinthian spirit."

David Turnbull was one of those pupils who would hurry from evening prep on a summer evening to watch Norman batting for the Masters XI, easing the ball through the covers, struggling through for a single rather sharper than he would have wished, and bowling a few overs of spin, with one hand or the other. David opened the bowling for the 1st XI, with David Larter, and was a successful goalkeeper for the hockey side.

"I was coached by Norman, particularly in my bowling as to the virtues of line and length. It was Norman's first year as coach, 1956 I think, after many years of Walter Winstanley. I remember him bowling left arm spinners in the nets. He was still playing for Devon in the Minor Counties Championship. He was quite lame by 1958, but he still played in hockey practices. He was particularly competitive and, although I say it myself, was rather annoyed when I managed to make a really good save from a well struck shot that he thought was destined to rattle the backboard. We bowled out Gresham's at Holt for 32 in 1958 on a rain affected wicket, with Robin Anderton getting a hat-trick, but Norman was none too pleased that we then lost three wickets in securing victory.

He was a good teacher of Geography, and I no doubt failed my A level because of too much cricket rather than his teaching! He was a disciplinarian, but was prepared to turn a blind eye to the team's occasional smoking and drinking when we were at the Oxford University Hockey Festival in 1958. We lost each of our matches 3-1. Maybe he should not have been so liberal.

He was a stickler for good manners. He was also a modest man for I never remember him talking about his past sporting achievements. I used to meet him at England hockey matches at Hurlingham Park in the early 1960's when he was chairman of the selectors and he always had time for a chat."

In the Spring of 1962, John Maulden, OF, College science master for 37 years, and enthusiastic sportsman if no great cricketer, approached Norman for his approval to convert the dreary College 2nd cricket section into a going concern by creating a team to play local villages. Norman gave the project his whole-hearted support and christened it The Haymakers. It catered for less talented but keen cricketers, and John found Norman was always prepared to allow the occasional 1st XI player to strengthen the side in order to match the opposition. When it was not otherwise being used, Norman was happy for

ABOVE: John Harris, left, was appointed by Norman as cricket coach in 1960. Here Harris attempts to coach the author, watched by Nick Horne, Jerry Caplen and Colin Lipman.

the 1st XI ground, the Back, to be used by the Haymakers, which was always popular with the village teams. John also had Norman's support for the concept, "an outrageous innovation in those days" of a drink after the game for both teams in the village pub.

In the summer vacation of that year Norman went to the Oval for the Test match starting on August 16th, when an England cricket cap was awarded to a Framlinghamian for the first time. And this Framlinghamian was one for whom Norman had had a short period of responsibility. For the fifth Test against the Pakistan touring side, the English selectors had rested a number of senior players, to give a chance to youth and to avoid calling heavily on those counties which were fighting for the County Championship. Trueman and Statham were amongst those rested, and Norman had an interest in both the replacements; first and foremost, 22 year old OF David Larter, but also Len Coldwell, now risen to dizzy heights from his early days opening the bowling for Devon.

Larter's entry to Test cricket was dramatic, claiming a wicket with his eleventh ball. Wisden described his debut as follows: 'Standing six feet seven and a half inches, Larter approached the crease with ten easy strides in a run of twenty yards. He maintained control over his length and direction and mixed his pace, putting the occasional ball down with some haste.' He ended the match with nine wickets for 145 runs and a run-out. He did not bat. Lest Len Coldwell be forgot, he took four wickets in the match, his second Test. In his first Test, the Lord's Test of the same series, he too, captured nine Pakistani wickets for 110 runs.

The College has only rarely produced cricketers of note. H. L. Wilson captained Sussex for 11 years after the First World

War and captained the Gentlemen against the Players in 1920.
Apart from Norman's three games for Essex, and the Norfolk
appearances of Gerald Mitchell and Ken Mayhew just after the
Second World War, the College had to wait until 1995 for
another prominent cricketer to emerge, when Ashley Cowan
began a 10 year career for Essex, in which he took 284 first
class wickets and went on England's tour to the West Indies in
1997-98, but did not make the Test side. Rob Newton
played for England Under 19s before making his first class
debut, and scoring his first century, for Larter's old county,
Northamptonshire, in 2010. The redoubtable Martin Pearse is a
double international at veterans level, having, in addition to his
senior England squash appearances, played cricket for England
Over 60s, including captaining the team to an 'Ashes' win over
Australia in 2009. He continues to score heavily for Norfolk
Over 50s and 60s, and for MCC.

Peter Over, pupil and now Governor at the school, will
always remember the first and last times he met Norman
Borrett. "The first time was in 1975 as a nervous 13 year old,
my first day at the College. He called me to his study and said
"I understand you are a hockey goalkeeper." I said "Yes". He
said "Are you any good?" and I said, trying my luck, "Very." He
said "Don't be so cocky boy – I will be the judge of that". But

*…I knew then that
Norman may not
have been quite as fit
as he once was but he
still had a razor sharp
sense of humour…*

he went the
extra mile for
me, insisting to
the selectors,
and succeeding,
that they pick
me for the
England
schoolboys
team. The last
time I saw
Norman was in
2002 when I
was playing
cricket for the Gents of Suffolk against the Quilibets on the
Back at Framlingham. I got a very lucky 94 and was out, trying
to hit a six. Feeling rather pleased with myself, whilst walking
back to the Pavilion I heard his dulcet tones shout out "Good
Lord boy, that was quite frankly the worst innings I have seen in
my life" – I knew then that Norman may not have been quite
as fit as he once was but he still had a razor sharp sense of
humour. I can honestly say that no other person made more of

an impression on me during my school days than Norman
Borrett – I am totally in awe of the man!"

John Harris left the college staff in 1964 for pastures new,
and later qualified as a distinguished first-class umpire. Norman
astutely signed as his replacement the ex-England and
Glamorgan all-rounder Alan Watkins, who proved a great
success with the boys, both as a genial coach and a cricket
raconteur of some style and wit.

Both Harris and Watkins played in their turn for Suffolk in
the long school holiday, sharing the County bowling attack
with the remarkable Cyril Perkins, coach and groundsman to
Ipswich School from 1946 to the 1970s. A slow left-armer,
Perkins had initially played for Northants from 1934 to 1937,
achieving the singular feat of never being on a winning side in
his 56 games for them, including the match when an 18 year
old Denis Compton scored his first first-class hundred. His
career for Suffolk began in 1939 and lasted beyond his 54th
birthday, by which time he had taken 779 wickets for the
county, including all ten against Hertfordshire for 23 runs in
1960 at the age of 49. Perkins' teams at Ipswich School were
always hard for Framlingham to beat and the wicket he
prepared was one of the best in the county. Perkins' links with
Framlingham went back to pre-war days when he played for
Suffolk alongside Phil Mead, then coach at the College. He
described Mead as "a funny chap. He'd take guard, stand right
away from his bat and do this shuffle towards the bat when the
bowler was running in. He was an awkward man to get out."

Mead's coaching career at Framlingham had sadly been cut
short by the Second World War and then by blindness in the
early 1940s, which led him to retire to Bournemouth. First
capped by England in 1911, he was one of the great English
cricketers, a batsman of remarkable consistency who scored
over 1,000 runs per season in each of his 27 county seasons and
made 153 centuries. In 1938 when the coach at the College,
suffering from rheumatism and failing eyesight, he topped the
Suffolk averages with over 76, and, in 1939, aged 53, averaged
over 71. In 1950, attending a Hampshire match, quite blind but
listening closely, Mead asked the young Hampshire batsman
who had just been dismissed to bring him his bat. Mead held it
for a while, running his fingers over the blade. "You're not
middling 'em yet" was his only comment.

Alan Watkins term as a popular and effective cricket
professional at the College, who had proved an inspired choice
by Norman, retired in 1970, to be replaced by another long
serving and popular county cricketer, Jack Oakes of Sussex.

6

FAMILY AND FRIENDS

RIGHT: An Allhallows family shot. Norman wearing his Cambridge hockey sweater, with Mullie with Anthony.

FAMILY AND FRIENDS

Norman would make the journey to Tonbridge occasionally to watch Anthony's progress on the hockey field. In his last hockey term there, in April 1960, Anthony was picked for the final trial for the English Schools XI. On leaving school that summer he went to France to study the language. He began work as a stockbroker in the City, playing hockey for Ipswich at weekends and in due course joining one of the top London sides, Dulwich, where he was immediately picked for the first team. He was to play for them for a number of years. He was soon asked to play in the county championship for Suffolk and made his debut against Essex in late 1961. Thus began a long county career, starting in his father's position of inside-left but going on to play in every position in the forward line.

The son shared his father's passion for sport. He threw himself into every sport he played with a gusto that on occasions verged on the reckless. He was a talented hockey player, and got close to an England cap. It is often said that it is of no benefit to a young keen son to have been preceded in his endeavours by a supremely talented father. Anthony did find this a difficulty, although he was passionately proud of his father's achievements. In turn his father was, like any other father, proud of Anthony's successes, and stood on the touchline of many cold, windswept hockey pitches urging the youngster on.

Following a successful county match against Bedfordshire in which he was described as the inspiration behind the Suffolk attack, he was selected for the East divisional trial in December 1962 as a late substitute, performed well, and forced his way into the East team for the season's first divisional match, against South on January 5th 1963, as outside-left. Divisional matches were still used by the English selectors as trials for the national side, and Anthony, as always, gave his all.

In February 1964, Anthony was again reported as showing '*brilliant form*', scoring in a 5-1 victory for the East over the Midlands at Norwich. Previewing Suffolk's match against Hertfordshire the following week, the EADT opined that '*Tony Borrett, who must have enhanced his England chances with a great display for the East, could be a match winner at inside left.*'

In the next season came an invitation to join the England Under 23 trial at Motspur Park. The Daily Telegraph's correspondent, R. L. Hollands, who had written so often about Norman's hockey, now found himself writing about the next generation. 'The only forward among the ten chosen for the trial with much experience of playing inside left in first class company is A. N. Borrett of Dulwich.' But competition for

places in the full England side was fierce and Anthony never got his chance. He continued to produce whole-hearted displays for Dulwich, Suffolk (where he played alongside OFs Norman Mayhew and Derek Moss) and the East, and in occasional representative matches for the Hockey Association.

Norman had attended a number of Suffolk's hockey matches over the years to watch Anthony play. In the 1970s county championship Anthony was to run into, occasionally literally, several of Norman's College protégés,

all of them full-backs, Tony Parsons, who had been picked for the first time by Sussex and went on to play for Wales and Great Britain, Jim Crosbie who was to be capped many times by Scotland, and Robin Anderton and Stephen Sayer who provided the Essex championship full-back pairing. OF Norman Porter was a regular in the Scottish national side at this time. Anthony's hockey career had reached its zenith; a serious knee injury was then to hamper further progress.

A good cricketer, Anthony captained Frinton Cricket Club. His early retirement from stockbroking in the City brought the prospect of many years of happy retirement with his wife Christine, but this was sadly not to be when she died at in 2007. He continues to live in Barnes, South West London, is a regular Test Match watcher at Lord's where he is a member of the MCC, and sees a lot of his son James, who made a delightful speech in honour of Mullie at her 90th birthday in early 2010. Anthony and his brother Tim are close, and regularly holiday together. Their childhood holidays were always spent at Frinton until they were about eight when the family would regularly holiday abroad, in France, Yugoslavia, Portugal and often in Spain: "Mum of course spoke fluent Portuguese and good Spanish, and for a year or two taught the latter at the College."

"Dad was a disciplinarian. Uncle Charles told us a story about how pernickety Dad was when he was a prefect at Fram. He would insist that boys line up so he could inspect their turn-out, in particular their shoes, which had to be immaculate. If there was a speck of dirt there would be hell to pay. As a grown-up he remained a perfectionist – and would go on with whatever he was doing until he got it right. This stubborn streak meant that he could be difficult; in such times I would turn to Mum. She has a wonderfully generous heart and would act as a mediator with Dad. He was quite a complex person; the arguments we used to have usually concerned money, which he didn't like to spend as I thought he ought! I used to think he could have done more with the money we had. Having said that, he was under this tough exterior quite soft-hearted, and was always positive in the support he gave Tim and me. He was difficult but I loved him. He was a loving father-in-law and grandfather. He was really pleased to meet OFs, and was delighted when they would seek him out. Teaching sport was really what made his life. He was interested in every sport."

And seek him out they did. A steady stream of OFs and of hockey and squash colleagues would ring the bell at the Readery, and later at Landermere, to say hello. Denys Carnill and his wife used to visit Norman in Framlingham nearly every year when they went to Aldeburgh. "A fine house he had, but too many stairs for him to cope with. 'Mother' or 'Mullie' looked after him marvellously."

Peter Smith, whose visits to Essex from Devon are now few and far between, was another visitor: "We tried to visit Norman and Mullie for each of his last few years, and both were extremely hospitable. I keep in touch with Mullie and we visited her in Frinton last Autumn, when having agreed that we would take her out to lunch she gave us a lovely lunch instead, with a bottle of wine! We both are very fond of Mullie who agrees that she did not have the easiest of lives, but we know they were a devoted couple."

Tim, who had followed Anthony to Brandeston Hall in 1958, left there in 1963, having boarded for his last two years, and went to Felsted School. "I didn't go to Fram for obvious reasons". At Felsted he came under the tutelage of Norman's old friend John Cockett, in whose House he was placed. Tim followed the family tradition of playing his hockey as an inside

left. Tim jokingly recalls that one of the most enjoyable goals he scored for the school was the only goal of the game to enable Felsted to beat Framlingham.

On leaving Felsted in 1968 Tim went to law school in Lancaster Gate, taking articles with solicitors Penningtons, a traditional, respected London law firm. After three years he decided to leave London and transfer his articles to Walton on the Naze, near home in Essex. After qualifying, he practised in Clacton on Sea and also opened a new solicitors' practice in Frinton. Divorced after seven years marriage, he found great happiness in his second marriage to Trudé, by whom he has two daughters, Alex and Katherine, born in 1984 and 1986. Tim and Trudé live in an Essex farmhouse near to the Borrett Frinton home, where they visit Mullie every day.

Tim agrees that his father was blunt and often irreverent, and as a father was strict, "but not too much". Tim exudes a laid-back attitude to life, at least in his retirement. "Yes, but it was different on the sports field! The Borrett DNA of determination and single-mindedness then kicked in. Perhaps the difference between me and brother Tony was that I knew my limitations and could accept the frustration of not succeeding, but Tony could not."

If the picture of

> 66 99
>
> *… Yes, but it was different on the sports field! The Borrett DNA of determination and single-mindedness then kicked in….*

Norman drawn in this memoir suggests a man whose only interest in life was sport, Tim adds another dimension: "I remember going into the College chapel with father, and finding it empty, he sat at the organ and played really well. Until then I had no idea he could even play the piano, let alone the organ. Perhaps he had learnt it when he was a pupil there. He also liked to collect antique maps and seascapes."

As Anthony has said, Norman was a complex personality. He was an intensely private person who had been brought up not to show his emotions. This meant that whilst by nature he was charming and well-mannered, he did not readily offer praise, nor convey to his family the warmth of the love which he no doubt felt for them. He never had much time for female children, although he did say he would have liked to have had a daughter.

An exception to this apparent alpha male preference was Katherine, Tim and Trude's daughter, who, as a young child, was happily permitted to sit on Norman's lap and cuddle him. Katherine recalls this bond, and of how her grandfather taught her how to play vingt et un with matchsticks at a very tender age, and of his calling her Shrimp as she was so small.

Her sister Alex's memories are mostly of her summer holidays on the beach at Frinton, "or of Grandpa always insisting that he had to carve the meat even when he needed two sticks to stand and do it. I was discussing with Mum how I remember Grandpa telling me that he used to shoot rabbits whilst sitting on the loo upstairs in the Readery at Framlingham. Mum tells me this was rubbish but I have spent years believing it was the truth!"

Trude's own abiding memory is of Norman's speaking to her as she was going into hospital to have Katherine: 'I hope you're not going to have another bloody girl'! Most of my memories are of that nature, where Norman enjoyed speaking frankly and with apparent unconcern at his listener's reaction. But I happily acknowledge that the frankness which ruffled feathers for some was taken by others as part of Norman's irreverence and wicked humour. He liked to be provocative."

Diana Turan, whose family have lived in Framlingham for decades, was often asked to do "Norman sitting" duty when her mother took out Mullie to give her a break from her tireless nursing routine. Diana had been one of the ladies in the mixed hockey games which Norman would organise in school holidays: "He would shout at us "what do you think you are doing woman?' but we all loved it. He didn't care what people thought of him, and would get away with murder in the things he said to people. I remember several instances: to the mother of the bride

at the wedding of a friend: 'What have you got on your head? Looks like a ruddy bird's nest!' To the Scottish telephone caller seeking to conclude a sale to Norman: 'Can't you put me on to someone who can speak ruddy English?' And the way he bossed Mullie around: 'Get up there woman, what's the matter with you?' as he encouraged her, well into her seventies, up the ladder to clean out the house guttering, or to prune the roses, whilst he waved his two sticks from below. He became very proficient with those sticks and could weed the garden by pinching them together. Yes he was difficult, but we all loved him. He would never permit the doctor to come to treat him, even when he was quite ill. I never heard him complain."

Trudé reflects: "He achieved a lot in his life, though he would never talk about it, and we all admired him. He was very demanding of Mullie and the family, and in his last years particularly so, which I think was due to the fact that the pain he had had to put up with for some fifty years became increasingly hard to bear. He was the most stoical person I have met. He would only

BELOW: Trudé did indeed have "another bloody girl". Norman was not famous for relating to babies, but he made an exception of Katherine.

FRAMLINGHAM

Photobank

Ivan Belcher

mention his pain when talking to me, as I, as his in-house pharmacist, discussed pain management with him. Mullie was such a wonderful wife to him, putting up with a lot but never failing to be positive and loving."

Norman was content in his immediate family environment, and did not make great efforts to spend time with his wider family. This is confirmed in the remarks of his nephew Andrew, Charles' son: "As children we rarely saw Norman and Mullie, let alone Tony and Tim, although my father and Norman were in regular contact by phone. There was a brotherly bond between them, but Dad would on occasion come off the phone fuming after a disagreement, usually about finance or about what had or had not been done by the family solicitor. Dad used to stay with Norman and Mullie at fairly regular times when he came to the Lodge at Framlingham, and as children we used to meet occasionally when we went to Frinton on holiday."

Tony and Christine's son James, asked for his memories of his grandfather, admitted: "it's made me quite emotional trying to think back. I don't think it ever really occurred to me what a sportsman he was. I knew from stories and photos I had heard and seen that he had achieved a great deal, but it didn't sink in until I was a bit older.

I remember that on one of the first times we walked

around Framlingham College I was thrown by the fact a new artificial pitch had been named after him. I was keen to play squash for the first time. I'm sure the rules, how to grip the racquet, where to be at any given moment, were all explained but I think I was more interested in trying to hit the ball as hard as I could. He couldn't swing through the shot because of his walking sticks, so they were removed, and he stood on the tee. I think he would have been angry at his lack of footwork, but I think I made up for it with the distance he made me run, chasing his wristy drops at the fore-court, and by my bizarre way of getting it down the line. Squash didn't really agree with me.

While I was at Tonbridge, both he and Vovoa (my pet name for Mullie - Brazilian for Granny) always tried to attend at least one match during the cricket and hockey seasons. I knew it was uncomfortable for him to make the journey and stand and watch, so that added to the pressure on me to perform, but there was always constructive criticism and flashes of dazzling dribbling skills with a walking stick. Oh and a meal or two out. My long-lasting memories of him will be at the Readery playing cricket on the lawn and tending his vegetable patch at the back of the garden."

ABOVE: The Readery, pictured in the 1950s and today.

7

...as always, he was on the touchline supporting, cajoling and criticizing - "Come on you fellows, hit the bloody ball!"

RETIREMENT FROM THE COLLEGE

At the end of the 1980 summer term Norman retired from the College staff, at the age of 62, after 30 years service. He had for the previous two years held the title of Deputy Headmaster, a role he had in reality fulfilled for a long time as Second Master.

1980 also included a Borrett family celebration, as they gathered to honour Norman's brother Charles, now Archdeacon of Stoke on Trent, on his appointment as a Chaplain to the Queen.

In retirement Norman and Mullie continued to holiday in Frinton at Landermere, the bungalow built in 1953 by his mother, Alice, when his father died, a few yards from the family home, so that she would not have the worry of looking after the large house. Norman and Mullie had used it as a holiday home since her death in 1966. Their home however remained the Readery in Castle Street, near Framlingham Castle, a house originally owned by Pembroke College for the use of Readers in nearby St. Michael's Church. They had lived there for all but the first five years since their arrival in Framlingham from Allhallows in 1950, and it was here that they planned to remain, entertaining friends and keeping in touch with College life.

Freely admitting what a difficult person he must have been to live with, Norman attributed his long and happy married life to the devotion and love of the long-suffering Mullie. Retirement gave him more time for children, grandchildren, travel with Mullie, and contact, within and without the sporting circle, with the large number of people who had become friends over the years. The Readery's front door bell would often be rung by OFs and old friends wanting to chat, and they would never be turned away, even those who arrived without warning and at odd hours. John Edwards was one of those former pupils who became a close friend of Norman and Mullie, and he recalls their great hospitality and kindness, typified by the wonderful party they gave to celebrate the 50th birthday of the much-respected OF Hon. Secretary Vinty Bromage.

Norman was a regular attender at Old Framlinghamian suppers and other functions. He had served his time as President of the SOF, back in 1970 and 1971, "an overdue accolade" in the words of Bob Gillett's The Second Sixty Years. Once or twice a year, Norman, accompanied often by Mullie, would get out to a reunion with a group of his cricket and hockey pupils of the early 1950s, John Gooderham, Ian Foster, David Mead, Bobby Osborne, and others, at local restaurants in Aldeburgh and elsewhere. In later years this involved Mullie pushing and propping Norman and his two sticks into a car, which he insisted on driving until well into his 80s, or into the passenger seat of a friend's car.

LEFT: Norman, Tim, Mullie and Anthony, in 1982.

Norman had always loved driving, which was fortunate for one who spent his life before retirement covering thousands of miles to get to sports events around the country. He enjoyed driving fast, as his succession of sports cars testifies, and he was evidently viewed, by some at least, as being skilled behind the wheel. Mullie recalls that around 1952 Norman received a remarkable invitation from a motoring friend: would he join him as co-driver of his Bentley at Le Mans in the annual 24 hour race? No doubt he would have loved to accept, and why he turned the invitation down is now beyond the recollection of the family.

Another invitation which he would have liked to accept, but was unable to as it involved taking two weeks out of school in the summer term, arose in the early post-war years. Tennis was then getting back on its feet, and to encourage players to return to top competition the All England Club issued invitations to players who had done well in regional events to play in the Wimbledon tournament. Norman had been a good tournament player pre-war, and post-war had accumulated a sufficient number of points to warrant an invitation.

With tennis and cricket to occupy him in the summer months, and squash and hockey in the winter, it is surprising that Norman had time, in the years of his sporting prime, for any other pursuits. But he did. In the 1950s he took up golf. The hip pain meant that the naturally rhythmical long swing was truncated more often than not, but the strength of wrist and forearm could compensate for the lack of hip rotation in propelling the ball down the Clacton – and occasionally Frinton - fairways. Within a year or so he was into single figures and eventually played to a handicap of four. He stopped playing in the late 1950s as the arthritis made it difficult to continue, and he did not resume it after the first hip replacement in 1963.

He was lucky to have been born, not only with ambi-dexterity, but also with remarkable hand-eye coordination. He could thus make a reasonable fist of any sport, and to play it to a reasonable standard if he devoted time to it. The following tale, from OF Stephen Sayer, is but one example:

"Back at Framlingham for the 1959 autumn term, a new boarding house, Moreau House, was opened. Bob Gillett, the new housemaster, proudly unveiled a small croquet lawn alongside the new building. He held Norman's sporting prowess in great regard, and invited him to strike the first ball to mark the opening of the lawn. Norman, modest as always, claiming he had never picked up a croquet mallet before, took aim and struck the ball clean through not just the first hoop but the second as well. Bob Gillett's reaction of praise and disgust in equal measure will evoke empathy in those readers who have experienced the frustration of us ordinary mortals when we find their honest toil eclipsed by casual genius."

Norman's claim never to have touched a mallet before was not quite correct. OF Andrew Towler innocently provides the background: "After Norman had retired to Frinton we met from time to time, and he was always very interested to find out how my career was progressing. He would always ask after my mother's garden in Frinton, not far from his own family house, as during the war years and post-war era the back garden was famous amongst the locals as a croquet lawn which Norman used, and he had fond memories of this."

Mullie knew that feeling of frustration at casual genius overwhelming honest endeavour. She recalls a badminton game in which she was playing. Norman arrived and insisted on "just trying a few shots" with her racket. He proceeded to strike winners from all over the court until Mullie in desperation demanded the return of her racket and the resumption of normal service.

Apart from playing, Norman had always been interested in the administration and management of the sports he loved. In 1977, not long before he retired from the College, he was appointed a vice-president of the Hockey Association. With his appointment in 1980 as president of the SRA, he thus maintained a close and rewarding involvement in the two games during retirement. Those ties were enhanced by other posts. One from which he got much enjoyment was the Travellers Hockey Club, a club formed mainly for ex-members of the Oxbridge Universities and members of Beckenham Hockey Club, and which toured abroad each year. Mike Bawden, a fine player, Cambridge Blue, Divisional player and England triallist, captained the Travellers at the time when Norman was its President:

"For many years during the 1970s and 1980s Norman was President of the Travellers. I was fortunate enough to go as its captain with Norman on three tours to South Africa, and many to Holland and Germany. Norman was very well known wherever he went and a fine ambassador; he was a great character and a very good member of a touring party. He had toured all of these countries when he was still playing, and was still respected for his talents.

He expected the team to play hard, but fairly, and looked to the highest standards of behaviour off the field, but still expected the Travellers to be the last to leave every party! We were fortunate that the teams that we took were good and able to win most of the games, despite the parties the night before. He got on well with every member of the team, be they young or old and always had a twinkle in his eye, especially when there were young ladies about! He was very supportive and helpful to me as a young captain of the side and remained a good friend ever since."

Norman's role on such tours was that of chief supporter, speech-maker, and meeter and greeter, sometimes to important people: on a Travellers tour to South Africa, on his 36th wedding anniversary, August 31st 1976, he and Mike Bawden were presented to Rhodesian Prime Minster, Ian Smith, at Smith's Salisbury office.

Ian Ferris, also a Traveller, saw two different sides to Norman, the player and the supporter. Ian, later to be a Hawks and Surrey player, in his last year at Cambridge in 1947 both played alongside and watched Norman: "On the hockey field and the squash court, it was evident that he was pretty 'definite', even ruthless: direct on the hockey field, and dominating from the centre of the squash court. These characteristics no doubt contributed to his success. Years later he joined us as an umpire on several Easter tours in Europe, for the Travellers. Although we did include some internationals, others like myself were of much lesser quality, but Norman was remarkably encouraging to us all: very supportive - a different side to him, perhaps that of a schoolmaster."

Norman's successor as Head of Geography at the College, and later as master in charge of hockey, was David Barker. An Oxford hockey blue and England indoor international, the modest Barker found he was filling some large shoes:

"Accounts of Norman's sporting ability, especially hockey, squash and cricket, were often referred to by members of both the College Common Room and OFs in after-match stories during the Quilibets cricket week in which I played before I joined the staff. These demonstrated the esteem in which he was held by many sportsmen who had known him. They nearly all had their Norman Borrett stories, which suggested that here was a person of real character as well as one of the finest amateur sportsmen in the country.

It was not until the summer term of 1979 that I first met him when invited for interview. Luckily for me (I have lived in this lovely market town now for over 30 years) I was appointed to take Norman's place. I believe that Norman and I have been two of only three Heads of Geography at the College since the Second World War. At that interview I was struck by his pleasant demeanour and his forthright manner. He was clearly a no-nonsense character who, without saying anything to them, had visible influence on pupils passing by as he showed me around College grounds, classrooms and corridors. It seemed that here was a schoolmaster who was very much respected and highly regarded by the boys.

The Geography department, and indeed the rest of the classroom block, did perhaps need some updating at this time; I still have the curved rubber stamp maps of the continents and the world which were used frequently by Geography masters in the 50s and 60s. I have too the old filmstrip projector which Norman used to plug into the light socket and some of the black and white filmstrips he used to teach the geography of various parts of the world. The subject itself has changed significantly since those days.

Over the next 20 years I met Norman and Mullie frequently in the Market Square, until he was unable to walk around. I remember Mullie being quite upset whenever I asked her how Norman was in those later years, largely because he was clearly very frustrated as he became more restricted in his movements. During that period, there was never a time when he didn't ask me about the Geography department, the College sport and my own family. As a Cambridge Geography graduate his interest in the subject never waned and he always showed a genuine interest in the department at the College; yet he never interfered, even though with his knowledge and experience he must have been tempted to. I often saw him wearing his blues hockey sweater in the town, although he rarely accepted my invitations to watch matches or to attend hockey functions at the College, no doubt mainly because of his difficulty in standing.

Over the years it was distressing to see him change from a very upright physically fit relatively young retiree in 1980 to someone who by the 21st century needed two sticks, built-up shoes and latterly to be driven by car to get around town. Even if it was the relentless sport which contributed to his hip problems, I am sure that like most sportsmen who have suffered later in life he would do it all again. We often had long conversations in the marquee at Speech Day until not long before he died; and even though he had to sit down and was clearly ageing, there was always a twinkle in his eye and he remained remarkably perceptive and retained his sharp wit.

Milton Keynes 1999
RIGHT: Norman with David Turnbull and Norman Porter.
FAR RIGHT: Norman with John Gooderham, seated. College Head Gwen Randall far right.

Although forthright in his views, he was an unassuming man who never talked about his own exploits, showing the humility and modesty characteristic of the great sportsmen."

Norman carefully kept his visits to the College to a minimum, not wishing to invade the territory of his successor. He did make a point of going to watch the College hockey team play Felsted, so he could meet John Cockett. The latter recalls this: "After Norman retired, I took the Felsted side to Framlingham and, as always, he was on the touchline supporting, cajoling and criticizing – 'Come on you fellows, hit the bloody ball!'"

He did return to the College occasionally, quietly, to pursue his interest in shooting. After retirement he continued to license and keep in the College armoury, a twelve bore shotgun and a .22 rifle. Malcolm Todd, who was in charge of the College armoury, used to collect Norman from the Readery and take him to the College so that he could shoot the rifle on the indoor range. This was one of the sports which he had managed to fit in around his main sporting commitments. Others included tennis, motoring and golf.

At the same time he stood aside as President of the SRA to permit Janet Morgan, the Women's SRA President, to become president of Squash England, the new body which amalgamated the men's and women's associations: as noted earlier, a well-received act of diplomacy. Norman's last act was to obtain the agreement of the Duke of Edinburgh to continue to act as Patron of the organisation in its new guise.

An accolade, late in life, which gave him much pleasure, was to be invited with Mullie as the guests of honour at the 1999 varsity match at the National Hockey Centre in Milton Keynes. The event marked the 60th anniversary of Norman's last Cambridge varsity match and was preceded by a luncheon with governors, staff, parents and OFs, and by a warm-up match in which the Framlingham College 1st XI, supported by five coach loads of pupils from the College and its prep school, Brandeston, played and beat Stowe. In tribute to Norman, the College flag flew over the ground. Introduced by the commentator as "one of the greatest sportsmen of our time", Norman handed tankards to each of the players and, his only regret of the day, the Deloittes trophy to Oxford who, having drawn the game 2-2, retained the trophy they had won in 1998. Eschewing the seats preferred by some of his younger graduate colleagues, Norman insisted on standing for a lot of the match.

At the age of 82 Norman's sense of fun showed little sign

of diminishing. He asked, through the columns of the Old Framlinghamian magazine, whether any reader could set his mind at rest by recalling for him the details of the incident in which Maths master Mr. Podd's Singer car had been found one morning parked sideways – virtually wedged – across the College's fives court.

In his last years Norman's awareness of what was happening at the College arose almost exclusively through contact with masters and old pupils. He did not visit the College much beyond occasional sports events such as Felsted's visits, and formal annual gatherings such as Speech Day and Remembrance Day. He was very lame and, even with sticks, it was a major effort to get about. He also found the inevitable changes in the way the College operated rather difficult to absorb. He had for so long possessed such strong and clear views of the proper, decent, way to bring up young men, that he was uncomfortable with modern methods. He has been brought up in what was in the 21st century regarded as a primitive, harsh, manner; boarding from the age of six, and succeeding through hard work, respect and discipline. He felt that the world had become a poorer place when it paid less attention to these elements.

In 2003 the Borretts gave up the Readery, when the difficulty of negotiating the stairs became insuperable for Norman, and after several painful falls. Mullie tells the story of one such fall, how he hit his head, leaving a massive cut, with blood everywhere. "Mop it up woman" was the order. The doctor arrived and said that it needed stitching at hospital. Norman hated hospitals, partly because he hated fuss. "You're a doctor aren't you - get on with it." And he did.

They moved to the greater convenience of their single storey Frinton house, where they were near to younger son Tim and the grandchildren. To help Norman move around the house live-in help was employed; but it was usually Mullie who was the nurse, the helper, the prop. She had done it for over 60 years and she wasn't going to stop now. Norman pretended to give orders, right up to the end, but he knew he was truly loved and he knew he owed everything to her.

8

THE ✦ TIMES

No. 68271 ■ THURSDAY DECEMBER 30 2004 ■ www.timesonline.co.uk ■

...arguably Britain's most talented post-war all round sportsman...

EPILOGUE

Norman died, peacefully, at Colchester General Hospital, on December 10th 2004, two months into his 88th year. The funeral at Frinton and the later memorial service at the College were attended by friends and sporting acquaintances from near and far.

The Jesters Club, whose membership included more multi-talented sportsmen than any other club, formally recorded Norman's death with the comment that he *'was arguably the greatest amateur all-rounder of his generation'*, language similar to that used in The Times obituary. Wisden's obituary followed the same path. The OF website attracted a number of old pupils' memories:

'I have fond memories of Norman. As John Birt has said he got a lot of practice with "Willie" – no doubt to sharpen up reflexes for the hockey and cricket teams. It was very appropriate that Norman's wife Mullie was honoured by the SOF for her great contribution to the College. On Sunday afternoons it was always a treat to be invited to have tea with Norman and Mullie. He will be sadly missed.'
Rory Brown.

'Two of my most vivid memories of Norman are: firstly Norman giving 'Dougal' Ellis an impromptu free haircut in class - he had ignored previous warnings to get it cut. Secondly, just before Norman was about to administer 'Willie' to me in front of class, he looked towards the big sash window and instructed that it be opened 'to give me a decent flight path'! A unique and inspiring person."
Tim Duncan.

'Nick Allan reminded me that apart from the sports and classroom memories it was the wonderful Aston Martin he drove that impressed us hugely. I remember getting a great thrill from the Aston's exhaust pipe's burbling noise as we passed through the narrow Oxford streets at the 1963 Oxford Hockey Festival where we beat all-comers save Kingston Grammar School!'
John Birt.

'I don't remember 'Willie' but I do know that I have never spelt 'lettuce' wrong since the day I was tanned by Norman for spelling it 'lettice'. He was an amazing man and teacher.'
Michael Thomson.

THE TIMES THURSDAY DECEMBER 30 2004

OBITU

NORMAN BORRETT

Amateur sportsman who excelled nationally and internationally in hockey, squash and cricket

NORMAN BORRETT was probably Britain's most talented postwar all-round amateur sportsman. Uniquely, he captained his country many times at hockey and squash, while also playing first-class and minor-county cricket. As a schoolmaster he inspired g[...]tions of pupils to achievement in [...]k and sport.

Born in Wanstead, Essex, where his father was a farmer, Norman Francis Borrett was educated at Framlingham College in Suffolk from the age of 13. There he revealed an outstanding talent for all athletic pursuits. He ended his school career as captain of hockey, cricket, squash, fives, athletics and swimming, secretary of the debating society and school captain. In the holidays of his last year he managed to fit in matches as fly-half for the Eastern Counties Schools rugby XV as well as winning the Evans Cup Public Schools Squash Handicap, playing cricket for Essex Young Amateurs and scoring 63 at Lord's in the Young Amateurs v Young Professionals match.

He went to Pembroke College, Cambridge, in 1936, read geography, won two hockey and three squash blues, captained the university in both, and won his first three England hockey ca[...] his last hockey term, 1939.

[...]r war service in the Army he became a schoolmaster, first at Allhallows School, Devon, from 1945 to 1950, then at Framlingham, from 1950 to 1980, where he eventually became second master.

At hockey Borrett played inside-left 30 times for England and 7 times for Great Britain, in an unbroken run of 15 years, captaining England 23 times and Great Britain 7. He led Great Britain to the silver medal at the 1948 Olympics. His ratio of goals to games played remains the highest by an English player.

Described in the press of the day as "the incomparable Borrett", he was without question the best player of his era, and in the view of many the most naturally gifted and skilful of all British players.

While at Cambridge he played twice for Essex at cricket, but not, strangely, for the university. After the war he was also picked for Essex, against Nottinghamshire in August 1946, his third and last match for the county. Thereafter he played for Devon in the Minor Counties championship each summer holidays, from 1947 to 1959, save for 1951 and 1955 when he was touring South Africa respectively with the British hockey team and the Great Britain squash team. He played 50 matches for Devon, scoring 2,408 runs at an average of over 36, with 4 centuries. He still holds the Devon record for the 4th wicket — an unbroken 262 against Oxfordshire in 1949, of which his share was 134 not out.

It was in squash that Borrett's remarkable talent stood out most starkly. While a virtual unknown, he won the English Amateur Championship in 1946, and again in each of the next four years, winning each final in straight games. He was a racing certainty to have won it in the sixth year but had to withdraw with food poisoning. But the astonishing aspect of his domination is that it was achieved without proper, or indeed any, competitive practice.

Squash was centred entirely on London in those days. Borrett lived in Devon, where there was no one he could play, so he had to use the first two or three rounds of the amateur championship each year to get his eye in. The other competitors all played regular top-class squash in London.

He captained the England and Great Britain squash teams, playing 12 times for England when hockey and school commitments permitted. Until 1952 he had lost only once to any amateur in the world since the war.

He played golf to a handicap of 4, accumulated enough tournament ranking points to qualify for the Wimbledon tennis championship, but was too busy to enter, and was invited by a friend to be his co-driver in the Le Mans 24-hour race — an invitation he declined. He was president of both the Squash Racquets Association and the Hockey Association as well as chairman of the England hockey selectors, president of the Travellers Hockey Club, a member of MCC, the Tramps, the Gentlemen of Essex, the Jesters and numerous other clubs. He wrote two well-received instructional books on hockey.

The war deprived him of the years between 22 and 29, otherwise his sporting record would have been even more extraordinary. At the age of 35 arthritis was diagnosed in both hips. He continued to play international squash until the age of 38, and Devon county cricket until 42, subsequently undergoing four hip replacements which left him crippled in later years.

He is survived by his wife Mullie, whom he married in 1940, and by their two sons, Anthony and Timothy.

Norman Borrett, amateur sportsman, was born on October 1, 1917. He died on December 10, 2004, aged 87.

Borrett: unknown when he won the amateur squash championship in 1946

In 2008 Mullie, accompanied by Norman Porter, was interviewed by Radio Essex, in a programme marking the 60th anniversary of the 1948 Olympics. Having looked at some of Norman's newspaper cuttings, retrieved from her garage, Mullie was asked about the GB hockey team. "I think he told me he had been selected. I only watched one match unfortunately, but I did see the opening ceremony, which was something I wanted to do very much. It was terrific, like going to a pop concert; seeing all the athletes and people, the fanfares and all that went with it, the chap with the torch running in and lighting the flame. To me it was absolutely wonderful.

I saw Norman play and I think score a goal. Although I only saw that one GB game, at other times I went quite often to see England games as they were easier to get to.

Of Norman's devotion to sport she expresses no concern or surprise: "People say that he was totally devoted, but I never thought anything about it. If that's what you like doing – do it! My family were all very interested in Norman's sport, but his family weren't quite so much."

She was asked about Norman's skill at various different games, including tennis and golf. "It used to be that if you were quite a good county tennis player as Norman was, you'd get an invitation to play at Wimbledon. That was then and he just couldn't do everything, so he didn't go! He wanted to take up golf as a professional in later life."

But he never had a special diet, Mullie explained: "He liked his food, as he was a hopeless cook! The only thing he used to do was to train perpetually."

Reminiscing in 2010 after her 90th birthday celebrations, Mullie expanded a little on what it was like to be married to a man devoted to sport: "I was always happy that he played sport, for that was what he loved doing. He never demanded that I be closely involved in following his successes; indeed he didn't talk about them at all, so the boys and I would only know what was going on if we read about it in the newspaper."

"Whilst he would socialize after matches he never stayed more than a polite period, maintaining his early belief that excessive drinking was not a good idea. On his Cambridge Muddlers Hockey Club trip to Germany before the war he had learnt that their opponents would produce 'hardened' drinkers to socialize with the visitors whilst the home team quietly excused themselves. It was a lesson he took to heart. So he would always make an effort to get home to me after sport, though of course he travelled a lot, abroad and in the UK, and I would hardly ever accompany him. I think I only went once to South Africa with him – we went on the Travellers tour to Natal in 1972, celebrating our 32nd wedding anniversary watching a match against Lauveld Nelspruit on 31st August; Norman's role on that trip was to umpire and to make speeches. I can't remember going on any UK trips save for once to Scotland and once to the North. When he did his annual August cricket tour with Devon I would stay with the children in Suffolk or Essex, sometimes with Norman's mother, Alice, who suffered badly from arthritis.

He cared about people – a fact which may not have been apparent to others as his style was not to show emotion,

...I fell in love with Norman because he made life fun, and although his arthritis took a terrible toll on him, he retained his enjoyment of life to the end....

and it amused him to appear rude and irreverent. I remember one pupil at Fram, a farmer's son who was being bullied. Norman took him under his wing and helped him through a difficult time. I fell in love with Norman because he made life fun, and although his arthritis took a terrible toll on him, he retained his enjoyment of life to the end. He would to outsiders appear brusque, for example when telling me while I was chattering away "You talk too much, woman!", but this was always with a twinkle in his eyes. He was difficult, but we survived happily."

LEFT: Celebrating Mullie's 90th: John Clements (ex Chairman of College Governors), Tim Borrett, Mullie, the author, Tony Borrett, and OFs Norman Mayhew, David Mead, John Gooderham and Norman Porter.
BELOW: from left: Evelyn Mansfield (Trudé's mother), Katherine, James, Tony, Mullie, Trudé, Alex and Tim.

9

...he was widely recognised, during the 1946 to 1952 period, as being outstanding amongst his peers at both squash and hockey.

ALL ROUND SPORTSMEN

In his obituary in The Times, Norman was described as *'probably Britain's most talented post-war all round amateur sportsman.'* Can this description be justified? A little research will immediately show just how many runners there are in this particular race.

It would in fact be somewhat surprising to find that an individual with a real gift for one sport had no talent for other sports. Thus there is nothing remarkable about the all-rounder. Where that relatively common multiple talent becomes special is when it occurs at international level. In any debate on the topic the examples which will be quoted will invariably be from the past. The reason for this is the socio-cultural change which has occurred in Britain and in other countries over the last 50 years. Before then the great all-rounders were almost always amateurs, who had the time and the financial resources to devote their year to the pursuit of different sports.

Most sports were amateur, soccer, golf and cricket being the main exceptions. Rugby, lawn tennis, athletics, hockey and the racket games were almost wholly amateur. Every effort was made to structure these sports to suit the amateur, and particularly the teachers at private schools, from whose ranks so many of the top sportsmen and women came. Norman's diary shows this clearly: the Amateur and the Open squash championships, the two flagship events of the squash season, were held respectively in the Christmas and Easter holidays to accommodate schoolmasters. The Home Countries and European hockey internationals were compressed into the Easter holiday period. The Minor Counties cricket season was contained almost exclusively within the school summer vacation.

The last of the annual Gentlemen versus Players cricket matches took place in 1962. As D. J. Taylor notes in his book "On the Corinthian Spirit", the early 1960s marked the end of amateurism's direct influence in British sport. The succeeding decades have seen an increasing trend to greater professionalism in every sport, and the day of the amateur is now well behind us. Of course multi-talented sportsmen and women continue to be born every day; but sadly for the romantic in us all, the advent of the professional attitude to all sport, and the consequent year round commitment that this entails, has meant that all-round talent will never be given the chance to flower, at least in a public setting. A recent example of a double international at two major sports is also a story of the pressures which have built up against the development of such diversity. Andy Goram, Scotland soccer goalkeeper, in 1989 played for his country at cricket against the touring Australians, in mid-July. His soccer club Hibernian fined him for it.

Norman was fortunate to have private means, inherited

from his parents, which supplemented his relatively modest schoolmaster's income and enabled him to bear the considerable travel and associated costs of playing two international sports. He was a true amateur, drawing merely the minimum expenses offered by the HA and the SRA for international matches, and nothing for his divisional, county or club fixtures. And so were his opponents and team-mates.

The drawing of comparisons between sportsmen and women of different eras, and of different combinations of sports, can never be a scientific exercise; it can only be a pleasant pastime from which no hard conclusions can be drawn. In seeking an answer to the question posed at the beginning of this chapter, the following review focuses solely on the amateur sportsmen and women of Norman's era, which started pre-war and blossomed post-war.

From the pre-war period, three all-rounders stand out, all of whom Norman played against. Excelling mainly in racket sports, was Kenneth Gandar-Dower, who in the 1930s represented Cambridge at seven sports - Eton and Rugby fives, billiards, squash rackets, rackets, real tennis and lawn tennis. He was also 12th man at Lord's for the Varsity cricket match. Runner-up in the Amateur squash championship in 1931, he won the event in 1938 and played squash and lawn tennis for England and tennis at Wimbledon. Maurice Turnbull played cricket for England, rugby and hockey for Wales, and won the South Wales squash championship. The last of this remarkable trio, a man whom Norman encountered several times, was David Milford, who was world champion at rackets and real tennis, a county squash player, and between 1930 and 1937 played 25 times at inside left for the England hockey team.

Straddling the war years, the little known Dr. Kevin O'Flanagan, whose simultaneous international participation in two sports replicates Norman's achievement, was a great all-rounder. He was 18 when he won, playing as an amateur, the first of four full soccer caps for Ireland, scoring in a World Cup match against Norway. In the 1938-39 season he scored a record 34 Irish League goals, and in the same season won the Irish 60 yards, 100 yards and long jump national titles. Post-war he lived in London, practising medicine and playing as an amateur right winger for Arsenal and at the same time as a wing three-quarter for London Irish. Astonishingly, on successive Saturdays in 1946 he played for Ireland against Scotland at soccer and against France at rugby union. His brother Mick also played for Ireland at both rugby and soccer.

Another with whom Norman played was Norman Yardley, who won Cambridge blues at cricket, squash, rugby fives and hockey, captaining at both squash and cricket. He became a

county hockey player, and would in all likelihood have played for, and quite probably captained, England at squash if his cricket, at which he captained England, had not occupied so much of his time. He played 20 Tests and 446 first class matches for Yorkshire between 1936 and 1955, scoring over 18,000 runs.

Described by Christopher Martin-Jenkins as *'one of the greatest amateur sportsmen of the 20th century'*, John Thompson was an England squash player, runner-up to Norman in the 1946 Amateur, British Open rackets champion, and a stylish Warwickshire batsman considered by C. B. Fry to be good enough for England.

Micky Walford, who, like O'Flanagan, Yardley and Norman, straddled the war period, played with and against Norman at both hockey and cricket. He was an outstandingly versatile sportsman, representing Oxford in the University rugby and hockey matches three times, and in the University cricket match twice. He would have had a blue for a fourth sport if he had not declined the offer to play for the soccer team; he played 17 times for England at hockey, of which six were as captain, played 97 first class cricket matches for Somerset in the school summer vacations and then 80 minor county matches for Dorset, the last at the age of 46. He was an England rugby triallist.

A wholly post-war all-round sportsman was Hubert Doggart, against whom Norman played squash. Having won Cambridge Blues at a record five sports, cricket, soccer, rackets, squash, and fives, captain in all except fives, he played cricket for Sussex and for England in two Tests. He played soccer for the Corinthian Casuals, squash for Sussex, and was a member of GB's Americas Cup sailing crew in both 1948 and 1953.

Of all these wonderfully gifted amateurs, it can be said that Milford, Yardley, and most recently Mike Corby, most closely mirrored Norman, in the sports at which they excelled and the success they achieved in their era. Corby represented England 59 times outdoor and 6 times indoor at hockey between 1961 and 1978, and won 33 GB caps, captaining GB at hockey in an Olympiad. He twice reached the final of the Amateur squash, losing to Jonah Barrington, and won a large haul of squash caps. A natural at all sports, he possessed marvellous hand/eye coordination which enabled him to perform, as a party piece, the waist-high volley of a golf ball struck with a wood down the fairway.

Norman's all round skills were no greater than these extraordinary sportsmen. What was unusual about him and can be said to distinguish him from them, was the dominance he attained in both his main sports. Not only did he captain his country at both, he was widely recognised, during the 1946 to 1952 period, as being outstanding amongst his peers at both sports.

SQUASH

Italics denotes did not play - either not available or scratched.

DATE	VENUE	FIXTURE	STRING	RESULT NFB	OPPONENT	RESULT TEAM
1935-36						
07.01.36	Queen's Club	Evans Cup - Public Schools Handicap - Final		won 3-0	R.S.Woodward	
21.01.36	Kensington C.Club	Kensington CC Schools Competition - Final		won 3-0	D.Yeats-Brown	
23.04.36	RAC	Drysdale Cup - 1st round		won 3-0	J.C.C.Coulston	
24.04.36	RAC	Drysdale Cup - 2nd round		won 3-0	P.B.Empson	
25.04.36	RAC	Drysdale Cup - 3rd round		lost 1-3	D.M.Beadle	
1936-37						
15.10.36	London	**Cambridge** v Bachelor's Club				
18.10.36	Cambridge	**Cambridge** v Jesters	2nd	lost 2-3	J.F.Stokes	
22.10.36	Cambridge	**Cambridge** v RAC	2nd	won		
24.10.36	Cambridge	**Cambridge** v Queen's Club	2nd	won		
29.10.36	London	**Cambridge** v International Sportsmen Club	2nd			
06.11.36	Cambridge	**Cambridge** v Royal Engineers	2nd			
08.11.36	Cambridge	**Cambridge** v United Hospitals	2nd			
10.11.36	London	**Cambridge** v Union Club	2nd			
15.11.36	London	**Cambridge** v Prince's Club	2nd			
19.11.36	Queen's Club	**Cambridge** v Queen's Club	2nd			
22.11.36	Cambridge	**Cambridge** v TCS Haywood's V	2nd			
25.11.36	Cambridge	**Cambridge** v University College Hospital	2nd			
15.11.36	Oxford	**Cambridge A** v Oxford A	1st	won 3-0	L.H.Waddy	
02.12.36	Cambridge	**Cambridge** v Junior Carlton Club	2nd	won		
04.12.36	Lansdowne Club	Amateur Squash Championship - 1st Round		lost 1-3	D.M.Backhouse	
15.12.36	Bath Club	**Cambridge** v Oxford	2nd	won 3-1	R.C.Riseley	won 5-0
28.01.37	London	**Cambridge** v United Hospitals	2nd			
04.02.37	London	**Cambridge** v University College Hospital	2nd			
25.02.37	London	**Cambridge** v Conservative Club	2nd			
04.03.37	Junior Carlton Club	**Cambridge** v Junior Carlton Club	2nd			
1937-38						
14.10.37	London	**Cambridge** v Bachelor's Club	2nd			
17.10.37	Cambridge	**Cambridge** v Jesters	2nd	won		
24.10.37	Cambridge	**Cambridge** v Queens Club	2nd	won 3-0	S.H.Skinner	won 4-1
28.10.37	London	**Cambridge** v International Sportsmen's Club	1st	lost 0-3	F.D.Amr Bey	
05.11.37	Cambridge	**Cambridge** v Royal Engineers	1st	lost 2-3	D. I. Burnett	
07.11.37	Cambridge	**Cambridge** v United Hospitals	1st			
11.11.37	London	**Cambridge** v Union Club	1st	won 3-0	H.D.Bradshaw	won 4-1
14.11.37	Cambridge	**Cambridge** v Prince's Club	1st			
18.11.37	Queen's Club	**Cambridge** v Queen's Club	1st			
21.11.37	Cambridge	**Cambridge** v TCS Haywood's V	1st			
01.12.37	Cambridge	**Cambridge** v Junior Carlton Club	1st			
02.12.37	RAC	**Cambridge** v RAC	1st	won		
03.12.37	Lansdowne Club	Amateur Championships - 1st Round		won 3-1	A.D.Leiper	
06.12.37	Lansdowne Club	Amateur Championships - 2nd Round		lost 0-3	R.F.Lumb	
14.12.37	Bath Club	**Cambridge** v Oxford	2nd	won 3-1	P.M.Whitehouse	won 3-2

SQUASH
continued

Italics denotes did not play - either not available or scratched.

DATE	VENUE	FIXTURE	STRING	RESULT NFB	OPPONENT	RESULT TEAM
01.02.38	London	**Cambridge** v University College Hospital	1st			
10.02.38	London	**Cambridge** v United Hospitals	1st			
24.02.38	London	**Cambridge** v Conservative Club	1st			
03.03.38	Junior Carlton Club	**Cambridge** v Junior Carlton Club	1st			
05.03.38	USA	**Cambridge** USA Tour	2nd			

1938-39

DATE	VENUE	FIXTURE	STRING	RESULT NFB	OPPONENT	RESULT TEAM
13.10.38	Cambridge	**Cambridge** v Bachelor's Past & Present	1st	won 3-1	A.G.Hazelrigg	won 4-1
16.10.38	Cambridge	**Cambridge** v Jesters	1st			
23.10.38	Cambridge	**Cambridge** v Queen's Club	1st			
27.10.38	Cambridge	**Cambridge** v International Sportsmens Club	1st	won		won 5-0
04.11.38	Cambridge	**Cambridge** v Royal Engineers	1st	lost 2-3	D.I.Burnett	won 4-1
06.11.38	Cambridge	**Cambridge** v United Hospitals	1st	won 3-0	E.M.Buzzard	won 5-0
10.11.38	London	**Cambridge** v Union Club	1st			
13.11.38	London	**Cambridge** v Prince's Club	1st			
17.11.38	Queen's Club	**Cambridge** v Queen's Club	1st			
20.11.38	Cambridge	**Cambridge** v TCS Haywood's V	1st	lost 0-3	K.C.Gandar-Dower	lost 0-5
30.11.38	Cambridge	**Cambridge** v Junior Carlton Club	1st			
01.12.38	Cambridge	**Cambridge** v RAC	1st	won 3-2	B.C.Phillips	lost 2-3
02.12.38	Lansdowne Club	Amateur Championship - 1st Round		won 3-0	R.G.Shaw	
05.12.38	Lansdowne Club	Amateur Championship - 2nd Round		won 3-1	A.R.Fyler	
06.12.38	Lansdowne Club	Amateur Championship - 3rd Round		lost 1-3	E.Snell	
09.12.38	Lansdowne Club	**Cambridge** v Oxford - captain	1st	won 3-0	R.S.Woodward	won 5-0
01.02.39	London	**Cambridge** v University College Hospital	1st			
02.02.39	London	**O.Framlinghamians** v O.Haileyburians	n/a		lost 1-4	
10.02.39	London	**Cambridge** v United Hospitals	1st			
15.02.39	Norwich	**Essex** v Norfolk	1st	won 3-1	J.A.L.Barrett	won 4-1
24.02.39	London	**Cambridge** v Conservative Club	1st			
03.03.39	Junior Carlton Club	**Cambridge** v Junior Carlton Club	1st			
06.03.39	Cambridge	**Cambridge** v U.S. Women's Squash Team	1st			
10.03.39	Cambridge	**Essex** v Cambridgeshire	1st	won 3-1	E.J.E.Readwin	won 3-2
18.03.39	*Harrogate*	*Essex v Yorkshire Q Final*		*n/a*		*Lost 3-2*

1939-45
No Play

1946-47
Season 1

DATE	VENUE	FIXTURE	STRING	RESULT NFB	OPPONENT	RESULT TEAM
02.12.46	Lansdowne Club	Amateur Championship - 1st Round	uns.	won 3-0	R.Pulbrook	
05.12.46	Lansdowne Club	Amateur Championship - 2nd Round		won 3-0	L.M.Minford	
06.12.46	Lansdowne Club	Amateur Championship - 3rd Round		won 3-0	D.G.Yeats-Brown	
09.12.46	Lansdowne Club	Amateur Championship - Quarter Final		won 3-1	Dr.Hildick-Smith	
10.12.46	Lansdowne Club	Amateur Championship - Semi Final		won 3-1	B.C.Phillips	
12.12.46	Lansdowne Club	Amateur Championship - Final		won 3-0	J.A.Gillies	
27.01.47	Wanstead SRC	**Essex** v Cambridgeshire	1st	won 3-0	H.G.Hay	won 5-0

SQUASH
continued

Italics denotes did not play - either not available or scratched.

DATE	VENUE	FIXTURE	STRING	RESULT NFB	OPPONENT	RESULT TEAM
1947-48						
Season 2						
17&22.12.47	*Lansdowne & RAC*	*Open Championship-Challenge (Karim 2-0)*		*n/a*		
30.12.47	Latymer Court SRC	Jesters v Exec Ctee of SRA	1st	won 3-0	B.C.Phillips	Draw 3-3
03.01.48	Lansdowne Club	Amateur Championship - 1st Round	1st	won 3-0	G.W.Vavasour	
05.01.48	Lansdowne Club	Amateur Championship - 2nd Round		won 3-0	P.Kershaw	
06.01.48	Lansdowne Club	Amateur Championship - 3rd Round		won 3-0	P.C.Samuelson	
08.01.48	Lansdowne Club	Amateur Championship - Quarter Final		won 3-0	J.F.Stokes	
10.01.48	Lansdowne Club	Amateur Championship - Semi Final		won 3-0	B.C.Phillips	
12.01.48	Lansdowne Club	Amateur Championship - Final		won 3-0	J.R.Thompson	
12.03.48	*Edinburgh*	*England v Scotland*		*clash*		
08-15.03.48	*Lansdowne Club*	*Open Championships (Karim)*		*n/a*		
11.04.48	*Hampstead SRC*	*Amateurs v Professionals*		*clash*		
1948-49						
Season 3						
03.12.48	London	**O.Framlinghamians** v O.Aldenhamians R2	1st	won 3-0	P.R.Thompson	won 4-1
15.12.48	London	**O.Framlinghamians** v O.Tonbridgians		n/a	B.C.Phillips	R3
19.12.48	Hurlingham	**Jesters** v Middlesex	1st	won 3-0	D.M.Bull	lost 2-3
29.12.48	*Latymer Court SRC*	*Jesters v **Executive Ctee of SRA***		*n/a*		
01.01.49	Lansdowne Club	Amateur Championship - 1st Round	1st	won 3-1	W.H.L.Gordon	
03.01.49	Lansdowne Club	Amateur Championship - 2nd Round		won 3-0	D.Chalk	
04.01.49	Lansdowne Club	Amateur Championship - 3rd Round		won 3-0	G.D.Evans	
06.01.49	Lansdowne Club	Amateur Championship - Quarter Final		won 3-0	R.B.R.Wilson	
08.01.49	Lansdowne Club	Amateur Championship - Semi Final		won 3-0	D.M.Bull	
10.01.49	Lansdowne Club	Amateur Championship - Final		won 3-0	B.C.Phillips	
17.01.49	*Hampstead S&RFC*	*Amateurs v Professionals*		*n/a*		
11.02.49	*Dublin*	***IRELAND v ENGLAND***		*n/a*		
08.03.49	*Copenhagen*	***DENMARK v ENGLAND***		*n/a*		
12.03.49	Torquay	**Devon** v Hampshire - QF	1st	won 3-0	M.H.Routh	lost 2-3
18.03.49	RAC	**ENGLAND** v SCOTLAND	1st	won 3-0	P.Harding-Edgar	won 5-0
15.04.49	Carlyon Bay	West of England Championship - 1st Rd		won 3-0	N.G.S.Marshall	
16.04.49	Carlyon Bay	West of England Championship - S.Final		won 3-0	J.Lloyd-Kirk	
18.04.49	Carlyon Bay	West of England Championships - Final		won 3-0	B.C.Phillips	
20.04.49	Lansdowne Club	Open Championship - 1st Round		won 3-0	J.M.Peake	
22.04.49	Lansdowne Club	Open Championship - 2nd Round		won 3-0	N.E.Hooper	
23.04.49	Lansdowne Club	Open Championship - Semi Final		lost 0-3	M.A.Karim	
1949-50						
Season 4						
18.11.49	Junior Carlton	**ENGLAND** v DENMARK	1st	won 3-0	O.Rasmussen	won 5-0 1
03.12.49	London	**O.Framlinghamians** v O.Haileyburians	1st	won 3-0	J.F.Stokes	lost 1-4
13.12.49		*SRA 21st anniversary matches*		*n/a*	*M.A.Karim*	
03.01.50	*Hampstead SRFC*	*Exec Ctee of SRA v Jesters*		*n/a*		
07.01.50	Lansdowne Club	Amateur Championship - 1st Round	1st	won 3-0	G.D.Evan	
09.01.50	Lansdowne Club	Amateur Championship - 2nd Round		won 3-0	R.Pulbrook	
10.01.50	Lansdowne Club	Amateur Championship - 3rd Round		won 3-0	W.S.M.Jameson	

SQUASH
continued

Italics denotes did not play - either not available or scratched.

DATE	VENUE	FIXTURE	STRING	RESULT NFB	OPPONENT	RESULT TEAM
12.01.50	Lansdowne Club	Amateur Championship - Quarter Final		won 3-1	A.Seymour-Hayden	
14.01.50	Lansdowne Club	Amateur Championship - Semi Final		won 3-0	R.B.R.Wilson	
16.01.50	Lansdowne Club	Amateur Championship - Final		won 3-0	H.Dagnall	
22.01.50	*New Grampians*	*Amateurs v Professionals*		*n/a*	*M.A.Karim*	
27.01.50	Cardiff	**Devon** v Glamorgan - Q Final	1st	won 3-1	D.H.Andrews	won 4-1
10.02.50	*RAC*	*ENGLAND v IRELAND*		*n/a*		
24.02.50	Torquay	**Devon** v Sussex - Semi Final	1st	won 3-2	N.E.Hooper	won 3-2
12.03.50	Cumberland Club	Middlesex v **Devon** - Final	1st	won 3-0	A.Seymour-Hayden	lost 2-3
17.03.50	*Edinburgh*	*SCOTLAND v ENGLAND*		*n/a*		
12.-17.04.50	Lansdowne Club	Open Championships		clash		

1950-51
Season 5

DATE	VENUE	FIXTURE	STRING	RESULT NFB	OPPONENT	RESULT TEAM
10.11.50	Lord's	**MCC** v RAC - Bath Club Cup	1st	lost 2-3	Dr.Hildick-Smith	lost 1-2
17.11.50	Bath Club	Bath Club v **MCC** - Bath Club Cup	1st	won 3-0	P.Maud	won 2-1
15.12.50	London	O.Framlinghamians v O.Aldenhamians R2	1st	won 3-0	K.H.Goodacre	won 3-2
18.12.50	*London*	***O.Framlinghamians** v Lancing O.B. - R3*		*n/a*		lost 0-5
03.01.51	Hampstead SRFC	Exec Ctee of SRA v Jesters	1st	won 3-0	B.C.Phillips	won 6-1
05.01.51	Lansdowne Club	Amateur Championship - 1st Round	1st	won 3-0	P.M.H.Robinson	
08.01.51	Lansdowne Club	Amateur Championship - 2nd Round		walk over	W.S.M.Jameson	
09.01.51	Lansdowne Club	Amateur Championship - 3rd Round		won 3-0	M.J.Perkins	
11.01.51	Lansdowne Club	Amateur Championship - Quarter Final		won 3-0	A.H.Fairbairn	
13.01.51	Lansdowne Club	Amateur Championship - Semi Final		won 3-2	R.B.R.Wilson	
15.01.51	Lansdowne Club	Amateur Championship - Final		won 3-0	Dr.Hildick-Smith	
21.01.51	New Grampians	Amateurs v Professionals	1st	won 3-1	J.P.Dear	won 4-3
27.01.51	Middleton SRC	Sussex v Devon	1st	won 3-1	N.E.Hooper	lost 1-4
09.02.51	*Dublin*	*IRELAND v ENGLAND*		*n/a*		
16.03.51	*RAC*	*ENGLAND v SCOTLAND*		*clash*		
04-09.04.51	*Lansdowne Club*	*Open Championships*		*n/a*		

1951-52
Season 6

DATE	VENUE	FIXTURE	STRING	RESULT NFB	OPPONENT	RESULT TEAM
12.10.51	Cambridge	Cambridge Univ v **Jesters**	1st	won 3-2	P.M.H.Robinson	won 4-2
Nov-51	Cambridge	Exhibition Match		lost	G.W.T.Atkins	
23.11.51	London	**O.Framlinghamians** v O.Millhillians R 2	1st	won 3-0	P.M.Johns	won 4-1
29.11.51	*Cardiff*	*WALES v ENGLAND*		*n/a*		won 5-0
07.12.51	London	**O.Framlinghamians** v O.Canfordians Rd 3	1st	won 3-0	M.E.Ash	won 4-1
02.01.52	Junior Carlton	**Exec Ctee of SRA** v Jesters	1st	lost 1-3	B.C.Phillips	lost 5-2
04.01.52	*Lansdowne Club*	*Amateur Championships*	*1st*	*ill*	*Food poisoning*	
20.01.52	New Grampians	**Amateurs** v Professionals	1st	lost 0-3	M.A.Karim	won 6-1
08.02.52	*RAC*	*ENGLAND v IRELAND - captain*		*hip*		
10.02.52	*Torquay*	*Devon v Middlesex*		*hip*		*lost 2-3*
25.02.52	London	**O.Framlinghamians** v O.Cranleighans QF	1st	won 3-0	W.D.N.Vaughan	lost 1-4
14.03.52	*Edinburgh*	*SCOTLAND v ENGLAND*		*clash*		
02-07.04.52	*Lansdowne Club*	*Open Championships*		*clash*		

SQUASH
continued

Italics denotes did not play - either not available or scratched.

DATE	VENUE	FIXTURE	STRING	RESULT NFB	OPPONENT	RESULT TEAM
1952-53						
Season 7						
19.11.52	Cambridge	Cambridge v **Jesters**	1st	won 3-1	D.A.Swales	won 4-2
03.12.52	*London*	*O.Framlinghamians v Lancing O.B.*		*n/a*		*lost 0-5*
29.12.52	*RAC*	*Jesters v Exec Ctee of SRA*		*n/a*		
02.01.53	*Lansdowne Club*	*Amateur Championships*		*did not enter*		
16.01.53	Cardiff	**ENGLAND** v WALES - **captain**	3rd	won 3-0	G.E.Needham	won 5-0
25.01.53	*Lansdowne Club*	***Amateurs** v Professionals*		*clash*		
07.02.53	Wanstead SRC	**Devon** v Essex - Quarter Final	1st	won 3-0	M.A.C.Lyon	won 5-0
11.02.53	Lansdowne Club	KG VI Memorial Doubles with D.G.Butcher		lost 1-2	Hextall & Keeble	lost 0-3
13.02.53	Dublin	IRELAND v **ENGLAND** - **captain**	2nd	won 3-0	J.P.McHale	won 4-1
21.02.53	Torquay	**Devon** v Hertfordshire - Semi Final	1st	won 3-1	A.W.H.Mallett	won 4-1
15.03.53	*Bath Club*	***Devon** v Sussex - final*	*1st*	*hip*	*N.E.Hooper*	*lost 1-3*
20.03.53	*RAC*	*ENGLAND v SCOTLAND*		*clash*		
25-30.03.53	*Lansdowne Club*	*Open Championships*		*n/a*		
1953-54						
Season 8						
09.11.53	Cambridge	Cambridge Univ v **Jesters**	1st	won 3-0	J.Partridge	drew 3-3
12.11.53	RAC	SRA v **Jesters** - Strawson Memorial match	1st	**lost 1-2 ret**	A.H.Fairbairn	lost 1-4
27.11.53	London	**O.Framlinghamians** v O.Aldenhamians	1st	won 3-0	D.Blake	won 4-1
04.12.53	*London*	*O.Framlinghamians v O.Haileyburians*	*1st*	*n/a*	*A.H.Fairbairn*	*lost-1-4*
11.12.53	Lansdowne Club	**ENGLAND** V NETHERLANDS	3rd	won 3-0	A.Blom	won 5-0
15.01.54	Naval & Military	**ENGLAND** v WALES - captain	4th	won 3-0	D.O.Bartlett	won 5-0
24.01.54	Lansdowne Club	**Amateurs** v Professionals	4th	**lost 0-3**	A.Bari	won 4-3
12.02.54	RAC	**ENGLAND** v IRELAND - c**aptain**	4th	won 3-1	G.P.Jackson	won 5-0
14.02.54	Torquay	**Devon** v Glamorgan	1st	won 3-0	D.J.O'Brien	won 5-0
27-28.02.54	Paris	Soc.Sportive de Jeu de Paume v **SRA**	1st	won 3-1	R.Lees	won 4-1
07.03.54	*Torquay*	*Devon v Sussex*		*n/a*		*lost 0-5*
19.03.54	Edinburgh	SCOTLAND v **ENGLAND** - **captain**	4th	won 3-0	C.N.Campbell	won 5-0
1954-55						
Season 9						
11.11.54	Lansdowne Club	SRA v **Jesters** - Strawson Memorial match	1st	**lost 0-3**	A.H.Fairbairn	won 3-2
25.11.54	Cardiff	WALES v **ENGLAND** - **captain**	2nd	won 3-0	R.Butterworth	won 4-1
02.12.54	London	**O.Framlinghamians** v O.Stoics 2nd rd	1st	won 3-0	R.Lush	won4-1
10.12.54	London	**O.Framlinghamians** v O.Salopians 4th rd	1st	won 3-0	L.M.Minford	lost 2-3
03.01.55	*Bath Club*	*Exec Ctee SRA v Jesters*		*n/a*		
06.02.55	Ipswich Aero	**Suffolk** v Cambridge University.	1st	won 3-1	J.R.Partridge	won 3-2
11.02.55	*Dublin*	*IRELAND v ENGLAND*		*n/a*		
20.02.55	*Torquay*	*Devon v Sussex - quarter final*		*n/a*		*lost 0-5*
27.02.55	Lansdowne Club	Abdul Bari Memorial Match	5th	**lost 0-3**	Safirullah	lost 0-5
18.03.55	*RAC*	*ENGLAND v SCOTLAND*		*n/a*		
15.03.55	Ipswich SRC	Suffolk Closed Championships - 2nd Round		won 3-0		
17.03.55	Ipswich SRC	Suffolk Closed Championships - Q Final		won 3-0		
19.03.55	Ipswich SRC	Suffolk Closed Championships - Semi Final		won 3-0		

SQUASH

continued

talics denotes did not play - either not available or scratched.

DATE	VENUE	FIXTURE	STRING	RESULT NFB	OPPONENT	RESULT TEAM
20.03.55	Ipswich SRC	Suffolk Closed Championships - Final	1st	won 3-0	B.H.Belle	
12.08.55	Salisbury	GB v N&S Rhodesia - **captain**	5th	won 3-0	R.S.Agar	won 5-0
13.08.55	Salisbury	GB v Mashonaland - **captain**	5th	won 3-0	D.Spafford	won 5-0
15.08.55	Bulawayo	GB v Rhodesia - captain	3rd	won 3-0	B.Suter	won 5-0
19.08.55	*Wanderers*	*GB v Transvaal B - captain*		*dnp*		won 5-0
20.08.55	Wanderers	GB v South Africa - 1st Test - **captain**	1st	**lost 1-3**	B.Callaghan	**lost 1-4**
24.08.55	Durban	GB v Natal - captain	3rd	won 3-0	H.M.Bull	won 5-0
26.08.55	Durban	GB v South Africa - 2nd Test - **captain**	1st	**lost 0-3**	B.Callaghan	won 4-1
28.08.55	Port Elizabeth	GB v Invitn E.Province Side - **captain**	3rd	won 3-0	W.Campbell	won 5-0
29.08.55	Port Elizabeth	GB v E.Province - captain	1st	won3-0	P.Prosser	won 5-0
02.09.55	*Cape Town*	*GB v Western Province - captain*		*dnp*		won 5-0
03.09.55	Cape Town	GB v South Africa - 3rd Test - **captain**	2nd	**lost 0-3**	D.Callaghan	**lost 2-3**
06.09.55	Wanderers	GB v Johannesburg SRC - captain	2nd	won 3-0	L.Levy	won 5-0
07.09.55	*Wanderers*	*GB v Transvaal - captain*		*dnp*		lost 1-4
08.09.55	Wanderers	SA Championships - 1st Round	3rd	won 3-0	D.Beagle	
09.09.55	Wanderers	SA Championships - 2nd Round		won 3-0	M.Berman	
10.09.55	Wanderers	SA Championships - 3rd Round		won 3-2	C.Kaplan	
12.09.55	Wanderers	SA Championships - Quarter Final		won 3-0	N.Lange	
13.09.55	Wanderers	SA Championships - Semi Final		**lost 1-3**	A.Seymour-Hayden	
16.09.55	Wanderers	GB v South Africa - 4th Test - **captain**	3rd	won 3-1	R.Jarvis	**lost 2-3**
17.09.55	Nairobi	GB v Kenya - captain	3rd	won 3-0	J.S.Crawford	won 5-0

1955-56
Season 10

DATE	VENUE	FIXTURE	STRING	RESULT NFB	OPPONENT	RESULT TEAM
15.10.55	Felixstowe	SRA v **East of England**	1st	won 3-2	B.C.Phillips	won 4-1
10.11.55	Lansdowne Club	**SRA** v Jesters - Strawson Memorial match	2nd	**lost 2-3**	R.B.Hawkey	lost 1-4
18.11.55?	*London*	*O.Framlinghamians v O.Cranleighans*		*n/a*		won 3-2
25.11.55	*RAC*	*ENGLAND v BELGIUM*		*n/a*		
09.12.55	London	O.Framlinghamians v O.Brentwoods	1st	won 3-0	K.A.Williams	lost 2-3
20.01.56	Hampstead SRC	**ENGLAND** v **WALES** - **captain**	5th	won 3-0	J.T.Evans	won 5-0
10.02.56	*Bath Club*	*England v Ireland*		*1st res*		
12.02.56	*Junior Carlton*	*Middlesex v Devon*	*1st*	*scr*		*lost 1-4*

1956-57
Season 11

DATE	VENUE	FIXTURE	STRING	RESULT NFB	OPPONENT	RESULT TEAM
03.12.56	London	**O.Framlinghamians** v O.Foresters	1st	**lost 2-3**	J.B.Taylorson	won 3-2
13.12.56	*London*	*O.Framlinghamians v O.Tonbridgians*	*1st*	*scr*	*B.C.Phillips*	*lost 1-4*
28.12.56	Junior Carlton	**Jesters** v South Africa	5th	won 3-2	H.W.P.Whiteley	won 3-2

Notes

In 11 post-war seasons 46/47-56/57 inc. he played 108 games, an average of 10 p.a. 15 of those were lost and 93 won.

His first post-war loss to an amateur was in the first match of his 5th season. The 2nd and 3rd were in his 6th season.
To the end of his 7th season, 52-53, when he effectively retired, he lost 5 times in 65 matches.
3 of those were to amateurs, Hildick-Smith, Atkins and Phillips, and 2 to a professional, Karim.
Internationals shown here total 10, although SRA records show variously 11 or 12.

He also played 5 times for GB, on the 1955 South African/Kenyan tour.

There are clearly matches not recorded here, particularly county matches in the 1940s.
If those missed were added, the total would increase by no more than 10%.

HOCKEY

ItItalics denotes did not play - either not available or scratched.

SEASON	DATE	VENUE	FIXTURE	RESULT	SCORE	GOALS NON-ENG	GOALS ENG
1936-37							
Season 1	18.10.36	Cambridge	**Wimbledon** HC v RAF	won	3-2		
	15.11.36	Cambridge	**Wimbledon** HC v Cambridge	lost	1-8		
	22.11.36	Cambridge	**Cambridge** v Richmond HC	won			
	29.11.36	Cambridge	**Cambridge** v Bromley	lost	3-6		
	25.03.37	Dusseldorf	**Cambridge** U.Muddlers v Dusseldorf	won			
	26.03.37	Duisburg	**Cambridge** U.Muddlers v Duisburg	won			
	28.03.37	Mulheim	**Cambridge** U.Muddlers v Mulheim	won			
1937-38							
Season 2	16.10.37	Beckenham	**Cambridge** v Beckenham	lost	1-3	1	
	30.10.37	Southgate	**Cambridge** v Southgate	won	4-3	3	
	21.11.37	Richmond	**Cambridge** v Richmond	lost	4-2	1	
	15.11.37	Cambridge	**Cambridge** v Essex	won	5-3		
	17.11.37	Wimbledon	**Cambridge** v Wimbledon	won	1-3	1	
	26.11.38	Cambridge	**Cambridge** v Bromley	won	3-2	2	
	18.12.37	Luton	East Final Trial - Whites v Colours	won	2-1	1	
	21.12.37	Beckenham	C.U.Wanderers v O.U.Occasionals	won	1-0	1	
	08.01.38	Bristol	West v **East**	lost	5-2		
	15.01.38	Cambridge	**Cambridge** v Richmond	lost	2-4		
	20.01.38	Cambridge	**Cambridge** v Essex	won	3-1		
	29.01.38	*Warrington*	*English Final Trial*	*n/a*			
	12.02.38	Beckenham	**Cambridge** v Oxford	drew	1-1		
1938-39							
Season 3	15.10.38	Cambridge	**Cambridge** v Beckenham	won	2-1		
	30.10.38	Wimbledon	**Cambridge** v Wimbledon	won	3-1	1	
	10.11.38	Richmond	**Cambridge** v Richmond	lost	1-3	1	
	12.11.38	Cambridge	**Cambridge** v Essex- East Trial	won	3-1		
	19.11.38	Northampton	**Cambridge** v Bacchanalians	won	7-0	3	
	26.11.38	Cambridge	**Cambridge** v Lampard-Vachtell's XI	lost	5-7	2	
	27.11.38	Dulwich	**Cambridge** v Tulse Hill	won	4-2	1	
	03.12.38	*Wandsworth*	*Cambridge v Spencer*	*clash*			
	10.12.38	Cambridge	**Cambridge** v Hampstead	drew	2-2	2	
	14.12.38	Cambridge	**Cambridge** P&P v H.A.				
	17.12.38	Cambridge	Final East Trial	drew	2-2	1	
	22.12.38	Bromley	**Cambridge** v Bromley	won			
	07.01.39	Brentwood	**East** v Combined Services	won	3-1		
	21.01.39	Shotley	**Cambridge** v Royal Navy	won	5-0	2	
	28.01.39	Norwich	**East** v Midlands	won	2-1		
	01.02.39	Cambridge	**Cambridge** v Army	lost	1-3		
	04.02.39	Beckenham	**Cambridge** v Beckenham (centre half)	won	3-2	1	
	08.02.39	Richmond	**Cambridge** v Mid Surrey (centre half)	won	1-0		
	11.02.39	Cambridge	**Cambridge** v Acrostics	won	12-1	6	
	18.02.39	Beckenham	**Cambridge** v Oxford	won	3-2	1	
	04.03.39	Beckenham	English Final Trial	drew	2-2		
	18.03.39	Oval	**ENGLAND** v WALES	won	4-1		1
	25.03.39	Edgbaston	**ENGLAND** v IRELAND	lost	0-1		
	01.04.39	Luton	**ENGLAND** v HOLLAND	won	3-0		1
1939-45							
No matches							
1946-47							
Season 3		Some Club Games	Taunton Vale say 8 games				
	00.11.46	Trent Bridge	Notts v **Essex**				
	16.11.46	Brentwood	**Essex** v Hertfordshire	lost			
	17.11.46	Taunton	Somerset Trial				
	11.01.47	Southgate	**East** v South	won	3-2	2	
	25.01.47	Watford	**East** v North	lost	0-5		
	08.03.47	*Rugby School*	*English Trial*	*postponed*			
	22.03.47	Guildford	English Final Trial	won	8-1	4	
	29.03.47	Dublin	IRELAND v **ENGLAND**	lost	2-1		
	30.03.47	Dublin	**Beckenham** v Dublin Railway Union				
	31.03.47	Dublin	**Beckenham** v Three Rock Rovers				
	04.04.47	Folkestone	Easter Festival - The Tramps.				
	05.04.47	Folkestone	Easter Festival - **ENGLAND** v FRANCE	won	2-1		1

HOCKEY

continued

IItItalics denotes did not play - either not available or scratched.

SEASON	DATE	VENUE	FIXTURE		RESULT	SCORE	GOALS NON-ENG	GOALS ENG
	12.04.47	Southgate	South v **East**		won	1-3		1
	19.04.47	Hawarden	WALES v **ENGLAND**		won	1-0		1
	26.04.47	Luton	**ENGLAND** v SCOTLAND		won	1-0		1
1947-48								
Season 5	Some Club Games		Taunton Vale say 8 games					
	06.12.47	Cambridge	East Trial					
	18.12.47	Beckenham	**C.U.Wanderers** v O.U.Occasionals		won	6-0	2	
	10.01.48	*St.Albans*	*East v Combined Services*		*clash*			
	24.01.48	Exeter	**West** v East		won	3-1		
	14.02.48	Liverpool	North v **West**		lost	2-1		
	28.02.48	Brentwood	English Trial	captain				
	06.03.48	Beckenham	English Final Trial	captain	won	4-1		
	13.03.48	Bristol	**ENGLAND** v WALES	captain	won	6-2		2
	03.04.48	Old Trafford	**ENGLAND** v IRELAND	captain	drew	2-2		
	10.04.48	Inverness	SCOTLAND v **ENGLAND**	captain	drew	1-1		
	24.04.48	Brussels	BELGIUM v **ENGLAND**	captain	drew	2-2		
	31.07.48	Park Royal	**Great Britain** v Switzerland	captain	drew	0-0		
	05.08.48	Chiswick Poly	**Great Britain** v USA	captain	won	11-0	6	
	07.08.48	Sudbury	**Great Britain** v Afghanistan	captain	won	8-0	4	
	09.09.48	Wembley	**Great Britain** v Pakistan - Semi Final	captain	won	2-0		
	12.08.48	Wembley	**Great Britain** v India - Final	captain	lost	0-4		
1948-49								
Season 6	Some Club Games		Taunton Vale say 8 games					
	16.10.48	Amsterdam	**Great Britain** v Holland		lost	1-4		
	17.10.48	Amsterdam	**Great Britain** v France		won	6-0	2	
	18.12.48	Taunton	West Trial					
	22.12.48	Beckenham	**C.U.Wanderers** v O.U.Occasionals		drew	3-3	1	
	29.01.49	Swindon	**West** v Combined Services		won	4-1	1	
	05.02.49	Evesham	Midlands v **West**		lost	3-1		
	19.02.49	Canford School	Dorset v **Somerset**		won	1-7	1	
	26.02.49	Rugby School	English Trial	captain	won	3-1		
	05.03.49	Cheltenham	English Final Trial	captain	won	6-1	1	
	12.03.49	Scarborough	**ENGLAND** v SCOTLAND	captain	drew	0-0		
	26.03.49	Abergavenny	WALES v **ENGLAND**	captain	won	0-7		3
	09.04.49	Dublin	IRELAND v **ENGLAND**	captain	lost	3-2		1
1949-50								
Season 7	Some Club Games		Taunton Vale say 8 games					
	03.12.49	Weston-s-Mare	Western County Hockey Tournament					
	07.01.50	*Exeter*	*West Trial*		*clash*			
	14.01.50	Reading	West v South		clash			
	04.02.50	Hereford	**West** v North		won	3-2	3	
	18.02.50	Glastonbury	**Somerset** v Dorset		drew	3-3		
	11.03.50	Watford	English Final Trial	captain	won	4-3	2	
	25.03.50	Bournemouth	**ENGLAND** v WALES		won	4-0		
	08.04.50	Folkestone	Easter Festival - The Tramps.					
	15.04.50	Edgbaston	**ENGLAND** v IRELAND		won	3-2		1
	22.04.50	Aberdeen	SCOTLAND v **ENGLAND**		won	2-5		
	30.04.50	Amsterdam	HOLLAND v **ENGLAND**		lost	3-0		
1950-51								
Season 8	Some Club Games		Norwich Grasshoppers say 6 games					
	20.12.50	Beckenham	**C.U.Wanderers** v O.U.Occasionals		won	4-3	1	
	23.12.50	*Tulse Hill*	*Tulse Hill v Schoolmasters*		*n/a*			
	13.01.51	*Broxbourne*	*East Trial*		*clash*			
	03.02.51	Folkestone	South v **East**	captain	drew	1-1		
	06.02.51	Motspur Park	HA v South African Universities		won	9-1	5	
	17.02.51	Lincoln	**East** v North		abandoned			
	22.02.50	Norwich	Norfolk v **Suffolk**		lost	4-3	2	
	03.03.51	Felsted	English Trial	captain	won	4-3	1	
	17.03.51	Northampton	English Final Trial	captain	won	6-1	2	
	23.03. 51	Felixstowe	Easter Festival - The East Anglians					
	31.03.51	Hawarden	WALES v **ENGLAND**		won	1-4		1
	07.04.51	Hove	**H.L.Lewis' XI** v Sussex					
	14.04.51	Dublin	IRELAND v **ENGLAND**		drew	1-1		
	21.04.51	Port Sunlight	**ENGLAND** v SCOTLAND	captain	won	4-2		1

HOCKEY
continued

ItItalics denotes did not play - either not available or scratched.

SEASON	DATE	VENUE	FIXTURE		RESULT	SCORE	GOALS NON-ENG	GOALS ENG
	12.05.51	Twickenham RFU	ENGLAND v BELGIUM	captain	lost	0-1		
	14.05.51	Twickenham RFU	ENGLAND v HOLLAND	captain	lost	2-3		
	15.05.51	Twickenham RFU	ENGLAND v FRANCE	captain	won	5-0		4
	29.07.51	Bulawayo	British & Irish XI v Rhodesia	(vice capt)	won	2-0	1	
	04.08.51	Bulawayo	B&I XI v Rhodesia Juniors		lost	2-3		
	08.08.51		B&I XI v Rhodesia		won	4-0	1	
	11.08.51	Griqua	B&I XI v Griqualand/Bechuanaland		won	3-0	1	
	15.08.51	Cape Town	B&I XI v Western Province		drew	1-1	1	
	18.08.51	Cape Town	1st Test v South Africa		won	3-1	1	
	20.08.51	Port Elizabeth	B&I XI v Eastern Province		won	3-0	1	
	22.08.51	Queenstown	B&I XI v Border		drew	5-5	2	
	25.08.51	Port Elizabeth	2nd Test v South Africa		drew	1-1	1	
	29.08.51	Pretoria	B&I XI v Transvaal		won	3-1	1	
	01.09.51	Durban	3rd Test v South Africa		lost	1-2		
	05.08.51	Bloemfontein	B&I XI v Orange Free State		won	2-0	1	
	08.09.51	Bloemfontein	B&I XI v SA Universities		drew	2-2		
	12.09.51	Pietermaritsburg	B&I XI v Natal		lost	0-2		
	15.09.51	Johannesburg	4th Test v South Africa		drew	1-1		

1951-52

SEASON	DATE	VENUE	FIXTURE		RESULT	SCORE	GOALS NON-ENG	GOALS ENG
Season 9	Autumn	Some Club Games	Norwich Grasshoppers - say 6 games					
	03.11.51	Edinburgh	ENG/WALES v SCOT/IRELAND		won	3-1		
	08.12.51	*Cambridge*	*East Final Trial*		*n/a*			
	19.12.51	Beckenham	C.U.Wanderers v O.U.Occasionals		won	2-1		
	21.12.51	Tulse Hill	Schoolmasters v Tulse Hill		won	4-1	1	
	12.01.52	Leicester	Midlands v East		lost	6-4	1	
	02.02.52	Watford	East v West		lost	3-4		
	01.03.52	The Leys	English Trial	captain	drew	4-4	1	
	15.03.52	Reading	English Final trial	captain	lost	0-1		
	22.03.52	*Peterborough*	*Lincolnshire v Suffolk*		*hip*			
	29.03.52	Bristol	ENGLAND v WALES	captain	won	5-0		3
	30.03.52	*Edgbaston*	*International XI v Bacchanalians*		*hip*			
	06.04.52	Boulogne	FRANCE v ENGLAND	captain	won	0-2		
	12.04.52	Lowestoft	Easter Festival - Racing Club de France					
	19.04.52	Park Royal	ENGLAND v IRELAND	captain	won	5-1		
	26.04.52	Glasgow	SCOTLAND v ENGLAND	captain	won	0-7		2

1952-53

SEASON	DATE	VENUE	FIXTURE		RESULT	SCORE	GOALS NON-ENG	GOALS ENG
Season 10	25.10.52	Brentwood	Invitation XI v Brentwood		won	9-1		
	26.10.52	Felixstowe	Suffolk Trial					
	02.11.52	Bury St.Edmunds	Suffolk v Essex	captain	won	3-2		
	15.11.52	Cambridge	East Trial					
	23.11.52	Cambridge	East v Cambridge University	captain				
	30.11.52	*Bury St.Edmunds*	*Suffolk v Hertfordshire*		*n/a*			
	06.12.52	Southend	East Trial		n/a			
	17.12.52	Beckenham	C.U.Wanderers v O.U.Occasionals		lost	1-3		
	19.12.52	Tulse Hill	Schoolmasters v Tulse Hill		lost	2-3	1	
	07.01.53	Sandhurst	Schoolmasters v RMA Sandhurst					
	10.01.53	*Peterborough*	*East v Combined Services*		*hip*			
	24.01.53	Swindon	West v East	captain	won	2-5		3
	21.02.53	Norwich	Norfolk v Suffolk	captain	lost	5-0		
	07.03.53	Charterhouse	First English Trial	captain	won	5-1	2	
	21.03.53	*Evesham*	*English Final Trial*	*captain*	*flu*			
	28.03.53	Newport	WALES v ENGLAND	captain	won	2-4		
	11.04.53	Guildford	ENGLAND v SCOTLAND	captain	drew	3-3		

1953-54

SEASON	DATE	VENUE	FIXTURE		RESULT	SCORE	GOALS NON-ENG	GOALS ENG
Season 11	19.12.53	Tulse Hill	Schoolmasters v Tulse Hill		lost	0-2		
	22.12.53	Beckenham	C.U.Wanderers v O.U.Occasionals		lost	0-3		
	02.01.54	*St.Albans*	*East Trial*		*hip trouble*			

Notes

There are 201 games listed above. In 10 seasons 1936-7 to 1952-53 he thus averaged 20 pa.
For England he played 30 times, 11 as captain; won 18, lost 6, drew 6, scoring 23 goals.
For GB he played 7 times, 5 as captain; won 4, lost 2, drew 1, scoring 12 goals.
In the 128 games where scores are known he scored 114 goals.
Clearly some matches are not recorded here, in particular some club county matches in 47 and 48.
If those missed were added in, the total would increase by no more than 15%

CRICKET

YEAR		DATE	VENUE	FIXTURE	BAT 1ST INN.	BAT 2ND INN.	BOWL 1ST INN.	BOWL 2ND INN.	RESULT
1936		Aug 7,8	Lord's	**Young Amateurs** v Young Professionals	63	8	3-2-1-0	4-1-8-1	lost 1w
		Aug 31	Oval	YA of Surrey v **YA of Essex**	38	4	13-1-39-4	18-3-71-1	lost 112runs
		Frinton CC 1936		*7 inns - 0 no - 397 runs - 152 highest - 56.70 average*					
				64.5 overs - 10 maidens - 208 runs - 12 wkts - 18.35 ave.					
1937		May 8,10,11	Fenners	**Tindall's** v Yardley's: Freshmens Trial	14		6-1-12-0		drawn
		May 15,17,18	Fenners	**Etceteras** v Perambulators	16		8-2-15-0		won 6w
		June 16,17	Brentwood	**Essex** v Cambridge University	2			2-1-1-0	won inns
1938		April 30, May 2,3	Fenners	**Brodhurst's** v Packe's: Seniors Match	7	18*	1-0-4-0	3-0-4-0	drawn
		May 25,26,27	Fenners	Cambridge University v **Essex**	9	15*			won 9w
1939		April 29, May 1,2	Fenners	Brodhurst's Side v **Wilson's Side**	4		1-0-8-0	5-0-23-4	drawn
		Aug 16,17	Nottingham	Sir Julian Cahn's XI v **Storks**	28				
1940-45		No cricket - War Years							
1946		Aug 14,15,16	Clacton	**Essex** v Nottinghamshire	dnb	7*	11-0-38-0	3-2-4-0	drawn
1947		Aug 30, Sep 1	Devonport	**Devon** v Royal Navy	63		4 for 79	5 for 34	won 8w
1948		No Devon cricket - Olympic Hockey							
1949	1	Aug 1,2	Oxford	Oxfordshire v **Devon** (stats est.)	*8*	*21*	*2 wkts*		lost inn & 55
		Aug 3,4	Torquay	**Devon** v A Somerset XI					
	2	Aug 5,6	Paignton	**Devon** v Dorset	134*	dnb			won 1st inn
	3	Aug 10,11	Exeter	**Devon** v Cornwall	0	dnb	9-1-26-0		lost 1st inn
	4	Aug 12,13	Instow	**Devon** v Oxfordshire	7	103			lost 4w
		Aug 15,16	Tavistock	A Devon XI v Tavistock CC	19	0*	3 for 18		won
	5	Aug 17,18	Torquay	**Devon** v Kent II	73*	109	21-6-54-2		lost 1st inn
	6	Aug 22,23	Torquay	**Devon** v Surrey II	3	42			lost 9w
	7	Aug 24,25	Dorchester	Dorset v **Devon** (stats est.)	28	27			lost 84runs
	8	Aug 31, Sep 1	Sidmouth	**Devon** v Glamorgan II	0	87	1 wkt		lost 1st inn
		Devon CC 1949		*14 inns - 3 no - 661 runs - 134* highest - 60.09 ave.*					
				148 overs - 416 runs - 13 wickets - 32.00 average					
		Seaton CC 1949		*10 inns - 4 no. - 584 runs - 106 highest - 97.33 ave.*					
				72 overs - 8 maidens -291 runs -19 wkts - 15.31 ave.					
1950		*July 22,24,25*	Lord's	**Minor Counties XI** v MCC	*n/a*				
	9	Aug 2,3	Instow	**Devon** v Cornwall	0	dnb	8-3-14-1		lost 1st inn
		Aug 6	UpLyme	**Uplyme & Lyme Regis** v Somerset XI					
	10	Aug 7,8	Canford	Dorset v **Devon** (stats est.)	*9*	*dnb*	*13-3-30-1*	*5-2-8-0*	won 1st inn
	11	Aug 16,17	Torquay	**Devon** v Kent II	16	dnb	12-5-12-0		NR
	12	Aug 23,24	Bristol	Gloucestershire v **Devon**	dnb	dnb			NR
	13	Aug 25,26	Exeter	**Devon** v Dorset (stats est.)	*7*	dnb	dnb		NR
	14	Aug 28,29	Exeter	**Devon** v Surrey II	32*	dnb			NR
		Devon CC 1950		*5 inns - 1 no - 64 runs - 32* highest - 16.00 average*					
				38 overs - 13 maidens - 64 runs - 2 wkts - 32.00 ave.					
1951		No Devon cricket - GB&I Hockey tour to S.Africa							
1952	15	Aug 1,2	Exeter	**Devon** v Berkshire	20	19			lost 1st inn
	16	Aug 4,5	Seaton	**Devon** v Dorset	2	dnb	13-2-40-0		won 1st inn
	17	Aug 11,12	Weymouth	**Devon** v Devon	69	dnb	12-5-20-1		won 1st inn
	18	Aug 13,14	Oxford	Oxfordshire v **Devon**	25	dnb	19-4-39-0	5-0-28-1	lost 1st inn
	19	Aug 15,16	Newbury	Berkshire v **Devon**	3	dnb	15-2-32-0		lost 1st inn
	20	Aug 18,19	Guildford	Surrey II v **Devon**	0	dnb	6-0-39-0		lost 1st inn
	21	Aug 22,23	Exmouth	**Devon** v Cornwall	22	0	3-0-6-0	4.4-0-8-1	won 5w
	22	Aug 25,26	Torquay	**Devon** v Oxfordshire	31	dnb	10-0-38-1	6-0-26-0	won-1st inn
	23	Aug 27,28	Plymouth	**Devon** v Surrey II	76	5	6-0-35-0		lost 157runs
		Devon CC 1952		*12 inns - 0 no - 272 runs - 76 highest - 22.66 average*					
				99 overs - 13 maidens - 311 runs - 4 wickets - 77.75 ave.					
1953	24	July 31, Aug 1	Exeter	**Devon** v Berkshire	12	25*		9-3-27-2	won 8w
	25	Aug 3,4	Seaton	**Devon** v Dorset	50*	14			won 78runs
	26	Aug 10,11	Weymouth	Dorset v **Devon**	20	dnb	4-0-12-0		won inn & 9
	27	Aug 12,13	Oxford	Oxfordshire v **Devon**	38	dnb	11-1-39-0		won 1st inn
	28	Aug 14,15	Newbury	Berkshire v **Devon**	71	15	6-0-28-2		lost 2w
	29	Aug 17,18	Guildford	Surrey II v **Devon**	20	40	1-0-6-0		lost inn & 16
		Devon CC 1953		*10 inns - 2 no - 305 runs - 71 highest - 38.12 average*					
				31 overs - 4 maidens - 112 runs - 4 wickets - 28.00 ave.					

CRICKET

continued

YEAR	DATE		VENUE	FIXTURE	BAT 1ST INN.	BAT 2ND INN.	BOWL 1ST 1NN.	BOWL 2ND INN.	RESULT
1954	30	July 30,31	Exeter	**Devon** v Berkshire	78	dnb			won 1st inn
	31	Aug 2,3	Seaton	**Devon** v Dorset	61	dnb			32
	32	Aug 9,10	Blandford	Dorset v **Devon**	1	dnb			lost 1st inn
	33	Aug 11,12	Banbury	Oxfordshire v **Devon**	dnb	dnb			NR
	34	Aug 13,14	Reading	Berkshire v **Devon**	3	35		3-0-11-0	won 6oruns
	35	Sep 13,14,15	The Oval	Surrey II v **Devon** (Challenge Match)	42	dnb			won 1st inn
		Devon CC 1954		6 inns - o no - 220 runs - 78 highest - 36.66. average					
				3 overs - o maidens - 11 runs o wkts					
1955		No Devon cricket - GB squash tour to S.Africa							
1956	36	Aug 3,4	Torquay	**Devon** v Berkshire	0	7	1-0-3-0	22-4-59-3	lost 83 runs
	37	Aug 6,7	Instow	**Devon** v Dorset	104	44	1-0-1-0	2-0-6-1	won 1st inn
	38	Aug 8,9	Plymouth	**Devon** v Cornwall	74*	28*	7-1-17-0		lost 1st inn
	39	Aug 13,14	Weymouth	Dorset v **Devon**	44	dnb	15-8-19-0		won 1st inn
	40	Aug 15,16	Oxford	Oxfordshire v **Devon**	3	dnb	5-2-9-0		NR
	41	Aug 17,18	Reading	Berkshire v **Devon**	9*	dnb			NR
		Devon CC in 1956		9 inns - 3 no - 313 runs - 104 highest - 52.16 average					
				53 overs - 15 maidens - 118 runs - 4 wickets - 29.50 ave.					
1957	42	Aug 2,3	Torquay	**Devon** v Berkshire	48	4	14.4-4-28-6	14-1-59-2	lost 121 runs
	43	Aug 5,6	Seaton	**Devon** v Dorset	3	0	3-0-22-0		lost 1st inn
	44	Aug 12,13	Dorchester	Dorset v **Devon**	28	23*		1-0-5-0	won 1st inn
	45	Aug 14,15	Oxford	Oxfordshire v **Devon**	1	dnb			won 6w
	46	Aug 16,17	Reading	Berkshire v **Devon**	14	8			lost 173 runs
		Devon CC 1957		9 inns - o no - 129 runs - 48 highest - 14.33 average					
				37overs - 5 maidens- 114 runs- 8 wickets - 14.25 ave.					
1958	47	Aug 1,2	Exeter	**Devon** v Berkshire	35*	25*			lost 1st inn
	48	Aug 4,5	Seaton	**Devon** v Cornwall	10	dnb			lost 1st inn
	49	Aug 11,12	Wimborne	Dorset v **Devon**	74*	dnb			won 1st inn
	50	Aug 13,14	Banbury	Oxfordshire v **Devon**	11	dnb			lost 1st inn
	51	Aug 15,16	Reading	Berkshire v **Devon**	67*	dnb			won 8w
		Devon CC in 1958		6 inns - 4 no - 222 runs - 74* - 111.00 average					
				Did not bowl					
1959	52	July 29,30	Torquay	**Devon** v Berkshire	12	7			won 4w
	53	31July, Aug 1	Falmouth	Cornwall v **Devon**	26	4*			won 1st inn
	54	Aug 3,4	Exeter	**Devon** v Somerset II	7	1			lost 57 runs
	55	Aug 5,6	Plymouth	**Devon** v Cornwall	83	dnb		14-1-13-0	won 1st inn
	56	Aug 7,8	Taunton	Somerset II v **Devon**	37	45			won 55 runs
		Devon CC 1959		9 inns - 1 no - 222 runs - 83 highest - 27.75 average					
				14 overs - 1 maiden - 13 runs - o wickets.					

Summary of Devon CC Career

	BATTING						BOWLING				
SEASON	INNS	N.O.	RUNS	HIGHEST	AVERAGE		OVERS	MAIDENS	RUNS	WKTS	AVERAGE
1949	14	3	661	134*	60.09		148.5	32	416	13	32.00
1950	5	1	64	32*	16.00		38	13	64	2	32.00
1952	12	0	272	76	22.66		99	13	311	4	77.75
1953	10	2	305	71	38.12		31	4	112	4	28.00
1954	6	0	220	78	36.66		0				
1956	9	3	313	104	52.16		53	15	118	4	29.50
1957	9	0	129	48	14.33		37	5	114	8	14.25
1958	6	4	222	74*	111.00		0				
1959	9	1	222	83	27.75		14	1	13	0	
	80	14	2408	134*	36.48		420.5	83	1148	35	32.80

4 centuries

INDEX

INDEX
continued

INDEX
continued

ACKNOWLEDGEMENTS

The compilation of this book would have been impossible without the generous help of a large number of people. Grateful thanks are due to the following for their kindness and their interest.

From the Borrett family: Norman – who started as a reluctant participant in the enterprise but was finally persuaded that others might welcome the chance to read and learn a bit more about him – the delightful and enthusiastic Mullie, Anthony and the late Christine, Tim and Trudé, and other members of the Borrett and Rowe families.

From Bath University, the archive for the Hockey Association's records: Lizzie Richmond; from the Hockey Association: Sandra Richards; from Pembroke College, Cambridge, the College archivist, Jayne Ringrose; and from the Squash Rackets Association's archivist, the late Ian Wright, whose help was unstinting.

From Devon County Cricket Club: Derek Cole, Ted Crowe, Deryck Fairclough, Stuart Mountford, Harold Shaw.

From Somerset County Cricket Club: John Harris.

From Devon County Squash Association: Bruce Coleman and Mike Tremellen.

From Framlingham College staff: Martin Irving (Hon. OF), John Maulden OF, Malcolm Todd, and David Barker (Hon.OF).

From Old Boys of Allhallows School: Stuart MacGregor and Tony Watson.

From Old Framlinghamians: Robin Anderton, James Barry, Jon Barry, Ben Barringer, Jim Blythe, David Boulton, Nick Chaplin (Hon.OF), Jim Crosbie, Guy Dawson, John Edwards, Tom Elliott, Chris Essex,

Michael Evans, Roger Fayers, Ian Foster, Bob Fox, Gerald and Mike Garnett, Peter Howard-Dobson, Nick Horne, Brian Ivory, Neil Joy, Ken Mayhew, Norman Mayhew, David Mead, Colin Micklewright, Chris Milner-Moore, Simon Molyneux, Peter Over, Tony Parsons, Ian Pearson, Martin Pearse, Norman Porter, the late Anthony Rosen, Brian Rosen, James Ruddock-Broyd, John Saul, Stephen Sayer, Brian Smith, Clive Smith, Malcolm Sneath, Andrew Towler, Humphrey Truman, David Turnbull, Graham Walsh, Andrew Wright; and also from Neil Flowerdew, the great nephew of OF Gordon Flowerdew VC.

From the world of hockey: Mike Bawden, Dil Bhara, Denys Carnill, John Cockett, Mike Corby, Sir Derek Day, Ian Ferris, Maurice Kittrell, Robin Manning, Tony Nunn, Balbir Singh, Peter Smith, and in particular the ever-helpful Pat Rowley, venerable hockey journalist and passionate fan of the game.

From the world of squash: Geoffrey Atkins, David Brazier, Jeremy Lyon, Michael Lyon, Bob Morris (Hon.OF), John Partridge, Mike Perkins, Bretton Priestley, Peter Robinson, John Thompson, Humphrey Truman, David Vaughan.

And grateful acknowledgement to the authors of the many books, newspaper and magazine articles listed hereunder whose scholarship has been liberally quoted in this memoir. In particular:

The Times; The Daily Telegraph; The London Evening Standard; The Manchester Guardian; The Evening News; The Observer; The Sketch; The Sunday Times; The Sunday Telegraph; The Western News; The Western Morning News; The Western Evening Herald; The East Anglian Daily News.

MCC Annual Reports; Wisden's Cricketer's Almanack; the Cricketer Magazine and the Wisden Cricketer Magazine; Christopher Martin-Jenkins' writings in Wisden; Frank Keating's articles in The Spectator; Glenn

Moore's article on cricket and soccer all-rounders in the 2004 Wisden; Jeremy Malies' book Sporting Doubles and Mick Collins study of Max Woosnam - All-Round Genius; On the Corinthian Spirit by D.J.Taylor; The Guinness Book of Olympic Records – McWhirter; The Oxford Companion to Sports and Games – Arlott.

Hockey World and Hockey News; 196 England Hockey Internationals by Pat Rowley; Improving Your Hockey by Norman Borrett; Hockey – for Men and Women by Norman Borrett; The Balsam Hockey Yearbook; The Great Britain Hockey Story by Bill Colwill.

British Lawn Tennis and Squash Magazine; A History of Devon Squash – by Michael Tremellen; Squash by Hashim Khan; The SRA Squash Annual; The History of Squash by John Horry.

Framlingham College – The First Sixty Years by John Booth; The Second Sixty Years by Leslie Gillett; N.F. Borrett Memorial Service - Address by OF Norman Porter.

I am indebted to Denys Carnill who graciously agreed to write the foreword to this book; to my good friend Roger Nokes, Old Felstedian, who so sadly died just before publication, who gave invaluable editorial advice; to my son, Jim, who took over Roger's editorial role; Jane Boyle for correcting my typing and helping with the lay-out. The support of a number of OFs has been crucial: Norman Porter, the indefatigable Hon.General Secretary of the SOF who has always been encouraging, Peter Howard-Dobson for publishing advice, and the Trustees of the SOF for their financial support. Above all I wish to thank Chris Keeble, dedicated and diligent designer and artistic guru whose skills have much enhanced this publication.

Finally, my thanks go to my wife Georgina, for her support, encouragement and patience throughout this project.